Race, Law and Hypercriminality

This book considers how neoliberal criminal law constructs racialised 'hypercriminals'.

In a world of fake news and virtual reality, where social media posts seem more real than the materiality of racial capitalism, this book develops the idea of 'hypercriminality', as a means of explaining how racial disproportionalities in the criminal legal system persist, despite discourses of a post-racial meritocracy. Drawing on critical race theory, the work of Judith Butler, and Jean Baudrillard's conception of the hyperreal, the book considers how neoliberal legal discourse constructs and reproduces hyperreal racialised legal subjects. The simulated violent figure of the racialised gang member, rioter, drug dealer, or sexual predator is made to appear 'real' through legal and evidential concepts such as dangerousness or bad character. The belief that this simulation is real is deployed to justify the carceral state and masks the structural, and racialised, violence of capitalism itself. Revealing the 'hypercriminality' of racialised legal subjects, the book thus offers a timely critical legal intervention that aims to advance the urgent project of decarceration, abolition, and transformative justice.

The book will appeal to scholars and students working in the areas of criminal law and evidence, criminology, criminal justice, socio-legal studies, and critical race theory.

Sarah Corbett-Batson is an Associate Professor at The University of Law, London, and a criminal defence barrister at One Pump Court.

Race, Law and Hypercriminality

Sarah Corbett-Batson

Routledge
Taylor & Francis Group
a GlassHouse Book

First published 2026
by Routledge
4 Park Square, Milton Park, Abingdon, Oxon OX14 4RN

and by Routledge
605 Third Avenue, New York, NY 10158

Routledge is an imprint of the Taylor & Francis Group, an informa business

A GlassHouse book

British Library Cataloguing-in-Publication Data
A catalogue record for this book is available from the British Library

ISBN: 978-1-032-99195-5 (hbk)
ISBN: 978-1-032-99197-9 (pbk)
ISBN: 978-1-003-60287-3 (ebk)

DOI: 10.4324/9781003602873

Typeset in Sabon
by Deanta Global Publishing Services, Chennai, India

Contents

Acknowledgements

Thank you to my family, friends, and colleagues for all their support. In particular, I owe a huge debt of gratitude to Professor Nadine El-Enany and Dr Piyel Haldar for their inspiration and encouragement. On a personal note, I would like to thank my parents, my sisters and Carl. This book is dedicated to the memory of Granny and Jacqueline.

Glossary

Capitalism / racial capitalism an economic system based on market forces and private profit rather than social need. The term 'racial capitalism' describes how capitalism is based not only on class differentiation but also on racial differentiation. See also 'Neoliberalism' (below).

Carceral abolition a society without police or prisons, where there are radical alternatives to punishment, such as transformative justice. See also 'Transformative justice' (below).

Colonialism controlling and dominating another country, including exploitation of its land, resources and people.

Colour-blindness / post-racial the belief that society has overcome racism and that everyone is treated equally, regardless of race. See also 'Meritocracy' (below).

Contradiction-closing case a Critical Race Theory term first used by Derrick Bell to describe a legal case that appears to resolve the contradiction between discourses of equality and continuing oppression. Such a case gives the impression that inequality has been overcome yet provides minimal material changes to the lives of oppressed people.

Character evidence evidence presented at criminal trials to show that a person is of 'good character' or of 'bad character'. Good character evidence is adduced at trial to show that someone is more likely to be telling the truth and/or less likely to have committed the alleged offence. In general, bad character evidence is adduced at trial to show that someone is less likely to be telling the truth, more likely to have committed the alleged offence and/or to discredit their defence.

Civilising mission the belief that Western societies were intellectually and culturally superior to the areas that they colonised. This contrasts the 'civilised' West with the 'uncivilised' areas colonised. The concept was, and continues to be, used to attempt to justify colonialism and imperialism.

Counternarrative a narrative that challenges mainstream or dominant discourses. Counternarratives can be a means of giving voice to members of marginalised and oppressed groups, who have been silenced in mainstream debates. It has been used as a methodology in some Critical Race Theory literature.

Critical Legal Studies (CLS) an academic movement primarily associated with US universities in the 1970s. CLS asserts that the law is political and that it operates to maintain unequal power structures in society while appearing to be neutral. CLS scholars argue that laws are indeterminate and contradictory and that legal decisions are political rather than purely legal.

Critical Race Theory (CRT) an academic and political movement that focuses on explaining and combating racism, including centring racism in discourses and research about the legal system, education, etc. The starting point is that race is a social construct (a creation of society) rather than having a biological basis and that racial inequality persists throughout contemporary society. Other concepts used in CRT include intersectionality, counternarrative, interest convergence, and the critique of rights.

Critique of rights a term used in CLS and CRT literature to argue that human rights victories are not necessarily progressive and that legal rights can be a distraction from achieving social and material equality.

Discourses written or spoken communications, including discussions and debates.

Empire areas controlled by a dominant state or ruler due to colonialism or imperialism.

Enlightenment a movement from the late 1600s to the early 1800s, primarily in Europe but also in North America, that focused on concepts such as the rule of law, science, government, and definitions of liberty. It is contrasted with pre-Enlightenment beliefs around religion, superstition, and monarchy.

Hyperreality Jean Baudrillard's theory that we have reached the historical stage where reality has been replaced by signs of reality that appear to be real. See also 'Simulacrum/simulacra' and 'Simulation' (below).

Imperialism the maintenance or expansion of power into other countries by a state.

Interest convergence a Critical Race Theory term first used by Derrick Bell to describe how civil rights for Black people are granted by courts or authorities only where they advantage White interests, or where they are the least damaging course of action for White elites seeking to safeguard their own position of privilege.

Intersectionality a term first used by Kimberlé Crenshaw to explain how different forms of oppression, such as race and gender, interact with each other. For example, Black women experience sexism in different ways to White women and experience racism in different ways to Black men, through the ways that these inequalities intersect with each other.

Although the concept originated in Critical Race Theory literature, it is now used more widely.

Meritocracy a belief that success is dependent upon ability and hard work, rather than on advantages and privileges. The concept of meritocracy is used to blame poor individuals and marginalised communities for their own disadvantaged situation.

Neoliberalism the current stage of capitalism, whereby the state promotes free market capitalism through deregulation and privatisation, as well as defunding social and welfare provisions.

Performativity a term used by Judith Butler to describe how repeated discourses or actions create identities. These are not neutral but are dependent on the society in which they occur. Identities are not stable and fixed but require constant repetition of discourses or actions to maintain them. Butler's main writing relates to gender and the way that this is performatively constituted.

Racial framing a term used by Judith Butler to describe how viewing the world through the lens of White privilege can lead to the perception that Black people are inferior or dangerous.

Racialisation a process of creating and maintaining the concept of race and of differentiating between people on that basis.

Simulacrum (singular) / simulacra (plural) a term used by Jean Baudrillard to describe a copy or image of something. He distinguished between different orders of simulacra. First order simulacra are copies that imitate and reflect reality: this is characterised by the counterfeit and associated with the period from the Renaissance to the Industrial Revolution. Second order simulacra are copies where there is no longer a discernible difference between the image and the original, such as objects made on assembly lines, and are associated with the Industrial Revolution. Third order simulacra are representations that are copies without originals that appear more real than reality, such that they are hyperreal.

Simulation a term used by Jean Baudrillard to describe a process whereby the signs of reality appear as reality, and the boundaries between truth and falsity are collapsed.

Transformative justice ways of responding to harm that do not rely upon prisons and other forms of state punishment. Transformative justice takes a holistic view and sees harm as rooted in social conditions. It seeks to respond to harm through community-based solutions, accountability, and social justice, rather than revenge and punishment.

Undeserving poor poor working class people who are deemed to be responsible for their own disadvantaged situation and who are contrasted with hardworking poor people (the deserving poor).

Ungrievable lives a term used by Judith Butler to describe how some lives are considered valuable (grievable) and how other lives are considered not to matter such that people from marginalised groups are deemed disposable (ungrievable).

White privilege the social, psychological, and economic advantages of being considered White in a racist society.

White supremacy beliefs, policies, practices, and structures that privilege those considered White over those not considered White.

Zemiology a theory primarily developed in UK academia from the late 1990s onwards that focuses on social harm rather than crime. Zemiologists critique mainstream criminology and argue that the legal system and processes of criminalisation are themselves sources of harm. Zemiologists argue that concepts of crime are socially constructed and reflect the power relations in a society, such that much significant social harm is not criminalised, including preventable deaths due to lack of access to resources, lack of health and safety provisions, and environmental harm.

Abbreviations

ASBO	Anti-social Behaviour Order
CBO	Criminal Behaviour Order
CDA	Crime and Disorder Act 1998
CJA	Criminal Justice Act 2003
CJPOA	Criminal Justice and Public Order Act 1994
CLS	Critical Legal Studies
CRT	Critical Race Theory
CTA	Criminal Tribes Act 1871
DTTO	Drug Treatment and Testing Order
HCA	Habitual Criminals Act 1869
IPP	Sentence of Imprisonment for Public Protection
KCPO	Knife Crime Prevention Order
PACE	Police and Criminal Evidence Act 1984
POA 1986	Public Order Act 1986
POA 2023	Public Order Act 2023
POV	Point of view imagery
PTA	Prevention of Terrorism (Temporary Provisions) Act 1974
s.60	Section 60, Criminal Justice and Public Order 1994

Introduction

In a world of fake news and virtual reality, where social media posts seem more real than the material inequalities of racial capitalism, the theory of hypercriminality[1] provides a means of explaining how racial disproportionalities in the criminal legal system persist despite discourses of a colour-blind, post-racial meritocracy. This book contends that criminal law, evidence, and the legal system are hyperreal and that they construct and reproduce 'hyper-

1 Note that there are other uses of the term 'hypercrime' which do not refer to the same phenomena described here. For example, Michael McGuire's concept of 'hypercrime' refers to that which 'is spatially rooted and which emerges specifically from the interactive possibilities of a hyperspace': Michael McGuire, *Hypercrime: The New Geometry of Harm* (Routledge-Cavendish 2007), 7. James Pinkerton refers to 'hypercrime' as extremely high crime levels due to community breakdown: James Pinkerton, *What Comes Next: The End of Big Government – and the New Paradigm Ahead* (Hyperion 1995). Brittany Slatton refers to the concept of 'hypercriminal black men' as an ideology that 'supports the unequal application of the law, which results in the intense surveillance, harassment, mass incarceration, and deaths of black men': Brittany C. Slatton, 'The Black Box: Constrained Maneuvering of Black Masculine Identity' in Brittany C. Slatton and Kamesha Spates (eds), *Hyper Sexual, Hyper Masculine? Gender, Race and Sexuality in the Identities of Contemporary Black Men* (Ashgate 2014), 35. Victor Rios uses the term to describe the 'youth control complex' used against Black and Latino Youth in the San Francisco Bay area, including racialised criminalisation and punitive measures from other institutions, such as schools: Victor M. Rios, 'The Hyper-Criminalization of Black and Latino Male Youth in the Era of Mass Incarceration' (2006) 8(2) *Souls* 40. Natalia Smirnov and Wan Shun Eva Lam refer to 'hypercriminalization' as 'the pervasive complex of social practices such as racial profiling' that deem young Black males as enduringly criminal: Natalia Smirnov and Wan Shun Eva Lam, '"Presenting Our Perspective": Recontextualising Youths' Experiences of Hypercriminalization Through Media Production' (2019) 1 *Written Communication* 1 <https://doi.org/10.1177/0741088319827594> accessed 18 December 2024. Although Richard Sherwin does not specifically use the term 'hypercriminal', he refers to Baudrillard and hyperreality: Richard K. Sherwin, *When Law Goes Pop: The Vanishing Line Between Law and Popular Culture* (The University of Chicago Press 2000), 242–243. A review of Sherwin's book refers to 'hyper-criminals': Ryan Alford, 'A Review of "When Law Goes Pop: The Vanishing Line Between Law and Popular Culture"' (2001) 8(2) *Journal of Criminal Justice and Popular Culture* 136, 138.

DOI: 10.4324/9781003602873-1

criminals': hyperreal racialised legal subjects who appear to be 'real' criminals. These constructions are situated within colonial discourses and processes of racialised criminalisation, yet this history is rendered invisible. Furthermore, it is argued that the criminal legal system is a source of harm, rather than the solution to social harm, and that social justice cannot be achieved through criminalisation and punishment. By theorising hypercriminality and applying it to criminal law and evidence, this book seeks to contribute to critical legal literature and advance the urgent project of decarceration, abolition, and transformative justice.

For readers unfamiliar with the theoretical approaches discussed, the glossary briefly explains the key terms. Additionally, Chapter 1 explains the relevant theories, and Chapter 2 sets out the historical background to put the later chapters into context. Although the arguments are inescapably theoretical, the glossary and explanations in the earlier chapters are intended to make these debates accessible not only to academics and students in the areas of law, criminology, and social science but to all anti-racist and abolitionist activists.

Criminal law is premised as being neutral and equally applicable to all, yet it produces racially disproportionate outcomes at all levels of the legal process, including stop and search, arrests, criminal charges, court convictions, and imprisonment. This book aims to explain this disproportionality through analysing the ways that neoliberal criminal law and evidence construct racialised hypercriminals. Through repeated and increasingly abstracted colonial discourses, criminal law constantly reproduces the simulation of racialised criminality. This simulation appears to close the contradiction between the neoliberal rhetoric of a colour-blind meritocracy and a legal system that disproportionately charges, convicts, and incarcerates racialised subjects. Under neoliberalism, constructed racialised legal subjects are hyperreal – simulations of reality that appear to be more real than the racist colonial discourses underpinning criminal law. They give the impression that Black[2] criminality is pathological, while making invisible both the colonial histories within which such constructions are situated and the violence of racial capitalism. Hyperreality naturalises colonial processes of racialised criminalisation while deploying civilising mission discourses to sustain this apparent reality.

The legal provisions considered in this book include the stop and search powers under s.60, Criminal Justice and Public Order Act 1994 (CJPOA); two categories introduced by the Crime and Disorder Act 1998 (CDA): hate

2 In this book, as is common in Critical Race Theory literature, the terms 'Black' and 'White' start with capital letters to reflect that race is a social construct. In this context, the term 'Black' refers to all people racialised as non-White and the term 'White' refers to people benefitting from White privilege.

crimes and anti-social behaviour, as well as subsequent related provisions including Criminal Behaviour Orders (CBOs), gang injunctions, and Knife Crime Prevention Orders (KCPOs); and two areas of law significantly altered by the Criminal Justice Act 2003 (CJA): dangerousness and bad character evidence. They have been chosen as examples of how neoliberal criminal law reproduces racialised constructions of criminality in ways that are increasingly abstracted, such that they create and recreate simulacra of criminality, despite the law appearing racially neutral or even racially progressive. Simulated hypercriminals appear more real than the harm caused by states and corporations under racial capitalism.

The theoretical approach used in this book combines the Critical Legal Studies' (CLS) critique of liberal law;[3] a materially grounded Critical Race Theory[4] (CRT) analysis of colonialism and continuing colonial practices against racialised people; the discourse analysis of Judith Butler's theory of performativity[5] and their work on racial framing[6] and ungrievable lives;[7] and Jean Baudrillard's theories of hyperreality, simulation, and simulacra.[8]

Judith Butler's theory of performativity explains how identities are created by discourses requiring constant repetition to sustain their apparent reality. Racialised individuals and populations are viewed through a racial frame that both reflects and reproduces historical processes. This theory enables a reading of the law that is anti-essentialist and accounts for fluctuating discourses and the possibility of agency and resistance. Butler's concept of ungrievable lives describes the ways that particular populations, as constructed by colonial processes, are deemed not only as disposable but as a threat to the lives of grievable populations. Neoliberal states divide humanity into those for whom the use of self-defence to preserve their way of life is justified and those they 'defend' themselves against. Carceral, violent, and coercive means are deployed against ungrievable people on the premise of protecting those considered worthy of living a good life.

3 Duncan Kennedy, *Legal Education and the Reproduction of Hierarchy* (article first published 1983, New York University Press 2004), 37.

4 Richard Delgado and Jean Stefancic, *Critical Race Theory: An Introduction* (3rd edn, New York University Press 2017).

5 Judith Butler, *Gender Trouble: Feminism and the Subversion of Identity* (2nd edn, Routledge 1990); Judith Butler, *Bodies That Matter* (Routledge 1993); Judith Butler, *Excitable Speech: A Politics of the Performative* (Routledge 1997).

6 Judith Butler, *Precarious Life: The Powers of Mourning and Violence* (Verso Books 2004), 57 and 90; Judith Butler, *Undoing Gender* (Routledge 2004), 10.

7 Judith Butler, *Frames of War: When Is Life Grievable?* (Verso Books 2016); Judith Butler, *The Force of Non-Violence* (Verso Books 2020).

8 Jean Baudrillard, *Simulacra and Simulation* (Sheila Faria Glaser tr, University of Michigan Press 1994); Jean Baudrillard, *Symbolic Exchange and Death* (Iain Hamilton Grant tr, SAGE Publications 2017).

The perceived identities reproduced by performative processes can be further analysed using Jean Baudrillard's concepts of simulation, simulacra, and hyperreality. Baudrillard explained how representations take increasingly abstracted forms over time.[9] He argued that we had reached the historical stage where the imaginary was indistinguishable from the real, such that reality had been replaced by hyperreality.[10] First order simulacra, associated with the pre-industrial period, were counterfeit copies that were less real than the originals.[11] Second order simulacra were connected with the Industrial Revolution, where commercial mass production created copies that were designed to be identical to the real item.[12] Third order simulacra are hyperreal – representations of representations that appear more real than reality.[13] Whereas under the previous eras described above, society was based on representation and production, under hyperreality it is based on simulation.[14] Simulation is a process of 'substituting the signs of the real for the real'.[15] These 'signs of the real' are simulacra – copies with no original or referent.[16] These concepts are explained in more detail in Chapter 1.

Baudrillard's theory of hyperreality can be used as a tool to interrogate neoliberal criminal law, a process whereby simulacra of criminality appear more real than the guilt or otherwise of a legal subject and where determinations of guilt are constructed through signs. It is argued that performative processes of simulation reproduce racialised subjects as criminals through repeated discourses situated within neoliberal racial capitalism,[17] particularly its colonial underpinnings. This occurs in an increasingly abstracted manner that creates hyperreal racialised legal subjects – hypercriminals. Criminal law and evidence rely upon racialised simulacra of criminality through concepts such as bad character, gangs, and dangerousness. It is not that the simulacra override the evidence but that the evidence itself is constructed through processes of simulation.

The origins of modern racism are intrinsically linked with the economics of slavery and with Enlightenment discourses. Criminal law and evidence are embedded in processes of racialisation through their colonial origins, which are obscured by the constant repetition of discourses that reproduce racialised constructions of criminality. This gives criminal law and evidence the veneer of neutrality and objectivity. Race, law, human rights, and the

9 Baudrillard, *Symbolic Exchange and Death*, 71.
10 Ibid., 24.
11 Ibid., 71–72.
12 Ibid., 75–78.
13 Ibid., 92.
14 Ibid., 71.
15 Baudrillard, *Simulacra and Simulation*, 2.
16 Ibid., 2 and 6; Baudrillard, *Symbolic Exchange and Death*, 81.
17 The meaning of racial capitalism is discussed in Chapter 2.

undeserving poor were second order simulacra constructed under the market law of value around the time of the Industrial Revolution and situated within Enlightenment discourses. However, under neoliberalism, racialised legal subjects are reproduced as criminals in increasingly abstracted ways. This abstraction results in the colonial roots of these simulations being erased from view, such that the simulated criminality of racialised subjects appears real, essential, and pathological – they become hypercriminals. They are third order simulacra, located within the symbolic realm, that circulate as signs of criminality. These processes of abstraction under neoliberalism construct and rework discourses around human rights, the undeserving poor, criminal law, and racialised criminality as third order simulacra. They are simulations of the second order simulacra referred to above, such that they are simulations of simulations: self-referential copies without originals.

While there is no shortage of academic literature on racism within the legal system, less has been written on how criminal laws and evidential provisions themselves contribute to these processes of racialisation, or the ways that seemingly neutral legal concepts such as character are situated within colonial discourses. While Critical Race Theory and Butler's theories have previously been used together, particularly in the field of education scholarship,[18] this theoretical combination has been underused in the legal field. Additionally, Baudrillard's concepts of simulacra, simulation, and hyperreality have been underutilised in legal and criminological academia. When explicitly situated within the context of colonialism and racial capitalism, these theories have explanatory power to show how processes of simulation construct racialised criminality and create hypercriminals. Neoliberal criminal legal processes are a continuation of the colonial project in order to secure the interests of White supremacy, while appearing natural and neutral. The abstracted neoliberal ideology of colour-blindness has replaced the explicit legal racism under slavery, colonialism, and the Empire. Ostensible legal equality is a façade that denies the materiality of continued racism.

In the UK, members of poor, racialised communities are stopped, arrested, charged, convicted, and imprisoned on a mass scale. Meanwhile, the major political parties are battling to be more punitive than each other and the far-right are deploying narratives of racialised criminality in order to gain popularity. Other neoliberal economies are in a similar position. Therefore, speaking out against the carceral logic of neoliberalism is an urgent project. Failure to challenge the simulation of racialised criminality will result in an intensification of these processes. The problem goes beyond police or court

18 Deborah Youdell, 'Identity Traps or How Black Students Fail: The Interactions Between Biographical, Sub-cultural, and Learner Identities' (2003) 24(1) *British Journal of Sociology of Education* 3; Charlotte Chadderton, *Judith Butler, Race and Education* (Palgrave Macmillan 2018).

racism. The very construction of criminal law is situated within colonial discourses and practices. Therefore, racism in the criminal legal system cannot be individualised and reduced to lack of diversity or unconscious bias. Failure to recognise this constrains our comprehension of the causes and continuation of racially disproportionate outcomes in the criminal legal system. Mainstream legal scholarship fails to appreciate that racialisation is embedded into criminal law and evidence. Rather than being a neutral phenomenon that is tainted by racist systems, criminal law is fundamental to the construction, maintenance, and reproduction of processes of racialisation.

An analysis of colonialism that seeks to make visible how the constructed signs of criminality appear as 'real' criminality is crucial to understanding racism in criminal legal processes. In particular, the concept of simulacra is key to elucidating how insidious these processes have become under the neoliberal third order simulacra of colour-blindness and meritocracy. Processes of simulation rely upon previous incarnations of racism and reproduce these in ways that construct ever more abstracted legal subjects within the symbolic realm. In this way, processes of racialisation have absorbed their own genealogy, such that they remain embedded in colonial discourses while making those histories invisible. Racism cannot be solved by neoliberal conceptions of human rights or meritocracy, as they are themselves simulacra. They are simulations of the Enlightenment discourses that were used as a justification for racism and therefore cannot eradicate racism. However, speaking back against processes of simulation can constitute a first step in challenging carceral responses to social issues and working towards social justice solutions. Through problematising the notion of criminality within a critique of racial capitalism, the theory of hypercriminality speaks to the increasing literature around zemiology[19] and carceral abolition.

Chapter 1 explains the theoretical perspectives that underpin the concept of hypercriminality: how neoliberal criminal law and evidence construct and reproduce hyperreal racialised legal subjects in increasingly abstracted ways. The Critical Legal Studies position that legal arguments are political discourses is outlined. This is followed by a detailed discussion of theories of racialisation and law, focusing on Critical Race Theory. Concepts including White privilege, White supremacy, counternarratives, the critique of rights, and contradiction-closing cases are considered. Judith Butler's work on performativity, racial framing, and ungrievable lives is analysed, and related to theories around the undeserving poor, biopolitics, and necropolitics. It is argued that race and law are performative processes, and a materially grounded reading of Butler is consistent with a Critical Race Theory

19 Zemiology can be described 'the study of harm beyond and outside of the context of crime, including harms of criminalisation': Victoria Canning and Steve Tombs, *From Social Harm to Zemiology: A Critical Introduction* (Routledge 2021), 65.

approach. This is followed by an exploration of Jean Baudrillard's theories of hyperreality, simulation, and simulacra. Different orders of simulation are explained and related to processes of racialisation. It is asserted that race has changed from a second order to third order simulacrum, such that it is hyperreal. Finally, it is argued that combining these theories can illuminate how neoliberal criminal laws are able to reproduce hypercriminals while simultaneously rendering invisible their colonial genealogy.

Chapter 2 analyses four key periods in the history of the criminal law and racial capitalism. The first half of the chapter focuses on three periods: the early stages of capitalism that conflated poverty with criminality through shifting definitions of property and theft; transatlantic slavery and the development of theories of racialisation; and British colonialism in India and discourses of racialised criminalisation. The second half of the chapter analyses neoliberalism, the hyperreal stage of racial capitalism. It is argued that criminal law has morphed from a second order simulacrum under earlier periods to an increasingly abstracted third order simulacrum under neoliberalism, such that it constructs hyperreal racialised legal subjects: hypercriminals. Neoliberalism combines upward redistribution of wealth with meritocratic discourses that frame society as post-racial. This serves to consolidate and maintain White supremacy. Discourses around poverty, race, and criminality are insidiously combined. Mass incarceration is an intrinsic element of neoliberalism that maintains social control, increases profitability, and warehouses poor racialised populations. It is argued that the simulacrum of racialised hypercriminality performs a contradiction-closing function: it appears to close the contradiction between racially disproportionate outcomes in the criminal legal system and neoliberal discourses of a colour-blind meritocracy.

Chapter 3 focuses on s.60, Criminal Justice and Public Order Act 1994, a provision that allows the police to stop and search people without reasonable cause in a designated area. It is argued that exceptional legal powers are hyperreal – an implosion of the rule of law and extreme powers justified by discourses around collective self-defence. Contemporary police powers are a continuation of the colonial practices within which they are situated. Section 60 orders deploy neoliberal discourses around risk management and are a contemporary reworking of the civilising mission. Racialised communities are constructed as sites of criminality requiring intensified surveillance. These orders are self-referential and hyperreal – increased policing leads to increased arrests which makes the perceived criminality of those living in that area appear real and leads to further orders. Communities are reproduced as hypercriminals and colonial subjects, with their local area occupied by the police during a s.60 order. This spatial containment of racialised communities is linked to the gentrification of urban areas, which sees property in terms of profit rather than housing need, and seeks to exclude the racialised poor. Rather than being an outlier, s.60 is part of a continuum of onerous powers used against racialised communities.

Chapter 4 considers a number of criminal provisions that rework previous discourses around the undeserving poor in the context of neoliberalism. The 'chav' discourse is discussed in relation to processes of racialisation and narratives of meritocracy. This is followed by an analysis of hate crime provisions, which are located within a post-racial framing of Britishness as tolerance, which not only blames poor White people rather than the state for racism but simultaneously names racialised communities as intolerant. This constructs the simulation that the state is progressive and civilising and that it protects its citizens against racism. The Stephen Lawrence case is considered in the context of contradiction-closing cases. Anti-social Behaviour Orders, Criminal Behaviour Orders, gang injunctions, and Knife Crime Prevention Orders are discussed, and it is asserted that these are self-referential provisions that create their own apparent reality by the imposition of an order that names the recipient as anti-social, criminal, a gang member, or a knife carrier in a way that collapses the boundaries between truth and falsity, such that these provisions are hyperreal. It is argued that these provisions are processes of simulation that are deployed to justify carceral solutions to social problems.

Chapter 5 considers how contemporary conceptions of violent and sexual danger have their genealogy in colonial discourses. The history of narratives around dangerousness is considered and related to processes of racialisation. Dangerousness legislation, including the Imprisonment for Public Protection sentence, is discussed. This is followed by an analysis of two specific forms of danger: violent and sexual. In relation to violent danger, with reference to Judith Butler's concept of racial framing, it is argued that Black bodies are viewed as physically threatening, which places them at risk of state violence premised as self-defence. Narratives around sexual danger are rooted in colonialism and frame Black male sexuality as a threat to White purity. In the United States, both the lynching of Black men and the rape of Black women were intrinsically linked to White patriarchal capitalist property relations. In the United Kingdom, discourses around child sexual abuse have framed Muslim men as misogynistic. Such discourses are situated within civilising mission discourses, including those relating to the War on Terror, where the Western state and carceral feminism are presented as saviours of women. These narratives construct racialised hypercriminals and render invisible the sexual harm of racial capitalism, including that of the carceral state.

Chapter 6 analyses the use of bad character evidence at trial. Following a brief outline of the legislation, it is argued that bad character provisions have become increasingly more abstracted such that they are hyperreal and replace direct evidence with codes for criminality. Moreover, character is situated within colonial discourses that associate bad character with Blackness and good character with Whiteness. Concepts of credibility are located within the racial frame and constitute an asset of White privilege denied to racialised defendants. The second half of the chapter focuses on bad character evidence in relation to gang membership and rap and drill music. It is argued that bad character provisions intersect with the racialised use of gang discourses at trial. The use of police officers as expert witnesses on gang membership privileges the voice of the state and silences the voices of defendants. Further, the use of rap and drill music as bad character evidence deems Black cultural expression intelligible only as criminality. The bad character provisions rely upon previous simulations of criminality and reproduce and intensify these processes, such that they are both racialised and racialising.

Chapter 7 starts by reiterating how neoliberal criminal law constructs hypercriminals through performative processes of simulation. The processes that dehumanise and criminalise racialised communities also render invisible the violence of colonialism and racial neoliberalism. Although the carceral state purports to solve social problems, not only is it unable to provide security, but it is a significant cause of social harm. A zemiological approach, which differentiates between harm and crime, can be used to disrupt the dominant discourses around criminal law that equate criminality with harm. Recentering significant social harm as that caused by racial capitalism, rather than by the racialised poor, leads to a rejection of carceral solutions. Speaking back against processes of hypercriminalisation by refusing to accept simulated racialised criminality as real, and naming it as hyperreal, can constitute an act of subversion. In this way, it is argued, the theory of hypercriminality can contribute to the growing body of literature around zemiology, carceral abolition, and transformative justice.

Working towards carceral abolition and transformative justice is a long-term project that requires social solidarity and resistance to neoliberalism. Academic work is an essential element of this endeavour. The theoretical perspectives discussed in this book build upon the intellectual labour and activism of countless others. For those unfamiliar with this literature, it is hoped that the references will be a springboard for further reading and research. This book does not pretend to have the answers, but it is hoped that it can provoke a dialogue and provide useful theoretical ammunition for abolitionists fighting for a world where all lives are valued.

Chapter 1

Hypercriminality and Racialisation

The central theme of this book is that neoliberal criminal law and evidence construct and reproduce racialised hypercriminals in increasingly abstracted ways. As will be outlined in this chapter, the starting point is the Critical Legal Studies (CLS) concept of legal indeterminacy and the position that law is an expression of politics. This is enhanced by a Critical Race Theory (CRT) approach that views law as a practice steeped in processes of racialisation and colonialism. CRT terms and concepts such as White privilege, White supremacy, and contradiction-closing cases are deployed to analyse legal and evidential provisions. This book also draws upon critical race scholarship more widely construed, and therefore not all of those referenced in the section below would define themselves as proponents of CRT. Judith Butler's theory of performativity is used to explain how these processes of racialisation are made to appear neutral and natural through repeated discourses situated within material inequalities, and how racialised populations are framed as ungrievable. This approach is augmented by the use of Jean Baudrillard's concept of simulation as an analytical device to show how hyperreal legal subjects appear real. These processes of simulation are performative in the ways that they construct categories such as bad character or dangerousness, and create hypercriminals.

Criminal laws and evidential provisions have roots in, and in turn perpetuate, White supremacy through performative processes of simulation that reproduce criminal legal subjects in increasingly nuanced and abstracted ways under neoliberalism, such that racialised criminality appears normal. Therefore, racially disproportionate outcomes in the legal system should be viewed as intrinsically linked with criminal law and evidence. They cannot be seen solely as the result of racist policing, although as will be argued in Chapter 3, police practices are embedded in their colonial origins. Neoliberal criminal law is constructed through the colonial racial frame and creates hypercriminals whose criminality appears real. Racialised criminality appears as pathological and essential while the violence of colonialism and racial capitalism is rendered invisible. In this hyperreality, the simulated figure of the racialised violent gang member, rioter, drug dealer, or sexual predator

DOI: 10.4324/9781003602873-2

appears more real than the material harm caused by corporations, governments, and law enforcement.

From Critical Legal Studies to Critical Race Theory

CLS provides a framework to analyse how the law disguises the power structures that constitute and maintain it. This theoretical position views the law as indeterminate. Rather than legal constructions, such as the doctrine of precedent, giving an inevitable and definitive outcome in a case, there are a number of philosophically contradictory positions that could be argued.[1] Even an appeal to human rights cannot provide finality, as there will be competing, contradictory rights.[2] However, rather than legal decisions being a matter of chance, this indeterminacy is resolved by political and economic relations of power, such that legal discourses are essentially political and economic discourses.[3] In other words, 'law is politics'.[4] CLS aims to unveil the assumptions and power structures that lie behind seemingly apolitical laws, procedural rules, and judgments and to demonstrate how 'legitimation' operates – the liberal 'rule of law' presents itself as natural and non-partisan but contributes to the maintenance of unequal power relations within society.[5] The 'trashing' of liberal legitimation aims to make these hidden power imbalances visible.[6] To use popular film culture as a metaphor, CLS aims to uncover *The Matrix*[7] and pull back the curtain from the so-called wizard in *The Wizard of Oz*.[8]

CLS scholars seek to demonstrate how the law falsely presents itself as coherent, fair, and equal by deconstructing the norms and values that underlie criminal legal doctrines and how these doctrines purport to solve social problems.[9] Later chapters of this book consider how constructions such as

1 Joseph William Singer, 'The Player and the Cards: Nihilism and Legal Theory' (1984) 94(1) *The Yale Law Journal* 1, 10.
2 Duncan Kennedy, 'The Critique of Rights in Critical Legal Studies' in Wendy Brown and Janet Halley (eds), *Left Legalism / Left Critique* (Duke University Press 2002), 196.
3 Duncan Kennedy, *Legal Education and the Reproduction of Hierarchy* (article first published 1983, New York University Press 2004), 37.
4 Mark V. Tushnet, 'Critical Legal Theory' in Martin P. Golding and William A. Edmundson (eds), *The Blackwell Guide to Philosophy of Law and Legal Theory* (Wiley-Blackwell 2005), 80.
5 Mark V. Tushnet, 'Critical Legal Studies: A Political History' (1991) 100 *The Yale Law Journal* 1515, 1526.
6 Mark Kelman, 'Trashing' (1984) 36(1–2) *Stanford Law Review* 293, 293.
7 Jerry L. Anderson, 'Law School Enters the Matrix: Teaching Critical Legal Studies' (2004) 54(2) *Journal of Legal Education* 201, 211–214.
8 Richard Michael Fischl, 'The Question that Killed Critical Legal Studies' (1992) 17(4) *Law and Social Enquiry* 779, 805.
9 David Nelken, 'Critical Criminal Law' (1987) 14(1) *Journal of Law and Society* 105, 110.

gangs, knife crime, and dangerousness are presented as social problems that criminal law purports to solve. However, it will be argued that these ostensibly neutral concepts are situated within a genealogy of colonialism and racialisation. These 'social problems' are constructed to justify the disproportionate criminalisation and incarceration of racialised people, and operate as a distraction from the material social harm that poor communities experience under racial capitalism.

CLS was criticised by legal academics including Kimberlé Crenshaw, Mari Matsuda, and Richard Delgado for neglecting issues of race, which led to the development of CRT.[10] A starting point of CRT is that race is a social construction, rather than a biological reality.[11] The use of skin colour as a signifier of differentiation is historically specific, rather than a natural or inevitable way of dividing populations.[12] Therefore, 'it is the *mark* of race that gives rise to distinctions between groups, not the *reality* of race'.[13] Furthermore, 'race is not so much a category but a practice: *people are raced*'.[14] This practice 'is a system of meanings *deployed* in the racing of individuals and, as a concept, race must be *maintained* in order to survive'.[15] Although race has no ontological reality, it operates 'through well-rehearsed narratives to position whiteness as superior to non-whiteness in Euro-American influenced society'.[16] Through constant repetition and adaption, the concept of race comes to appear as natural.[17] Later in this chapter, it is argued that these processes are performative.

As will be discussed in Chapter 2, modern racism has an economic basis and was a justificatory discourse for transatlantic slavery. Enlightenment thinkers including Immanuel Kant, Voltaire, John Locke, David Hume, and Thomas Jefferson expressed views that race existed and that there was a hierarchy whereby White people were superior and capable of rationality, unlike other races.[18] Charles Linnaeus's *General System of Nature*, first

10 Kimberlé Crenshaw, 'The First Decade: Critical Reflections, or A Foot in the Closing Door' (2002) 49 *UCLA Law Review* 1343, 1354–1359.

11 Richard Delgado and Jean Stefancic, *Critical Race Theory: An Introduction* (3rd edn, New York University Press 2017), 9.

12 Robert Miles, *Racism and Colonialism: Essays on Ideology and Social Structure* (Routledge 1982), 89.

13 Barbara Perry, *In the Name of Hate* (Routledge 2001), 57 (original italics).

14 D. Marvin Jones, 'Darkness Made Visible: Law, Metaphor and the Racial Self' in Richard Delgado and Jean Stefancic (eds), *Critical White Studies* (Temple University Press 1997), 67 (original italics).

15 Nadine Ehlers, *Racial Imperatives: Discipline, Performativity, and Struggles Against Subjection* (Indiana University Press 2012), 16 (original italics).

16 Philip S.S. Howard, 'White Privilege: For or Against? A Discussion of Ostensibly Antiracist Discourses in Critical White Studies' (2004) 11(4) *Race, Gender and Class* 63, 66.

17 Ehlers, 17.

18 Kehinde Andrews, *The New Age of Empire* (Allen Lane 2021), 7–11.

published in 1735, classified people into four categories: White Europeans, Red Americans, Yellow Asians, and Black Africans.[19] From the tenth edition onwards, different behavioural characteristics were ascribed to each category.[20] Enlightenment discourses deployed racialising concepts and tools that categorised humanity into civilised White Europeans and uncivilised racialised non-Europeans.[21]

Kehinde Andrews explains that, 'the Enlightenment was essential in providing the intellectual basis for Western imperialism, justifying White supremacy through scientific rationality'.[22] The Enlightenment social contract was an exclusionary 'racial contract',[23] of which 'all whites are *beneficiaries* ... though some whites are not *signatories*'.[24] Rationality and science were an advance on the earlier religious superstitious conceptions of good and evil that conflated criminality with wickedness and sin.[25] However, these distinctions continued in different guises, with Enlightenment discourses asserting that racialised slaves lacked rationality, such that they were located outside the social contract.[26] Religious differentiation, which distinguished between Christian and 'infidel', was replaced by racialised differentiation.[27] Furthermore, as one can convert to Christianity, race was a stronger and more permanent symbol of demarcation.[28]

In Cedric Robinson's words: 'The tendency of European civilization through capitalism was ... to differentiate – to exaggerate regional, subcultural, and dialectical differences into "racial" ones'.[29] As slaves were taken from Africa, this required African people to be deemed inferior in order to justify this practice.[30] Thus, racial categories were created and deployed to legitimise economic expropriation, particularly slavery.[31] In the nineteenth century, the concept of race as a biological category linked positivist scientific

19 Nikki Sullivan, *A Critical Introduction to Queer Theory* (Edinburgh University Press 2003), 57.
20 Ibid., 57.
21 Emmanuel Chukwudi Eze (ed), *Race and The Enlightenment* (Blackwell Publishing 1997), 5.
22 Andrews, xiii.
23 Charles Wade Mills, *The Racial Contract* (Cornell University Press 1997), 64.
24 Ibid., 11 (original italics).
25 Biko Agozino, *Counter-Colonial Criminology: A Critique of Imperialist Reason* (Pluto Press 2003), 13.
26 Ibid., 16.
27 Mills, 23.
28 Ibid., 54.
29 Cedric J. Robinson, *Black Marxism: The Making of the Black Radical Tradition* (The University of North Carolina Press 2000), 26.
30 Alana Lentin, 'Race' in William Outhwaite and Stephen Turner (eds), *The SAGE Handbook of Political Sociology* (SAGE Publications 2018), 866.
31 Eric Williams, *British Capitalism and British Slavery* (first published 1944, Diasporic African Press edn, The University of North Carolina Press 2013), 7.

ideas of evolution and natural selection with a justification for colonialism and imperialism.[32] Scientific categorisation was linked with legal categorisation, with blood-related legal definitions of race premised on eugenicist notions of biological difference.[33] Modernity, including the concept of the rule of law, can be understood as a project of exclusion based on racial ordering, where this exclusion is made to appear natural.[34]

The practice of racism varies spatially and temporally. Although it has a material origin, racism can manifest in both material and ideological forms – material through inequality in relation to access to resources such as housing or employment, and ideological through discourses around deficit and criminality. These two aspects of racism are mutually reinforcing. In Chapter 2, it is argued that racism is able to rework itself in different historical and economic settings. For example, the myth of the colour-blind meritocracy under neoliberalism obscures the colonial roots and continuation of material racial inequalities, in conjunction with insidiously linking poverty and disadvantage with criminality. Racism can be seen as a means of maintaining divisions and of disciplining those who transgress them.[35]

Although mainstream contemporary social science has accepted that race is a social construct,[36] many outside this branch of academia do not have knowledge of, or do not accept, such an understanding of processes of racialisation.[37] Even within the humanities, there was some resurgence in biological racism and classism during the 1990s, with 'underclass' theory and Bell Curve arguments.[38] More recently, the popularity of DNA testing kits claiming to identify percentages of geographic ancestry has reinstated the concept of genetic racial identity.[39] Under Donald Trump's first presidency, there was a resurgence of biological racism from the alt-right, and arguments that intelligence was racially differentiated and innate were deployed to oppose affirmative action policies.[40]

32 Michael Rowe, *Race and Crime* (SAGE Publications 2012), 3–6.
33 Cheryl I. Harris, 'Whiteness as Property' (1993) 106(8) *Harvard Law Review* 1707, 1738–1741.
34 David Theo Goldberg, *The Racial State* (Blackwell Publishing 2002), 9–10.
35 Jones, 59.
36 Lentin, 'Race', 861.
37 Michelle Brattain, 'Race, Racism and Antiracism: UNESCO and the Politics of Presenting Science to the Postwar Public' (2007) 112(5) *The American History Review* 1386, paras 80–81 <https://doi.org/10.1086/ahr.112.5.1386> accessed 18 December 2024.
38 Charles Murray, *The Emerging Underclass* (Institute of Economic Affairs 1990); Richard J. Hernstein and Charles Murray, *The Bell Curve* (Basic Books 1994).
39 David Theo Goldberg, *The Threat of Race* (Blackwell Publishing 2008), 7; Alana Lentin, *Why Race Still Matters* (Polity Press 2020), 28–29.
40 Gavin Evans, 'The Unwelcome Revival of "Race Science"' *The Guardian* (2 March 2018) <www.theguardian.com/news/2018/mar/02/the-unwelcome-revival-of-race-science> accessed 18 December 2024.

A CRT approach not only enables one to deconstruct the political constitution of criminal law and evidence but foregrounds how processes of colonialism and racialisation are key to understanding this lack of neutrality. The law not only reflects but is engaged in processes of racialisation.[41] During slavery, there was a legal presumption in the United States that White people were free and Black people were slaves.[42] Subsequently, differential treatment under segregation laws required definitions of those included and those excluded from full participation in society. US states had differing definitions of who was considered Black, including reference to percentages of descent such that 'in the name of racially regulating behaviour, laws *created* racial identities'.[43] In some states, anyone who had one Black great-great-grandparent was determined to be Black, and in other states any Black ancestry was sufficient for a person to be legally defined as Black.[44] As Neil Gotanda argues, if a 'drop of blood' makes one Black, this implies that Blackness is a 'contaminant' that nullifies Whiteness and that 'a white racial identity is a declaration of racial purity and an implicit assertion of racial domination'.[45] Not only is racial privilege associated with white skin tone, both historically[46] and contemporaneously,[47] but a study by Ellis Monk concluded that in relation to Black people in the United States, when controlling for other factors, the darker their skin, the more likely they were to be arrested and imprisoned, such that 'being perceived as *blacker*' increased contact with law enforcement.[48] Research by Mark Bennett and Victoria Plaut also found evidence to suggest that darker skin tone and facial features perceived to be more 'Afrocentric' intensified the racial bias in legal outcomes.[49]

41 Amanda Carlin, 'The Courtroom as White Space: Racial Performance as Noncredibility' (2016) 63 *UCLA Law Review* 450, 458.
42 Dorothy E. Roberts, 'The Genetic Tie' in Richard Delgado and Jean Stefancic (eds), *Critical White Studies* (Temple University Press 1997), 187.
43 Ian Haney López, *White by Law: The Legal Construction of Race* (New York University Press 2006), 83 (original italics).
44 Ibid., 83.
45 Neil Gotanda, 'A Critique of "Our Constitution is Color-Blind"' in Kimberlé Crenshaw and others (eds), *Critical Race Theory: The Key Writings that Formed the Movement* (The New York Press 1996), 259.
46 W.E.B. Du Bois, 'The Souls of Black Folk' in Nathan Huggins (ed), *Writings* (article first published 1903, The Library of America 1986), 372.
47 Howard, 73–74.
48 Ellis P. Monk, 'The Color of Punishment: African Americans, Skin Tone, and the Criminal Justice System' (2018) 42 *Ethnic and Racial Studies* 1, 14 (original italics).
49 Mark W. Bennett and Victoria C. Plaut, 'Looking Criminal and the Presumption of Dangerousness: Afrocentric Facial Features, Skin Tone and Criminal Justice' (2018) 51(3) *UC Davis Law Review* 745, 802–803.

Racialisation and criminalisation are symbiotic and mutually constituting processes.[50] A person's criminal history and risk assessment affect how they are treated in the legal system, yet these classifications, which present as being race neutral, are dependent on racial bias at earlier stages and are then reproduced and compounded while appearing objective.[51] Particular examples of this are the dangerousness and bad character provisions considered in Chapters 5 and 6, respectively. Racism within the legal system is cumulative and self-perpetuating, and racial meanings are reproduced by criminal law and evidence.[52] This bias, manifesting as colour-blindness, operates at every stage of the legal process, particularly where there is scope for discretion by those enforcing the law.[53] The s.60 stop and search powers considered in Chapter 3 are illustrative of the link between greater discretion and increased racial disproportionality. The neoliberal rhetoric of colour-blind jurisprudence veils the ways that inequality is maintained and perpetuated by the law. However, it is not just that the legal system compounds prior inequality. More fundamentally, criminal law and evidence construct racialised and criminalised subjects through processes situated within colonialism. Rather than being one variable within the legal system, race is a central and defining element.[54] Exposing the purported neutrality of the law as fictitious entails uncovering not only that it constitutes a political discourse but moreover, that it is situated within colonial discourses and processes of racialisation.

The CRT concepts of White supremacy and White privilege can be used to analyse criminal law. White supremacy refers to 'the operation of forces that saturate the everyday mundane actions and policies that shape the world in the interests of White people' rather than being restricted to far-right fascist ideology.[55] White privilege describes how all White people benefit in some way from racism.[56] Cheryl Harris describes Whiteness as a form of property[57] that constitutes 'the legal legitimation of expectations of power and control that enshrine the status quo as a neutral baseline, while masking the maintenance of white privilege and domination'.[58] This has taken various historical forms, with the most blatant example being White ownership of Black

50 Nicole Gonzalez Van Cleve and Lauren Mayes, 'Criminal Justice Through "Colorblind" Lenses: A Call to Examine the Mutual Constitution of Race and Criminal Justice' (2015) 40(2) *Law and Social Inquiry* 406, 409.
51 Ibid., 422–424.
52 Ibid., 426–427.
53 Ibid., 424.
54 Ibid., 423.
55 David Gillborn, *Racism and Education: Coincidence or Conspiracy?* (Routledge 2008), 35.
56 Dolores Delgado Bernal and Octavio Villalpando, 'An Apartheid of Knowledge in Academia' in Edward Taylor, David Gillborn and Gloria Ladson-Billings (eds), *Foundations of Critical Race Theory in Education* (2nd edn, Routledge 2016), 80–81.
57 Harris, 1709.
58 Ibid., 1715.

slaves,[59] as discussed in Chapter 2, where the absence of Whiteness 'meant being the object of property'.[60] Whiteness shares a number of features with property rights, including the right to use and enjoy certain opportunities,[61] and the right to exclude others.[62]

Even for poor White people, the benefits conferred by White privilege include a 'public and psychological wage'.[63] Peggy McIntosh lists 46 benefits of White privilege, such as, 'I can go shopping alone most of the time, pretty well assured that I will not be followed or harassed'.[64] Indeed, the mere fact of rarely having to think of one's race because it is seen as the norm is itself a form of privilege.[65] The offence taken by some White people in relation to a journalist commenting on a pro-Brexit demonstration, 'I've never seen so many white people in one place', demonstrates how White people find the idea of being identified by their race to be completely alien to their experiences; they perceive their racial identity to be a neutral state of affairs.[66] In Western culture, 'hegemonically, "race" is taken to refer to people other than "whites", elevating "whiteness" to the status of the *racially* unmarked; the norm'.[67] In other words, White people tend to see themselves as unraced.[68]

An example of the operation of White privilege in criminal law discourses and practices is the way that only particular types of criminal offences are racialised. Whereas street robberies[69] and riots[70] have been racialised as Black, it is difficult to find offences portrayed as committed by White people, even where there is evidence to suggest that most of the perpetrators are White. As David Gillborn argues, 'White people do not generally risk demonization and stereotyping as a result of criminal or other negative acts by other White

59 Ibid., 1718–1721.
60 Ibid., 1721.
61 Ibid., 1734.
62 Ibid., 1736.
63 W.E.B. Du Bois, *Black Reconstruction in America* (first published 1935, Russell and Russell 1963), 700.
64 Peggy McIntosh, 'White Privilege and Male Privilege: A Personal Account of Coming to See Correspondences through Work in Women's Studies' in Richard Delgado and Jean Stefancic (eds), *Critical White Studies* (Temple University Press 1997), 293–294.
65 Haney López, 111.
66 Myriam François, 'The Fury of "White People" with Jon Snow Shows a Total Lack of Self-Awareness on Race' *The Guardian* (12 April 2019) <www.theguardian.com/commentisfree/2019/apr/12/jon-snow-white-people-brexit-rally> accessed 18 December 2024.
67 Caroline Braunmühl, *Colonial Discourse and Gender in U.S. Criminal Courts* (Routledge 2012), 25 (original italics).
68 Perry, 57.
69 Stuart Hall and others, *Policing the Crisis: Mugging, the State, and Law and Order* (Macmillan 1978).
70 Michael Rowe, *The Racialisation of Disorder in Twentieth Century Britain* (Ashgate Publishing Limited 1998), 157.

individuals'.[71] The significant social cost of financial crime, which is primarily committed by wealthy White males,[72] as well as the murder of over 200 people by Dr Harold Shipman,[73] could be used to justify the mass stopping and DNA profiling of White male graduate professionals on the basis that this demographic are dangerous, criminal, and adept at concealing their wrongdoing.[74] However, such a suggestion would seem unintelligible as the actions of White criminals are individualised rather than used to name entire White communities as criminal.[75] This is discussed further in Chapter 5 in relation to sexual grooming cases. Race is rarely raised as a relevant consideration in relation to the harm caused by White elites, such that there is an 'effective de-racialization of corporate and state crimes in contrast to the ready racialization of violent crime, particularly serious youth violence'.[76] The linking of race with specific types of harm ignores the circumstances and contexts in which actions take place, and operates to pathologise racialised populations as having certain proclivities and an innate propensity for particular activities. The racial framing of street crime as being committed by young Black males is considered in Chapter 2, with reference to the work of Paul Gilroy[77] and Stuart Hall,[78] the racialisation of knife crime is analysed in Chapters 3 and 4, and the racialisation of riots is discussed in Chapters 3–6.

Discourses around terrorism are a further example of how Black people are racialised whereas White people are seen as individuals. White perpetrators of terror-related attacks are frequently seen as 'lone wolves', whereas a Muslim person carrying out such an action is viewed as part of a community comprising a security threat.[79] Further, while Muslim terrorists are dehumanised and their actions attributed to their religion, White far-right terrorists often retain their humanity in media discourses, where they are presented as suffering from personal trauma or mental health issues.[80] Indeed, in many

71 David Gillborn, 'Risk-Free Racism: Whiteness and So-Called Free Speech' (2009) 44(2) *Wake Forest Law Review* 535, 554.

72 Ibid., 540.

73 Ibid., 541.

74 Ibid., 540–542.

75 Ibid., 542.

76 Coretta Phillips and others, 'Dear British Criminology: Where Has All the Race and Racism Gone?' (2020) 24(3) *Theoretical Criminology* 427, 430.

77 Paul Gilroy, 'The Myth of Black Criminality' (1982) 19 *The Socialist Register* 47 <https://socialistregister.com/index.php/srv/article/view/5474> accessed 18 December 2024; Paul Gilroy, *There Ain't No Black in the Union Jack* (Routledge 1987); Paul Gilroy, *Postcolonial Melancholia* (Columbia University Press 2005).

78 Hall and others, *Policing the Crisis*.

79 Arun Kundnani, 'Blind Spot? Security Narratives and Far-Right Violence' (2012) 23(2) *Security and Human Rights* 129, 129.

80 Caroline Mala Corbin, 'Terrorists Are Always Muslim but Never White: At the Intersection of Critical Race Theory and Propaganda' (2017) 86(2) *Fordham Law Review* 455, 466–469.

cases White terrorists are not referred to as terrorists. Caroline Mala Corbin adds 'even if I use violence ... to intimidate a civilian population, odds are I will not be called a terrorist' to Peggy McIntosh's list of the benefits of White privilege referred to above.[81] Additionally, while terrorist offences by a Muslim are often followed by calls for Muslim people to denounce the attack,[82] White people are never asked or expected to denounce terrorist acts by other White people.[83] To be White is to be seen as an individual rather than being defined by race or religion.

The terms White privilege and White supremacy have been criticised by some Marxist academics who are sympathetic to aspects of CRT but argue that the theory gives insufficient attention to class.[84] Mike Cole argues that the term White supremacy should be restricted to the narrower definition of conscious racism by the far-right.[85] However, as Paul Warmington argues, 'to treat white supremacy as a marginal extremist activity, as opposed to being integral to the social and political formation, is a category error in the first place'.[86] Critical legal scholarship has, as outlined above, attempted to uncover that which is hidden and appears neutral. The term White supremacy can be seen as 'an analytical tool for understanding covert racism' that seems natural because it is such an intrinsic part of society.[87] This does not conflate it with fascism but recognises how racism permeates the organisation and structure of society, as opposed to being something that is perpetrated only by extremists.

Rather than seeing a binary distinction between 'mainstream' racism and 'extreme' racism that needs to be maintained discursively by reserving the term White supremacy to the latter, we should understand that the racist practices in, for example, education and the legal system have their origins

81 Ibid., 466.

82 Roy Greenslade, 'Why It's Wrong to Demand that Muslims Condemn ISIS' *The Guardian* (24 November 2015) <www.theguardian.com/media/greenslade/2015/nov/24/why-its-wrong-to-demand-that-muslims-condemn-isis> accessed 2 February 2025.

83 Corbin, 472.

84 Mike Cole, *Critical Race Theory and Education: A Marxist Response* (2nd edn, Palgrave Macmillan 2017), 48–52; Dave Hill, 'Race and Class in Britain: A Critique of the Statistical Basis for Critical Race Theory in Britain and some Political Implications' (2009) 7(2) *Journal for Critical Education Policy Studies* 1.

85 Mike Cole, '"A Bright Future" for "Something New and Highly Significant" or a Bit of a Damp Squib?: (Neo-) Marxist Reflections on Recent Theoretical Developments in "BritCrit" in the Journal Race, Ethnicity and Education' (2017) 15(3) *Journal for Critical Education Policy Studies* 57, 59–60.

86 Paul Warmington, 'Critical Race Theory in England: Impact and Opposition' (2020) 27(1) *Identities* 20, 30.

87 Charlotte Chadderton, 'UK Secondary Schools Under Surveillance: What are the Implications for Race? A Critical Race and Butlerian Analysis' in Antonia Kupfer (ed), *Power and Education: Contexts of Oppression and Opportunity* (Palgrave Macmillan 2015), 78.

in slavery and colonialism. They can be seen as the legacies of the 'colonial matrix of power', a term used by Walter Mignolo, drawing on the work of Aníbal Quijano, which is described as having 'four interrelated domains: control of the economy, of authority, of gender and sexuality, and of knowledge and subjectivity'.[88] As Mignolo argues, 'the colonies were not a secondary and marginal event in the history of Europe ... on the contrary, the colonial history is the non-acknowledged centre in the making of modern Europe'.[89] Colonialism is intrinsically linked with modernity,[90] and the racial classifications in contemporary society have colonial roots.[91]

The classification of colonial populations as less than human shares the logic of the Holocaust, which led Aimé Césaire to argue that, 'the very distinguished, very humanistic, very Christian bourgeois of the twentieth century ... has a Hitler inside him', and that Hitler 'applied to Europe colonialist procedures which until then had been reserved exclusively' for racialised people in Algeria, India, and Africa.[92] The uniqueness of the Holocaust was its use of mass murder by Europeans against Europeans, rather than against non-Europeans, yet this genocide was nonetheless based on processes of racialisation.[93] This demonstrates how, as discussed below, the boundaries of Whiteness are subject to change, such that European ethnic or religious populations are not immune from being racialised, and from being subjected to exclusion and to the violence of White supremacy, including torture and genocide. The ideologies of racial inferiority and supremacy used to justify colonialism share the premise of fascist ideology.[94] To draw a strict demarcation between the two is to succumb to the liberal illusion of justice that CRT seeks to challenge.

Contrary to Mike Cole's argument that the CRT concept of White supremacy 'homogenizes all white people together as being in positions of power and privilege' and fails to account for poverty in White communities,[95] the concepts of White supremacy and White privilege recognise that not all

88 Walter D. Mignolo, *The Darker Side of Western Modernity: Global Futures, Decolonial Options* (Duke University Press 2011), 8.
89 Ibid., 140.
90 Aníbal Quijano and Michael Ennis, 'Coloniality of Power, Eurocentrism and Latin America' (2000) 1(3) *Nepantla: Views from South* 533, 548.
91 Ibid., 533.
92 Aimé Césaire, *Discourse on Colonialism* (Joan Pinkham tr, Monthly Review Press 2000), 36.
93 Mills, 102–103.
94 Ibid., 106.
95 Mike Cole, 'On "White Supremacy" and Caricaturing, Misrepresenting and Dismissing Marx and Marxism: A Response to David Gillborn's "Who's Afraid of Critical Race Theory in Education?"' (2009) 7(1) *Journal for Critical Education Policy Studies* 30, 31.

White people benefit from racism to the same degree.[96] Ultimately, the main beneficiaries of White supremacy are rich elites who will sacrifice the interests of poor White people in order to safeguard their own interests in particular situations, for example by blaming racism on the constructed 'White working class' rather than on their own racist rhetoric or on material inequalities.[97] This is discussed in Chapter 4 in relation to hate crimes. CRT acknowledges that millions of White people live in conditions of poverty, but it does recognise that, when all other factors are equal, their chances of transcending this are higher than their Black peers.[98] Thus, the theory does not discount class nor does it homogenise all White people, as it recognises that White privilege is deployed unequally on the basis of class position and furthermore, that it is used tactically to bolster the power of White elites.[99] Indeed, the concept of 'White supremacy' can be used to draw a distinction between Whiteness as an ideology and White people.[100] The invention of the 'White race' and the corresponding White privilege afforded to poor Whites has been used as a 'safety valve' to prevent them from combining with Black people to oppose their shared exploitation under capitalism.[101] Fundamentally, under capitalism, class distinctions and racial ordering are intrinsically linked, as explained in Chapter 2.

Another principle central to CRT enables one to consider how other inequalities, such as class and gender, interact with processes of racialisation. Intersectionality was introduced into the literature by Kimberlé Crenshaw[102] and is now used more widely in social science and popular discourses. This approach demonstrates how different identities and inequalities impact upon one another. For example, Black women experience sexism in different ways to White women but also experience racism in different ways to Black men.[103] An intersectional approach is not immune from essentialism. It could be interpreted as considering how various essentialised identities interact, such that there is an authentic Black working class female identity, for example.[104] Judith Butler has argued that intersectionality can assume the pre-existence

96 David Gillborn, 'The White Working Class, Racism and Respectability: Victims, Degenerates and Interest-Convergence' (2010) 58(1) *British Journal of Educational Studies* 3, 4.
97 Ibid., 21–22.
98 Howard, 70.
99 Warmington, 25.
100 Ibid., 25.
101 Theodore W. Allen, *The Invention of the White Race* (Verso Books 2021), Volume 2, 259.
102 Kimberlé Crenshaw, 'Demarginalizing the Intersection of Race and Sex: A Black Feminist Critique of Antidiscrimination Doctrine' (1989) 1989 *University of Chicago Legal Forum* 139.
103 Kimberlé Crenshaw, 'Mapping the Margins: Intersectionality, Identity Politics and Violence Against Women of Color' (1991) 43(6) *Stanford Law Review* 1241.
104 Charlotte Chadderton, *Judith Butler, Race and Education* (Palgrave Macmillan 2018), 35.

of these types of identity whereas their theory of performativity, which is discussed below, provides a way of avoiding essentialism by considering how identities are not innate but are performatively constituted.[105] However, they do accept that an intersectional analysis may challenge the concept of reductive, universal categories.[106]

A nuanced, non-essentialist approach to intersectionality can demonstrate how categories of oppression have the capacity to reinforce each other and take different forms in various situations. This requires a historically and materially grounded approach, otherwise the theory lacks explanatory force. The reasons why categories interact with each other in varying ways, for example, why racial discrimination against Muslim women differs from racial discrimination against Muslim men, are not due to free-standing ideological conceptions of race, class, or gender. They can be explained by the ways that those inequalities are rooted in patterns of colonialism, imperialism, migration, and globalisation, and how they emerge and play out in the context of racial capitalism.[107] An intersectional approach needs to locate processes of racialisation in the context of different stages of racial capitalism, and to see these processes as intrinsically linked with the ways that gender and sexuality are constructed. As Françoise Vergès argues, racism and patriarchal processes have intersected to deem racialised women unworthy of protection, as discussed in Chapter 5.[108]

Contrary to arguments that CRT fails to account for 'non-colour-coded racism',[109] the theory posits that racialised categories are socially constituted – 'the white race consists of those who partake of the privileges of the white skin in this society'.[110] Daniel Rubin has coined the term HebCrit to describe 'a new facet of CRT that specifically addresses the needs of the Jewish people' as a racialised group.[111] The experiences of Jewish people illustrate how a group can benefit from some aspects of White privilege yet remain racialised, and thus suffer racism.[112] Materialist critical race scholars, such as Richard Delgado, locate changes to the racialisation of particular groups within an

105 Ibid., 36.

106 Judith Butler, *Gender Trouble: Feminism and the Subversion of Identity* (2nd edn, Routledge 1990), 4–5.

107 Avtar Brah and Ann Phoenix, 'Ain't I a Woman? Revisiting Intersectionality' (2004) 5(3) *Journal of International Women's Studies* 75, 83 <https://vc.bridgew.edu/cgi/viewcontent.cgi?article=1543&context=jiws> accessed 18 December 2024.

108 Françoise Vergès, *A Feminist Theory of Violence* (Melissa Thackway tr, Pluto Press 2022), 32–33.

109 Cole, *Critical Race Theory and Education*, 42.

110 Noel Ignatiev, *How the Irish Became White* (Routledge 1995), 2.

111 Daniel Ian Rubin, 'HebCrit: A New Dimension of Critical Race Theory' (2020) 26(4) *Social Identities* 499.

112 Ibid., 507.

analysis of economic factors, including colonialism and imperialism.[113] David Roediger explains that several groups now considered White were initially regarded as 'nonwhite, or of debatable racial heritage' following their arrival in the United States.[114] Italian and Irish immigrants to the United States were considered White only when they pledged allegiance to the Democratic Party and sided with White elites against their Black neighbours.[115] The Democratic Party won the support of Irish Catholic immigrants by 'appeals to an "American race" of "white men"'.[116] This defined labour privileges as based on Whiteness rather than on length of time in the United States, with Irish workers consolidating their newly acquired Whiteness by campaigning to exclude Chinese immigrant workers from California.[117] In New York, Irish workers attacked tobacco factories, forcing them to stop hiring Black workers.[118] As Noel Ignatiev argues, in order to gain a competitive advantage in labour markets, many Irish immigrants chose the privileges of Whiteness over solidarity with Black workers.[119]

Irish immigrants to Britain were in a different position – they were racialised due to Britain's colonial relationship to Ireland.[120] The treatment of Irish immigrants around the time of the Industrial Revolution is discussed in Chapter 2. In the 1950s, it was not uncommon for rental properties in Britain to have 'No Blacks, No Dogs, No Irish' signs in the window.[121] However, although Irish people in Britain suffered economic deprivation not dissimilar to Caribbean and Asian immigrants in the post-war period,[122] they were advantaged in relation to immigration law.[123] Processes of racialisation are constantly contested and renegotiated such that those groups at the margins of Whiteness may be at risk of losing their partial White privilege when it no longer serves the interests of White elites, such as during a recession or during periods of resistance to colonialism or imperialism. As discussed in Chapter

113 Richard Delgado, 'Two Ways to Think About Race: Reflections on the Id, the Ego, and Other Reformist Theories of Equal Protection' (2008) 89 *Georgia Law Journal* 2279, 2283–2285.
114 David Roediger, *Towards the Abolition of Whiteness* (Verso Books 1994), 184.
115 Delgado, 'Two Ways to Think About Race', 2285.
116 Roediger, 190.
117 Ibid., 190.
118 Allen, 191.
119 Ignatiev, 3.
120 John Corbally, 'The Jarring Irish: Postwar Immigration to the Heart of Empire' (2009) 104 *Radical History Review* 103, 104.
121 Ibid., 103.
122 Ibid., 115.
123 Ibid., 110–111.

3, from the 1970s to the 1990s, the use of the Prevention of Terrorism Acts constructed Irish people in Britain as a 'suspect community'.[124]

The upward mobility of some groups, such as Jewish people, has been deployed by White elites as an ideological weapon to present society as meritocratic and to justify post-racial discourses where 'in time and with hard work, every ethnic group would get a piece of the pie'.[125] This 'project of racial uplift' relies upon a reworking of colonial civilising mission discourses.[126] Whiteness is positioned as superiority, and something for colonial subjects or immigrants to aspire to emulate. 'Model minority' discourses use the educational and economic success of particular racialised groups to assert that they have overcome adversity.[127] This denies continued racism against those groups by suggesting that they have 'recovered from histories of exclusion, internment, exploitation, and colonialism'.[128] Further, it attributes the continued disadvantage of other racialised groups to their inherent deficiencies.[129] The neoliberal myth of meritocracy that operates to justify such discourses is considered in Chapter 2, and the civilising mission is discussed throughout this book.

Some CRT literature deploys counternarrative as a device to disrupt processes of racialisation that would otherwise seem natural, and to reveal voices silenced by the law or by mainstream academia. Daniel Farber and Suzanna Sherry critique this methodology, arguing that narrative needs to include reason and legal analysis to be sufficiently rigorous to count as academic output[130] and to enable the work to invite further dialogue rather than being solely an autobiographical anecdote to which other academics are unable to respond.[131] They also argue that academics from oppressed groups cannot claim to speak for all members of their race or gender and that, rather than allowing silenced voices to speak, such an approach may give voice to unrepresentative views or atypical experiences and silence others from the same group.[132] Similarly, Douglas Litowitz argues that CRT

124 Paddy Hillyard, *Suspect Community: People's Experience of the Prevention of Terrorism Acts in Britain* (Pluto Press 1993), 257–258.

125 Karen Brodkin Sacks, 'How Did Jews Become White Folks?' in Richard Delgado and Jean Stefancic (eds), *Critical White Studies* (Temple University Press 1997), 401.

126 Victor Bascara, *Model-Minority Imperialism* (University of Minnesota Press 2006), 75.

127 Ibid., 1.

128 Ibid., 4.

129 Denise Ferreira Da Silva, *Towards a Global Idea of Race* (University of Minnesota Press 2007), 264.

130 Daniel A. Farber and Suzanna Sherry, 'Telling Stories Out of School: An Essay on Legal Narratives' in Edward Taylor, David Gillborn and Gloria Ladson-Billings (eds), *Foundations of Critical Race Theory in Education* (2nd edn, Routledge 2016), 328 and 332.

131 Ibid., 331.

132 Ibid., 325.

makes the mistake of seeing storytelling as being inherently progressive, as well as criticising the methodology on the basis 'that it plays on emotion, instead of reason'.[133]

In response, Mark Tushnet argues that critics such as Daniel Farber and Suzanna Sherry do not appreciate the importance of narrative in legal theory more generally, and that narrative form has been more successful than earlier abstract work in 'constructing a social theory that made sense of the claims about the processes by which ideological domination or hegemony was created'.[134] Patricia Williams has used autobiographical accounts of discrimination as part of a broader analysis of racist practices, such as her account of being told that a Benetton shop that she wanted to enter was closed even though others were still in there.[135] As she argues, law is all about narratives, particularly trial advocacy, so 'the idea that somehow critical race theorists introduced storytelling into the legal academy is ridiculous'.[136] Therefore, in Richard Schur's words, for critics of narrative in legal scholarship, 'the problem therefore is not storytelling in itself, but whose story is being told'.[137] He highlights how Patricia Williams unveils the hidden discrimination and lack of neutrality that underlie concepts in contract and property law,[138] and how she relates personal narratives to legal cases.[139] In this way, her work articulates 'how legal concepts rely on racial fictions, and how notions of self and autobiography are products of liberal legal theory'.[140] The recounting of the Benetton incident is not merely an anecdote but a means to demonstrate how private property rights are deployed in racialised ways.[141]

Similarly, Richard Delgado points out that narrative is a fundamental part of the law and that mainstream, or in his words 'majoritarian', accounts are also stories, but the key difference is that those stories are not subjected to

133 Douglas E. Litowitz, 'Some Critical Thoughts on Critical Race Theory' in Edward Taylor, David Gillborn and Gloria Ladson-Billings (eds), *Foundations of Critical Race Theory in Education* (2nd edn, Routledge 2016), 303.
134 Tushnet, 'Critical Legal Theory', 88.
135 Patricia J. Williams, *The Alchemy of Race and Rights* (Harvard University Press 1992), 44–45.
136 Patricia J. Williams, 'Interview with Cornel West' in Cornel West and Kelvin Shawn Sealey (eds), *Restoring Hope: Conversations on the Future of Black America* (Beacon Press 1997), 149.
137 Richard Schur, 'Critical Race Theory and the Limits of Auto/Biography: Reading Patricia Williams's "The Alchemy of Race and Rights" Through/Against Postcolonial Theory' (2002) 25(3) *Biography* 455, 459.
138 Ibid., 469.
139 Ibid., 458–459.
140 Ibid., 470.
141 Ibid., 468–469.

interrogation about their veracity or reliability.[142] Counternarratives have a different purpose – 'outsider scholarship is often aimed not at understanding the law, but at changing it'.[143] Such accounts are likely to seem unintelligible to those who have viewed the law as neutral and not previously questioned its assumptions or foundations. Within an unequal legal system, a neutral legal narrative cannot exist – any account that purports to be neutral and colour-blind is situated within the dominant discourse of neoliberal White supremacy.

The criticism of the use of counternarratives may also be seen as an example of Edward Said's concept of Orientialism – binary distinctions whereby the West is seen as rational, advanced, and civilised, in contrast with the non-West, which is viewed as backward.[144] This racialised view of non-Western inferiority cannot be divorced from the ways that counternarratives by members of marginalised groups are dismissed as lacking reason and rigour, whereas narratives grounded in White European superiority are viewed as objective, enduring, and universal. Discourses around valid academic knowledge can be understood as part of a colonial worldview, grounded in Enlightenment modernity, that decides what is legitimate and what is dismissed as 'superstition or folk knowledge'.[145] The negative response by some academics to Patricia Williams' account of the Benetton incident is illustrative of attempts to present counternarratives as lacking credibility, and to silence racialised accounts of the law.[146] Counternarratives can disrupt existing paradigms of knowledge and enter those spaces of discourse to seek to redefine which voices and experiences have epistemic validity. This can make visible processes of racialisation that would otherwise be disappeared in legal literature and can counter the dehumanisation of racialised people.

Another theme in critical race literature is the critique of rights. Earlier in this chapter, it was argued that legal indeterminacy means that an appeal to human rights cannot guarantee a particular outcome.[147] A case may involve competing rights, such as the right to free speech against the right not to be verbally abused.[148] Therefore, human rights cases still entail a political choice between two competing positions. Furthermore, as with liberal law

142 Richard Delgado, 'On Telling Stories In School: A Reply to Farber and Sherry' in Edward Taylor, David Gillborn and Gloria Ladson-Billings (eds), *Foundations of Critical Race Theory in Education* (2nd edn, Routledge 2016), 334.

143 Ibid., 337.

144 Edward W. Said, *Orientalism* (2003 edn, Penguin Random House 1978), 206–207.

145 William Jamal Richardson, 'Understanding Eurocentrism as a Structural Problem of Undone Science' in Gurminder K. Bhambra, Dalia Gebrial and Kerem Nişancioğlu (eds), *Decolonising the University* (Pluto Press 2018), 234.

146 Schur, 467–469.

147 Mark V. Tushnet, 'The Critique of Rights' (1994) 47(1) *SMU Law Review* 23, 33.

148 Kennedy, 'The Critique of Rights in Critical Legal Studies', 196.

generally, legal rights can 'obscure (or legitimate) hierarchical social arrangements and the unequal distribution of power'.[149] This critique of rights was formulated by CLS and further developed by CRT. They were not the first to formulate a critique of rights. Karl Marx had asserted that granting rights to workers under capitalism did not stop their exploitation and, moreover, created the illusion of equality.[150]

While rights may pertain to be universal,[151] they are defined within the parameters of the normative values of a particular society, such that they are not inherently progressive.[152] Indeed, the concept of human rights was forged under Enlightenment reason where only White property–owning men were considered fully human, thus excluding by definition racialised populations, women, and the poor.[153] Thus, the origin of human rights discourses is located within the inequality of racial capitalism and the dehumanisation of racialised people. Lisa Lowe explains that, 'the genealogy of modern liberalism is ... a genealogy of modern race; racial differences and distinctions designate the boundaries of the human'.[154] If a person is not defined as human, then human rights have no application to them. As Gurminder K. Bhambra and John Holmwood remind us, 'rights, when limited, become privileges'.[155] It will be argued in Chapter 3 that the Enlightenment construction of human rights constitutes a second order simulacrum but neoliberal conceptions of human rights have become third order simulacra.

Under neoliberalism, human rights discourses are likely to lend themselves to right-wing individualism and free market ideologies rather than social solidarity.[156] Thus, rights may be used for conservative causes,[157] such as White people arguing that their rights have been infringed by affirmative action.[158] Further, additional legal rights for marginalised groups do not necessarily translate into actual safeguards, and there is a tendency for courts to apply legal rights increasingly restrictively over time.[159] Dominant groups, who believe that too much has been conceded, may seek to claw back and con-

149 David O. Friedrichs, 'Critical Legal Studies and the Critique of Criminal Justice' (1986) 11 *Criminal Justice Review* 15, 17.
150 Kennedy, 'The Critique of Rights in Critical Legal Studies', 215.
151 Ibid., 185.
152 Robin West, *Normative Jurisprudence: An Introduction* (Cambridge University Press 2011), 122–123.
153 Andrews, 20–23.
154 Lisa Lowe, *The Intimacies of Four Continents* (Duke University Press 2015), 7.
155 Gurminder K. Bhambra and John Holmwood, *Colonialism and Social Theory* (Polity Press 2021), ix.
156 West, 127.
157 Tushnet, 'The Critique of Rights', 27 and 33.
158 Tushnet, 'Critical Legal Theory', 86.
159 Francisco Valdes, 'Insisting on Critical Theory in Legal Education: Making Do While Making Waves' (2001) 12 *Berkeley La Raza Law Journal* 137, 143.

solidate their perceived loss of power.[160] An appeal to legal rights can be a diversion from full equality – it expresses rights in relation to 'equal protection' rather than socio-economic equality.[161] Even seemingly progressive rights may be problematic as they may create the illusion of meritocracy and thus legitimate continued inequality.[162] The use of human rights discourses as a justificatory alibi for the neoliberal simulacrum of meritocracy is discussed in subsequent chapters. Similar arguments in relation to the use of international human rights discourses as a justificatory alibi for imperialism are made in Chapter 3.

Notwithstanding these issues with human rights laws, some critical race scholars have argued that formal legal rights constitute a safeguard for racialised people. Patricia Williams contrasts her experience of renting a flat with that of a White male colleague – while he took a more informal approach to negotiating the agreement, viewing legal formalities as alienating, she opted for a detailed written contract.[163] As a Black woman, the formalisation of her rights gave her security; she did not have the privilege of being able to rely upon agreements based solely on trust. In Chapter 3, it will be argued that stop and search provisions that give greater discretion to the police are used in a more racially disproportionate way than those requiring reasonable suspicion. In other words, for racialised individuals, tightly defined legal provisions may provide some element of protection against racist practices when compared with those drafted in vague terms.

In the context of the overruling of *Roe v Wade*[164] in relation to abortion rights in the United States, it may appear inappropriate to speak of a critique of rights, given that the loss of such rights is likely to impact disproportionately on marginalised communities. However, as Mari Matsuda argues, there may be times when one argues that the legal system has no legitimacy yet other times when one deploys human rights discourses tactically to achieve a particular result.[165] Mark Kelman also argues that it is possible to argue for reforms, both as a way of securing practical gains and of exposing how these gains do not solve the fundamental issues in the legal system – a critical legal academic may 'advocate particular legal reforms, hoping both to better the short-term position of the reform's beneficiaries *and* to expose the limits of

160 Edward Taylor, 'The Foundations of Critical Race Theory in Education: An Introduction' in Edward Taylor, David Gillborn and Gloria Ladson-Billings (eds), *Foundations of Critical Race Theory in Education* (2nd edn, Routledge 2016), 2.
161 Kennedy, 'The Critique of Rights in Critical Legal Studies', 182.
162 West, 111 and 123.
163 Williams, *The Alchemy of Race and Rights*, 146–147.
164 410 US 113 (1973).
165 Mari J. Matsuda, 'When the First Quail Calls: Multiple Consciousness as Jurisprudential Method' (1992) 14 *Women's Rights Law Reporter* 213, 214.

legal reform'.[166] This last point is key as part of a strategy to move beyond legal equality to socio-economic justice.

The critique of rights has focused primarily on civil cases dealing with equality issues. Within the criminal context, discourses around victims' rights that argue in favour of carceral solutions have been critiqued by critical legal scholars, including Dean Spade and Sarah Lamble.[167] Any increase in criminalisation or punitive sentencing is likely to fall upon those sections of society already disproportionately prosecuted, with the paradoxical effect of further incarceration of the disadvantaged groups whose rights the law purports to protect. These points are considered in Chapter 4 in relation to hate crime.

Human rights arguments may seek the decriminalisation of activities that disproportionately criminalise marginalised groups. However, even when the law appears to grant increased freedom through placing previously criminalised activities outside the reaches of law and punishment, it may contain within it a countervailing tendency to intensify its punitive powers in relation to those related activities that stay within its realm. This can result in an increase in criminalisation and incarceration by strengthening the penalties for related activities, while also serving to bolster the legitimacy of the law. For example, sexual offences legislation in the late 1950s and 1960s decriminalised particular activities but strengthened the penalties for others.[168] While the Street Offences Act 1959 resulted in fewer convictions for street prostitution through driving sex workers off the streets, it dramatically increased the imprisonment rate of those convicted.[169] Similarly, after the Sexual Offences Act 1967 partially decriminalised homosexuality, the number of convictions for indecency between males rose significantly.[170] The impetus behind such legislation was 'to construct a "civilised form of social life" appropriate to a civilised and modernised capitalism'.[171] This maintained and consolidated the authority of the law, such that it could be seen to be responding to shifts in public opinion by selective liberalisation in order to avoid appearing outdated and unduly punitive. Without this reframing, excessive criminalisation could threaten the legitimacy of criminal law. Such processes draw a sharp

166 Kelman, 298 (original italics).

167 Dean Spade, 'Laws as Tactics' (2011) 21(2) *Columbia Journal of Gender and Law* 40; Morgan Bassichis and Dean Spade, 'Queer Politics and Anti-Blackness' in Jin Haritaworn, Adi Kuntsman and Silvia Posocco (eds), *Queer Necropolitics* (Routledge 2014) 191–210; Dean Spade, *Normal Life* (Duke University Press 2015), 42–49; Sarah Lamble, 'Queer Investments in Punitiveness' in Jin Haritaworn, Adi Kuntsman and Silvia Posocco (eds), *Queer Necropolitics* (Routledge 2014), 151–171.

168 Stuart Hall, 'Reformism and the Legislation of Consent' in National Deviancy Conference (ed), *Permissiveness and Control* (Macmillan 1980), 17–18.

169 Victoria Greenwood and Jock Young, 'Ghettos of Freedom' in National Deviancy Conference (ed), *Permissiveness and Control* (Macmillan 1980), 161.

170 Ibid., 166.

171 Hall, 'Reformism and the Legislation of Consent', 33.

dichotomy by redefining those whose activities remain criminalised as having a greater degree of criminality than previously, and in doing so both remake and reinforce the boundaries between those populations deemed worthy of inclusion in society and granted access to the benefits of privilege, and those categorised as a threat to civilised society, who are subjected to the harshness of criminal punishment. For this reason, it is crucial that well-meaning activists do not advocate for law reforms that ultimately further criminalise marginalised groups and strengthen the carceral state.[172]

As part of the CRT critique of rights, Derrick Bell's theory of 'interest convergence' asserted that civil rights victories for Black people were granted by courts or authorities only when they advantaged White interests, or when they were the least damaging course of action for White elites in order to safeguard their own position.[173] Bell used the term in his analysis of *Brown v Board of Education*,[174] a landmark case that marked the end of racially segregated schools in the United States. He argued that the judgment was fundamentally about benefitting the United States both internationally and domestically rather than a commitment to racial equality.[175] It operated to safeguard the US reputation among developing nations in the context of the Cold War, as well as preventing unrest from Black citizens who had fought in the Korean War and would be unlikely to accept continuing segregation following their sacrifices in the name of the United States.[176]

Derrick Bell described *Brown* as a 'contradiction-closing case',[177] as it appeared to resolve the tension between the rhetoric of equality and the lived experiences of oppressed groups – 'the blatant credibility gap between our democratic precepts and our racist practices'.[178] The contradiction was closed by giving the impression that inequality was being addressed while providing minimal material changes.[179] Such a case, in Richard Delgado's words, will 'allow business as usual to go on even more smoothly than before, because now we can point to the exceptional case and say, "See, our system is really

172 Spade, *Normal Life*, 48.

173 Derrick Bell, 'Brown v Board of Education and the Interest Convergence Dilemma' (1980) 93(3) *Harvard Law Review* 518, 524.

174 347 US 483 (1954).

175 Bell, 'Brown v Board of Education', 524–525.

176 Ibid., 524–525.

177 Derrick Bell, 'Foreword: The Civil Rights Chronicles (The Supreme Court, 1984 Term)' (1985) 99 *Harvard Law Review* 4, 32.

178 Derrick Bell, 'Black Faith in a Racist Land: A Summary Review of Racism in American Law' (1971) 20 *Journal of Public Law* 409, 416.

179 Bell, 'Foreword: The Civil Rights Chronicles', 32.

fair and just. See what we just did for minorities or the poor"'.[180] Nearly two decades after *Brown*, desegregation was not achieved.[181]

More fundamentally, Derrick Bell argued, segregation was a manifestation of racism in education rather than the cause, and desegregation alone did not provide Black children with equal educational outcomes to White children.[182] Apparent equal rights masked a divided educational system that both reflected and perpetuated the unequal socio-economic position of Black children. As Cheryl Harris explains, 'White privilege accorded as a legal right was rejected, but de facto white privilege not mandated by law remained unaddressed'.[183] Within a system of White supremacy, Black children attending racially mixed schools were more likely to underachieve or be excluded.[184] In this way, ostensible equal rights masked material inequalities. Where Blackness is equated with deficiency, Black students will be seen as successful only where they assimilate into White norms and values.[185] Under neoliberalism, contradiction-closing cases can reinforce the myth of a post-racial meritocracy, whereby this apparent equality is deployed to support arguments that any failings on the part of Black people can no longer be accounted for by oppression and therefore must be due to their own deficiencies. Contradiction-closing cases in the context of neoliberalism will be discussed at the end of Chapter 2, and the concept of contradiction-closing provisions will be used throughout this book as a means of analysing criminal law and evidence.

CRT is a broad church, and one point of debate has been the tension between a materialist approach and discourse analysis. Richard Delgado criticises those who see racism as based solely on ideological factors.[186] He argues for a materialist analysis, pointing out that although the lives of oppressed people will be less unpleasant without hateful comments and caricatures, an attention to racist discourses alone will not lead to equality, as racism has an economic basis.[187] Referring to the concept of differential racialisation discussed above, he argues that this change in attitude to different groups over time can be explained by changing material forces and not by unconscious

180 Richard Delgado, 'Rodrigo's Committee Assignment: A Skeptical Look at Judicial Independence' (1999) 72 *Southern California Law Review* 425, 445.
181 Derrick Bell, 'Serving Two Masters: Integration Ideals and Client Interests in School Desegregation Legislation' (1976) 85(4) *Yale Law Journal* 470, 471.
182 Ibid., 487.
183 Harris, 1753.
184 Bell, 'Serving Two Masters', 488.
185 Daniel G. Solorzano and Tara J. Yosso, 'Critical Race Methodology' in Edward Taylor, David Gillborn and Gloria Ladson-Billings (eds), *Foundations of Critical Race Theory in Education* (2nd edn, Routledge 2016), 133.
186 Delgado, 'Two Ways to Think About Race', 2279–2282.
187 Ibid., 2281–2282.

impulses.[188] He uses the case of *McCleskey v Kemp*,[189] to illustrate ideological and material racism. The case involved a Black defendant sentenced to death for killing a White police officer during a robbery. His appeal was based on an academic empirical study which showed that prosecutorial discretion as to whether to request the death penalty was influenced by the race of both the victim and the defendant. Although the court accepted the results of the study, they found that discretion was a vital component of the system such that Mr McCleskey was not discriminated against.

Richard Delgado argues that while an idealist would see the case as reflecting the unconscious bias inherent in stereotypes of Black criminality, a materialist would consider how the carceral state and death penalty operate as a means of socio-economic control linked to labour market and voter disenfranchisement.[190] Nevertheless, discourses are not merely reflections of the material base but also operate to constitute and maintain identities, which in turn have material consequences. Racism is perpetuated through discourse. Without its ideological aspect, racism would not be able to persist, as it relies upon the *belief* that there are different races.[191] Racism has a material origin, with discourse later used to justify this inequality, as in the case of slavery where economic exploitation preceded the racism that was subsequently used as justification.[192] In Delgado's words:

> The sequence, then, is as follows: We treat minorities badly because we stand to gain material advantage. We then develop and propagate attitudes and beliefs that justify what we have done; other actors, including legal ones, join in. Oppression entrenches, making the next round of exploitation that much easier to carry out.[193]

As outlined earlier, a strength of CLS is its ability to combine an analysis of indeterminacy, philosophical instability and flux within the law itself with a materially and politically grounded analysis of why cases are decided in a particular way. CRT builds upon this by seeking to demonstrate how 'the Court's rulings with respect to race may more plausibly be deemed a result of a tactical political choice among competing doctrinal possibilities, any of which could have been legally defensible'.[194] This analysis, which considers how discourses are unstable but have material origins and consequences,

188 Ibid., 2286.
189 481 US 279 (1987).
190 Delgado, 'Two Ways to Think About Race', 2290.
191 Perry, 57.
192 Delgado, 'Two Ways to Think About Race', 2285.
193 Ibid., 2288.
194 Kimberlé Crenshaw, 'Introduction' in Kimberlé Crenshaw and others (eds), *Critical Race Theory: The Key Writings that Formed the Movement* (The New York Press 1996), xxviii.

can be enhanced further by another theoretical approach that considers how legal and evidential provisions can construct and reproduce different types of legal subjects by naming them in particular ways: Judith Butler's theories of performativity, racial framing, and ungrievable lives.

Judith Butler: Performativity, Racial Framing, and Ungrievable Lives

Judith Butler's theory of performativity asserts that there is no essential self, such that individuals are not inherently a particular gender but are so named by discourses and by 'doing' gender.[195] These discourses are performative; they are repeated actions or speech acts that create our identities, but are involuntary and situated within the constraints of a particular society, while hiding their historically situated specificity.[196] They are unstable and therefore require constant reproduction in order to maintain the illusion that particular categories are fixed.[197] This creates the possibility for them to be disrupted and subverted through the agency of the subject.[198]

Butler describes how the performative speech act, 'It's a girl!', serves to gender immediately after birth those with particular sexual organs.[199] Moreover, this naming as a girl carries with it assumptions around heterosexuality and femininity.[200] This gendering is then reinforced throughout one's life by disciplinary boundaries and social norms around gender that make one intelligible as a girl and a woman, although these processes of naturalisation may be contested.[201] Butler argues that parody has the potential to disrupt performativity in relation to gender.[202] Rather than exposing that the identity being parodied is 'the original', the parody exposes that there is no original, such that 'the parody is *of* the very notion of an original'.[203] The gender roles being parodied are not essentialist but are performatively constituted.[204] As will be argued later in this chapter, this idea of a copy without an original can be seen as consistent with Jean Baudrillard's theory of hyperreality.

Gender is Butler's primary focus, but their later work considers the ways that race is constructed through historically situated discourses by means of

195 Butler, *Gender Trouble*, 34.
196 Judith Butler, *Bodies That Matter* (Routledge 1993), 12.
197 Butler, *Gender Trouble*, 198–199.
198 Ibid., 201.
199 Butler, *Bodies That Matter*, 176–177.
200 Ibid., 176.
201 Ibid., xvii.
202 Butler, *Gender Trouble*, 43.
203 Ibid., 188 (original italics).
204 Ibid., 200.

'racial and ethnic frames',[205] with Islam framed as barbaric in contrast to Western 'civilisation'.[206] As outlined earlier, Butler argues for an intersectional approach that considers how, for example, race and gender interact with each other in particular contexts with each treated as non-essentialist and performativity constituted.[207] Performativity and CRT, as anti-essentialist theories of race, can complement each other and have been combined by education scholars, such as Charlotte Chadderton[208] and Deborah Youdell.[209] Chadderton argues that 'Butler's work gives us the tools to view race, rather than a fixed or innate aspect of identity, as a hegemonic, subjectifying norm, calling into question its ontological status'.[210] Some of Chadderton's work touches on criminal law, for example, the construction of Muslim students as terror suspects.[211] There is scope for applying these theoretical tools to criminal law more broadly.

Butler's analysis lends itself well to the law given that criminal law and evidence can be viewed as a series of repeated performative discourses that name people as legal subjects. Performativity within the law makes the legal categories that it creates seem natural and neutral. Thus, the law is self-legitimating through its own discourses. As Butler explains, 'the law produces and then conceals the notion of "a subject before the law" in order to invoke that discursive formation as a naturalized foundational premise that subsequently legitimates the law's own regulatory hegemony'.[212] However, there is the possibility of disrupting law's legitimacy and resisting these framings. Butler argues that a subject constituted by discourses still has the potential to challenge this – 'the culturally enmired subject negotiates its constructions, even when those constructions are the very predicates of its own identity'.[213]

Performativity enhances a non-essentialist CRT approach by enabling us to analyse how identities that appear natural and normal are produced and reproduced through processes of racialisation situated within economic relations. As Charlotte Chadderton argues, Butler's analysis of 'framing', particularly the concept of 'racial frames', is a useful way of conceptualising

205 Judith Butler, *Precarious Life: The Powers of Mourning and Violence* (Verso Books 2004), 57 and 90.
206 Ibid., 2 and 91.
207 Butler, *Gender Trouble*, 4–5.
208 Chadderton, *Judith Butler, Race and Education*.
209 Deborah Youdell, 'Identity Traps or How Black Students Fail: The Interactions Between Biographical, Sub-cultural, and Learner Identities' (2003) 24(1) *British Journal of Sociology of Education* 3.
210 Chadderton, *Judith Butler, Race and Education*, 48.
211 Chadderton, 'UK Secondary Schools Under Surveillance', 82–88; Chadderton, *Judith Butler, Race and Education*, 149–164.
212 Butler, *Gender Trouble*, 3.
213 Ibid., 195.

racialisation, as it 'offers a way of understanding the paradox of race: how race is a social and discursive construction yet is perceived (and thus mostly lived and experienced) as an essential aspect of identity'.[214] Framing can be seen as 'a collection of discourses that shapes perception'.[215] This shaping of perception, such that discourses appear to be true, can lead to material consequences for those framed. It does not escape Butler's attention that framing can also mean criminalisation: 'to be framed is to be set up, or to have evidence planted against one that ultimately "proves" one's guilt'.[216] As Butler argues, framing can also be the surrounding for a picture, which is linked to how the picture is interpreted, and this process of seeing something in a particular way can result in people drawing particular conclusions.[217] In this way, it is analogous with framing in the sense of a false accusation which is upheld because 'a "frame" is constructed around one's deed such that one's guilty status becomes the viewer's inevitable conclusion'.[218] This process is not, however, infallible, and it is possible to disrupt it and 'call the frame into question' by introducing something that challenges the conventional way of viewing and reproducing it, for example, by contextualising it in a different way.[219]

Although not always used explicitly, the term 'racial frame' is implicit throughout Butler's later work when discussing racism, given the central position of framing in their work generally.[220] As Charlotte Chadderton explains, this analysis, which draws on the work of Frantz Fanon in relation to racial gaze,[221] makes it clear 'that the "racial frame" shapes the way in which arbitrary acts, events and interaction are perceived'.[222] Butler also uses the term 'racial phantasmagoria' to describe how social conscious and unconscious imaginations constitute particular racialised populations as violent or threatening, such that state violence against them is considered legitimate.[223] Discriminatory policing can be seen as a consequence of viewing Black people through a colonial gaze or racial frame, which creates and sustains racial categories, as in the Rodney King case considered in Chapter

214 Charlotte Chadderton, 'Towards a Research Framework for Race in Education: Critical Race Theory and Judith Butler' (2013) 26(1) *International Journal of Qualitative Studies in Education* 39, 50.
215 Ibid., 50.
216 Judith Butler, *Frames of War: When Is Life Grievable?* (Verso Books 2016), 8.
217 Ibid., 8.
218 Ibid., 8.
219 Ibid., 9.
220 For examples of Butler's specific use of the term 'racial and ethnic frame' see Butler, *Precarious Life*, 57 and 90; Judith Butler, *Undoing Gender* (Routledge 2004), 10.
221 Frantz Fanon, *Black Skin, White Masks* (2008 edn, Pluto Press 1952), 82–108.
222 Chadderton, *Judith Butler, Race and Education*, 51.
223 Judith Butler, *The Force of Non-Violence* (Verso Books 2020), 142–143.

5.[224] It is not just that this overcomes the evidence in the case; the evidence itself is constituted through this form of seeing, which is saturated with colonial discourses.

In order to explain how particular communities are racialised in specific historical contexts, racial framing needs to be materially grounded. Discourse analysis has the potential to slip into relativism. An emphasis on cultural rather than material factors can result in the collapsing of economic inequalities into a matter of semantics.[225] In a Marxist critique, Peter McLaren and Ramin Farahmandpur acknowledge the contribution of Butler but emphasise the necessity of viewing performativity 'as a material practice ... produced within existing social relations of production'.[226] As Charlotte Chadderton argues, it is crucial that Butler is read materially, and combining performativity with a CRT analysis of White supremacy can provide a more complete understanding of processes of racialisation, and of how the production and reproduction of racialised subjects can be disrupted.[227]

Butler's later work, in particular, is grounded in a historical and material analysis of racism, particularly in relation to vulnerability to risk.[228] Butler argues that the belief in race separates populations into those deemed grievable and those deemed ungrievable.[229] War is a prime example of the categorisation of people into those 'whose lives are considered valuable, whose lives as mourned, and whose lives are considered grievable' and those who are ungrievable – 'one that cannot be mourned because it has never lived, that is, it has never counted as a life at all'.[230] While Butler's analysis is centred on the West's actions in the Middle East, they consider how the concept of 'war' can extend to domestic racialised populations due to 'the framing of immigration issues as a "war at home"',[231] and the detention and torture of Muslim prisoners in Guantanamo Bay by the US state.[232] For Butler, grievable populations are those 'entitled to self-defence and to the preservation of their lives'.[233] Those deemed ungrievable are constituted as the threat of violence that requires the use of self-defence, a theme that is explored in more

224 Chadderton, *Judith Butler, Race and Education*, 50–51.
225 Peter McLaren and Ramin Farahmandpur, 'Breaking Signifying Chains' in Dave Hill and others (eds), *Marxism Against Postmodernism in Educational Theory* (Lexington Books 2002), 49.
226 Ibid., 52.
227 Chadderton, 'Towards a Research Framework for Race in Education', 50–52.
228 Butler, *Frames of War*, 28.
229 Ibid., 24.
230 Ibid., 38.
231 Ibid., 26.
232 Ibid., 55–62.
233 Butler, *The Force of Non-Violence*, 143.

detail in Chapters 3 and 5.[234] These distinctions are constructed through processes of racialisation.[235]

Butler's notion of ungrievability is conceptually similar to the work of Michel Foucault,[236] Achille Mbembe,[237] Henry Giroux,[238] Gargi Bhattacharyya,[239] Ruth Wilson Gilmore,[240] and Dean Spade[241] in relation to the ways that racialised populations are considered disposable. Michel Foucault viewed his own concept of biopower, 'the right to make live and to let die',[242] as central to state racism.[243] He argued that, 'racism ... is the pre-condition for exercising the right to kill', which includes not only murder 'but also every form of indirect murder: the fact of exposing someone to death, increasing the risk of death for some people, or, quite simply, political death, expulsion, rejection, and so on'.[244] In this way, he linked biopower with the emergence of modern racism.[245] He argued that colonialism required a justification for the killing of particular populations, and evolutionary racism provided the alibi for this genocide.[246] This was extended to anyone who was deemed to be a threat to the strength and purity of the state, including war-time enemies, criminals, and mentally ill people, which meant that those categories became racialised.[247] The concept of the social body was based on 'the principle that the death of others makes one biologically stronger'.[248] The death or exclusion of particular populations was considered fundamental to the health of the dominant race.[249]

Achille Mbembe's theory of necropolitics builds upon Foucault's concept of biopolitics.[250] Mbembe argues that not only does the state have the right to decide who lives and dies, but racialised populations live under conditions of 'the subjugation of life to the power of death' such that they have 'the

234 Ibid., 143.
235 Ibid., 142–143.
236 Michel Foucault, *Society Must be Defended* (David Macey tr, Penguin Books 1997).
237 Achille Mbembe, *Necropolitics* (Duke University Press 2019).
238 Henry A. Giroux, *Stormy Weather: Katrina and the Politics of Disposability* (Paradigm Publishers 2006).
239 Gargi Bhattacharyya, *Rethinking Racial Capitalism* (Rowman and Littlefield International 2018).
240 Ruth Wilson Gilmore, *Golden Gulag: Prisons, Surplus, Crisis, and Opposition in Globalizing California* (University of California Press 2007).
241 Spade, *Normal Life*.
242 Foucault, *Society Must be Defended*, 241.
243 Ibid., 258.
244 Ibid., 256.
245 Ibid., 257.
246 Ibid., 257.
247 Ibid., 258.
248 Ibid., 258.
249 Ibid., 255.
250 Mbembe, 66.

status of the *living dead*'.[251] Henry Giroux writes that under neoliberalism, there is a 'new biopolitics of disposability'[252] where 'people marginalized by class and race are considered either dangerous or worthless, left to fight off society's misfortunes alone'.[253] Further, 'biopolitics ... is linked to the securing of borders to prevent the influx of immigrants, the production of human waste mechanisms to dispose of those populations considered dangerous or redundant'.[254] As Gargi Bhattacharyya argues, under racial capitalism those populations deemed surplus suffer from racialised processes of 'differential exploitation, expropriation and expulsion'.[255] Similarly, Ruth Wilson Gilmore describes racism as, 'state-sanctioned or extralegal production and exploitation of group-differentiated vulnerability to premature death'.[256] Dean Spade uses the term 'subjection' to describe the complex power relations underpinning norms based on the separation of people into 'the national population' and those 'others' that they must be protected from or who will 'drain' their resources.[257] Administrative systems, including welfare provision, housing, education, and law enforcement, appear neutral but operate on the basis of these norms and determine the life chances of those populations marginalised due to their race, gender, sexuality, class, or nationality.[258] This theme of racialised, criminalised populations being considered disposable and vulnerable, not only to a heightened risk of death but also to a life not worth living, is central to a system of criminal law that is embedded in colonialism. Additionally, the concept of the undeserving poor, which, as Robbie Shilliam argues, is a racialised categorisation,[259] is key to understanding processes of criminalisation under neoliberalism. In subsequent chapters, I will be deploying the concept of ungrievable lives to conceptualise the dehumanisation of racialised communities.

A related concept in Butler's work is that of 'intelligibility'. In the context of gender, they describe intelligibility as identities that 'in some sense institute and maintain relations of coherence and continuity among sex, gender, sexual practice and desire'.[260] Those identities that do not conform to these norms are deemed unintelligible and viewed as flawed or 'logical impossibilities from within that domain'.[261] In their later work, Butler discusses intelligi-

251 Ibid., 92 (original italics).
252 Giroux, *Stormy Weather*, 47.
253 Ibid., 63.
254 Ibid., 65.
255 Bhattacharyya, 182.
256 Gilmore, *Golden Gulag*, 28.
257 Spade, *Normal Life*, 5.
258 Ibid., 5–7.
259 Robbie Shilliam, *Race and the Undeserving Poor* (Agenda Publishing 2018), 6.
260 Butler, *Gender Trouble*, 23.
261 Ibid., 24.

bility as 'the general historical schema or schemas that establish domains of the knowable' and links this to being grievable.[262] They argue that, 'a life has to be intelligible *as a life*, has to conform to certain conceptions of what life is, in order to become recognizable'.[263] Those who are deemed unintelligible can be considered ungrievable.[264]

Law is performative: it contributes to the social construction of race and to legal categories such as criminal, anti-social, dangerous, and bad character. Butler refers to 'whiteness as a practice of superiority over minorities' and argues that 'its claim to dominance is fortified through daily acts which may not seem racist at all precisely because they are considered "normal"'.[265] Therefore, both law and race can be seen as performative practices that construct and maintain racialised legal subjects and conceptions of criminality through constant repetition. One additional theoretical perspective can refine the analysis further and is of particular use in explaining how performativity can produce and reproduce identities that appear real, such that the boundaries between truth and falsity are collapsed: Jean Baudrillard's concepts of hyperreality, simulation, and simulacra.

Jean Baudrillard: Hyperreality, Simulation, and Simulacra

A particular challenge for critical race scholarship is how to analyse the nuanced forms that racism takes under neoliberal criminal law. A materially grounded account of racial capitalism and colonialism is key when considering how concepts such as criminality, dangerousness, and character are racialised. Additionally, as set out above, Judith Butler's theory of performativity assists in explaining how these socially constructed racialised categories seem natural and neutral. To take the analysis further, Jean Baudrillard's concepts of simulacra, simulation, and hyperreality are tools to explain how the disproportionate criminalisation of Black people is perpetuated, and how this takes particular forms under neoliberalism through the use of signs such as gang member or violent rioter, such that racialised people are viewed as criminals. The durability and strength of these signs in constructing guilt provides a means of analysing the legal and evidential provisions described in subsequent chapters, and the ways that these provisions both rely upon and reproduce abstracted simulated legal subjects.

For Baudrillard, society had moved on from the commodity production stage of capitalism to a condition where meaning was produced by signs or

262 Butler, *Frames of War*, 6.
263 Ibid., 7 (original italics).
264 Ibid., 13–15.
265 George Yancy and Judith Butler, 'What's Wrong With "All Lives Matter"?' *The New York Times* (12 January 2015) <https://opinionator.blogs.nytimes.com/2015/01/12/whats-wrong-with-all-lives-matter/> accessed 18 December 2024.

codes,[266] such that it was 'a question of substituting the signs of the real for the real'.[267] He argued that there were four stages in this process.[268] At the first stage, the image still has meaning – it reflects, imitates, and represents reality.[269] The significant shift comes at the second stage, as it 'inaugurates the era of simulacra and simulation' such that the sign 'masks and denatures a profound reality'.[270] At the third stage, 'it masks the *absence* of a profound reality' such that there is only the image and no original, with the image appearing to be 'real', and at the fourth stage, 'it has no relation to any reality whatsoever: it is its own pure simulacrum'.[271]

Additionally, Baudrillard located simulacra in three historical orders.[272] The first order, which he referred to as 'the natural law of value', dated from the Renaissance to the Industrial Revolution, and was characterised by the counterfeit – there remained a discernible difference between the original and the copy, such that the copy was less real.[273] The second order took place during the Industrial Revolution and was based around reproducibility and commercial mass production, such that it was no longer possible to distinguish between the original and the copy – objects on assembly lines were made to be identical.[274] This operated on 'the market law of value'.[275] The third order of simulacra operates on 'the structural law of value'.[276] Baudrillard described this as hyperreality, a simulation of a simulation that appeared more real than reality.[277] He later added a fourth order – the fractal or virtual stage where there is no longer any law of value, only an 'epidemic of value' where all points of reference have disappeared and concepts are completely dissociated from their ideologies.[278]

The key point about simulated reality, or hyperreality, is not that it disguises difference and meaning but that it 'threatens the difference between the "true" and the "false," the "real" and the "imaginary"'.[279] It 'effaces the

266 Jean Baudrillard, *Symbolic Exchange and Death* (Iain Hamilton Grant tr, SAGE Publications 2017), 71.
267 Jean Baudrillard, *Simulacra and Simulation* (Sheila Faria Glaser tr, University of Michigan Press 1994), 2.
268 Ibid., 6.
269 Ibid., 6.
270 Ibid., 6.
271 Ibid., 6 (original italics).
272 Baudrillard, *Symbolic Exchange and Death*, 71.
273 Ibid., 71–72.
274 Ibid., 75–78.
275 Ibid., 71.
276 Ibid., 71.
277 Ibid., 92.
278 Jean Baudrillard, *The Transparency of Evil: Essays on Extreme Phenomena* (James Benedict tr, Verso Books 1993), 5–7.
279 Baudrillard, *Simulacra and Simulation*, 3.

contradiction of the real and the imaginary'.[280] Baudrillard argued that this makes it '*impossible to isolate the process of the real*, or to prove the real'.[281] Therefore, the question is not how to reclaim reality but rather, 'is there anything but a *discourse* of the real and the rational?'[282] For Baudrillard, the perfect crime is 'the murder of reality', where reality is so bound up with simulation that it can no longer be detached.[283] Hyperreality appears to be reality. In this way, 'we are in a world where the essential function of the sign is to make reality disappear and at the same time to mask that disappearance'.[284] Rather than reality and simulation existing alongside each other, as in previous historical stages, they have become so enmeshed that simulated, subjective cultural codes are produced and reproduced as objective reality.[285] What we deem to be reality is 'produced and reproduced by simulation' such that 'the proliferation of reality ... is our true catastrophe'.[286] The problem is our belief that hyperreality is reality.

Perhaps Baudrillard's most controversial work was his provocatively titled trilogy of essays – *The Gulf War Will Not Take Place*, *The Gulf War: Is it Really Taking Place?* and *The Gulf War Did Not Take Place*, where he argued that the Gulf War was a simulacrum that was 'not measured by being waged but by its speculative unfolding in an abstract, electronic and informational space, the same space in which capital moves'.[287] Thus, the signifying value of the war was greater than the military aspect: 'our wars ... have less to do with the confrontation of warriors than with the domestication of the refractory forces on the planet'.[288] As Richard Sherwin argued, 'the violent and tragic reality of war itself simply vanished' and became hyperreal such that 'whether the images we saw constituted disinformation (to demoralize the enemy) or were reality-based no longer seemed to matter'.[289] For the West, the simulated media images of the conflict took the appearance of reality. The conflict was read through signs that were themselves based on simulations constructed through Orientalist views of the Middle East.

Baudrillard had previously written that the Vietnam War was 'no less atrocious for being only a simulacrum – the flesh suffers just the same, and

280 Baudrillard, *Symbolic Exchange and Death*, 92.
281 Baudrillard, *Simulacra and Simulation*, 21 (original italics).
282 Jean Baudrillard, *The Perfect Crime* (Chris Turner tr, Verso Books 2008), 136 (original italics).
283 Ibid., xi–xii.
284 Jean Baudrillard, *Screened Out* (Chris Turner tr, Verso Books 2014), 125.
285 Baudrillard, *The Perfect Crime*, 18–19.
286 Ibid., 17.
287 Jean Baudrillard, *The Gulf War Did Not Take Place* (Paul Patton tr, Indiana University Press 1995), 56.
288 Ibid., 86.
289 Richard K. Sherwin, *When Law Goes Pop: The Vanishing Line Between Law and Popular Culture* (The University of Chicago Press 2000), 242–243.

the dead and former combatants are worth the same as in other wars'.[290] The theorisation of an event as hyperreal does not preclude a materialist analysis. Biko Agozino asserts that 'the Iraq War did not take place precisely because it was not a war, it was a colonial invasion'.[291] The aim was to consolidate Western hegemony and communicate a message of superiority, such that it 'ended in a technological demonstration which provided the illusion of power (of virtual omnipotence)'.[292] This was then exploited by the imperialist victor in the carving up of contracts for the 'rebuilding' of Iraq.[293] The bombing of Iraq continued after the official end of the war thus destroying the barriers, both discursive and material, between war and peace.[294] Baudrillard argued that the West had used Saddam Hussein in their own interests against Iran and then 'bumped off' this 'hired gun' when he became too powerful.[295] Discourses around factual events were superseded by those around good versus evil.[296]

Since Baudrillard wrote *Simulacra and Simulation*, processes of simulation have intensified. Under the bureaucratic managerialism of neoliberalism, meeting targets appears to take priority over the 'real' aims of institutions, as illustrated by hospitals that perform more routine operations at the expense of seriously ill patients, or by schools that focus on getting students through examinations rather than on educating them.[297] However, the issue is not that they are not fulfilling their 'real' role but that neoliberal institutions have an 'indeterminacy of functions' and therefore their role is hyperreal rather than real.[298] Education operates as a system of signs which deploys use value as an alibi, or justification, for handing out endless qualifications – 'a simulacrum of work exchanged against a simulacrum of a diploma'.[299] It is not that no teaching or learning takes place but that courses serve to 'resemble a "real" relation'.[300] John Canning argues that the Teaching Excellence Framework (TEF) is an example of a hyperreal simulacrum as it is detached

290 Baudrillard, *Simulacra and Simulation*, 37.

291 Biko Agozino, 'The Iraq War Did Not Take Place: Sociological Implications of a Conflict That Was Neither a Just War nor Just a War' (2004) 14(1) *International Review of Sociology* 73, 73.

292 Baudrillard, *Screened Out*, 72.

293 Subhabrata Bobby Banerjee, 'Necrocapitalism' (2008) 29(12) *Organization Studies* 1541, 1552.

294 Agozino, *Counter-Colonial Criminology*, 102.

295 Baudrillard, *The Perfect Crime*, 136.

296 Ibid., 112.

297 Mark Fisher, *Capitalist Realism* (Zero Books 2009), 43–44.

298 Baudrillard, *Simulacra and Simulation*, 77–78.

299 Ibid., 156.

300 Ibid., 156.

from teaching practice and relies instead on metrics, such as employability.[301] He argues that the simulated definition of 'teaching excellence', that presents as real, deprives lecturers of the language that they need to improve teaching and learning.[302]

Baudrillard used the example of a simulated robbery of a bank to argue that the law is incapable of distinguishing between the simulation of crime and the act of crime.[303] Because the signs of a simulated robbery will be so similar to a 'real' robbery, and the consequences may be the same in relation to the trauma caused to witnesses, the actions by the police, and so on, it is impossible to determine truth from falsity.[304] Furthermore, because actions such as bank robberies are embedded in media discourses around previous robberies, including both actual robberies and those depicted in popular culture, and therefore exist within the symbolic order, they are already 'hyperreal events'.[305] The inability of the law to distinguish between simulations and acts of crime will be discussed further in Chapter 6 in relation to drill music and bad character evidence.

In respect of law enforcement, Murray Lee and Alyce McGovern argue that while British policing has always deployed imagery to legitimise itself, 'the difference is that now the representation of policing *is* policing – or at least a simulation or simulacra of traditional policing'.[306] Observational documentaries, police social media, and news stories provided by the force to journalists are simulations of policing, which in turn affect police practices themselves, such that policing becomes hyperreal.[307] As with other so-called 'reality' television programmes, the act of being recorded mediates the behaviour of the participants, such that it is impossible to know what would be different if the cameras were not there.[308] Yet the way that such programmes are presented works to give the illusion that the presence of the cameras makes no difference, thus making the hyperreal appear real.[309] Production companies edit and select the footage in such a way as to ensure their continued relationship with police.[310] Through their use of the media, 'the police, as knowledge brokers, have increasing capacities to produce and disseminate

301 John Canning, 'The UK Teaching Excellence Framework (TEF) as an illustration of Baudrillard's Hyperreality' (2019) 40(3) *Discourse: Studies in the Cultural Politics of Education* 319.
302 Ibid., 328.
303 Baudrillard, *Simulacra and Simulation*, 20–21.
304 Ibid., 20.
305 Ibid., 21.
306 Murray Lee and Alyce McGovern, *Policing and Media: Public Relations, Simulations and Communications* (Routledge 2014), 72 (original italics).
307 Ibid., 168.
308 Baudrillard, *Simulacra and Simulation*, 27–30.
309 Ibid., 28.
310 Lee and McGovern, 168.

preferred narratives and images'.[311] The public then view these images as constituting 'real' policing, and expect the police to behave accordingly in their own interactions with them, such that the simulation shapes their actions and responses to being policed.[312] These processes of simulation construct police practices as ahistorical and dislocated. This disappears their colonial genealogy and the ways that police practices reproduce colonial relations against domestic racialised communities, as discussed in Chapter 3.

A Baudrillardian analysis enables us to question the ontological status of criminal law.[313] Richard Sherwin has described how the law 'comes to be dominated by image and perception' such that 'law enters the domain of the hyperreal'.[314] He argues that verdicts are increasingly reliant on signs and narratives rather than on evidence, with television, film, and media representations interacting with trial processes.[315] In this way, facts become blurred with image, fiction, and fantasy.[316] Bruce Arrigo argues that the media narratives around Aileen Wuornos were such that 'the social construction of homicide and serial killing was abstracted beyond recognition'.[317] Arrigo's account raises the prospect of using the concept of simulacra to analyse how criminality is reproduced. This process of simulation cannot take place without the earlier stages that construct criminality based upon historical performative discourses. In other words, Wuornos could only be reproduced as this simulacrum due to the underlying historical and material processes, such as the treatment of women who do not comply with expected female norms, that had already produced her as a criminal prior to her reproduction as a media image. The intersectionality of her gender, sexuality, and class was key to this. Simulacra of criminality are situated within a sign system that is embedded in colonialism and material inequalities, and located within the racial frame. Positioning the analysis in such a way can build on the work of Sherwin and Arrigo and enable these concepts to be used to theorise how neoliberal criminal law and evidence reproduce racially disproportionate outcomes.

Baudrillard considered law and the legal system to be second order simulacra.[318] A central argument of this book is that neoliberal criminal law and evidence have reached the stage of third order simulacra, with hyperreal

311 Ibid., 77.
312 Ibid., 168.
313 Bruce A. Arrigo, 'The Ontology of Crime: On the Construction of the Real, the Image, and the Hyperreal' in Bruce A. Arrigo and Christopher R. Williams (eds), *Philosophy, Crime, and Criminology* (University of Illinois Press 2006), 52.
314 Sherwin, 141.
315 Ibid., 217–218.
316 Ibid., 146 and 152.
317 Arrigo, 61.
318 Baudrillard, *Simulacra and Simulation*, 21.

simulations of guilt. They cannot be separated from the signs or simulacra of criminality that threaten the distinction between truth and falsity. Law and evidence are themselves constructed within processes of simulation. The issue is not that signs are being substituted for reality-based evidence, it is that the evidence itself is a simulation such that it is not possible to extract 'real' evidence.[319] Concepts of criminality, credibility, character, anti-social behaviour, and dangerousness are constructed through a racial frame, which is itself situated within colonial genealogies. As discussed below, race can be viewed as a second order simulacrum. However, under neoliberalism, processes of racialised criminalisation have become third order simulacra that collapse the boundaries between truth and falsity. These abstracted forms of criminality have their genealogy in previous orders of simulacra yet have absorbed this history, such that they are an implosion of the past and present. In this way, they are embedded in processes of racialisation and colonialism, but these processes are rendered invisible. As racism has become more abstracted, from biological to cultural to colour-blind, these simulacra have correspondingly become more abstracted.

Baudrillard recognised racism as located within modernity, with Enlightenment Reason premised on the concept of the universal man, which purported to be inclusionary yet excluded certain populations.[320] He asserted that, 'the progress of Humanity and Culture are simply the chain of discriminations with which to brand "Others" with inhumanity, and therefore with nullity'.[321] Baudrillard argued that there had been 'an increasingly racist definition of the "normal human"'.[322] He wrote that, 'the more hybrid our cultures become, and the more the theoretical and genetic bases of racism crumble away, the stronger it grows',[323] such that racism had 'become an immanent, viral and everyday reality'.[324] He argued that the 'fetishistic system of difference' means that 'the whole trend of our culture is towards a fanatically pursued differential construction'.[325] The West defined other cultures as different, because it saw itself as universal.[326] Baudrillard considered critiques of racism as limited; they addressed racism as a 'biological illusion' or 'obsession with difference' without considering whether biology

319 Note that this refers to 'real' evidence as evidence based on reality rather than evidence based on falsity. This is different from the usual definition of real evidence in criminal law, such as a physical object or demeanour in the witness box.
320 Baudrillard, *Symbolic Exchange and Death*, 146–147.
321 Ibid., 146.
322 Ibid., 147.
323 Baudrillard, *The Perfect Crime*, 131.
324 Baudrillard, *The Transparency of Evil*, 149.
325 Baudrillard, *The Perfect Crime*, 131–132.
326 Baudrillard, *The Transparency of Evil*, 155.

and difference were themselves illusionary concepts.[327] Colonialism imposed binary distinctions in relation to race and gender by defining Western concepts of biological difference as universal.[328] Therefore, it is crucial to view these binaries as historically specific products of colonialism rather than as enduring realities, and to appreciate that these concepts of binary distinctions and biological difference are themselves social and political constructions.

Stuart Hall had advanced the argument that race was 'a discursive construct, a sliding signifier'[329] that served to essentialise the notion of race after biological grounds for racism had been widely discredited.[330] He explained how race had maintained its apparent reality through the way that, since the Enlightenment, science had functioned as a 'regime of truth' that 'makes difference function discursively'.[331] Physical features such as skin colour became 'signifiers of an invisible code that writes difference upon the black body'.[332] Therefore, overcoming biological racism was not sufficient to move beyond the notion of racial markers of difference, as these markers then functioned to indicate cultural difference.[333] As Paul Gilroy contends, essentialist concepts of Black culture have slipped into viewing Blackness as a signifier for criminality, such that racialised people in the UK are viewed as existing within a 'culture of criminality and inbred inability to cope with that highest achievement of civilisation – the rule of law'.[334] All of these forms of racism are situated within Enlightenment discourses around the distinction between civilisation and barbarism.[335] Therefore, while scientific racism may appear to have been transcended, science as a discursive regime of classification permeates all of these constructions.[336] Blackness as a signifier of criminality then serves to naturalise racially disproportionate outcomes in the legal system, such that the discourse of post-racial colour-blindness is able to circulate under neoliberalism.

327 Ibid., 149.

328 For discussion of how gender binaries were imposed by colonialism see Oyèrónkẹ́ Oyěwùmí, *The Invention of Women: Making an African Sense of Western Gender Discourses* (University of Minnesota Press 1997); Maria Lugones, 'The Coloniality of Gender' (2008) 2 *Worlds and Knowledges Otherwise* 1; Judith Butler, *Who's Afraid of Gender* (Allen Lane 2024).

329 Stuart Hall, *The Fateful Triangle: Race, Ethnicity, Nation* (Harvard University Press 2017), 32.

330 Ibid., 59–60.

331 Ibid., 57.

332 Ibid., 63.

333 Ibid., 64.

334 Gilroy, 'The Myth of Black Criminality', 48.

335 Hall, *The Fateful Triangle*, 64.

336 Ibid., 64.

Maria Grahn-Farley's work is particularly pertinent as she links the simulacrum of law with the simulacrum of race.[337] As she argues: 'The rule of law is the rule of the white-adult-male hegemony. Out of this comes the hyperreal, the identities of the minorities, the ones who have less'.[338] The 'law functions as the alibi of a naturalized social hierarchy'[339] through its abstraction of racialised people and women, who become simulated essentialised legal subjects.[340] In this way, the law creates hyperreal legal subjects who appear real,[341] and are judged in relation to their perceived essential characteristics rather than on their actions.[342] Similarly, Simone Bull has argued that in New Zealand, Māori communities have been constructed as criminals through hyperreal processes whereby signifiers of apparent criminality appear as real.[343] These concepts can be deployed to analyse racialised criminalisation under neoliberalism more widely.

The theory of hyperreality enables a conceptualisation of contemporary racism as a simulacrum that has absorbed and rendered invisible previous incarnations of racism, such that it is located within Enlightenment and scientific regimes of classification and differentiation but serves to deny their existence. An understanding of hyperreality equips us to resist not only biological racism but also the discourses of differentiation that underpin the concept of Black criminality. It can illuminate the ways that racism becomes more abstracted and insidious over time. Viewing race as a simulacrum enables an analysis that challenges the perception that populations should be differentiated and categorised, and rejects discourses that position Whiteness as neutrality. The problem is not hyperreality as such, it is our belief that hyperreality constitutes reality.[344]

Race is a second order simulacrum located within the market law of value – an Enlightenment construct based on the definition of who was considered human in order to justify colonial expropriation. However, under neoliberalism, signs such as pimp, gang member, drug dealer, mugger, and rapist have become increasingly abstracted such that they act as signifiers for race, which in turn is a code for criminality. In this way, they have entered the realm of

337 Maria Grahn-Farley, 'The Law Room: Hyperreal Jurisprudence and Postmodern Politics' (2001) 36(1) *New England Law Review* 29, 44.

338 Maria Grahn-Farley, 'A. Taking Schlag to (the) Task: Reconstructing Rights, Reason, and Politics: A Theory of Child Rights' (2003) 57 *University of Miami Law Review* 867, 927.

339 Grahn-Farley, 'The Law Room', 44.

340 Ibid., 45.

341 Ibid., 46.

342 Ibid., 44.

343 Simone Bull, 'Crime and Māori in the Media' in Antje Deckert and Rick Sarre (eds), *The Palgrave Handbook of Australian and New Zealand Criminology, Crime and Justice* (Springer 2017), 743–745.

344 Baudrillard, *The Perfect Crime*, 17–20.

third order simulacra. These signs are a simulation of the simulation of race – they are a copy with no original. They operate to 'mask the *absence* of a profound reality'.[345] In other words, essentialised racialised legal constructions operate to hide that race is itself a simulation.[346] They make race, and racially disproportionate criminality, appear real. The origins of practices of racialised criminalisation have been made invisible through a process of distancing neoliberal criminalisation from its colonial roots. Hyperreality, simulation, and simulacra can be deployed as analytical devices to strengthen the CRT concept of contradiction-closing cases by explaining how criminal law and evidence use signs of criminality to appear to close the contradiction between racially disproportionate outcomes in the legal system and supposed equality while appearing neutral. Contradiction-closing cases are discussed further at the end of Chapter 2 and are deployed as an analytical device throughout this book.

Performative Processes of Simulation

Judith Butler's concept of performativity and Jean Baudrillard's theory of hyperreality can complement each other. As outlined above, Butler argues that gender is performatively constituted and there is no essential original gender.[347] Therefore, 'genders can be neither true nor false, but are only produced as the truth effects of a discourse of primary and stable identity'.[348] Additionally, Butler writes that 'certain cultural configurations of gender take the place of "the real" and consolidate and augment their hegemony through that felicitous self-naturalization'.[349] In other words, gender is a construction that collapses the boundaries between truth and falsity, and appears as real – it is hyperreal. A number of scholars have interpreted Butler's work through the lens of Baudrillard's theories. Karen Sichler uses the concept of hyperreality to enhance Butler's analysis by arguing that queerness can be viewed as a 'hyperreal gender', a simulation without an original.[350] This can liberate queer bodies and identities from being considered as an unintelligible or lesser form of gender, as it removes the notion that heterosexuality is the original or 'real' form of gender.[351] Similarly, Ridley Handley argues that in Butler's writing, 'gender adheres precisely to Baudrillard's definitions of hyperreality, an imitation without an original, a continuous reapproximation

345 Baudrillard, *Simulacra and Simulation*, 6 (original italics).
346 Grahn-Farley, 'The Law Room', 46.
347 Butler, *Gender Trouble*, 200.
348 Ibid., 186.
349 Ibid., 45.
350 Karen Sichler, 'Post Queerness: Hyperreal Gender and the End of the Quest for Origins' (2010) 30(2) *Post Identity* 46, 54.
351 Ibid., 46.

of simulated heterosexual ideals'.[352] As Victoria Grace writes, performativity is 'the dominant logic of discourse in an era where the relation of language and world is structured in accordance with sign value'.[353] The ways that performativity produces identities that appear real can be viewed as synonymous with hyperreality.[354]

By naming something, we construct it as an image, such that it is a representation.[355] In doing this to things, 'we call them into existence and at the same time hasten their doom, subtly detach them from their brute reality'.[356] Through the performative processes whereby human beings seek to give things meaning, the representation is seen as real and perceived as true.[357] In this way, simulacra are performative, and reproduce the initial representation in ever more abstracted forms, such that the subjectivity of the initial naming is disappeared and the concept appears to be objective, as with race, gender, and sexuality. In the case of hypercriminality, not only does this abstracted form belie its material histories by absorbing its colonial genealogy and so making it invisible, but it constructs the concept of Black criminality and White innocence as objective and real. The sign of the criminal overtakes the actions of the racialised individual in determining involvement with the law, including practices such as stop and search and the gang discourse at trial, and ultimately in establishing guilt.

Butler's concept of ungrievable lives can further enhance this analysis of hypercriminality. Marginalised communities are more prone to being abstracted as signs as they have already been dehumanised through previous processes of simulation. As Ruth Wilson Gilmore argues, racism is itself 'a practice of abstraction'.[358] Being ungrievable and being a hypercriminal can be seen as symbiotic processes that reinforce and reproduce each other, making racialised individuals increasingly abstracted. The challenge is to destabilise, disrupt, and interrupt these processes.

While critical legal theory may assist us in understanding how criminal law is one of the matrices of power that operate to preserve the structure of White supremacy, we cannot simply exit the matrix of racialised neoliberalism and escape the simulated viewpoint that reproduces Black communities as criminal. To refer back to the popular culture analogies considered earlier

352 Ridley Handley, 'Gender? I Hardly Know Her. Exploring the Hyperreality of Gender and Sexual Identities' *The University of British Columbia, Arts One* <artsone.arts.ubc.ca/student-journal/gender-i-hardly-know-her/> accessed 18 December 2024.

353 Victoria Grace, *Baudrillard's Challenge: A Feminist Reading* (Routledge 2000), 124.

354 Ibid., 124–125.

355 Jean Baudrillard, *Why Hasn't Everything Already Disappeared?* (Chris Turner tr, Seagull Books 2009), 11.

356 Ibid., 11.

357 Ibid., 12.

358 Ruth Wilson Gilmore, *Abolition Geography* (Verso Books 2023), 136.

in this chapter, it is not a question of discovering that the Matrix exists or pulling back the curtain that conceals the Wizard of Oz. There is no underlying reality to uncover. The issue is that what appears as reality is hyperreality.

The contention that there is nothing outside the simulation, nothing outside the place where truth and falsity no longer have any meaning, may be seen as negative. However, Baudrillard argued that his work had been misunderstood and that 'one must fight all charges of irresponsibility, nihilism or despair. Radical thought is never depressive'.[359] A theory of simulation 'is not a form of illusion, but opposed to illusion, a way of getting rid of the fundamental illusionality of the world'.[360] Baudrillard argued that Disneyland appeared as an imaginary world in order to make Los Angeles appear real, and to hide that Los Angeles itself is hyperreal and a simulation: 'It is no longer a question of a false representation of reality (ideology) but of concealing the fact that the real is no longer real, and thus of saving the reality principle'.[361] The problem is not the lack of reality – the problem is the belief that the simulacra are real. Thus, in relation to the issues considered in this book, the belief in race as a reality and the belief that hypercriminals are criminals are the problems. As Paul Gilroy writes, race can be viewed as 'a virtual reality given meaning only by the fact that racism endures'.[362]

Baudrillard argued that the system of hyperreality itself constitutes a nihilism of meaning, such that it prevents the 'active nihilism of radicality' by the implosion of meaning.[363] However, Baudrillard did leave open the possibility of resistance: 'if the world is fatal, let us be more fatal than it. If it is indifferent, let us be more indifferent. We must conquer the world and seduce it through an indifference that is at least equal to the world's'.[364] In Chapter 7, it is argued that being indifferent to the values of racial neoliberalism by refuting private property, competition, and individualism and replying with social justice, carceral abolition, and community solidarity can constitute a form of resistance. Speaking back and asserting that racialised legal subjects are hypercriminals rather than criminals can serve as an act of subversion to challenge dominant concepts of criminal law and oppose carceral solutions. In this way, the theory of hypercriminality can speak to abolitionist literature.

This book does not attempt to adopt Baudrillard's work wholesale but to appropriate his concepts of hyperreality, simulation, and simulacra within a particular context. Combining Baudrillard's theories with a materialist

359 Baudrillard, *The Perfect Crime*, 104.
360 Rex Butler, *Jean Baudrillard: The Defence of the Real* (SAGE Publications 1999), 23–24.
361 Baudrillard, *Simulacra and Simulation*, 12–13.
362 Gilroy, *There Ain't No Black in the Union Jack*, xxii.
363 Baudrillard, *Simulacra and Simulation*, 163.
364 Jean Baudrillard, *The Ecstasy of Communication* (Bernard and Caroline Schutze trs, Semiotext(e) 1988), 101.

reading of CRT may appear to be a contradiction in terms. When describing orders of simulacra, Baudrillard identified a break between the industrial era, which was based on production, and 'the current code-governed phase' where 'simulation is the dominant schema'.[365] He asserted that this constituted 'the end of a "materialist" history'.[366] However, he also wrote, 'are we still within a capitalist mode? It may be that we are in a hyper-capitalist mode' and 'if ... capital is a *mode of domination*, then we are always in its midst'.[367] It is contended that Baudrillard's work can lend itself to a reading that is both materially and historically contingent. As will be argued in Chapter 2, neoliberalism can be viewed as the hyperreal stage of capitalism where finance capital is self-referential and trades on codes of value rather than production value, yet this has immense material consequences for racialised populations.

Baudrillard argued that the orders of simulation were 'the reabsorption of all genealogy'.[368] Third order simulacra of criminality can be viewed as the culmination of historical processes where one order subsumes the former in an increasingly abstracted way that finds its epitome under neoliberalism. Baudrillard's work can explain how signs of racialised criminality are divested of their history of slavery, colonialism, and imperialism. This history is absorbed into the hyperreal realm and disappeared.[369] In the context of the built environment, Stephanie Malia Hom has used her theory of 'simulated imperialism' to demonstrate how simulacra interact with colonial and imperial processes[370] and 'bring[s] the colonial past into the hyperreal present'.[371] As she argues, processes of simulation create distance such that the colonial origins of contemporary simulacra are made invisible, yet their effect is amplified.[372] This can be deployed to analyse racialised criminalisation under neoliberalism. Dislocation and disjuncture hide the ways that signs themselves are based in colonial practices and discourses. They seem disconnected, such that there appears to be no historical context behind the image of the Black body as dangerous, threatening, or violent. The 'perfect crime' is this disappearance of colonial history – it is disseminated into the criminal law where it is reabsorbed and rendered invisible.[373] This disappearance of colonialism enables neoliberal criminal law and evidence to name

365 Baudrillard, *Symbolic Exchange and Death*, 71.
366 Ibid., 33.
367 Ibid., 32 (original italics).
368 Jean Baudrillard, *Forget Foucault* (Nicole Dufresne tr, Semiotext(e) 2007), 76.
369 Baudrillard, *Screened Out*, 18–21.
370 Stephanie Malia Hom, 'Simulated Imperialism' (2013) 25(1) *Traditional Dwellings and Resettlements Review* 25, 26.
371 Ibid., 27.
372 Ibid., 33.
373 Baudrillard, *The Perfect Crime*, 101.

racialised individuals and communities as uncivilised, ungrievable criminals, while portraying itself as post-racial and colour-blind.

Resisting these processes of disappearance is an urgent project. If the histories of colonialism, racial injustice, and struggle are not remembered, we cannot 'challenge the historical amnesia that feeds neoliberalism's ahistorical claims to power and the continuity of its claims to common sense'.[374] The next chapter will analyse the historical processes of colonialism, racialisation, and criminalisation that have culminated in the construction and reproduction of hypercriminals under neoliberalism.

374 Henry A. Giroux, *America on the Edge: Henry Giroux on Politics, Culture and Education* (Palgrave Macmillan 2006), 167.

Chapter 2

Racial Capitalism, Colonialism, and Simulation

This chapter focuses on four historical periods that illuminate processes of racialised criminalisation, particularly the ways that performative discourses construct and reproduce racialised legal subjects as simulacra, including the shift from second order to third order simulacra. The criminal provisions considered in subsequent chapters require an understanding of Britain as a colonial state, and of how processes of racialisation and criminalisation interact during various stages of capitalism. The periods considered in this chapter are: the early stages of capitalism that conflated poverty with criminality through shifting definitions of property and theft; transatlantic slavery and the development of theories of racialisation; British colonialism in India and the similarities between discourses of criminalisation used against those deemed lower caste in India and the poor in Victorian Britain; and finally criminal law under neoliberalism, with increased punitivity and mass incarceration located within meritocratic, colour-blind discourses. Through analysing these periods, this chapter will seek to demonstrate how processes and practices of racialised criminalisation are key to the operation of racial capitalism, and how this maintains and consolidates capital accumulation for White elites. Further, discourses around racialised criminality attempt to close the contradiction between ostensible legal equality and racially disproportionate outcomes in the criminal legal system. It will be argued that the first three of these periods created legal subjects as second order simulacra, and that the fourth, current period constructs third order simulacra: hypercriminals.

Throughout this book, I refer to 'racial capitalism'. Destin Jenkins and Justin Leroy describe this as 'the process by which the key dynamics of capitalism – accumulation/dispossession, credit/debt, production/surplus, capitalist/worker, developed/underdeveloped, contract/coercion, and others – become articulated through race'.[1] Capital accumulation required the

1 Destin Jenkins and Justin Leroy, 'Introduction: The Old History of Capitalism' in Justin Leroy and Destin Jenkins (eds), *Histories of Racial Capitalism* (Columbia University Press 2021), 3.

DOI: 10.4324/9781003602873-3

forcible dispossession of particular populations, and this process created and sustained racial differentiation.[2] Racist discourses made the resulting inequalities appear natural and rational.[3] Cedric J. Robinson explains that as 'the development, organization, and expansion of capitalist society pursued essentially racial directions, so too did social ideology'.[4] While there had been ethnic and cultural differences between populations under feudal systems, capitalism intensified these and turned them into enduring racial distinctions.[5]

For colonial and imperial projects to gain moral legitimacy, those whose land and resources were taken had to be framed as less than human. This enabled invasion and theft to be reframed as a civilising mission over dehumanised populations: 'since none may enslave, rob or kill his fellow-man without committing a crime, they lay down the principle that the native is not one of our fellow-men'.[6] Thus, it was central to the narrative of colonialism that White Europeans were civilised, whereas the inhabitants of the areas of the world they occupied were savage. Theodore Allen writes that 'resistance to conquest and the ways of colonial exploitation was interpreted in terms of an incapacity for civilization'.[7] Colonial and imperialist discourses drew a binary distinction between the civilised, advanced West and the uncivilised, backward non-West.[8] The latter was viewed as spiritually[9] and intellectually[10] underdeveloped and valuable only in relation to its utility to the entitled West.[11] As Homi Bhabha argued, 'the objective of colonial discourse is to construe the colonized as a population of degenerate types on the basis of racial origin, in order to justify conquest and to establish systems of administration and instruction'.[12] These processes of racialised dehumanisation were intrinsically linked with criminalisation.

As argued below, modern racism can be seen as a consequence rather than the cause of transatlantic slavery.[13] The aim of colonialism was to make a

2 Ibid., 3.
3 Ibid., 3.
4 Cedric J. Robinson, *Black Marxism: The Making of the Black Radical Tradition* (The University of North Carolina Press 2000), 2.
5 Ibid., 26.
6 Frantz Fanon, *The Wretched of the Earth* (Penguin Books 1961), 13.
7 Theodore W. Allen, *The Invention of the White Race* (Verso Books 2021), Volume 1, 31.
8 Edward W. Said, *Orientalism* (Penguin Random House 2003), 206–207.
9 Ibid., 60.
10 Ibid., 36.
11 Ibid., 221.
12 Homi K. Bhabha, 'The Other Question: Difference, Discrimination and the Discourse of Colonialism' in Francis Barker and others (eds), *Literature, Politics and Theory: Papers from the Essex Conference 1976–1984* (Routledge 1986), 154.
13 Eric Williams, *British Capitalism and British Slavery* (Diasporic Africa Press 2013), 7.

profit, not to institute a system of racism.[14] In Patrick Wolfe's words, 'race is colonialism speaking ... colonialism came before race, which it created. To say otherwise – that race created colonialism – would be to subscribe to colonialism's own justification'.[15] While the modern concept of race finds its origins in colonialism and the Enlightenment, racism has become mutualistic and symbiotic with capitalism. Rather than being specific to a particular phase, type, or expression of capitalism, racism is endemic to capitalism.[16] However, it takes different forms at various stages of capitalism, such that it is continually reworked, both reflecting and impacting upon other ideologies during each period.[17] Gargi Bhattacharyya writes that, 'racial capitalism is characterised, in all its variety, by the manner in which powerful actors seek to requisition the means of life and value and to gain benefit from the mobilisation of racialised distinctions'.[18] As Stuart Hall argued, capitalism not only reproduces class relations but structures them through racial differentiation.[19]

Race can be viewed as a second order simulacrum constructed through Enlightenment discourses around rationality and civilisation. The concept of race was deployed to justify slavery and colonialism, which were means of securing capital accumulation through expropriation and exploitation. As outlined in Chapter 1, the act of naming a representation commences the performative processes through which it becomes ever more abstracted yet appears as real, such that its initial subjectivity is disappeared.[20] As racial capitalism developed, the racialising processes rooted in colonialism were used in ever more nuanced and insidious ways, such that they changed from second order to third order simulacra.

The perpetuation of racism in neoliberal societies operates to maintain the power and privilege of White elites. It will be argued that neoliberalism is the hyperreal phase of racial capitalism where stock values are self-referential rather than based on production. The drive to maintain the rate of profit necessitates further processes of criminalisation of the racialised poor through the simulacrum of meritocracy, which is a contemporary reworking of undeserving poor discourses. Processes of racialised criminalisation are increasingly abstracted, such that their colonial roots are rendered invisible

14 Patrick Wolfe, *Traces of History: Elementary Structures of Race* (Verso Books 2016), 57; Gargi Bhattacharyya, *Rethinking Racial Capitalism* (Rowman and Littlefield International 2018), 37 and 77.
15 Wolfe, 57.
16 Jenkins and Leroy, 1.
17 Stuart Hall, 'Race, Articulation and Societies Structured in Dominance' in David Morley (ed), *Essential Essays, Volume 1* (Duke University Press 2018), 217.
18 Bhattacharyya, 176.
19 Hall, 'Race, Articulation and Societies Structured in Dominance', 216.
20 Jean Baudrillard, *Why Hasn't Everything Already Disappeared?* (Chris Turner tr, Seagull Books 2009), 11–12.

and the racialised poor become hypercriminals. These processes are simulations of the second order simulacra of race and the undeserving poor, such that they are third order simulacra. They are simulations of previous simulacra, copies without an original. In this way, processes of racialisation have morphed from the economic to the symbolic realm while reabsorbing their genealogy. These processes operate to consolidate capital accumulation by White elites at the expense of the racialised poor.

The USA is discussed extensively in two sections of this chapter – trans-atlantic slavery and neoliberalism. While there are key differences between Britain and the USA, this book resists taking a comparative approach, which can lead 'to the erroneous suggestion that states can be looked at in isolation as though ideas of race do not circulate globally'.[21] Although the plantations were in the Americas, Britain's wealth was built on slavery and colonialism. Further, Britain remains a colonial state; racism is situated within the history of Empire and colonialism, with racial boundaries enforced by immigration laws.[22] In relation to criminal legal practices under neoliberalism, the second order simulacra of race and the undeserving poor are absorbed into the construction of third order simulacra of racialised hypercriminals in similar ways in Britain and the USA. Therefore, although this book focuses on criminal law in England and Wales, these provisions cannot be understood in isolation and the theory of hypercriminality is applicable to all neoliberal economies.

Emerging Capitalism and the Undeserving Poor

Capital accumulation requires the dispossession of particular populations, who are reduced to labouring for the propertied classes. In the early period of capitalism, this was enabled by changing definitions of property and ownership, including access to natural resources, such as land, plants, and minerals, as well as autonomy over one's own body. Civil and criminal law operated in tandem to define and enforce property relations. Processes of criminalisation, particularly those relating to property offences such as theft, facilitated the development of racial capitalism.

Enclosure, which can be defined as the privatisation of land that had previously been communal, significantly changed land use from the 1600s onwards. Prior to enclosure, this common land had been used by the local community to keep and graze animals, and extract materials, such as wood

21 Alana Lentin, *Why Race Still Matters* (Polity Press 2020), 78.
22 Nadine El-Enany, 'From Love to Justice: Families' Interrogation of Racial State Violence' (2022) 32 *Social and Legal Studies* 1, 10.

for building or fuel.[23] Enclosure displaced the customs that enabled rural communities to use land for agriculture.[24] Although some of the earlier enclosure period predated capitalism, enclosure was key to the transition from feudalism to early capitalism.[25] In most cases, the commissioners who distributed land under the Enclosure Acts were able to ignore the customary rights to the common land previously enjoyed by the rural poor and award them nothing, thus taking away their subsistence.[26] Even those successful in obtaining a small plot of land were often unable to meet the costs required, which could include fencing and hedging, as well as losing the benefits of the use of larger common areas, so had to sell their land to the large landowners.[27] Initially there was differentiation within the rural poor, as some lost everything and others became small proprietors who benefitted from rising yields.[28] However, for many, this newly won entry into the propertied classes would soon dissipate as they became subject to the mercy of market forces.[29]

The enclosure of land can be seen as a means of exercising spatial power to discipline and contain.[30] As Courtney Wade Mason argues in the context of reservation land in North America, to enclose a piece of land is a means of exercising disciplinary power that differentiates it from other land and establishes a hierarchy.[31] The gentrification of urban areas under neoliberalism can be seen as a contemporary form of this, as discussed in Chapter 3. Such processes redefine particular enclosed spaces as productive and efficient sites.[32] Furthermore, they exclude those populations considered surplus. To justify enclosure, marketised agriculture was framed as a productive, efficient, and legitimate use of the land whereas communal use of natural resources was portrayed as backward, inefficient, and undisciplined. In this way, 'the social violence of enclosure consisted precisely in the drastic, total imposition upon the village of capitalist property-definitions'.[33] The emerging discourses around capitalism and ownership of the means of production

23 Jerome Blum, 'English Parliamentary Enclosure' (1981) 53(3) *The Journal of Modern History* 477, 478.
24 E.P. Thompson, *The Making of the English Working Class* (Penguin Books 1980), 239.
25 Karl Marx, *Capital*, vol. 1 (first published 1867, Penguin Classics 1976), 878 and 895; Richard Burt and John Michael Archer (eds), *Enclosure Acts: Sexuality, Property, and Culture in Early Modern England* (Cornell University Press 1994), 1.
26 Blum, 485.
27 Ibid., 487–491.
28 Thompson, *The Making of the English Working Class*, 241.
29 Ibid., 242.
30 Burt and Archer, 2–4.
31 Courtney Wade Mason, *Spirits of the Rockies: Reasserting an Indigenous Presence in Banff National Park* (University of Toronto Press 2014), 38–40.
32 Ibid., 40.
33 Thompson, *The Making of the English Working Class*, 238.

were performative – they renamed the practice of taking certain resources as legitimate and the taking of others as theft. Once this ideology had been reinforced by repeated performative legal discourses and actions, capitalist conceptions of property became accepted as natural. Resistance against them was deemed unintelligible, and named as theft or criminal damage.

E.P. Thompson describes enclosure as 'a plain enough case of class robbery, played according to fair rules of property and law laid down by a parliament of property-owners and lawyers'[34] and argues that 'social discipline' was part of the move to enclosure, with the existence of smallholders seen as detrimental to the interests of large landowners who wanted the freedom to employ them for low paid seasonal work.[35] Former smallholders were reduced to waged labourers.[36] Robbie Shilliam contends that enclosure 'facilitated the "marketization" of agriculture, which can be understood ... as a shift from moral obligations regarding the provision of subsistence to a far less personal and amoral mechanism of supply and demand'.[37] The establishment of capitalist property relations marked the start of processes of abstraction and simulation where land use became mediated by the profit motive and distanced from its original aim of providing food for the community. Furthermore, the concept of land as primarily an asset for making profit and the accompanying narrow concepts of who was deemed worthy of owning property were intrinsically linked with colonial expropriation of land.[38]

Although there is academic debate around the extent to which enclosure led to high levels of migration from the countryside to towns and cities, it is agreed that such migration took place.[39] Many of the rural poor who had lost their means of living from the land became reliant on the Poor Laws, and some were displaced to the cities, where they became the urban poor. Although enclosure was not the only factor that impacted on the rural poor during this period, most historians accept that it contributed to increased spend on poor relief during the late eighteenth and early nineteenth centuries.[40] Those subjected to the discipline of the wage system were viewed as the deserving poor, with those subjected to the discipline of the Poor Laws deemed the undeserving poor.[41] After poor relief was cut by the Poor Law

34 Ibid., 237–238.
35 Ibid., 242–243.
36 J.D. Chambers, 'Enclosure and Labour Supply in the Industrial Revolution' (1953) 5(3) *The Economic History Review* 319, 336.
37 Robbie Shilliam, *Race and the Undeserving Poor* (Agenda Publishing 2018), 9–10.
38 Gurminder K. Bhambra and John Holmwood, *Colonialism and Social Theory* (Polity Press 2021), 33–38.
39 Chambers, 339–340.
40 Blum, 499.
41 Shilliam, 13.

Amendment Act 1834, those without the means to support themselves had little alternative but to submit to the custody of the workhouse.[42]

Around this period, links between unemployment and criminality were embedded.[43] The undeserving poor were framed as criminal, and as having chosen a life of begging, prostitution, or theft due to aversion to work.[44] While the workers in the new industrial society, in Marxist terms, owned nothing but their own labour power, there were limitations on the extent to which they owned even that. Employment law and criminal law were blurred, as labourers were prevented from withdrawing their labour.[45] The Master and Servants Act 1823 exemplified this. Workers who breached the employment contract were criminalised and punished by up to three months' imprisonment with hard labour. In contrast, breaches by employers were regarded as a matter for the civil law. The Poor Laws performed a similar hegemonic purpose – refusal to participate in waged labour was equated with criminality, with the workhouse effectively serving as imprisonment and removal from respectable society. As Robbie Shilliam argues, analogies began to be drawn between slaves in the colonies and domestic workhouse residents, with both groups framed as the undeserving poor who lacked the moral qualities of industriousness and worked only through compulsion.[46] These performative discourses sought to racialise and 'blacken' the poor to separate them from 'respectable' White society.[47] The concept of the undeserving poor can be viewed as a second order simulacrum located within the market law of value. Under neoliberalism, these discourses around the undeserving poor continue in a more abstracted form as third order simulacra, as discussed in Chapter 4.

The taking of common land from the rural poor was accompanied by the criminalisation of customary rights or 'customs', which had enabled craft and trade workers to recover some of the fruits of their labour, such as taking offcuts of raw materials, in order to provide themselves with sustenance.[48] This corresponded with the establishment of the wages system in the growing urban areas.[49] Customs included 'socking' (river workers taking tobacco),[50]

42 Ibid., 26–27.
43 Martin J. Wiener, *Reconstructing the Criminal: Culture, Law, and Policy in England, 1830–1914* (Cambridge University Press 1990), 25 and 47.
44 Ibid., 25.
45 D.C. Woods, 'The Operation of the Master and Servants Act in the Black Country 1858–1875' (1982) 7(1) *Midland History* 93, 93.
46 Shilliam, 19 and 30.
47 Ibid., 31.
48 Peter Linebaugh, *The London Hanged* (2nd edn, Verso Books 2006), 172.
49 Ibid., 172.
50 Ibid., 181.

'clicking' (shoemakers taking leather, which was criminalised in 1723),[51] and dockers taking chips of wood.[52] Additionally, it was not uncommon for servants to take small items from their employers, such as pieces of silk.[53] While the taking of land from the poor was deemed as progress, the reappropriation of goods by the poor was reclassified as theft and subject to the harshness of criminal law, including the death penalty. This criminalisation of customs used the law to consolidate the concept of private property and reduce workers' remuneration solely to wages.[54] Through defining customs as theft, processes of criminalisation sought to reframe worker resistance to low wages as unintelligible and illegitimate. Criminal law served a performative function, as it redefined the boundaries of payment and property, with market forces operating as the mediating factor between employer and employee, and replacing the previous informal arrangements. Customary usage was reframed as theft, while enclosure of the land was deemed progressive rather than as theft from the community.

The increasing use of the death penalty in London in the 1700s arose in the context of the development of capitalism and the accompanying working class resistance. Hangings for theft, in common with the threat of the workhouse, were a means to discipline the working class in general, not just those who were subjected to such punishment, and to produce and reproduce the hegemony of private ownership of the means of production.[55] As Peter Linebaugh explains, 'most of those hanged had offended against the laws of property, and at the heart of the "social contract" was respect for private property ... so each hanging repeated the lesson: "Respect Private Property"'.[56] While protecting private property was key to the extensive use of the death penalty during this period, criminal law was also concerned with protecting structures of power, although of course the two were intrinsically linked.[57] Thus, law enforcement was not limited to defending private property itself but was fundamentally concerned with establishing and maintaining the class relations required for an economy based upon private property.[58] These underpinning class interests were obscured by the commutation of hangings through the use of mercy[59] and by the occasional imposition of the death sentence on rich offenders.[60] This gave the illusion of fairness and

51 Ibid., 234.
52 Ibid., 378.
53 Ibid., 407–409.
54 Ibid., 172.
55 Ibid., xxii.
56 Ibid., xxii.
57 Douglas Hay and others, *Albion's Fatal Tree* (revised edn, Verso Books 2011), 31.
58 Linebaugh, 434–435.
59 Hay and others, 40–49.
60 Ibid., 33–34 and 39.

uphold the legitimacy of the law.[61] In this way, the law was portrayed as applying equally to all, while processes of simulation operated to construct the second order simulacrum of the disposable, undeserving poor.

Later in this chapter, *Policing the Crisis* by Stuart Hall and others,[62] which builds upon Stanley Cohen's classic work, *Folk Devils and Moral Panics*,[63] is discussed in relation to the state's need to create folk devils in order to increase social control and maintain hegemony during the 1970s, a time of economic crisis.[64] There is scope to analyse the 1700s in similar terms. During the 1970s, elites responded to working class resistance against declining real wages by deploying discourses around law and order to criminalise the racialised poor. In the 1700s, during the emergence of capitalism, the challenge for the ruling class was to force workers to accept a new wage system. Key to this aim was the criminalisation of those who resisted, including those who took customary benefits to maintain a subsistence living. Throughout racial capitalism, the classification and differentiation of populations through criminalisation is central to the processes of simulation that enable elites to dehumanise the poor in furtherance of capital accumulation.

For John Locke, those who did not respect the capitalist ethos of private ownership of property were exempt from Reason. Indeed, he saw their execution as being justified for the greater public good.[65] The use of the death penalty during this period can be interpreted through the lenses of Michel Foucault's theory of biopolitics,[66] Achille Mbembe's concept of necropolitics,[67] and Judith Butler's work on precarious lives[68] and ungrievable lives.[69] Those whose lives were ended at the scaffold in the name of protecting private property were dehumanised by the state. They were deemed dispensable and ungrievable in the pursuit of industrialism and capitalism. For the poor, criminalisation was an occupational hazard of doing what needed to be done in order to survive. They lived under constant precarity, where poverty and starvation were as much of a threat to their existence as the noose. Some resisted their framing as disposable communities, with scenes of protest at public hangings.[70] This included attempts by relatives and the crowd to remove the deceased's body before they were taken away

61 Ibid., 55.
62 Stuart Hall and others, *Policing the Crisis: Mugging, the State, and Law and Order* (Macmillan 1978).
63 Stanley Cohen, *Folk Devils and Moral Panics* (3rd edn, Routledge 2011).
64 Hall and others, *Policing the Crisis*.
65 Linebaugh, 49–50.
66 Michel Foucault, *Society Must be Defended* (David Macey tr, Penguin Books 1997), 241.
67 Achille Mbembe, *Necropolitics* (Duke University Press 2019), 66.
68 Judith Butler, *Precarious Life: The Powers of Mourning and Violence* (Verso Books 2004).
69 Judith Butler, *Frames of War: When is Life Grievable?* (Verso Books 2016).
70 Hay and others, 98.

for dissection by surgeons.[71] For the Irish in particular, 'execution ballads' mourned the condemned, as well as having a celebratory and bawdy element which saw death as an 'escape from oppression' with the hanging being 'an occasion to display a fearless defiance towards the repressive terror of official punishment'.[72]

While the English rural poor had suffered dispossession of their land, the situation was even worse for the rural Irish Catholics. The Penal Code banned them from certain occupations and education, and severely curtailed their ability to inherit land and to own or rent property.[73] The amount of Irish land owned by Catholics fell to around 5–7% by the mid-eighteenth century.[74] Irish Catholics were racialised, and differentiated from the Protestant ruling elite.[75] Protestant Dissenters were also subject to the Penal Code and had a standard of living not dissimilar to Catholics but were not racialised in the same way, so had the psychological advantage of seeing themselves as part of the 'dominant race'.[76] Irish Catholics were excluded from the benefits of citizenship because they were seen as loyal to the Pope rather than the King, and therefore as a 'security risk'.[77] Their resistance to British colonialism was dealt with by racialisation and by criminalising their culture. The Penal Code sought to suppress cultural identity, with music, poetry, and language restricted.[78] This can be related to contemporary legal provisions, such as Criminal Behaviour Orders and the use of rap and drill music as bad character evidence at trial, as discussed in Chapters 4 and 6, respectively. These provisions allow the state to suppress the music of racialised individuals by deeming it as an expression of criminality, rather than as an art form.

Following their repression and the potato famine, tens of thousands of Catholics migrated to Britain, predominantly to the main industrial cities, particularly London, Manchester, and Liverpool.[79] Despite being a fundamental part of the working class, often employed as labourers,[80] they were frequently viewed as the undeserving poor who lacked the Protestant work

71 Ibid., 81.
72 Linebaugh, 324–325.
73 T. Arkins, 'The Commercial Aspect of the Irish Penal Code' (1912) 1(2) *Studies: An Irish Quarterly Review* 257; Noel Ignatiev, *How the Irish Became White* (Routledge 1995), 40–41.
74 Ignatiev, 42 (7%); Linebaugh, 289 (5%).
75 Ignatiev, 41–42.
76 Ibid., 42.
77 R.E. Burns, 'The Irish Penal Code and Some of its Historians' (1959) 21(1) *The Review of Politics* 276, 290.
78 Linebaugh, 290.
79 Thompson, *The Making of the English Working Class*, 469.
80 Ibid., 474.

ethic.[81] As Peter Linebaugh argues, their activities while living in London need to be seen in the context of their dispossession by British colonialism, and their consequent poverty.[82] During the eighteenth century, a disproportionately high 14% of those hanged at Tyburn were Irish born, with a significant proportion in employment.[83] Indeed, the occupations of those hanged reflected the structure of the working class generally.[84] Thus, there was not a criminal underclass defined by a refusal to work and constant offending – the poor as a whole were vulnerable to criminalisation and punishment.

Prior to the Irish immigration of the eighteenth and nineteenth centuries, the sixteenth and seventeenth centuries saw Flemish cloth workers and Huguenot handloom weavers arrive in London.[85] As Cedric J. Robinson argues, it is a mistake to speak of 'the English working class', as immigrant and migrant labour has always been a key feature of European economies.[86] Further diversification of working class cultures resulted from the influence of returning sailors.[87] Having worked with African and African-American crew, they spoke a dialect drawing on various languages.[88] This was described by one magistrate as being 'entirely discharged from the common bands of humanity' and 'the language and behaviour of savages'.[89] While rural workers were seen as embodying the English work ethic, those who had migrated to the cities were increasingly racialised.[90] Working class communities in London were described by journalists, authors, and charity organisers of the time as 'another race', a 'caste apart',[91] and 'a race apart'.[92] Processes linking racialisation and criminalisation gathered pace. Early criminologists such as Francis Galton promoted eugenics and social Darwinism, categorising the urban poor as degenerate and barbaric.[93] In this way, rather than being attributed to economic disadvantage resulting from increasing industrialisation and new production methods, poverty was increasingly essentialised. This ensured that White privilege would not only be denied to those racialised through slavery but also the domestic urban poor. Performative

81 Linebaugh, 293.
82 Ibid., 288–289.
83 Ibid., 288.
84 Ibid., 107 and 110.
85 Robinson, *Black Marxism*, 23–24.
86 Ibid., 23.
87 Linebaugh, 134–135.
88 Ibid., 134–135.
89 Ibid., 135.
90 Shilliam, 62–63.
91 Ibid., 48.
92 Lydia Morris, *Dangerous Classes: The Underclass and Social Citizenship* (Routledge 1994), 22.
93 Ibid., 24–25; Shilliam, 49.

discourses that described working class communities as uncivilised operated to pathologise criminality.[94]

While clear distinctions must be drawn between the conditions of the poor in Britain and those enslaved in the colonies, the discourses underlying both groups stemmed from the same processes of simulation; processes that were used to create and consolidate the power and wealth of White elites.[95] The second order simulacra of race and the undeserving poor were situated within discourses around White, middle and upper class, patriarchal supremacy. These processes of simulation cannot be understood without analysing their genealogy in colonial and Enlightenment discourses that required the racialisation of particular populations in order to justify their expropriation, exploitation, and captivity, as discussed below.

Slavery and the Establishment of White Supremacy

The doctrine of racism served to resolve the contradiction between the Enlightenment rhetoric of liberty and equality, and the existence of slavery. By constituting Black people as inhuman, ungrievable, and lacking the capacity for free will, it was possible to exclude them from the scope of Reason and human rights. This enabled colonial states to maintain their stated commitment to rights and progress while denying those rights to slaves thereby creating a system of 'racialized "justice"'.[96] The development of racism was grounded in capitalist exploitation, economic processes, and the emergence of the colonial state.[97] As Gurminder Bhambra and John Holmwood argue, it is incorrect to say that Britain and other European powers became nation states during the period of modernity.[98] Rather than being nation states with empires, these were imperial or colonial states from their modern inception.[99] Therefore, the 'post-imperial claim of an underlying essential nation to which empire itself was merely a contingent phenomenon' was a means of restricting access to the spoils of colonialism.[100] In other words, framing Britain as a nation state rather than a colonial state enabled it to differentiate between 'national citizens and colonial subjects',[101] with the former entitled to the

94 Wiener, 31–33.
95 Shilliam, 31.
96 Mike Cole, *Critical Race Theory and Education: A Marxist Response* (2nd edn, Palgrave Macmillan 2017), 167.
97 Robert Miles, 'Explaining Racism in Contemporary Europe' in Ali Rattansi and Sallie Westwood (eds), *Racism, Modernity and Identity on the Western Front* (Polity Press 1994), 206.
98 Bhambra and Holmwood, 8–9.
99 Ibid., 9 and 126.
100 Ibid., 9.
101 Ibid., 213.

proceeds arising from the expropriation of the latter.[102] These distinctions continue to operate in relation to immigration law[103] and discourses around entitlement to the welfare state.[104]

Racism was a fundamental aspect of the formation of modern law. As argued above, race was a second order simulacrum situated within discourses around economic utility that excluded Black people from humanity as a means of justifying colonial exploitation and expropriation. Discourses around race and human rights were intrinsically linked. Enlightenment concepts of human rights operated as a process of simulation that served to construct and justify the racial differentiation deployed to extract wealth from the colonies. European powers viewed themselves as having a 'right to colonise' justified by the civilising mission.[105] Therefore, human rights discourses during this period can also be viewed as second order simulacra.

Patricia Tuitt explains that the early stages of the market economy required a concept of materiality in relation to that which could be owned and regulated as part of legal contracts.[106] As this 'material world' included not only goods and natural resources but also human slaves, slavery is intimately connected with the origins of contract law.[107] Law can be viewed as 'enabling' the market economy.[108] Rather than defining the law as, in Marxist terms, part of the superstructure, it is better seen as an element of the economic base 'to the extent that it defined the property relations that constituted capitalism as an economic system'.[109] Criminal law, along with contract and property law, produced legal categories of people. The law during this period was a second order simulacrum that constructed other simulacra through performative processes. This relied upon and reproduced the developing colonial conceptions of racialisation that were embedded within modernity, particularly in relation to slavery. The simulation that race existed was deployed to justify slavery, empire, and colonialism, such that race was given meaning within this economic context.

Those who initially laboured in the Americas were taken from indigenous populations rather than from Africa, but they suffered from illnesses brought

102 Ibid., 83, 111 and 130.
103 Nadine El-Enany, *(B)ordering Britain: Law, Race and Empire* (Manchester University Press 2020).
104 Bhambra and Holmwood, 214.
105 Ibid., 7 and 174.
106 Patricia Tuitt, *Race, Law, Resistance* (The GlassHouse Press 2004), 8.
107 Ibid., 8.
108 Ibid., 9.
109 Mark V. Tushnet, 'Critical Legal Theory' in Martin P. Golding and William A. Edmundson (eds), *The Blackwell Guide to Philosophy of Law and Legal Theory* (Wiley-Blackwell 2005), 84.

by the colonisers and were limited in numbers.[110] The next batch of labour consisted of poor Europeans; either convicts arriving involuntarily or indentured servants who had agreed to serve for a number of years as payment for transportation.[111] While many of the latter were glad for the chance to start a new life albeit after a period of indentured labour, as the ownership of labour became more profitable, the poor were coerced, induced, or even kidnapped and taken to the colonies.[112] Transportation to the colonies was the prescribed sentence for a number of petty offences, leading Eric Williams to conclude that 'there was some connection between the law and the labour needs of the plantations'.[113] Transportation of the poor also reduced poor relief costs.[114] There were reports of defendants being pressured to plead guilty in order to be sentenced to transportation rather than hanging.[115] Those seen as enemies of the British state were also transported, including Quakers who refused to swear allegiance to the Crown, and the Irish and Scottish taken prisoner by Cromwell's forces.[116] While the death penalty can be seen as a means of disposing of poor individuals and communicating a warning to others, transportation did the same but with the added bonus to the capitalist class of providing free labour in the colonies. Transportation established the loss of the right to reside in one's country of birth as a punishment, thus framing nationality and residence as privileges that could be withdrawn from surplus populations deemed as criminal, even those claiming birthright. Such discourses continue to the present day. As outlined in Chapter 6, racialised people convicted of criminal offences are liable to deportation from the UK in certain circumstances.

The surplus population of sixteenth-century Europe was insufficient to provide the labour required for the plantations in the Americas, and therefore the taking of Africans as slaves was seen by the emerging capitalist class as the only economically viable means to undertake this task.[117] As sugar prices increased and the supply of indentured labour became more difficult, the market for slaves boomed in the mid-seventeenth century.[118] In Eric Williams' words, 'a racial twist has thereby been given to what is basically an economic phenomenon. Slavery was not born of racism: rather, racism

110 Williams, 7–9.
111 Ibid., 9.
112 Ibid., 10–11.
113 Ibid., 12.
114 Ibid., 10.
115 Ibid., 15.
116 Ibid., 13.
117 Ibid., 6.
118 William A. Green, 'Race and Slavery: Considerations on the Williams Thesis' in Barbara Lewis Solow and Stanley L. Engerman (eds), *British Capitalism and Caribbean Slavery: The Legacy of Eric Williams* (Cambridge University Press 1988), 45–47.

was the consequence of slavery'.[119] Slavery was central to emergent capitalism in both Britain and the United States through production of the three major cash crops – sugar, tobacco, and cotton.[120] Most English and Welsh industrial towns benefitted in some way from the slave trade by the mid-eighteenth century.[121] In what was known as the 'triangular trade', British ships travelled to Africa with manufactured goods that were traded at a profit for Africans, who were transported to the colonies where they were traded at a profit, then the crops produced by slaves were taken back to Britain to be sold at yet another profit.[122] This provided the capital necessary to fund the Industrial Revolution.[123] Culture was also rooted in the spoils of slavery, with the arts funded by the apparent benevolence of those profiting from the plantations.[124] Cotton production was key to the development of North American capitalism, as it was the United States' most lucrative export.[125]

In the early 1680s, Slave Codes gave legal definition to the rights of White non-slaves and the lack of rights of Black slaves, thus creating racialised legal subjects with distinct statuses.[126] Thus, 'whiteness became a shield from slavery'[127] and 'was the characteristic, the attribute, the property of free human beings'.[128] A key difference between indentured or convict labour from Europe and slaves taken from Africa was that slavery was in perpetuity – not only did it continue until death, but, significantly, it was hereditary such that the child of a slave was born a slave, as discussed below.[129] This distinction between perpetual servitude and legal liberty created race as a defining feature, with European bond-labourers accorded higher social status, despite living in poverty with little or no social mobility.[130] White elites had been shaken by the unity between Black and White labourers during Bacon's Rebellion in 1676–1677.[131] The invention of Whiteness as a category

119 Williams, 7.
120 Ibid., 23.
121 Ibid., 52.
122 Ibid., 51–52.
123 Ibid., 52.
124 Mbembe, 19.
125 Sven Beckert and Seth Rockman, 'Introduction' in Sven Beckert and Seth Rockman (eds), *Slavery's Capitalism* (University of Pennsylvania Press 2016), 26–27.
126 Cheryl I. Harris, 'Whiteness as Property' (1993) 106(8) *Harvard Law Review* 1707, 1718.
127 Ibid., 1720.
128 Ibid., 1721.
129 W. Haywood Burns, 'Law and Race in Early America' in David Kairys (ed), *The Politics of Law: A Progressive Critique* (3rd edn, Basic Books 1998), 280.
130 Allen, Volume 2, 248–249.
131 Ibid., 248.

served to prevent poor Whites from uniting with their Black neighbours to challenge the plantocracy.[132]

The law created and sustained chattel slavery through racialised property relations producing 'legislated societal racism'.[133] As Patricia Tuitt writes, 'the slave as the only human subject and thus distinct from animal, weapons and jewels and so on at the dawn of the modern law, reveals herself as a form of chattel but as chattel's *exception*'.[134] The commodification of the slave, as an exceptional form of property, defined Africans as non-human.[135] This was so all-consuming that reproduction by female slaves became a means of increasing property for slave owners.[136] As Shauna Sweeney argues, 'if race became the self-evident mark of hereditary slavery at the heart of eighteenth-century racial capitalism, black women's wombs were the incubators of capital accumulation'.[137] The simulacrum of race was deployed to justify these processes of dehumanisation, appropriation, and exploitation.

As with other forms of property, slaves could be inherited,[138] bought and sold, and used to settle a debt.[139] When a captain threw overboard 132 slaves who were being transported, the case was dealt with as a civil rather than criminal matter, and Lord Chief Justice Mansfield ordered compensation of £30 per slave, commenting that, 'the case of slaves was the same as if horses had been thrown overboard'.[140] Through these processes of racialised commodification, 'enslaved people became numerical abstractions that filled shipping logs, manifests, and margins as exchange values'.[141] Meticulous accounting practices enabled slaveowners to manage and increase productivity, enforced by violence.[142] Balance sheets recorded the appreciation and depreciation in the value of each slave,[143] as with capital assets such as vehicles.[144] When slaves took their own lives, the slaveowner could recoup the

132 Ibid., 249.
133 Haywood Burns, 280.
134 Tuitt, 14 (original italics).
135 Ibid., 10 and 14.
136 Harris, 1719.
137 Shauna J. Sweeney, 'Gendering Racial Capitalism and the Black Heretical Tradition' in Justin Leroy and Destin Jenkins (eds), *Histories of Racial Capitalism* (Columbia University Press 2021), 59.
138 Harris, 1720.
139 Ibid., 1720.
140 Williams, 46.
141 Sweeney, 59.
142 Caitlin Rosenthal, 'Slavery's Scientific Management: Masters and Managers' in Sven Beckert and Seth Rockman (eds), *Slavery's Capitalism* (University of Pennsylvania Press 2016), 63.
143 Ibid., 80.
144 Ibid., 83.

cost of replacing them through insurance policies,[145] such that slaves could be considered property even after death.[146]

Having defined the property relations central to slavery, the law in the United States upheld and reinforced these relations. To enforce the legal definitions of racialised inequality and protect the 'property' of the slaveowners, slave patrols would return escaped slaves and generally police those enslaved to prevent revolts.[147] In the North Carolina case of *State v Mann* in 1829,[148] Supreme Court Justice Thomas Ruffin held that a White man who had abused and shot his rented female slave could not be guilty of her murder on the basis that slaves would not accept their inferior status unless they were forced to do so.[149] Slavery, and any violence used to enforce enslaved labour, was seen as legitimate, whereas the idea that the slave had the right to bodily autonomy or even life itself was considered unintelligible. The slave was ungrievable to the legal system – one whose life 'cannot be lost, and cannot be destroyed, because they already inhabit a lost and destroyed zone; they are, ontologically, and from the start, already lost and destroyed'.[150] In the 1857 case of *Scott v Sandford*,[151] Dred Scott, a slave who was living in a state where slavery was illegal, unsuccessfully sued for his freedom, with the Supreme Court holding that Black people were not considered by the US Constitution to be citizens and that they were inferior to Whites and subject to White authority. Thus, the law operated as a performative racialising discourse, excluding Black people from liberty, freedom, and equality and deeming them ungrievable.

White privilege was used strategically by the property-owning classes to gain support from poor Whites. Through appeals to unity due to their 'shared Whiteness', slaveowners gained the support of poor Whites against revolts or escape attempts by slaves.[152] Indeed, the slave patrols were comprised mainly of the poorest Whites, such that 'propertyless European-Americans were the principal element in the day-to-day enforcement of racial oppression'.[153] After the abolition of slavery, these slave patrols 'morphed into apartheid white citizens' militias' which in turn later developed 'into what would become

145 Ibid., 162.
146 Beckert and Rockman, 18.
147 Allen, Volume 2, 252.
148 13 NC 263 (1829).
149 Alfred L. Brophy, 'The Market, Utility, and Slavery in Southern Legal Thought' in Sven Beckert and Seth Rockman (eds), *Slavery's Capitalism* (University of Pennsylvania Press 2016), 265–266.
150 Butler, *Frames of War*, xix.
151 60 US 393 (1857).
152 Derrick Bell, 'Wanted: A White Leader Able to Free Whites of Racism' in Richard Delgado and Jean Stefancic (eds), *The Derrick Bell Reader* (New York University Press 2005), 330–331.
153 Allen, Volume 2, 252.

the foundations for modern police'.[154] Thus, slave patrols can be seen as the precursors of US policing.[155] The links between colonialism and policing are explored further in Chapter 3.

During the mid-nineteenth century, when the abolition movement was gathering strength in England, scientific justifications for racism became more prevalent as an ideological tool for resisting abolition.[156] In France, proponents of biological arguments in favour of slavery suggested that it had a civilising influence on slaves.[157] Even some of those in favour of abolition advocated the view of distinct races and White superiority, with their anti-slavery sentiments based on charitable concerns, rather than a belief in equality.[158] The abolition of slavery can be seen as an example of interest convergence. The Republicans were against the expansion of slavery to the Northern States for economic reasons,[159] despite many of them having profited from investments in the Southern cotton trade.[160] They believed that if slavery moved further north, it would hamper the long-term economy through stunting educational and technological investment.[161] Similarly, the British advocated the abolition of slavery in the Caribbean as a means of eliminating the West Indian monopoly.[162] When slavery was abolished, slaveowners were paid extremely large sums as compensation.[163] In this way, 'crimes against the person [were] re-narrated as crimes against property'.[164] The end of slavery did not bring material equality for former slaves.[165] White labourers, including those of Irish descent, were paid just enough more than

154 Dylan Rodríquez, 'The Obsolescence of "Police Brutality"' in Chris Cunneen and others (eds), *The Routledge International Handbook on Decolonizing Justice* (Routledge 2023), 127.

155 Michael A. Robinson, 'Black Bodies on the Ground: Policing Disparities in the African American Community – An Analysis of Newsprint from January 1, 2015, Through December 31, 2015' (2017) 48(6) *Journal of Black Studies* 551, 553.

156 Seymour Drescher, 'The Ending of the Slave Trade and the Evolution of European Scientific Racism' in Joseph E. Inikori and Stanley L. Engerman (eds), *The Atlantic Slave Trade: Effects on Economies, Societies and Peoples in Africa, the Americas, and Europe* (Duke University Press 1992), 368–369.

157 Ibid., 382.

158 Ibid., 376.

159 John Majewski, 'Why Did Northerners Oppose the Expansion of Slavery? Economic Development and Education in the Limestone South' in Sven Beckert and Seth Rockman (eds), *Slavery's Capitalism* (University of Pennsylvania Press 2016), 277.

160 Ibid., 278.

161 Ibid., 280.

162 Williams, 169.

163 Bhattacharyya, 92.

164 Ibid., 93.

165 Bell, 'Wanted: A White Leader Able to Free Whites of Racism', 331.

their Black counterparts to secure their loyalty to White supremacy so that they continued to identify in terms of race rather than class interests.[166]

Whiteness continued to be a determinant of social relations and the ability to partake in a host of activities, including travel, education, work, and voting, such that it became 'a form of racialized privilege ratified in law'.[167] This enduring perception of racial superiority prevented poor Whites from rebelling against their own economic exploitation. In Derrick Bell's words, 'the ideology of whiteness continues to oppress whites as well as blacks' by using the psychological advantages of White privilege to distract them from their disadvantaged class position and prevent them from uniting with Black workers.[168] The sense of entitlement to preferential treatment can be seen as 'a property right in whiteness'.[169] Joy James argues that, 'the encoding of slavery or criminality onto blackness reflected a counterpart construction: the inscription of "whiteness" and nonincarceration as freedom and civility, hence as property or existential wealth'.[170] As outlined in Chapter 1 with reference to the work of Cheryl Harris, Whiteness can be seen as a form of property that has taken various historically and materially contingent forms.[171]

Racial distinctions were maintained through legislation. When counting populations for political representation, a Black person was considered to be 60% of a person.[172] The Black Codes in the South regulated social relations such as work, marriage, and movement to try to keep the former slaves tied to working on the land.[173] This meant that apparently emancipated Black former slaves were effectively forced to work for very little payment.[174] The racialisation of undeserving poor discourses continued through vagrancy provisions such as the Mississippi Black Codes, whereby, as Angela Davis writes, 'vagrancy was coded as a black crime', punishable by work on the former slave plantations.[175] Additionally, in the same way that the post-enclosure newly urbanised English poor often had to steal in order to survive, so newly emancipated Black people were compelled to do the same

166 Allen, Volume 1, 198.
167 Harris, 1745.
168 Bell, 'Wanted: A White Leader Able to Free Whites of Racism', 331.
169 Ibid., 331.
170 Joy James (ed), *The New Abolitionists: (Neo)Slave Narratives and Contemporary Prison Writings* (Albany 2005), xxv.
171 Harris.
172 Haywood Burns, 281.
173 Ibid., 282.
174 Ruth Thompson-Miller and Joe R. Feagin, 'The Reality and Impact of Legal Segregation in the United States' in Pinar Batur and Joe R. Feagin (eds), *Handbook of the Sociology of Racial and Ethnic Relations* (2nd edn, Springer 2018), 204.
175 Angela Y. Davis, *Are Prisons Obsolete?* (Seven Stories Press 2003), 29.

and punished with forced labour.[176] The law maintained White supremacy to keep Black populations serving the economic interests of White landowners.[177] The Black Codes ended in 1866, but the Jim Crow legal segregation provisions had already started to take effect in the South and border states, where they lasted until the 1960s.[178] Jim Crow laws regulated racial segregation at restaurants, schools, and water fountains[179] with 'Whites Only' and 'Colored Only' signs.[180] In the North, workplaces and accommodation were segregated.[181]

The case of *Plessy v Ferguson*[182] involved Homer Plessy, a mixed-race man who had used a Whites-only railroad carriage. He was chosen for this political action to test the segregation legislation as he was able to 'pass' as White, and therefore able to board the carriage without being refused initial entry. Plessy's action 'was read by the Supreme Court as an act of appropriation, as an unqualified theft of an identity imagined as property – as that which is properly and privately owned by a "legitimate" white subject'.[183] The judgment named 'the reputation of being a white man' as a form of property that Mr Plessy did not possess.[184] The court ruled that racially segregated facilities were lawful and constitutional if they were equal in quality – known as 'separate but equal'.[185] However, 'only the "separate" part of segregation policy was taken seriously and rigorously enforced'.[186] Denise Ferreira Da Silva writes that, 'by naming these matters local, private or social rather than national, public, or political the court situated blacks outside the ethical terrain occupied by the US American people' and therefore placed them outside Constitutional rights.[187] As set out later in this chapter, under neoliberalism the private sector is used as a means of excluding racialised people and restricting usage rights to White communities and individuals. Desegregation was not abolished in law until the *Brown* case[188] in the mid-1950s and

176 Ibid., 33.
177 Haywood Burns, 282.
178 Thompson-Miller and Feagin, 205.
179 Edward E. Baptist, *The Half Has Never Been Told* (Basic Books 2014), 409.
180 Thompson-Miller and Feagin, 206.
181 Baptist, 411.
182 163 US 537 (1896).
183 Amy Robinson, 'Form of Appearance and Value: Homer Plessy and the Politics of Privacy' in Elin Diamond (ed), *Performance and Cultural Politics* (Routledge 1996), 238.
184 Ibid., 243.
185 Michael J. Klarman, *From Jim Crow to Civil Rights: The Supreme Court and the Struggle for Racial Equality* (Oxford University Press 2004), 21.
186 Derrick Bell, 'Time for the Teachers' in Richard Delgado and Jean Stefancic (eds), *The Derrick Bell Reader* (New York University Press 2005), 226.
187 Denise Ferreira Da Silva, *Towards a Global Idea of Race* (University of Minnesota Press 2007), 212.
188 *Brown v Board of Education* 347 US 483 (1954).

the Civil Rights Act 1968.[189] However, formal legal equality did not bring material or social equality. As discussed later in this chapter, human rights discourses served to legitimise material inequality by deploying narratives around colour-blindness and meritocracy.

Empire, Colonialism, and Simulacra of Criminality

When considering the history of criminal law, a study of the British Empire in India can illustrate how processes of racialisation and criminalisation are symbiotic. While 'the enslavement of Africans was a fundamental reference point for the initial racialization of deserving and undeserving characteristics, with the "slave" – and thereby the condition of blackness – exemplifying the latter', this discourse continued as 'other subjects of empire were "blackened" in the process of also being made to carry undeserving characteristics', as happened in India.[190] The conflation of race and class under the caste system and the criminalisation of Indian tribes, as described below, is an example of how the simulacra of race and the undeserving poor are mutually constituted.

Discourses around civilisation were used to legitimise Britain's expropriation of other countries' land and resources.[191] John Locke's theory of property asserted that working the lands provided the colonialist with property rights that were defendable by force and superseded those of indigenous populations, such that he 'conjoined the empire's rule of law to its theory of just war, bridging the gap between colonial justice and colonial violence'.[192] The indigenous populations of the colonies were considered barbaric and savage, and there were fears that 'inferior races' could pollute and contaminate Europeans.[193] However, rather than being underdeveloped prior to British rule, India had thriving textile, iron-working, and shipbuilding industries that were ruined by tariffs designed to create and maintain markets for British manufactured goods,[194] as well as by direct physical violence, including amputation of the thumbs of Bengali master weavers.[195] The plunder of Indian raw materials for the use of British industry required 'the de-industrialisation of India – its forcible transformation from a country of combined agriculture and manufacture into an agricultural colony of British

189 Thompson-Miller and Feagin, 205.
190 Shilliam, 7.
191 Elizabeth Kolsky, *Colonial Justice in British India: White Violence and the Rule of Law* (Cambridge University Press 2010), 3.
192 Ibid., 3.
193 Preeti Nijhar, *Law and Imperialism* (Routledge 2009), 24.
194 Peter Fryer, *Aspects of Black History* (Index Books 1993), 22–24.
195 Subhabrata Bobby Banerjee, 'Necrocapitalism' (2008) 29(12) *Organization Studies* 1541, 1542.

capitalism'.[196] The textiles produced in Britain, using cotton obtained from slave plantations in the Americas, could then be sold to India, while Indian produce was exported to Britain, leading to poverty and starvation for many Indian people as landowners prioritised cash crops for export.[197]

Meanwhile, laws codifying racial inequality were 'exported' to the colonies.[198] In this way, 'the rule of law was a tool of empire that served both practical and ideological functions' – it enabled control of the Indian population in order to achieve colonial economic aims while advancing justificatory civilising mission discourses.[199] Indeed, the law has been a fundamental element of civilising mission narratives throughout the history of colonialism and imperialism.[200] As Elizabeth Kolsky argues, 'not only was physical violence a persistent and integral feature of British rule in India, law was its most reliable and consistent accomplice'.[201] Criminal law imposed and maintained racial differentiation, and legitimised force by the colonisers.

The case of *The Indian Chief* in 1800 held that the settlements of the East India Company were English territories governed by English law, such that Indian communities were no longer subject to their own rules and jurisdiction but to those of the colonial forces.[202] However, while the early legal system had authority over the Company's employees and the Indian population, initially it did not cover those Europeans in India who were not involved in the Company.[203] A system of courts was set up in the eighteenth century, but the Company Courts in the *mofussil* or rural areas had jurisdiction over non-British Europeans and Indians only, although British subjects could sue Indians in those courts so the position was not reciprocal.[204] Until 1793, the British could only be tried in the Supreme Courts in relation to both criminal and civil cases.[205] White people who killed Indians were often charged with lesser offences of manslaughter or assault rather than murder,[206] or even had charges dropped,[207] while others relied on biologically racist defences that the cause of death was the weak Indian constitution rather than the ferocity of

196 Fryer, 22–23.
197 Arun Kundnani, *What Is Anti-racism? And Why It Means Anti-capitalist* (Verso Books 2023), 45–46.
198 Nijhar, 26–27.
199 Kolsky, 232.
200 Peter Fitzpatrick and Richard Joyce, 'The Normality of the Exception in Democracy's Empire' *Birkbeck ePrints* (2007) 11 <https://core.ac.uk/download/pdf/6543.pdf> accessed 18 December 2024.
201 Kolsky, 30.
202 Ibid., 30–31.
203 Ibid., 31.
204 Ibid., 31 and 33.
205 Ibid., 33.
206 Ibid., 57–63.
207 Ibid., 189.

the attack.[208] In relation to the plantations of Assam, the colonial government took the view that physical coercion, including extreme violence by British settlers against Indians, was a necessary means of ensuring the success of the plantations and the British Empire more generally, and therefore such behaviour was, in essence, decriminalised.[209]

The colonialists not only distinguished themselves from the Indian population but also buttressed the distinctions in the caste system, which was a synthesis of class and racialisation. They accomplished this 'insidiously ... in the construction of caste as the core symbol of Indian tradition'.[210] Positivist Lombrosian theories around biological criminality were combined with the caste system to classify, regulate, and criminalise lower caste Indians.[211] They were seen as a race apart from other Indians, and their criminality was viewed as innate and inherited.[212] This racialised criminalisation operated to position 'the "criminal" tribes and castes outside the notion of modernity and progress'.[213] Meanwhile, higher caste Indians were differentiated from the general population and assimilated into the bureaucracy of the legal system, a tactic that ensured their support for the colonial project and provided the law with legitimacy.[214] The perception of lower caste criminality was shared by the higher castes.[215]

The Criminal Tribes Act 1871 (CTA), s.3 enabled 'any tribe, gang or class of persons' to be designated as a 'criminal tribe' if it was believed that 'they were addicted to the commission of non-bailable offences'.[216] Those so designated could be prevented from leaving their local area, required to report to the police station, and generally subjected to supervision and surveillance from the authorities.[217] Whole racialised communities were pathologised, named as criminal and subjected to exceptional powers whether or not they were guilty of any offence. Such a declaration operated performatively to create a space of simulated criminality based around classed and racialised classifications. As will be argued in Chapter 3, this continues in a more abstracted form in contemporary Britain in relation to the use of s.60 powers against racialised communities.

208 Ibid., 135–140.
209 Ibid., 157.
210 Nicholas B. Dirks, *Castes of Mind: Colonialism and the Marking of Modern India* (Princeton University Press 2001), 80.
211 Nijhar, 112–113.
212 Ibid., 111.
213 Santhosh Abraham, 'Colonialism and the Making of Criminal Categories in British India' (2011) 6(1) *NALSAR Law Review* 151, 165.
214 Ibid., 165; Nijhar, 102.
215 Nijhar, 117.
216 Ibid., 125.
217 Ibid., 125.

The racialised criminalisation of parts of Indian society had a dual purpose. It consolidated the ideology of Western supremacy, and delegitimised resistance to colonialism.[218] Because certain tribes had been categorised as inherently and pathologically criminal, their actions could be deemed as violent crime rather than as insurgency. Thus, the law operated to depoliticise rebellion against colonial rule.[219] The CTA was used against those in agricultural communities resisting the imposition of waged labour.[220] As with the hangings in England considered earlier in this chapter, the criminalisation of those failing or refusing to comply with capitalist relations of production served as a process of simulation to define the material interests of White elites as legally and morally legitimate. Colonial discourses towards sections of the Mappila, the Muslim communities living in the Malabar region of India, illustrate the slippage between racialised constructions of criminality and those relating to terrorism. Whereas initially the Mappila's collective action against the colonial East India Company resulted in colonialists referring to them as criminals, bandits, and robbers, by the late nineteenth century, they were defined as 'fanatics'.[221] As will be discussed in Chapters 3 and 5, racialised definitions of ungrievable communities are intimately connected with performative discourses that name them as dangerous, with the construction of the terrorist embedded in colonial and racialised simulations of criminality.

The positivist conception of particular populations as inherently criminal had much in common with domestic Victorian discourses. Preeti Nijhar draws parallels between the CTA in India and the Habitual Criminals Act 1869 (HCA) in Britain.[222] The latter also constructed the concept of 'a criminal class' and gave the police increased surveillance powers.[223] This legislation effectively punished the poor for being 'suspicious', dangerous, or of bad character.[224] As Arvind Verma argues, the CTA was more onerous as it covered the entire community, whereas the HCA punished an individual, but nonetheless these two pieces of legislation shared a common ideology of 'dangerous classes'. [225] The domestic urban poor were framed as inherently criminal, although the legislation against them was less oppressive than that

218 Abraham, 152.
219 Ibid., 156.
220 Ibid., 153.
221 Ibid., 164–165.
222 Nijhar, 15.
223 Ibid., 56.
224 Ibid., 105 and 144.
225 Arvind Verma, 'Consolidation of the Raj: Notes from a Police Station in British India, 1865-1928' in Louis A. Knafla (ed), *Crime, Gender, and Sexuality in Criminal Prosecutions* (Greenwood Press 2002), 125.

used in the colonies. Discourses around the undeserving poor were deployed, with unemployment and homelessness linked to criminality.[226]

These processes of simulation reflected Victorian scientific views of criminals and the perceived need to categorise, regulate, and discipline the biologically racialised Other.[227] Links were made between 'savages' in the metropolis and those in the colonies.[228] This led to a symbiotic relationship between processes of criminalisation and racialisation in Britain and the colonies. Some aspects of criminal law were transposed to the colonies while conceptions of criminality taken 'from colonial India [were] applied to the "dangerous" classes of Victorian England'.[229] The second order simulacra of race and the undeserving poor were constructed during the period of the Enlightenment, the British Empire, and the Industrial Revolution. As will be argued below and in subsequent chapters, these simulacra have been reproduced in ever more abstracted forms under neoliberalism, as they have absorbed and reworked civilising mission discourses. This can be seen in the anti-social and criminal behaviour laws considered in Chapter 4, the dangerousness provisions considered in Chapter 5, and the bad character evidential rules considered in Chapter 6, all of which construct and reproduce the third order simulacra of hypercriminals.

Racial Neoliberalism and Colour-Blindness

In the post-civil rights era, it may appear that the worst aspects of racism have been overcome. The blatant discrimination faced by the Windrush generation in the 1950s when landlords put up 'No Blacks' signs[230] is prohibited and legislation such as the Equality Act 2010 ostensibly provides protection against discrimination, leading to discourses that we are living in a colour-blind society. Yet despite seeming legal equality, racial inequalities persist, from disproportionate outcomes in the legal system to overrepresentation in Covid-19 cases and deaths.[231] In order to understand why these inequalities remain, it is necessary to consider the project of neoliberalism and its relationship to processes of racialisation and simulation.

Neoliberalism may be summarised as, 'the political project designed to create the conditions for capital accumulation based on the upward distribution

226 Wiener, 25.
227 Nijhar, 71.
228 Wiener, 33.
229 Nijhar, 14.
230 Ron Ramdin *The Making of the Black Working Class in Britain* (Verso Books 2017), 195.
231 Zubaida Haque, 'Why Does Covid-19 Affect Ethic Minorities So Badly? It Isn't to Do with Biology' *The Guardian* (22 June 2020) <www.theguardian.com/commentisfree/2020/jun/22/covid-19-britain-ethnic-minorities-government-race-inequality-epidemic> accessed 18 December 2024.

of resources, and an ideological adherence to meritocratic notions of individual success and personal responsibility'.[232] This includes defunding social and welfare provisions, and blaming the racialised poor for their own disadvantage arising from this exclusion and disinvestment.[233] Rather than being purely *laissez faire* and leaving the free market to its own devices, neoliberalism entails the state taking pro-active steps to promote the market,[234] and to secure private property rights.[235] Neoliberalism requires state intervention to bolster markets and support businesses, such that 'neoliberal markets have not required state roll-back so much as state-repurposing'.[236] Neoliberal economic policies include the deregulation of private industry and privatisation of public services, combined with lower taxes for corporations and wealthy individuals.[237]

Neoliberalism is a global phenomenon; a restructuring of racial capitalism whereby elites maintain, consolidate, and increase capital accumulation by combatting both workers' resistance to falling living standards in the West, and anti-colonial liberation movements in the Global South.[238] In the West, the neoliberal project concentrates greater wealth in the hands of the ruling elites, while the accompanying increases in poverty and homelessness, cuts to welfare and public services, and declining real wages have a disproportionate impact on racialised communities.[239] In the Global South, as discussed below, neoliberal policies operate to keep poor countries poor, and continue the colonial practices of exploitation and extraction of wealth through new methods.

Neoliberalism can be understood as the hyperreal stage of capitalism.[240] Money is able 'to escape into infinite speculation, beyond all reference to a real of production, or even to a gold-standard'.[241] Jon Baldwin argues that President Nixon's suspension of the gold standard in 1971 can be viewed

232 Randolph Hohle, *Race and the Origins of American Neoliberalism* (Routledge 2015), 1.
233 Lambros Fatsis, 'Policing the Beats: The Criminalisation of UK Drill and Grime Music by the London Metropolitan Police' (2019) 67(6) *The Sociological Review* 1300, 1301.
234 Emma Bell, *Criminal Justice and Neoliberalism* (Palgrave Macmillan 2011), 140–141.
235 David Harvey, *A Brief History of Neoliberalism* (Oxford University Press 2005), 2.
236 James Trafford, *The Empire at Home* (Pluto Press 2021), 119.
237 Randolph Hohle, 'The Color of Neoliberalism: The "Modern Southern Businessman" and Postwar Alabama's Challenge to Racial Desegregation' (2012) 27(1) *Sociological Forum* 142.
238 Kundnani, *What Is Anti-racism?*, 157–158.
239 Jordan T. Camp, *Incarcerating the Crisis: Freedom Struggles and the Rise of the Neoliberal State* (University of California Press 2016), 16.
240 Jon Baldwin, 'Baudrillard and Neoliberalism' (2015) 12(2) *International Journal of Baudrillard Studies* <https://baudrillardstudies.ubishops.ca/baudrillard-and-neoliberalism/> accessed 18 December 2024.
241 Jean Baudrillard, *Symbolic Exchange and Death* (Iain Hamilton Grant tr, SAGE Publications 2017), 29.

as the moment when capital became hyperreal as money lost its referent.[242] Rather than being tied to the materiality of gold, finance capital became self-referential.[243] According to Jean Baudrillard, the US national debt was 'released from any economic contingency, moving in a parallel universe, having escaped, by its very acceleration, from any relapse into the banal universe of production, value and use'.[244] As Elton McGoun explains:

> Decisions affecting production and employment are made on the basis of stock price and not on the basis of production and employment. It is not the 'real' economy that shapes 'reality', but activity in the financial economy. The financial economy is thereby more 'real' than the real economy itself; it is a hyperreal economy.[245]

Whereas the 1929 stock market crash had catastrophic economic consequences due to the link between stock value and the economy at that time,[246] the 1987 crash did not have a comparable effect on production and employment.[247] However, while the financial system may be a simulacrum trading on sign value rather than economic value, it nonetheless has material consequences.[248] The belief in hyperreality creates its own 'reality', such that rather than production determining stock values, changes in share prices influence decisions around production.[249] Although a stock market crash is a hyperreal event,[250] the *belief* that the financial system is real is used to justify the narrative that austerity measures are necessary to 'save' the economy.[251] In Slavoj Žižek's words, the huge amounts of public money spent on the bailout of the banks in 2008, 'were spent not on some clear "real" or concrete problem, but essentially in order to *restore confidence* in the markets, that is, simply to change people's beliefs!'.[252] The simulation of the burst financial bubble is an opportunity to further redistribute wealth upwards at the expense of the racialised poor through public sector cuts, and the simulacrum of meritocracy naturalises these material inequalities. As discussed below, neoliberalism reworks the second order simulacra of the undeserving poor into the

242 Baldwin.
243 Ibid.
244 Jean Baudrillard, *Screened Out* (Chris Turner tr, Verso Books 2014), 146.
245 Elton G. McGoun, 'Hyperreal Finance' in Norman B. Macintosh and Trevor Hopper (eds), *Accounting, The Social and the Political: Classics, Contemporary and Beyond* (Elsevier 2005), 319.
246 Baudrillard, *Screened Out*, 23; McGoun, 320.
247 Baudrillard, *Screened Out*, 25; McGoun, 320.
248 McGoun, 319.
249 Baudrillard, *Screened Out*, 96.
250 McGoun, 320.
251 Baldwin.
252 Slavoj Žižek, *First as Tragedy, Then as Farce* (Verso Books 2009), 80 (original italics).

third order simulacra of racialised hypercriminals, and meritocracy is a key aspect of this process.

Jo Littler argues that meritocracy can be seen as the interaction between the language of liberation movements and discourses around individual success and competition.[253] This seeming contradiction means that meritocracy operates 'to absorb the language of equality …into entrepreneurial self-fashioning'.[254] Success is measured as upward mobility, with working class communities and cultures associated with failure – 'as abject zones and lives to flee from'.[255] Discourses of social mobility date back to the onset of capitalism and the Protestant work ethic, and were located within Enlightenment discourses around equality and human rights, for those deemed to be human.[256] However, under the neoliberal narrative of meritocracy, the absorption of feminist, anti-racist, and queer liberation language into discourses around self-advancement has served to negate claims that inequalities persist. Meritocracy is hyperreal – it disappears discourses of liberation by reabsorbing and assimilating them, and in so doing diffuses them of meaning. Through such processes of simulation, anti-racism is commodified as an advert for Coca-Cola with a diverse looking collection of people singing together, rather than as a movement for socio-economic equality.[257] The harm caused by the Coca-Cola company, particularly in the Global South, including child labour, health and safety violations and actions against trade unionists, is rendered invisible.[258] The sign value of the brand as a code for happiness, friendship, and unity prevails.

Meritocracy is a third order simulacrum that gives the appearance that society has transcended inequalities such as race, class, gender, and sexuality, while acting as a justificatory alibi for economic policies and practices that increase inequality. Discourses of post-feminism and post-racism, which assert that gender and race equality have been achieved, attribute continued inequalities to poor choices by deficient individuals, as discussed in Chapter 4.[259] Shelley Rawlins posits that post-feminism is hyperreal – an abstraction that 'is dependent on *its own production* of feminism to exist'.[260] The assertion that gender inequality has been overcome and that feminism is

253 Jo Littler, *Against Meritocracy* (Routledge 2018), 2.
254 Ibid., 2.
255 Ibid., 7.
256 Ibid., 27.
257 Ibid., 57.
258 Mark Thomas, *Belching Out the Devil* (Ebury Press 2008).
259 Littler, 64–65.
260 L. Shelley Rawlins, 'Kellyanne Conway and Postfeminism: "The Desert of the Real"' (2019) 18(7) *Kaleidoscope: A Graduate Journal of Qualitative Communication Research* 61, 78 (original italics) <https://opensiuc.lib.siu.edu/cgi/viewcontent.cgi?article=1354&context=kaleidoscope> accessed 18 December 2024.

simultaneously constraining women from achieving their goals by encouraging them to 'choose' to be victims and disadvantaging men, positions post-feminism as the 'real' force for gender equality.[261] Post-feminism can be seen as a copy without an original – a third order simulacrum that purports to have transcended feminism but has absorbed and negated it, thus constituting a simulation of feminism, empty of liberatory content. Post-racial discourses operate to delegitimise claims of ongoing structural racism and, as discussed below, blame poor racialised people for their own disadvantage.

David Theo Goldberg argues that neoliberalism can be seen as a reaction to 'concern about the impending impotence of whiteness' whereby moves towards equality in the public sector led conservatives to attempt to reclaim the privatised sphere as exempt from racial equality provisions.[262] Similarly, Randolph Hohle's work illuminates how 'the racial meaning of neoliberalism is embedded in the language of privatization'.[263] He explains how Southern US business interests were able to win support for neoliberal policies through ostensibly neutral language that deployed racial imagery and gained them the backing of those who were overtly racist.[264] Thus, 'the fusion of the liberal business class and segregationists resulted from elite struggles to protect their white privilege'.[265] As public facilities in the United States became desegregated, Blackness became associated with the public sector, whereas private spaces could remain segregated and exclusive, and thus White.[266] Racialised discourses around the undeserving poor were deployed.[267] Privatisation was framed as efficient, superior, and White,[268] while the public sector was deemed inefficient and 'associated with black, with poverty, with shame, with failure'.[269] Neoliberal discourses were 'organized around the white-private / black-public binary'.[270] In this way, racism was privatised.[271]

In the UK, although racialised communities, particularly the Windrush generation, experienced blatant racist discrimination, there was no formal segregation comparable to the Jim Crow provisions. Therefore, discourses around the public and private sectors in the UK are not as explicitly racialised. However, although the association between Blackness and the public sector

261 Ibid., 81.
262 David Theo Goldberg, *The Threat of Race* (Blackwell Publishing 2008), 337.
263 Hohle, 'The Color of Neoliberalism', 143.
264 Ibid., 159.
265 Hohle, *Race and the Origins of American Neoliberalism*, 2–3.
266 Ibid., 5.
267 Randolph Hohle, *Racism in the Neoliberal Era: A Meta History of Elite White Power* (Routledge 2018), 110 and 118.
268 Hohle, 'The Color of Neoliberalism', 159.
269 Ibid., 156.
270 Hohle, *Race and the Origins of American Neoliberalism*, 4.
271 David Theo Goldberg, 'Racisms Without Racism' (2008) 123(5) *Publications of the Modern Language Association of America* 1712, 1713.

is perhaps more subtle in the UK when compared with the United States, these narratives remain situated within a post-racial framing of meritocracy and the undeserving poor, particularly in relation to discourses around immigration and the welfare state, as discussed below.

Neoliberal meritocratic discourses perform a hyperreal function by making increased race and class inequality appear fair. The belief that meritocracy is real leads to the conclusion that poor, racialised communities are responsible for their own disadvantage. As discussed above, in earlier periods of capitalism, those dependent on the Poor Laws were branded the undeserving poor. Enslaved and colonial populations were constructed in similar terms, combining the second order simulacra of race and the undeserving poor. Therefore, these two constructions can be seen as linked throughout their history. These discourses are reworked under neoliberalism, with those communities in receipt of welfare benefits judged similarly. This abstracts racism through processes of simulation where the public sector, social housing and welfare are signifiers of the racialised undeserving poor. As will be argued below, discourses around criminality function in a similar way, reproducing and amplifying racism while appearing colour-blind. The second order simulacra of racist discourses used to justify slavery and colonialism have been redeployed to fit colour-blind, post-racial ideologies and neoliberal economic systems, and are increasingly dislocated from their genealogy, which is absorbed and disappeared, thus creating a third order simulacrum: the hyperreal figure of the racialised undeserving poor criminal.

In the UK context, discourses around welfare provision rely on signifiers of immigrants being prioritised for social housing and benefits at the expense of White communities.[272] The economic interests of White elites are presented in racial terms in order to attract the support of poor White people, despite such policies being against their material interests,[273] with poverty in the UK rising significantly from 1979 onwards.[274] In the United States, the sign of the lazy 'Black welfare queen' who saw claiming benefits as a way of life has been used by White elites to gain support among White people for welfare cuts.[275] As Henry Giroux writes:

> The twin images of the young black male 'gangsta' and his counterpart, the 'welfare queen' became the primary vehicles for selling the Amercian public on the need to dismantle the welfare state, ushering in an era of

272 Shilliam, 162.
273 Ibid., 163.
274 Susanne MacGregor, 'The Welfare State and Neoliberalism' in Alfredo Saad-Filho and Deborah Johnston (eds), *Neoliberalism: A Critical Reader* (Pluto Press 2004), 144–145.
275 Ibid., 123–124; Michelle Alexander, *The New Jim Crow: Mass Incarceration in the Age of Colorblindness* (The New Press 2010), 48–49.

> unprecedented deregulation, downsizing, privatization, and regressive taxation.[276]

Following the 1992 Los Angeles uprising, when President George Bush Senior talked about the rise in babies born to unmarried mothers, there was an unspoken understanding that he was referring to Black mothers.[277] As Denise Ferreira Da Silva argues, the issue is not only that discourses around 'welfare queens' use such terms as a code for race 'but that the association of criminality and material (economic) dispossession has become the new signifier of the affectability of the racial subaltern'.[278] Discourses around race, poverty, unemployment, and criminality intersect in the construction of the neoliberal third order simulacrum of the hypercriminal. These processes of simulation are deployed to justify neoliberal policies, including the expansion of the carceral state discussed below.

Neoliberalism appears to contain contradictions. The rhetoric of free market forces assumes agents acting in their own interests, regardless of race, class, or gender, where everyone is able to succeed if they play the game well. However, racial inequalities persist. In order for markets to operate without hindrance, free movement of workers appears to be an essential component, yet border controls limit migration. As Arun Kundnani argues, it is incorrect to see racism under neoliberalism as merely a 'hangover' from previous eras.[279] Processes of racialisation re-enact themselves in new forms under neoliberalism. In Cedric J. Robinson's words:

> with the development of corporate structures and the myth of the intensively rationalized and rational society, Blacks became the irrational, the violent, criminal, caged beast. The cage was civilization and Western culture, obviously available to Blacks but inexplicably beyond their grasp.[280]

The framing of market forces as the exemplar works to name those populations not embracing or materially succeeding within this economic system as backward, lacking both intelligence and civilisation.[281] In this way, 'the logic of neoliberalism itself draws the project towards a racial-civilisation

276 Henry A. Giroux, *Stormy Weather: Katrina and the Politics of Disposability* (Paradigm Publishers 2006), 2.
277 David Roediger, *Towards the Abolition of Whiteness* (Verso Books 1994), 8.
278 Da Silva, 265.
279 Arun Kundnani, 'The Racial Constitution of Neoliberalism' (2021) 63(1) *Race and Class* 51, 52; Kundnani, *What Is Anti-racism?*, 170.
280 Robinson, *Black Marxism*, 187.
281 Kundnani, 'The Racial Constitution of Neoliberalism', 60–62.

discourse'.[282] Those unable or unwilling to achieve the neoliberal dream of self-enrichment are deemed to be deficient and are dehumanised in a contemporary reworking of colonial processes of exclusion.

Neoliberal practices increase inequality and bolster the position of White elites both within and between countries. Trade agreements and financial institutions such as the International Monetary Fund keep the Global South poor by imposing conditions such as austerity measures and the production of cash crops for export rather than food for their inhabitants, resulting in preventable deaths.[283] This can be seen as a continuation of colonial practices through new methods, such that countries in the Global South are kept under the control of their former colonisers through the use of debt finance.[284] The enduring wealth disparities between countries are then deployed to perpetuate the civilising mission narrative that poorer countries are incapable of managing their own affairs and in need of paternalistic guidance from their former colonisers. The neoliberal project also includes military action to quell insurgency in poor countries, using 'a scale of violence little different from the older forms of imperialism'.[285] The United States has supported, and in some cases imposed, pro-Western authoritarian regimes across much of the Global South to secure access to natural resources and extremely cheap labour for multinational corporations.[286] While neoliberalism deploys the simulacrum of a post-racial meritocracy, it constitutes a refashioning of the imperialist project to expropriate resources from those populations deemed disposable.

Neoliberal policies endeavour to consolidate and fortify White supremacy by continuing the exploitation of the former colonies, and maintaining the economic, geographic, and discursive barriers between racialised ungrievable populations and those benefitting from White privilege. Therefore, measures such as border controls are not an anomaly within neoliberalism but are part of its inherent logic to assure continued capital accumulation.[287] As Nadine El-Enany argues, UK immigration controls are a continuation of colonial ordering, whereby racialised people from the former colonies are denied entry to the UK and thus excluded from access to the spoils of colonialism, including welfare and healthcare.[288] Border controls keep poor racialised workers in the Global South, where they are paid poverty wages, rather than

282 Ibid., 63.
283 Dean Spade, *Normal Life* (Duke University Press 2015), 23.
284 Ibid., 24.
285 Kundnani, *What Is Anti-racism?*, 177.
286 Ibid., 189–190.
287 Kundnani, 'The Racial Constitution of Neoliberalism', 66.
288 Nadine El-Enany, *(B)ordering Britain*.

allowing them to seek higher wages in the West.[289] Further, this outsourcing of production to the Global South at lower wages has also weakened the power of British trade unions and depressed wage growth, leading to falling living standards for working class people in the UK.[290] Thus, neoliberal racial ordering facilitates further expropriation in the former colonies, as well as increasing exploitation and precarity for workers in the West, particularly racialised workers who are disproportionately represented in minimum wage and insecure jobs.

If one accepts that racism is not an aberration but a fundamental constituting element of neoliberal economies, then it follows that racism cannot be overcome by measures such as diversity training around unconscious bias.[291] Neoliberalism uses the language of equality, diversity, and inclusion while exploiting, colonising, or excluding racialised populations. Racial capitalism commodifies racialised people as 'signs of diversity, no more than symbols to be exchanged in the effort to accrue the benefits flowing to institutions perceived to be diverse'.[292] Baudrillard explains that:

> by integrating Blacks on the basis of white criteria, this metahumanism merely extends the boundaries of abstract sociability, *de jure* sociality. The same white magic of racism continues to function, merely whitening the Black under the sign of the universal.[293]

Civilising mission discourses endure, with upward mobility and assimilation into White neoliberal values presented as synonymous. The neoliberal discourse of a post-rights colour-blind society where individuals determine their own success acts as a simulation to erase the continuing operation of racism.[294]

Racial neoliberalism 'extends by building silently on the structural conditions of racism while evaporating the very categories of their recognizability'.[295] Such discourses are based upon 'the assumption of the history-free subject before law'.[296] Both racism and its effects are individualised rather than viewed as historically and materially grounded. This allows the colonial roots of racism to be hidden and their ongoing legacies denied. In David Theo Goldberg's words, 'the universalizing politics of "All Lives

289 Aviah Sarah Day and Shanice Octavia McBean, *Abolition Revolution* (Pluto Press 2022), 141.
290 Ibid., 141.
291 Kundnani, *What Is Anti-racism?*, 86–87.
292 Bhattacharyya, 158.
293 Baudrillard, *Symbolic Exchange and Death*, 207 fn 1.
294 Angela Y. Davis, *The Meaning of Freedom* (City Lights Books 2012), 169.
295 Goldberg, 'Racisms Without Racism', 1716.
296 Bhattacharyya, 88.

Matter" is one of racial dismissal, ignoring, and denial'.[297] Such a slogan misses the point that Black lives are not considered to matter in the same way as White lives, both historically and contemporaneously, and often do not count as lives at all.[298] As Alana Lentin argues, 'Black and other racialised people are no longer permitted, in a post-racial era, either to identify racially and, more crucially, to mobilise, collectivise, or seek redress on the basis of race'.[299] Not only are acts of racism divorced from their colonial roots, but racialised populations are deemed solely responsible for their disadvantaged position within society at large, and for their disproportionate criminalisation and imprisonment.[300]

Neoliberal colour-blind meritocratic discourses can be understood as third order simulacra that seek to explain away racial disparities. Criminality is racialised in increasingly abstracted ways. In this way, as David Theo Goldberg explains, 'the language of racial reference becomes coded, embedded'[301] and 'the geopolitical reality principle embeds what in effect is racial characterization while at once evaporating any and all explicit or even conscious racial reference'.[302] Therefore, racism becomes a process without referent – a simulation of a simulation. Neoliberalism is the stage of capitalism where simulations of race shift from second order to third order simulacra, such that racism becomes hyperreal. Similarly, the second order simulacra of human rights forged during the Enlightenment period have become third order simulacra. Human rights discourses are now hyperreal – they circulate as signs and act as a justificatory alibi for the simulacrum of meritocracy. This is a self-referential and circular process whereby the simulation of a post-racial society constructs the apparent reality of a meritocracy, which in turn reproduces the belief that poor racialised individuals have equality. The belief in meritocracy serves to link Blackness with criminality. If racially disproportionate outcomes in the criminal legal system cannot be accounted for by inequalities, the implication is that they must be the result of racially disproportionate criminality.

297 David Theo Goldberg, 'Why "Black Lives Matter" Because All Lives Don't Matter in America' *Huffington Post* (25 September 2015) <https://www.huffpost.com/entry/why-black-lives-matter_b_8191424> accessed 18 December 2024.

298 Ibid.; George Yancy and Judith Butler, 'What's Wrong With "All Lives Matter"?' *The New York Times* (12 January 2015) <https://opinionator.blogs.nytimes.com/2015/01/12/whats-wrong-with-all-lives-matter/> accessed 18 December 2024.

299 Alana Lentin, 'Race' in William Outhwaite and Stephen Turner (eds), *The SAGE Handbook of Political Sociology* (SAGE Publications 2018), 872.

300 Davis, *The Meaning of Freedom*, 171.

301 Goldberg, 'Racisms Without Racism', 1714.

302 Ibid., 1715.

Racialised Folk Devils as Third Order Simulacra

As Henry Giroux argues, 'neoliberal racism calls for a hollowing out of the social welfare functions of the state, except for its role in safeguarding the interests of the privileged and in strengthening its policing functions'.[303] Similarly, in Jordan T. Camp's words:

> the neoliberal carceral state emerged from a bipartisan consensus forged during the Cold War about the necessity of prioritizing security – a consensus that has justified the withdrawal of the social wage and created an increasingly central role for military action, national security policies, aggressive policing, and mass prison-building programmes in the counter-insurgency governance of neoliberal racial capitalism.[304]

Just as the establishment of capitalism required the criminalisation of those resisting enclosure and the new wage system, so racially disproportionate punitivity under neoliberalism can be seen as a reaction to the threat of militancy from the racialised poor to defend their economic position.[305] The increased racialisation of crime is a strategy by White elites to maintain and consolidate their privilege. The response of the state can be seen as 'counter-insurgency as a strategic response to a crisis of legitimacy'.[306] The processes of simulation that produce links between disorder, criminality, and race have been described by Vesla Weaver as a 'frontlash'.[307] Whereas backlash is used to refer to a populist, conservative reaction to a perceived increase in equality for minority groups, frontlash is a process whereby 'elites aim to control the agenda and resist changes through the development of a new issue and appropriation and redeployment of an accepted language of norms'.[308] She argues that the punitive turn in criminal law and the construction of crime as a major political agenda issue was a strategy by those White elites who opposed civil rights for racialised people.[309] This approach not only defined crime as a racial issue but simultaneously served to depoliticise struggles for racial equality and redefined them as issues of public disorder and criminality.[310]

Such processes are hyperreal; they construct their own apparent reality. Politicians galvanised support for punitive policies by reframing civil

303 Henry A. Giroux, *America on the Edge: Henry Giroux on Politics, Culture and Education* (Palgrave Macmillan 2006), 161.
304 Camp, 8–9.
305 Ibid., 4–5.
306 Ibid., 5.
307 Vesla M. Weaver, 'Frontlash: Race and the Development of Punitive Crime Policy' (2007) 21 *Studies in American Political Development* 230, 265.
308 Ibid., 238.
309 Ibid., 263 and 265.
310 Ibid., 265.

rights activism as criminal disorder. This was widened to form discursive links between race and criminality more generally. Racially disproportionate policing in response to perceived racialised criminality led to racially disproportionate arrests, which gave credibility to the simulacrum that particular communities were inherently criminal, such that it appeared true. The process of simulation resulted in outcomes that fed and reproduced the racist simulacrum, thus reproducing racialised hypercriminals. Racialised political activists were viewed as an enemy within. Paul Gilroy argues that the use of policing methods taken from Northern Ireland against racialised populations in mainland Britain was a practice of 'counter-insurgency'.[311] The state viewed the policing of those seeking to advance civil rights or to defend their economic position as a militarised fight against insurgents. The links between colonial policing and the policing of domestic racialised populations are developed further in Chapter 3.

In the UK during the 1970s, the Metropolitan police took the decision to publish selective statistics for some types of robbery and theft, or 'muggings' as they became popularly known, to give the impression of a Black crime wave and a crisis of law and order.[312] In the seminal work, *Policing the Crisis*, which draws upon Stanley Cohen's theory of folk devils and moral panics,[313] combined with a historical materialist approach and Antonio Gramsci's concept of hegemony, Stuart Hall and others argued that this racialised moral panic over muggings had to be seen in the context of the economic and political situation of the 1970s.[314] The events in France in 1968 and countercultural challenges to the established order, as well as an escalation of the troubles in Northern Ireland with British troops sent there in August 1969, formed the backdrop to a period when the existing hegemony was being questioned.[315] Capitalism was in crisis with a falling rate of profit and rising inflation.[316] This had a particularly significant effect on the British economy, which lost its share of manufacturing industry against existing and emerging competitors.[317] An increase in working class militancy and industrial unrest erupted into strikes, threatening plans to hold down wages.[318] The state invoked discourses around the breakdown of law and order to justify a crackdown on union militants and other activists, including those involved in political

311 Paul Gilroy, 'The Myth of Black Criminality' (1982) 19 *The Socialist Register* 47, 49 <https://socialistregister.com/index.php/srv/article/view/5474> accessed 18 December 2024.

312 Paul Gilroy, *There Ain't No Black in the Union Jack* (Routledge 1987), 118.

313 Cohen; Hall and others, *Policing the Crisis*, 16–18.

314 Hall and others, *Policing the Crisis*, 218.

315 Ibid., 258–262.

316 Ibid., 263.

317 Ibid., 263.

318 Ibid., 263–264.

campaigns against racism.[319] Legislation was enacted to deal with those constructed as a threat to the security of the state, including trade unionists, drug users, and immigrants.[320]

Within this context, the moral panic over a perceived rather than actual rise in street robberies was used to justify increasingly high-profile and interventionist policing focused on young Black males in urban areas.[321] These discourses created racialised folk devils associated with images of danger and mob rule.[322] Paul Gilroy argues that cultural racism pathologised Black communities as predisposed to criminal behaviour due to dysfunctional families while ignoring disproportionate policing and racial profiling.[323] Discourses around broken families and young offenders were deployed in a racialised manner and used as a signifier for Black communities.[324] Such discourses, rooted in colonial conceptions of Black moral inferiority, sealed the discursive links between race, poverty, and crime. As Michael Rowe writes, following the unrest at Broadwater Farm estate in Tottenham, North London in 1985, discussions about problems with youths in the inner cities effectively became a code for referring to young Black males such that commentators could invoke racist imagery without appearing racist.[325] This code constructed those communities as hypercriminals – the neoliberal third order simulacrum of the racialised undeserving poor.

Increased class consciousness among Black workers, combined with their particular vulnerability to unemployment, represented 'the synchronisation of the race and class aspects of the crisis' such that 'policing *the blacks* threatened to mesh with the problem of policing *the poor* and policing *the unemployed*'.[326] As discussed above, the simulacra of race and the undeserving poor are intrinsically linked throughout the history of racial capitalism. The government and media constructed the folk devil of the dangerous Black mugger requiring intensive policing and lengthy custodial sentences, thus manufacturing public support for increased social control.[327] As Stuart Hall argued, 'devils do, indeed, have to be *summoned*'.[328] The folk devil of the mugger was a simulacrum that framed young Black men as a danger to the property and physical safety of White communities.

319 Ibid., 280.
320 Ibid., 288–289.
321 Ibid., 16–17 and 327.
322 Ibid., 161–162.
323 Gilroy, 'The Myth of Black Criminality', 52.
324 Michael Rowe, *The Racialisation of Disorder in Twentieth Century Britain* (Ashgate Publishing Limited 1998), 41–42.
325 Ibid., 157.
326 Hall and others, *Policing the Crisis*, 332 (original italics).
327 Ibid., 17.
328 Ibid., 162 (original italics).

This moral panic was used to shore up support for the police at a time when their legitimacy was being questioned.[329] This enabled racist police tactics to be framed as collective self-defence of White civilised society against barbarism. Racially disproportionate policing and discursive links between race and criminality paved the way for significant increases in the imprisonment of racialised communities. Simulated constructions of criminality created a self-fulfilling prophecy of racially disproportionate outcomes. This state of hyperreality, where simulacra of criminality appeared more real than the racism of the criminal law and policing practices, served a performative contradiction-closing function to disappear police racism and construct hypercriminals. Further, these simulacra operated to name poor Black young men, rather than increased poverty and the defunding of the public sector, as the main threat to the public. Such a construction also acted performatively to reinforce the framing that the public interest was synonymous with that of White communities, thus bolstering the racial distinction between grievable and ungrievable populations.

As Michael Keith argues, the racialisation of criminality has taken place in various historically specific forms:

> In Britain, at a crude level, the succession of racist images of (gender specific) Afro-Caribbean criminality have followed on from the pimp of the 1950s, to the Black power activist of the 1960s, to the mugger of the 1970s, to the rioter of the 1980s and, quite possibly, to the ultimate folk devil, the underworld 'Yardie' of the 1990s.[330]

However, rather than follow a chronology, each image overlaps with and absorbs the previous ones. The simulacra of mugger, rioter, and gangster continue to endure, combined with discourses around knife and gun crime. The ways that discourses around dangerousness and gangs reproduce racialised hypercriminals are explored in more detail in Chapters 5 and 6. Racist images of South East Asian criminality have also taken specific forms, such as the terrorist and the paedophile, as discussed in Chapters 3 and 5. The moral panic over knife crime in recent years, including the s.60 powers discussed in Chapter 3 and the KCPOs discussed in Chapter 4, can be seen in the context of the need to create racialised folk devils and manufacture support for expanded police powers against a backdrop of falling living standards for all but the rich.

As will be argued below and in later chapters, these images have become increasingly abstracted such that they act as simulacra for criminality. It is

329 Gilroy, *There Ain't No Black in the Union Jack*, 120.

330 Michael Keith, *Race, Riots and Policing: Lore and Disorder in a Multi-racist Society* (UCL Press 1993), 245.

not just that racialised people are more likely to be arrested than White people. More fundamentally, neoliberalism closes its contradictions of racially disproportionate outcomes by creating racialised simulacra abstracted from the original criminalising processes. This naming of Black people as criminals, whether as gang members or sexual predators, is so distanced from the explicitly racist colonial representations that it appears to have a factual basis and to be racially neutral. In this way, simulacra of Black criminality operate performatively to reproduce images that appear more real than the continued racism and colonial practices in which they are embedded.

Neoliberalism and Mass Incarceration

Under neoliberalism, incarceration rates have increased significantly in both the UK and the United States.[331] Black people are significantly overrepresented in this carceral expansion.[332] Not all Western capitalist economies pursued similar policies of prison expansion, with Nordic countries taking a more rehabilitative approach.[333] There is evidence of a negative correlation between welfare spending and imprisonment rates – countries that spend a higher proportion of their GDP on welfare have lower imprisonment rates.[334] Research has shown that as a country becomes more neoliberal economically, its legal system becomes more punitive.[335]

In the UK, the drivers behind increased incarceration included greater use of recall to prison for licence breaches, and the use of indeterminate sentences, in particular Imprisonment for Public Protection (IPP) for 'dangerous' offenders, as discussed in Chapter 5.[336] In 1990, there were 44,975 prisoners in the UK with this figure rising significantly throughout the decade.[337] Under the Tony Blair government elected in 1997, the adult prison population rose from nearly 61,500 to over 80,000 in ten years, but this was not racially neutral with the number of Black prisoners increasing at over four times the rate of the increase in the general prison population between 1999 and

331 David Garland, *The Culture of Control* (Oxford University Press 2001), 135.

332 Ibid., 132; Nicole Gonzalez Van Cleve and Lauren Mayes, 'Criminal Justice Through "Colorblind" Lenses: A Call to Examine the Mutual Constitution of Race and Criminal Justice' (2015) 40(2) *Law and Social Inquiry* 406.

333 James Dignan and Michael Cavadino, 'Penal Policy in Comparative Perspective' (2007) 70 *Criminal Justice Matters* 15, 15–16.

334 David Downes and Kirstine Hansen, 'Welfare and Punishment in Comparative Perspective' in Sarah Armstrong and Lesley McAra (eds), *Perspectives on Punishment: The Contours of Control* (Oxford University Press 2006), 154.

335 Dignan and Cavadino, 16.

336 Michael Teague, 'Neoliberalism, Prisons and Probation in the United States and England and Wales' in Philip Whitehead and Paul Crawshaw (eds), *Organising Neoliberalism: Markets, Privatisation and Justice* (Anthem Press 2012), 54.

337 Ibid., 53.

2002.[338] In England and Wales in September 2024, just over 26% of prisoners were categorised as Black, Asian, mixed race, or other ethnic groups.[339] Given that the population of England and Wales was around 18.3% Black, Asian, mixed race, or other ethnic groups according to the 2021 census,[340] this shows a significant racial disproportionality in imprisonment rates.[341] In June 2023, the government at the time predicted that the prison population would rise to between 93,100 and 106,300 by March 2027.[342]

While the increased cost of penal expansion is considered by some as the antithesis of neoliberal economics,[343] increased punitivity is an inherent aspect of neoliberalism. In economic terms, mass incarceration contributes to the neoliberal project through the privatisation of prisons, the use of cheap prison labour that reduces wages more generally, and the containment of surplus populations. As Loïc Wacquant argues, 'the invasive, expansive and expensive penal state is not a deviation from neoliberalism but one of its constituent elements'.[344] The insecurity and inequality caused by other aspects of neoliberalism, such as increased precariousness at work, unemployment, and welfare cuts, require an enhanced level of disciplinary containment in order to avoid public disorder.[345] However, rather than being solely coercive to quell such dissent, penal expansion also acts hegemonically to maintain the legitimacy of the state[346] and reinforce the distinctions between the deserving and undeserving poor.[347] This bolsters the simulacrum of a colour-blind

338 Joe Sim, *Punishment and Prisons: Power and the Carceral State* (SAGE Publications 2009), 104.

339 Ministry of Justice, *Prison Population* (2024) <www.gov.uk/government/collections/offender-management-statistics-quarterly> accessed 18 December 2024.

340 UK Government, *Population of England and Wales* (2022) <www.ethnicity-facts-figures.service.gov.uk/uk-population-by-ethnicity/national-and-regional-populations/population-of-england-and-wales/latest> accessed 18 December 2024.

341 Although the figures do not exactly accord with each other, as the census figures are for 2021 and the prison figures are for 2024, nonetheless they enable a rough calculation to be made. On the basis of these figures, the incarceration rate for Black, Asian, mixed race, and other minority groups in England and Wales is approximately 1.43 of the population rate (where a figure of 1 means that the percentage of a racialised group in the prison population is the same as the percentage of that group in the general population, a figure of 2 means that the percentage in the prison population is double the percentage of that group in the general population).

342 Jacqueline Beard, 'The Prison Estate in England and Wales' (Briefing Paper No. 5646, House of Commons Library, 29 June 2023), 5 <https://researchbriefings.files.parliament.uk/documents/SN05646/SN05646.pdf> accessed 18 December 2024.

343 Bell, *Criminal Justice and Neoliberalism*, 3–4; Harvey, 77.

344 Loïc Wacquant, *Punishing the Poor* (Duke University Press 2009), 308.

345 Ibid., 307–308; Harvey, 77.

346 Wacquant, 299.

347 Ibid., 295 and 313.

meritocracy by attributing the incarceration of the racialised poor to their own deficiencies and inherent criminality.[348]

According to David Garland, this neoliberal turn is synchronous with the 'criminology of the Other' which acts to 'demonize the criminal, to excite popular fears and hostilities, and to promote support for state punishment'.[349] Rather than a means of crime prevention, penal expansion is a political choice by governments keen to appear forceful on crime in an unequal society.[350] Constructions of crime are key. In the UK, there has been a clear contrast between the lack of prosecutions in relation to white collar and corporate crimes and increased punitivity towards poor, racialised communities.[351] This fits the neoliberal logic of freeing up the market through ignoring social harm by corporations and controlling resistance to the social effects of austerity policies.[352] These processes of simulation name the racialised poor rather than the state and corporations as the source of harm.

Racial disparities in the United States led Joy James to describe prison as 'the modern day manifestation of the plantation'.[353] Loïc Wacquant views racialised mass incarceration as one of four institutions of containment that 'operated to define, confine and control African Americans over the centuries in the history of the United States', with the previous three being chattel slavery, Jim Crow segregation in the South, and ghettos in the North.[354] Michelle Alexander also draws parallels between Jim Crow segregation and mass incarceration of Black people in the United States,[355] while noting that explicit racism has been replaced by discourses of colour-blindness.[356] She argues that contemporary racialised mass incarceration creates a 'racial caste'.[357] As Angela Davis points out, some academics have misinterpreted Michelle Alexander's analysis by viewing mass incarceration 'as a primarily US problem that emanates from the failure to comprehensively address the economic, political, and cultural consequences' of slavery.[358] Not only do such readings fail to account for the growth of incarceration in other neoliberal economies such as the UK, but they have led to suggestions that the issue can be overcome by reformist measures to reduce the imprisonment of

348 Camp, 16.
349 David Garland, 'The Limits of the Sovereign State: Strategies of Crime Control in Contemporary Society' (1996) 35(4) British Journal of Criminology 445, 461.
350 Ibid., 462.
351 Sim, 27–29.
352 Ibid., 26.
353 James, xxiii.
354 Wacquant, 196.
355 Alexander, 4.
356 Ibid., 141.
357 Ibid., 21 and 30.
358 Angela Y. Davis and others, *Abolition. Feminism. Now.* (Penguin Books 2022), 62.

specific communities, without recognising that mass incarceration is intrinsically linked to global racial capitalism.[359]

Increased incarceration cannot be explained by a rise in crime as there was no such rise during the period of penal expansion.[360] Mass incarceration ingrains the fallacy of colour-blindness by naming the racialised urban poor as inherently dangerous and criminal through an insidious process that links poverty with criminality, and consolidates the neoliberal project. This builds upon, reproduces, and reworks previous discourses of Black criminality, inferiority, and unworthiness. Racialised communities are reproduced as uncivilised and as requiring containment and exclusion. Whereas the Enlightenment project excluded racialised populations on grounds of rationality and civilisation, neoliberal racism not only reinforces this exclusion but reframes it as meritocratic, premised on the failure of poor communities to engage with the logic of market forces such that, as described above, conceptions of racialised criminality have moved from second to third order simulacra.

Under the Reagan administration in the United States, key policies included welfare cuts, increased spending on prisons, and the inception of private prisons.[361] This was intensified in the Clinton era when 'zero tolerance' policing targeted poor racialised communities and increased the prison population.[362] In the 1990s, prisons were built in rural White towns that had suffered from the economic downturn, as this was seen as 'a recession-proof economic policy'.[363] This was squared with the austerity of public sector spending cuts through the privatisation of prisons.[364] Drawing on aspects of Keynesian demand management and Marxist economics, Ruth Wilson Gilmore argues that the impetus behind mass incarceration in the United States was the crisis of capitalism and a need to deal with the surplus of capital, land, and labour generated during recessions[365] to stave off the falling rate of profit.[366] Mass incarceration became a central part of the Californian economy through investment in prison infrastructure and staffing.[367] Whereas previously surplus labour and capital had been employed in the arms economy, the new expansion of prison capacity can be viewed as a 'permanent crisis workfare-warfare state, whose domestic militarism is

359 Ibid., 62–64.
360 Teague, 'Neoliberalism, Prisons and Probation', 53.
361 Hohle, *Racism in the Neoliberal Era*, 204.
362 Ibid., 206.
363 Ibid., 207.
364 Ibid., 208.
365 Ruth Wilson Gilmore, *Golden Gulag: Prisons, Surplus, Crisis, and Opposition in Globalizing California* (University of California Press 2007), 69, 77 and 83.
366 Ibid., 71 and 79.
367 Ibid., 126.

concretely recapitulated in the landscapes of depopulated urban communities and rural prison towns'.[368] For those employed at the new prisons, 'the prison economy created a real material interest for rural middle class whites on the continued racist zero-tolerance policing and imprisonment of racial minorities'.[369] However, while some gained employment through the location of prisons in their town, mass incarceration had devastating consequences for those whose jobs were replaced by prison labour, as well as dragging down working class wages more generally.[370]

Rather than being a conspiracy between private companies and the state, penal expansion may be seen as the convergence of various elite interests, where the impetus to contain the poor presented profit-making opportunities.[371] It was seized upon by opportunistic corporations.[372] The American Legislative Exchange Council spent huge sums on political lobbying in favour of higher sentences.[373] This organisation included private prison companies as well as large corporations intending to benefit from cheap prison labour, including McDonald's and Walmart.[374] As Angela Davis writes, 'black bodies are considered dispensable within the "free world" but as a major source of profit in the prison world'.[375] The explosion of prison building removed poor people from the welfare system and simultaneously made money for the owners of high-occupancy, non-unionised private prisons.[376] Nonetheless, mass incarceration required substantial state investment, particularly in relation to 'unprofitable' areas such as housing high-risk prisoners.[377] Moreover, the vast majority of prisons remained publically owned and funded.[378] However, even public prisons were 'tied to the corporate economy and constitute[d] an ever-growing source of capitalist profit' as private corporations entered lucrative contracts to sell their goods to prisons.[379]

In the UK, the first private prison of the twentieth century was opened in 1992 and by 2010, 11.3% of prisoners in England and Wales were in private

368 Ibid., 86.
369 Hohle, *Racism in the Neoliberal Era*, 128.
370 Heather Ann Thompson, 'The Prison Industrial Complex: A Growth Industry in a Shrinking Economy' (2012) 21(3) *New Labor Forum* 39, 42.
371 Gilmore, *Golden Gulag*, 88; Bell, *Criminal Justice and Neoliberalism*, 174; Wacquant, xx; Hohle, *Racism in the Neoliberal Era*, 207.
372 Ruth Wilson Gilmore, *Abolition Geography* (Verso Books 2023), 273.
373 Thompson, 'The Prison Industrial Complex', 41.
374 Ibid., 41.
375 Davis, *Are Prisons Obsolete?*, 95.
376 Hohle, *Racism in the Neoliberal Era*, 209.
377 Ibid., 209.
378 Gilmore, *Abolition Geography*, 273.
379 Davis, *Are Prisons Obsolete?*, 100.

prisons, compared to 7.2% in the United States.[380] The figure was even higher in Scotland, with around 20% of prisoners in private prisons.[381] By 2018, around 15% of British prisoners were incarcerated in private prisons, a percentage higher than the United States and only surpassed by Australia.[382] Under the Private Finance Initiative (PFI), the UK government issued contracts for the construction and management of prisons.[383] PFI used private sector debt capital and equity, underwritten by the public, to deliver services previously provided by the public sector. For those employed in the new private prisons, wages and pensions were lower and working hours longer, with increased staff turnover, lack of experience, and high levels of violence.[384] Prison labour in the UK is used by over 300 companies, with prisoners' minimum *weekly* wage lower than the minimum *hourly* wage for those on the outside.[385] The use of prison labour can be seen as a way of extending the 'workfare' requirements imposed on the non-imprisoned poor to the imprisoned poor at lower cost.[386]

In the United States, the War on Drugs dramatically increased Black incarceration rates through policing practices and higher sentencing powers.[387] As Kojo Koram argues, drugs are themselves a social and legal construction formed through processes of criminalisation.[388] Legislation and enforcement of drug prohibition have focused on racialised groups throughout history, from opium laws aimed at Chinese immigrants onwards.[389] Police targeting of poor Black neighbourhoods ensured that the moral panic from the perceived threat of drugs fell on Black working class people.[390] The War on Drugs originated during a period of political crisis for the right-wing in America, with Nixon deploying the strategy as a means to appeal to White Southerners, using discourses around law enforcement as a code for racist policies.[391] Furthermore, by constructing discursive links between race, radicalism, and drug taking, Nixon created a seemingly legitimate reason to

380 Teague, 'Neoliberalism, Prisons and Probation', 65; Bell, *Criminal Justice and Neoliberalism*, 181.
381 Bell, *Criminal Justice and Neoliberalism*, 181.
382 Jonathan Ford and Gill Plimmer, 'Momentum Stalls on UK's Private Prisons' *Financial Times* (12 February 2018) <www.ft.com/content/3c356914-0d9c-11e8-839d-41ca06376bf2> accessed 18 December 2024.
383 Bell, *Criminal Justice and Neoliberalism*, 67.
384 Ibid., 67–68.
385 Trafford, 78.
386 Wacquant, 208.
387 Alexander, 96–97.
388 Kojo Koram (ed), *The War on Drugs and the Global Colour Line* (Pluto Press 2019), 11–12.
389 Ibid., 15.
390 Ibid., 97–98.
391 Alex S. Vitale, *The End of Policing* (Verso Books 2018), 133.

crack down on activists, particularly Black leaders, during the late 1960s, a time of intense political struggle.[392]

The War on Drugs was a process of simulation that constructed racialised legal subjects such as 'crack fiends'[393] and evil drug pushers as simulacra that appeared real, while racist policing and differential sentencing were disappeared,[394] as were the colonial histories that constructed drugs as a racialised legal category. Kojo Koram explains how the fear of contamination from drugs is viewed through the lens of racism, meaning that the 'metaphysical quality read into drugs is easily transferred into the very material bodies of those already traditionally constructed as being a threat to the boundaries of humanity: racially othered populations'.[395] The War on Drugs reproduced Black criminality as a contaminant, threatening to poison respectable (White) communities with illegal deadly substances, corrupt their children, or endanger their property.

The moral panic of White communities being 'blackened' by illegal drug use also acts as a metaphor for Black people entering into areas deemed to be White spaces. As Simon Flacks writes, discourses around drugs are often premised upon protecting childhood innocence, which is a classed and racialised concept.[396] Such discourses draw a distinction between those risks 'posed *to* children and those posed *by* them'.[397] Black children are not afforded the White privilege of being seen as innocent and vulnerable – they are deemed dangerous and ungrievable. While initially it may appear that the adultification of Black children and the infantilisation of marginalised communities are contradictory processes, both stem from the same colonial discourses that dehumanise racialised populations. Childhood innocence and adult autonomy are the preserve of what it means to be considered fully human under White supremacy. The simulacra of untamed Black teenagers roaming the streets wielding knives and pushing drugs and the simulacra of lawless racialised communities requiring firm control by the colonial state due to their inability to look after themselves are two sides of the same coin. These narratives are fundamental to the provisions considered in Chapters 3 and 4.

While Black and White Americans have similar rates of illegal drug use, Black people are ten times more likely to be imprisoned for drug offences.[398]

392 Ibid., 133–134.
393 Koram, 17.
394 Ibid., 5.
395 Ibid., 15.
396 Simon Flacks, *Law, Drugs and the Politics of Childhood: From Protection to Punishment* (Routledge 2021), 75.
397 Ibid., 148 (original italics).
398 Anjali Om, 'Chekhov's Corner: The Opioid Crisis in Black and White: The Role of Race in our Nation's Recent Drug Epidemic' (2018) 40(4) *Journal of Public Health* 614, 615.

The contrast between the treatment of opiate users and that of crack cocaine users is striking. Almost 90% of those addicted to opiates in the United States are White.[399] Opiate addiction has been viewed by the government and media as a health crisis, in contrast to crack cocaine addiction, which is framed solely as a criminal law issue.[400] The differentially racialised discourses around drugs serve to name Black users as criminals, while White users are seen as victims, vulnerable or corrupted by Blackness.

Jordan T. Camp points out that even excluding those sentenced for drugs offences, the United States still has the highest incarceration rate in the world.[401] Similarly, Dylan Rodríguez argues that an emphasis on the War on Drugs as the problem can lead to the misleading narrative that if it ended, then the system could be satisfactorily reformed.[402] Furthermore, the UK did not have a comparable policy of mass imprisonment for drug use, yet it has experienced a significant increase in racially disproportionate incarceration, as described above. However, not only did the War on Drugs increase the imprisonment rates of Black people, but it also performed a hegemonic function as a process of simulation to reproduce the third order simulacra of the undeserving racialised poor, choosing welfare, drugs, and crime over legitimate work. The War on Drugs operated 'to *produce* race itself, giving material form to old ideas about humanity and sub-humanity in this supposedly post-racial era'.[403] The sign of the Black drug dealer epitomised the dangerous gangster and helped to cement the discursive links between race, gangs, and weapons. In this way, the simulated War on Drugs not only reproduced the racialisation of drug crime but also intensified discourses that linked Blackness, poverty, and criminality more generally, allowing Black hypercriminality to appear as real.

Following Loïc Wacquant's argument that mass incarceration is the fourth institution to control and confine Black people in the United States, Reuben Jonathan Miller argues that the 'supervised society' of post-imprisonment control and exclusion serves as the fifth such institution.[404] The state of Illinois has 1,463 laws and regulations that control and restrict the freedoms of those convicted, New York State has over 1,300, and Michigan has nearly 800.[405] This results in the involuntary supervision and exclusion of those

399 Ibid., 614.
400 Ibid., 615.
401 Camp, 8.
402 Dylan Rodríguez, 'Abolition as Praxis of Human Being: A Foreword' (2019) 132 *Harvard Law Review* 1575, 1593.
403 Koram, 17 (original italics).
404 Reuben Jonathan Miller, 'All Leviathan's Children: Race, Punishment and the (Re-) Making of the City' in John Flint and Ryan Powell (eds), *Class, Ethnicity and State in the Polarized Metropolis* (Palgrave Macmillan 2019), 223.
405 Ibid., 222.

with convictions – landlords may be prohibited from renting to them, and their families may risk eviction by taking them in.[406] In this way 'criminal records shape *informal* interactions *outside* the purview of state institutions and influence the nature of even the most intimate or mundane relationships'.[407] Neoliberal discourses around risk management act performatively to reproduce simulacra of racialised criminality while appearing objective, ensuring that hypercriminality is a perpetual condition for the racialised poor with convictions.

Similarly in the UK, the ethos of the probation service changed substantially from the 1990s onwards, with increased managerialism.[408] As Michael Teague argues, this can be seen as intrinsically linked to neoliberalism and the privatisation of the probation service, such that 'what had been, in essence, an organisation engaged in social welfarist intervention was metamorphosing into a more punitive, target-driven agency, propelled by the twin imperatives of enforcement and compliance'.[409] These changes included greater supervision and surveillance of the increasing number of people on parole.[410] Instituting breach proceedings, potentially leading to prison recall, became a significant part of the probation officer's role, thus co-opting them into the policing and regulatory mechanisms controlling the life of the ex-prisoner. The dynamic of the relationship shifted from supportive to carceral.[411] The extensive number of recalls to prison, often for non-criminal actions, for those subjected to the life licence requirements of IPP sentences is discussed in Chapter 5.

These processes have operated to consolidate the belief in racialised criminality, such that, as Michelle Alexander argues, 'what it means to be criminal in our collective consciousness has become conflated with what it means to be black, so the term *white criminal* is confounding, while the term *black criminal* is nearly redundant'.[412] By way of example, in August 2022 during a discussion on ITV's *Good Morning Britain* about the murder of nine-year-old Olivia Pratt-Korbel, journalist Andrew Pierce commented that gun crime 'is an issue in our black community in many of our inner cities and it has to be addressed, you have to be not afraid to say so'. At the time of his comments, the identity of the perpetrator was unknown, but a White man was

406 Ibid., 224.
407 Ibid., 226 (original italics).
408 Teague, 'Neoliberalism, Prisons and Probation', 56.
409 Michael Teague, 'Probation, People and Profits: The Impact of Neoliberalism' (2016) 14(1) *British Journal of Community Justice* 133, 134–135.
410 Bell, *Criminal Justice and Neoliberalism*, 87–88.
411 Ian Brownlee, 'New Labour – New Penology? Punitive Rhetoric and the Limits of Managerialism in Criminal Justice Policy' (1998) 25(3) *Journal of Law and Society* 313, 328.
412 Alexander, 193 (original italics).

later arrested and convicted of murder. Although Pierce's comments were challenged, for many people the shooting of a child was assumed to be the work of a dangerous Black man. In the United States, the media coverage of Hurricane Katrina in 2005 presented a narrative of Black 'looters' and White 'finders' of essential goods.[413] Images of Blackness made the activity intelligible only as crime, whereas 'without a black body, the same action was interpreted as a (white) survival strategy'.[414] Blackness, poverty, and criminality are seen as synonymous through neoliberal reworkings of undeserving poor discourses. These simulated conceptions of criminality mean that the racialisation of crime and criminality is ever more abstracted, and its material and colonial roots are made invisible.

Jordan T. Camp argues that against a background of increased economic inequality, 'purportedly color-blind discourses of law and order, safety, and security became the key legitimating narratives for securing consent to carceral resolutions of social crises'.[415] As will be argued in more detail in later chapters, White elites deploy the simulacra of racialised criminality to frame the carceral state as self-defence for grievable populations. Therefore, speaking back against this hyperreality is necessary to advance the urgent project of carceral abolition and social justice.

Contradiction-Closing Cases Revisited

Derrick Bell's concept of contradiction-closing cases was outlined in Chapter 1, and it is argued throughout this book that processes of racialised criminalisation serve a contradiction-closing function. There are, however, differences between the ways that contradiction-closing civil cases operated during the civil rights era and how contradiction-closing criminal cases operate under contemporary neoliberalism. Contradiction-closing civil cases, such as *Brown*, appeared to resolve the contradiction between discourses of equality and the materiality of continued oppression by extending civil legal rights, notwithstanding their limitations in practice. In the era of colour-blind, post-rights discourses, criminal prosecutions for racist offences perform a contradiction-closing function by explaining away continuing racism as an anomaly perpetuated by backward individuals, rather than a fundamental aspect of neoliberalism, and by presenting the carceral state as the solution. Examples of this are the hate crime provisions and the Stephen Lawrence case, both considered in Chapter 4. In relation to criminal prosecutions of racialised defendants, the contradiction between apparent equality and continuing

413 Lisa Marie Cacho, *Social Death* (New York University Press 2012), 1–3.
414 Ibid., 2.
415 Camp, 16.

racial disparities in the criminal legal system is seemingly accounted for by the deficiencies, particularly the innate criminality, of racialised communities.

As Baudrillard wrote:

> what is politically effective is the creation not of a situation in which contradiction is replaced by equality and equilibrium, but of one in which contradiction is replaced by difference. The solution to social contradiction is not equalization, but differentiation.[416]

Neoliberal criminal law and evidence operate to naturalise disproportionate criminalisation through colonial discourses that differentiate racialised communities from Whiteness. The neoliberal simulacrum of meritocracy that is deployed to justify material inequalities also operates to blame racialised communities for their higher rates of criminalisation and incarceration. The law seeks to resolve its own contradictions through the simulation of difference: the simulacra of racialised criminality. In this way, contradiction-closing provisions in criminal law serve a hyperreal function – as third order simulacra, they mask 'the *absence* of a profound reality'.[417] In other words, they hide that there is only hyperreality; that there is only the simulacrum, rather than the reality, of racially disproportionate criminality. In this way, they operate to close the contradiction between discourses of colour-blindness and meritocracy and practices of racially disproportionate stop and search, arrests, charges, convictions, and incarceration.

The History of Criminal Law: From Second Order to Third Order Simulacra

This chapter has illustrated how criminalisation and punishment under racial capitalism are inseparable from concepts of property and labour. The periods discussed in this chapter illustrate how definitions of property have changed and been racialised. As capitalism developed, resources shifted from communal access to private property ownership, with theft redefined to reflect these changing property relations. Communal use of land was framed as backward while colonial taking of land and natural resources was deemed as progressive and rational. In this way, the values of Whiteness were used to define and justify property use. More fundamentally, those subjected to chattel slavery were commodified and defined as property owned by slaveowners rather than as free human beings. Enforced labour in various forms has

416 Jean Baudrillard, *The Consumer Society: Myths and Structures* (SAGE Publications 1998), 94.

417 Jean Baudrillard, *Simulacra and Simulation* (Sheila Faria Glaser tr, University of Michigan Press 1994), 6 (original italics).

been a form of punishment throughout capitalism, whether through prison labour, workhouse labour, community orders, or deportation to work in the colonies. Additionally, punishment is used as a means of disciplining and controlling the racialised poor more generally in order to create a compliant labour force. The forms that this punishment takes may vary during different stages of racial capitalism, but they all require definitions of criminality and processes of criminalisation. The racialised concept of the undeserving poor provides the ideological justification for the disposal of surplus populations. Under earlier stages of capitalism this was through prison, the workhouse, the gallows, and transportation, while under neoliberalism lethal injection, immigration detention, deportation, and mass incarceration serve a similar purpose. In this way, discourses around the racialised undeserving poor can be seen as closely linked to ungrievability.

As illustrated by the periods covered in this chapter, the second order simulacra of race and the undeserving poor are intrinsically linked. This continues under the more abstracted conception of racialised criminalisation through the neoliberal simulation of meritocracy, which is deployed to legitimise both material inequality and the carceral state. As Baudrillard wrote, 'history isn't over, it's in a state of simulation'.[418] There is a 'reabsorption of all genealogy' such that previous orders of simulacra are present within third order simulacra but rendered invisible.[419] Colonial constructions of second order simulacra are absorbed into the neoliberal criminal practices that construct racialised hypercriminals. In this way, colonialism continues to impact on racialised populations in the UK.

The following four chapters will analyse particular provisions from criminal law and evidence and the ways that they act as performative discourses to reproduce racialised legal subjects as third order simulacra of criminality – hypercriminals. Such provisions perform a contradiction-closing function; they serve to explain away the racial disproportionality in criminal legal outcomes as a reflection of essentialised Black criminality, such that hypercriminality appears to be real. In this way, hypercriminality operates as an alibi for the neoliberal carceral state.

418 Jean Baudrillard, *Forget Foucault* (Nicole Dufresne tr, Semiotext(e) 2007), 72.
419 Ibid., 76.

Chapter 3

Stop and Search Powers under Section 60

This chapter focuses on section 60 of the Criminal Justice and Public Order Act 1994, a provision that allows the police to stop and search people in a particular area without reasonable cause. Located within colonial discourses and operating through the racial frame, s.60 designates particular geographical areas as sites of criminality in order to justify these stop and search procedures. By deploying neoliberal discourses around risk management and a contemporary reworking of the civilising mission, s.60 constructs racialised communities as ungrievable, dangerous, and requiring intensified surveillance, monitoring, and restraint. As such, it can be viewed as an abstracted form of the CTA and HCA considered in the previous chapter.

Racialised communities who have already been produced as criminals by neoliberal legal practices are subjected to s.60 orders. The consequent intense police activity in those areas results in increased arrests and charges, which are then presented as evidence of localised criminality, justifying further s.60 orders. Therefore, s.60 is a circular, self-referential, and hyperreal process. The simulation of racialised criminality that led to the imposition of the initial order leads to a further simulation of criminality in that area, and the community are reproduced as hypercriminals. Meanwhile, the colonial discourses that underlie the disproportionate policing of racialised communities are rendered invisible.

Due to the lack of a requirement for reasonable cause, it has been argued that s.60 is an exceptional power.[1] This chapter will start by considering how exceptional powers can be considered hyperreal. This will be followed by a discussion around the policing of racialised communities, and how this is embedded within colonial discourses and practices, prior to focusing on s.60.

1 Michael Shiner and Rebekah Delsol, 'The Politics of the Powers' in Rebekah Delsol and Michael Shiner (eds), *Stop and Search: The Anatomy of a Police Power* (Palgrave Macmillan 2015), 37.

DOI: 10.4324/9781003602873-4

Hyperreal Exceptional Powers

Exceptional powers can be used to expose how the law itself contains the potential for legalised tyranny and dictatorship. Through the use of violence to maintain the law, 'the rule of law … directly appears as its own self-negation'.[2] Carl Schmitt, a political theorist for Hitler's Nazi Party, sought to demonstrate how liberal law was inherently contradictory.[3] He argued that the law had the potential to impose the will of the leader through imposing a state of emergency, which was within the constitution and therefore both democratic and legal.[4] However, the very concept of a state of emergency and the granting of extraordinary powers to the executive could contain the seeds of the end of the rule of liberal democratic law.[5] Thus, the rule of law may result in its own destruction through providing the legal means for processes that could ultimately lead to the establishment of dictatorship.

While Schmitt wrote about how the state of exception is a means for the sovereign power to break from the normal legal order, for Giorgio Agamben, the state of exception is a permanent feature in modern liberal states.[6] Furthermore, this state of exception is contradictory as it is both within and outside the law – 'an emptiness of law'.[7] In other words, it is an extra-judicial power and therefore not part of the law, yet at the same time it can only come into existence because it is provided for under legal powers and is thus part of the law. One cannot draw a binary distinction between legal and exceptional powers as the former contains the latter within it – the legal power to dispense with legality. Binoy Kampmark describes the state of exception as hyperreal, as it constitutes 'a juridical-political category where illegality and legality blur before the justification of emergency'.[8] In this way, the state of exception can be seen as a site of implosion where the rule of law and the use of extreme powers cannot be distinguished from each other.

An analysis of the processes, practices, and discourses whereby exceptional provisions are normalised can expose the law's partiality, and illuminate

2 Slavoj Žižek, *The Courage of Hopelessness: Chronicles of a Year of Acting Dangerously* (Allen Lane 2017), 247.

3 David Dyzenhaus, 'Why Carl Schmitt?' in David Dyzenhaus (ed), *Law as Politics: Carl Schmitt's Critique of Liberalism* (Duke University Press 1998), 12.

4 Ibid., 12.

5 Ibid., 12.

6 Peter Fitzpatrick and Richard Joyce, 'The Normality of the Exception in Democracy's Empire' *Birkbeck ePrints* (2007), 3 <https://core.ac.uk/download/pdf/6543.pdf> accessed 18 December 2024.

7 Giorgio Agamben, *State of Exception* (Kevin Attell tr, The University of Chicago Press 2005), 6.

8 Binoy Kampmark, 'Murder in the Simulacrum: Bin Laden, Unbelievable Deaths and Depictions of Legal Exceptionality' (C-Theory: Theory Beyond the Code, 10 April 2012) <https://journals.uvic.ca/index.php/ctheory/article/view/14948/5844> accessed 18 December 2024.

how seemingly exceptional provisions are a sustained aspect of neoliberal law, rather than an aberration. The continuation of powers initially seen as temporary, such as the Prevention of Terrorism (Temporary Provisions) Act 1974 (PTA),[9] 'pushes back the threshold of repression by normalising the extraordinary'.[10] Moreover, the PTA is illustrative of how 'a symbiotic relationship develops between the ordinary criminal law and the emergency legislation'.[11] The extraordinary detention powers under the PTA were significantly lengthier than the regular detention powers under the Police and Criminal Evidence Act 1984 (PACE).[12] The existence of these longer PTA detention powers made it easier to justify the subsequent extension of detention powers under PACE, albeit not to the same degree.[13]

As Subhabrata Bobby Banerjee and Yehouda Shenhav point out, Giorgio Agamben provides a useful analysis of the operation of the state of exception but neglects the role played by colonialism and imperialism.[14] Exceptional powers are premised as a response to a threat to the security of the state. The framing of who constitutes this threat is situated within processes of colonialism and racialisation. Exceptional powers dehumanise, and abstract to the point of simulacra, the people against whom they are used. These simulacra may be insurgents in colonised areas, states deemed hostile, or those considered enemies within a state, such as the organised working class. The law acts performatively to define who constitutes a threat to national and global security. This is intrinsically linked to concepts of grievable and ungrievable populations. The simulated War on Drugs, discussed in the previous chapter, deployed exceptional powers to maintain and perpetuate neoliberal socio-economic inequality and consolidate White supremacy. Increasingly punitive measures achieve their simulation by constructing the racialised poor as a threat to society that requires collective self-defence by means of the intensification of the carceral state. The sacrifice of ungrievable individuals or groups is presented as legitimate to protect those deemed worthy of inclusion in humanity. Such processes are rooted in colonial discourses, such that they are inherently racialised.

9 Paddy Hillyard, *Suspect Community: People's Experience of the Prevention of Terrorism Acts in Britain* (Pluto Press 1993), 263.
10 Joe Sim and Philip A. Thomas, 'The Prevention of Terrorism Act: Normalising the Politics of Repression' (1983) 10(1) *Journal of Law and Society* 71, 72.
11 Hillyard, *Suspect Community*, 263.
12 Ibid., 93.
13 Ibid., 263.
14 Subhabrata Bobby Banerjee, 'Necrocapitalism' (2008) 29(12) *Organization Studies* 1541, 1545; Yehouda Shenhav, 'Imperialism, Exceptionalism and the Contemporary World' in Marcelo Svirsky and Simone Bignall (eds), *Agamben and Colonialism* (Edinburgh University Press 2012), 19.

Fundamentally, the rule of law under racial capitalism operates to maintain, rather than confront, White supremacy. As discussed in previous chapters, the modern concept of the rule of law was formed within Enlightenment discourses of racialisation and cannot serve as a means of liberation from racism. Therefore, those who appeal to the rule of law as a bulwark against racism and fascism are misguided. As Walter Benjamin wrote, 'the "state of exception" in which we live is not the exception but the rule ... it is our task to bring about a real state of emergency, and this will improve our position in the struggle against fascism'.[15] Similarly, Slavoj Žižek argues that 'when a state institution proclaims a state of emergency, it does so by definition as part of a desperate strategy to *avoid* the true emergency and return to the "normal course of things"'.[16] When challenged, states deploy the spectre of dangerous enemies to justify the use of emergency powers as self-defence. The simulacra of the War on Terror and the War on Drugs operate to construct racialised folk devils and hide that 'business as usual' is a conflict against the racialised poor, who are 'simply collateral damage in the construction of a neoliberal order' to increase elite wealth.[17] As Jude McCulloch and Dean Wilson point out: 'The world is still waiting for the "war on global warming"'.[18]

Influenced by Giorgio Agamben, as well as Michel Foucault's work on governmentality and sovereign power,[19] Judith Butler views governmentality as co-existing with sovereign power rather than replacing it.[20] Butler posits that one should view 'the act of suspending the law as a performative one which brings a contemporary configuration of sovereignty into being or, more precisely, reanimates a spectral sovereignty within the field of governmentality'.[21] Butler considers how the suspension of rights of those detained at Guantanamo Bay constitutes 'an indefinite state of emergency'.[22] As Charlotte Chadderton argues, Butler enhances Agamben's work through their concept of racial framing, which seeks to explain how racialised populations are dehumanised.[23] The concept of racial framing was discussed in Chapter 1 and is used throughout this book to theorise performative processes of racialised criminalisation. In relation to Guantanamo Bay, Butler

15 Walter Benjamin, 'Theses of the Philosophy of History' in Hannah Arendt (ed), *Illuminations* (Harry Zohn tr, Schocken Books 1968), 257.
16 Slavoj Žižek, *Welcome to the Desert of the Real* (Verso Books 2012), 136 (original italics).
17 Henry A. Giroux, *Stormy Weather: Katrina and the Politics of Disposability* (Paradigm Publishers 2006), 11.
18 Jude McCulloch and Dean Wilson, *Pre-crime: Pre-emption, Precaution and the Future* (Routledge 2015), 142–143.
19 Judith Butler, *Precarious Life: The Powers of Mourning and Violence* (Verso Books 2004), 51–68.
20 Ibid., 52–54 and 60.
21 Ibid., 61.
22 Ibid., 63.
23 Charlotte Chadderton, *Judith Butler, Race and Education* (Palgrave Macmillan 2018), 154.

asks, 'to what extent is there a racial and ethnic frame through which these imprisoned lives are viewed and judged such that they are deemed less than human, or as having departed from the recognisable human community?'[24] They later answer this point by considering how processes of racialisation categorise particular groups as 'dangerous' in the context of the War on Terror, such that their legal rights are suspended on the grounds of national security.[25]

By framing resistance to globalisation and imperialism as terrorism, the discourse of collective self-defence can be used as a justification for the removal of rights from racialised suspects. Such narratives are premised on the argument that, in Achille Mbembe's words, 'the suspension of the rights and lifting of the guarantees that protect individuals are presented as the condition of the survival of those same rights'.[26] The violence used by capitalist states is displaced to 'nonplaces', formerly the colonies and the plantations, and now prisons and detention camps,[27] where racialised bodies are subjected to 'nonlaw' – exceptional powers that are normalised on the premise of preserving the law.[28] In this way, 'to protect the state of law against terror, it is deemed, violence must be done to the law, or we must constitutionalize what only yesterday was seen as an exception or outright lawlessness'.[29] Civilising mission discourses name Muslims as 'pre-modern, who have not yet entered into the secular terms of the liberal state'.[30] Such a framing legitimates exceptional state powers that violate the bodies of those deemed outside rationality in order to 'civilise' them – 'torture can be understood in this regard as a technique of modernization'.[31] Later in this chapter, it is argued that s.60 powers are grounded in civilising mission discourses, such that intense surveillance of racialised communities is framed as being for their own good.

The state of exception allows the state to subject racialised communities to 'necropolitical discipline'.[32] Elena Loizidou writes that this 'totalises narratives, it precludes those that are deemed a threat from providing us with a counter-narrative, it precludes the possibility of a legitimate trial ... it gives licence to kill'.[33] She gives the example of the fatal shooting by UK police of Jean Charles de Menezes at an underground station in London, after he was

24 Butler, *Precarious Life*, 57.
25 Ibid., 76–77.
26 Achille Mbembe, *Necropolitics* (Duke University Press 2019), 33.
27 Ibid., 27.
28 Ibid., 33.
29 Ibid., 33.
30 Judith Butler, *Frames of War: When Is Life Grievable?* (Verso Books 2016), 124.
31 Ibid., 129–130.
32 David Theo Goldberg, *The Threat of Race* (Blackwell Publishing 2008), 334.
33 Elena Loizidou, *Judith Butler: Ethics, Law, Politics* (Routledge-Cavendish 2007), 92.

incorrectly believed to be a terror suspect.[34] He was dehumanised, such that the racialised sign of him as a terrorist became the entirety of his being. The perceived enemies of the state are abstracted as signifiers of threat, danger, and contamination, such that they become simulacra of terrorism.

As outlined above, the state of exception can be described as hyperreal – an implosion of the rule of law and extreme legal powers justified by discourses around collective self-defence. Neoliberal international human rights discourses can also be viewed as hyperreal. Jean Baudrillard wrote that under conditions of globalisation, 'democracy and human rights circulate just like any other global product – like oil or capital'.[35] Human rights and the rule of law were Enlightenment constructions embedded in colonialism, class relations, and patriarchy, and as such were second order simulacra. They were linked to the period of industrialisation, with legally enshrined racial inequality forcibly exported to India by colonial Britain along with British manufactured goods, as described in Chapter 2. However, under neoliberalism, international human rights have now become third order simulacra, as Western nations purport to export human rights to the Middle East pursuant to the simulation of the War on Terror. Human rights discourses exist in the symbolic realm and are an implosion of meaning such that the apparent imposition of rights and the infliction of rights abuses have become blurred. These discourses are located within civilising mission narratives that act as processes of racial differentiation in furtherance of imperialist aims, positioning the West as advanced and rational, and dehumanising racialised populations. Conflicts between the West and Islam are 'not ... a clash of civilizations or religions'[36] but a 'clash of *economic* interests, and of the geopolitical interests of the United States itself'.[37] Civilising mission discourses operate as a justificatory alibi for the project of imperialism.

In Baudrillard's words, 'what the West now wishes to foist on the whole world, in the guise of universality, is not its – completely unhinged – values, but its absence of values'.[38] Neoliberal human rights discourses have become an abstracted simulation of the second order simulacrum of Enlightenment human rights, such that they 'mask the *absence* of a profound reality'.[39] Ashley Woodward writes that, 'simulated systems which have lost their reference in the real hide this loss by producing an imaginary, an opposite, which maintains the illusion that this reference still operates by upholding

34 Ibid., 92.
35 Jean Baudrillard, *The Spirit of Terrorism* (Chris Turner tr, Verso Books 2003), 90.
36 Ibid., 11.
37 Žižek, *Welcome to the Desert of the Real*, 52 (original italics).
38 Jean Baudrillard, *Screened Out* (Chris Turner tr, Verso Books 2014), 70.
39 Jean Baudrillard, *Simulacra and Simulation* (Sheila Faria Glaser tr, University of Michigan Press 1994), 6 (original italics).

the binary oppositions which require this reference'.[40] Human rights discourses are deployed to signify that justice, equality, and fairness are a reality in the West, which is contrasted with the rest of the world, in a contemporary reworking of Orientalism. This hides the empty content of neoliberal human rights discourses and the continued lack of social justice in the West.

Such narratives operate to exclude collective transformative justice solutions to inequality and social issues by positioning hyperreal Western conceptions of human rights as liberatory.[41] In this way, as Aidan Hehir argues, the project of imperialism seeks to recreate other countries not as the West but as the hyperreal image of an idealised version of the West.[42] This simulacrum names human rights and freedom as Western concepts, tied to notions of individualism and meritocracy. Western narratives around bestowing human rights on Muslim countries reproduce the myth that the West has transcended patriarchy, racism, homophobia, and repressive laws. The point that laws criminalising homosexuality in the Global South are frequently a legacy of colonial rule is absent from these narratives.[43] The civilising mission discourse has mutated from the colonisers' condemnation of homosexuality as a primitive and morally backward practice, to the neoliberal simulacrum that homophobia exists only in less developed, barbaric countries and has been surpassed in the West.

The binary divide reproduced by these imperialist discourses on an international level also impacts on domestic racialised populations and amplifies processes of racialised criminalisation in the UK. Charlotte Chadderton argues that 'the discourse of "state of emergency" ... functions to actually produce the state of emergency as a "reality"'.[44] This perceived 'reality', or hyperreality, is a simulation whereby Muslims become hyperterrorists. These processes of simulation are located within a history of imperialism and colonialism, and a desire to erase this through invoking civilising mission discourses that position Muslims as the source of violence and repression.[45] In Chapter 5, it will be argued that similar narratives are deployed by the state and the media in relation to child sexual abuse, with the West

40 Ashley Woodward, 'Was Baudrillard a Nihilist?' (2008) 5(1) *International Journal of Baudrillard Studies* <https://baudrillardstudies.ubishops.ca/was-baudrillard-a-nihilist/> accessed 19 December 2024.

41 Slavoj Žižek, 'Against Human Rights' (2005) 34 *New Left Review* 115, 126.

42 Aidan Hehir, 'Hyper-reality and Statebuilding: Baudrillard and the Unwillingness of International Administrations to Cede Control' (2011) 32(6) *Third World Quarterly* 1073, 1074.

43 Enze Han and Joseph O'Mahoney, *British Colonialism and the Criminalization of Homosexuality: Queens, Crime and Empire* (Routledge 2018); Hannah McCann and Whitney Monaghan, *Queer Theory Now: From Foundations to Futures* (Bloomsbury 2020), 163.

44 Chadderton, *Judith Butler, Race and Education*, 149–150.

45 Ibid., 150.

presented as post-patriarchal, and Islam portrayed as backward and misogynistic. Chadderton argues that the increased surveillance of racialised school students in the UK is part of the process of normalising the state of exception, with these students being constructed as a threat against the background of the War on Terror.[46] These surveillance techniques, particularly the Prevent agenda, are not only a response to racialised discourses but also reproduce and extend these narratives – they 'produce the recognisability of white bodies as lives, and minority ethnic bodies as threat, therefore maintaining the structures of white supremacy'.[47]

While Muslims have been constructed as a 'suspect community' within Britain since September 2001,[48] Irish people were framed as suspicious from the 1970s to the early 1990s.[49] A 'suspect community' is constructed by 'the complex interplay between the legal machinery of the state and social and political discourses'.[50] The exceptional powers under the PTA created a racialised 'dual system of criminal justice in Britain'.[51] As Paddy Hillyard argues, 'individualized notions of suspicion and response [were] replaced by aggregate classification systems for the purposes of surveillance, arbitrary detention, and control'.[52] Risk was deemed to be situated within the Irish community, such that the state sought to 'optimize public safety through the efficient management of this section of the population'.[53] Neoliberal managerialism targets law enforcement resources on particular communities on the premise of efficiency, yet concepts of risk are constructed through racial framing. As discussed in more detail in Chapter 5, narratives around dangerous communities are embedded in colonial discourses.

The construction of a suspect community relies upon previous processes of racialisation, but also operates as a process of racialisation.[54] In this way, discourses around the perceived justification for exceptional powers, as well as the legal powers themselves, can be viewed as both racialised and racialising. Suspect communities become simulacra for danger, such that they are constructed in the symbolic hyperreal realm and their colonial genealogy is reabsorbed and disappeared. Through a self-referential process, the simulation

46 Charlotte Chadderton, 'UK Secondary Schools Under Surveillance: What are the Implications for Race? A Critical Race and Butlerian Analysis' in Antonia Kupfer (ed), *Power and Education: Contexts of Oppression and Opportunity* (Palgrave Macmillan 2015), 87.
47 Ibid., 86.
48 Christina Pantazis and Simon Pemberton, 'Restating the Case for the "Suspect Community"' (2011) 51 *British Journal of Criminology* 1054.
49 Hillyard, *Suspect Community*, 257–258.
50 Pantazis and Pemberton, 1056.
51 Hillyard, *Suspect Community*, 261.
52 Paddy Hillyard, 'Irish People and the British Criminal Justice System' (1994) 21(1) *Journal of Law and Society* 39, 52.
53 Ibid., 52.
54 Hillyard, *Suspect Community*, 2–4 and 258.

of criminality leads to members of those communities being arrested and charged, which perpetuates this simulation, such that suspect communities become hypercriminals. It is argued below that s.60 powers operate in such a way, and create areas of hypercriminality. In order to understand these processes, it is necessary to consider the relationship between exceptional powers, colonialism, and the policing of racialised communities.

Policing the Simulation

Our understanding of processes of racialisation criminalisation can be enhanced by analysing the colonial practices within which criminal law and policing are embedded. The Metropolitan Police was established in London for the purposes of quelling unrest, strikes, and protests, as well as enforcing the vagrancy laws.[55] This social control was a means to an economic end – to create the complaint labourers necessary for industrial capitalism and to protect private property.[56] However, as Lambros Fatsis and Melayna Lamb argue, it is 'an unpardonable blind spot in police scholarship' to interpret British policing as solely class based, and to treat it as separate from the history of policing the colonies.[57] As outlined in Chapter 2, slave patrols were the precursors of US policing.[58] To see this as unrelated to British policing is 'to think of imperial Britain as a non-imperial nation'.[59] Contemporary British policing models constitute 'the reincarnation of the pre-professional colonial, slave-catching militias, with the plantation *overseer* being the forerunner of the metropolitan *officer*'.[60] Colonial policing techniques used in Caribbean plantations, India, and Ireland laid the foundations for British police forces.[61] Additionally, practices used by the British Army in Kenya and Malaysia were deployed as counter-insurgency techniques in Northern Ireland and later utilised in mainland Britain.[62] Colonialism was not only fundamental to the initial form taken by British policing but continues to infuse its methods and operations.

For Aimé Césaire, the 'boomerang effect of colonization' meant that those colonising other countries not only dehumanised others but also became

55 Alex S. Vitale, *The End of Policing* (Verso Books 2018), 36.
56 Ibid., 36.
57 Lambros Fatsis and Melayna Lamb, *Policing the Pandemic: How Public Health Becomes Public Order* (Policy Press 2022), 26.
58 Vitale, 45–47; Michael A. Robinson, 'Black Bodies on the Ground: Policing Disparities in the African American Community – An Analysis of Newsprint from January 1, 2015, Through December 31, 2015' (2017) 48(6) *Journal of Black Studies* 551, 553.
59 Fatsis and Lamb, 26.
60 Ibid., 26 (original italics).
61 Ibid., 27.
62 Arun Kundnani, 'Total Policing and the Global Surveillance Empire Today' in Jordan T. Camp and Christina Heatherton (eds), *Policing the Planet* (Verso Books 2016), 90–91.

dehumanised themselves through this brutality.[63] This 'boomerang effect' meant that while the West imposed its own legal and socio-political practices on the colonies, the imposition of these techniques of power in turn affected their use in the originating nation.[64] In this way, in Foucault's words, 'a whole series of colonial models was brought back to the West, and the result was that the West could practice something resembling colonisation, or an internal colonialism, on itself'.[65] The French army suppressed the 1848 uprisings using techniques they had used previously in the colony of Algeria, and many of those involved in the unrest were punished by transportation to Algeria.[66] During their occupation of the Philippines, the United States set up a constabulary to monitor and police anti-colonial resistance.[67] This formed the blueprint for the establishment of the Pennsylvania State Police in 1905, which used similar techniques to suppress strikes by miners and factory workers.[68]

In the 1960s and early 1970s, anti-guerrilla and military surveillance techniques first used in Vietnam were deployed against US civil rights protestors.[69] US police departments received surplus weapons from the Vietnam War, as well as their own military-grade weapons.[70] During the 1965 uprising in Watts, Los Angeles, the police chief described the situation as 'very much like fighting the Viet Cong'.[71] Black Panther co-founder Bobby Seale understood this practice of treating domestic racialised communities as colonial subjects when he argued, 'The racist military police force occupies our community just like the foreign American troops in Vietnam'.[72] Military-style policing of racialised communities was framed as a civilising mission. The performative processes of simulation that dehumanised colonial subjects were applied against those resisting the state.

63 Aimé Césaire, *Discourse on Colonialism* (Joan Pinkham tr, Monthly Review Press 2000), 41.

64 Michel Foucault, *Society Must be Defended* (David Macey tr, Penguin Books 1997), 103.

65 Ibid., 103.

66 Gurminder K. Bhambra and John Holmwood, *Colonialism and Social Theory* (Polity Press 2021), 86.

67 Vitale, 40–41.

68 Ibid., 40–42.

69 Robin D.G. Kelley, 'Thug Nation: On State Violence and Disposability' in Jordan T. Camp and Christina Heatherton (eds), *Policing the Planet* (Verso Books 2016), 23; Jordan T. Camp, *Incarcerating the Crisis: Freedom Struggles and the Rise of the Neoliberal State* (University of California Press 2016), 41.

70 Elizabeth Hinton, *America on Fire: The Untold History of Police Violence and Black Rebellion Since the 1960s* (Williams Collins 2021), 11.

71 Joshua Bloom and Waldo E. Martin Jr, *Black Against Empire: The History and Politics of the Black Panther Party* (University of California Press 2016), 29.

72 Stuart Schrader, *Badges Without Border: How Global Counterinsurgency Transformed American Policing* (University of California Press 2019), 3.

In relation to British policing, Tanzil Chowdhury argues that Northern Ireland 'provided an important space for logistical and strategic experimentation with the policing of dissent and anti-colonial resistance', with those techniques subsequently used to police racialised communities in Britain.[73] Emma Bell explains that 'Irish colonial policing cultures actually shared much in common with English policing cultures, with Ireland often providing the model'.[74] This is supported by the comments of Sir Robert Mark, Metropolitan Police Commissioner for much of the 1970s, who admitted that tactics used by the police in London had been previously used in Northern Ireland by both the Royal Ulster Constabulary (RUC) and the army.[75] Ron Ramdin notes that the troubles in Northern Ireland 'would prove good training for controlling and disciplining Britain's black communities'.[76] The Special Patrol Group, a mobile unit of the Metropolitan Police used for stop and search operations, demonstrations, and industrial action,[77] took its name from a similar unit used by the RUC.[78]

Standard policing techniques have long existed in conjunction with aspects of militarised policing, with the potential for policing to shift into occupation of communities, as in Northern Ireland.[79] Paramilitary techniques developed to suppress resistance in the colonies were deployed by the British police in relation to peace protestors in the 1980s, anti-drug operations in Black communities in the late 1980s, acid house parties in 1989, and poll tax protests in 1990.[80] Methods taken from colonial policing in Hong Kong were used at Orgreave during the miners' strike of 1984–85[81] and during the uprisings in Brixton, Handsworth, and Tottenham in 1985.[82] The use of colonial strategies of social control against domestic populations is particularly marked during times of economic crisis and working class resistance to racial

73 Tanzil Chowdhury, 'From the Colony to the Metropole: Race, Policing and the Colonial Boomerang' in Koshka Duff (ed), *Abolishing the Police* (Dog Section Press 2021), 86.

74 Emma Bell, 'Normalising the Exceptional: British Colonial Policing Cultures Come Home' (2013) 10 *Mémoire(s), Identité(s), Marginalité(s) Dans Le Monde Occidental Contemporain* 1, 4.

75 Chowdhury, 89.

76 Ron Ramdin, *The Marking of the Black Working Class in Britain* (Verso Books 2017), 473.

77 Brian Roberts, 'The Debate on "Sus"' in Ellis Cashmore and Barry Troyna (eds), *Black Youth in Crisis* (Routledge 1982), 117.

78 Liz Fekete, 'Total Policing: Reflections from the Frontline' (2013) 54(3) *Race and Class* 65, 68.

79 Gargi Bhattacharyya, *Dangerous Brown Men* (Zed Books 2008), 76.

80 Ellis Cashmore and Eugene McLaughlin, 'Out of Order' in Ellis Cashmore and Eugene McLaughlin (eds), *Out of Order? Policing Black People* (Routledge 1991), 15 and 29–37.

81 Connor Woodman, 'How British Police and Intelligence are a Product of the Imperial Boomerang Effect' *Verso* (10 June 2020) <https://www.versobooks.com/blogs/4390-how-british-police-and-intelligence-are-a-product-of-the-imperial-boomerang-effect> accessed 19 December 2024.

82 James Trafford, *The Empire at Home* (Pluto Press 2021), 67–70.

capitalism. When White elite privilege is at risk, processes of racialisation intensify. This includes a proliferation in the dehumanisation of populations deemed surplus, or those challenging White supremacy. Therefore, crises in racial capitalism are inseparable from an acceleration in the processes of simulation that construct hyperreal legal subjects.

Liz Fekete describes the links between the justification used for militaristic policing in Northern Ireland and in urban areas of the UK where racialised communities live, such as Tottenham, North London:

> In much the same way as areas like Ardoyne are portrayed as a breeding ground for a murderous Republicanism and pathological hatred of the British state, the residents of Broadwater Farm have been stigmatised in the media as inhabitants of a lawless zone, lost to postcode gangs, guns and anti-police hatred.[83]

As Paul Gilroy notes, the police are aware of the symbolism of inner city areas as places of resistance to police practices, such that 'the struggle over signs and images, particularly those which involve blacks, has become more important for the maintenance of order than the actual law-breaking that they denote'.[84] In order to continue the simulation that law enforcement is legitimate and cannot be resisted successfully, 'Black crime and disorder must be extinguished ... because they signify the limits to the order of public authority, with which the police are identified'.[85] During the late 1970s and early 1980s, there was 'an enhanced sense of the spatial and geographical dimensions to policing', with targeting of particular areas.[86] Black people were simultaneously excluded from places such as the West End and subjected to frequent stop and search in their local areas, with police resources focusing on South London and Hackney in East London.[87] These practices of 'containment', where those living in certain areas were treated as inherently criminal and had their ability to move freely in public spaces restricted, were used more generally by police later in the 1980s.[88] These techniques can be seen as precursors of the s.60 powers discussed below.

During the 2011 uprising, which started in Tottenham following the fatal shooting of Mark Duggan by the police, not only were organised, militaristic police tactics deployed on the streets, but the full force of the carceral state came to bear on those involved. Courts sat through the night, and defendants

83 Fekete, 67.
84 Paul Gilroy, *There Ain't No Black in the Union Jack* (Routledge 1987), 139.
85 Ibid., 140.
86 Ibid., 123.
87 Ibid., 123.
88 Ibid., 123–124.

with no previous convictions charged with relatively minor offences were refused bail and ultimately given custodial sentences, following political pressure on the courts to disregard the sentencing guidelines that they would be expected to follow in usual circumstances.[89] These higher sentences can be understood as fulfilling a symbolic function. Resistance to police practices was deemed to signify not only criminality but a level of criminality that justified immediate incarceration. The simulacrum of the dangerous, undeserving poor rioter was used to frame punitive sentencing as collective self-defence of society, in an attempt to bolster the legitimacy of the state and the police. In this way, the neoliberal state used legal and symbolic force to exert its authority, while simultaneously silencing narratives around racist policing, the defunding of public services, and working class immiseration.

This demonstrates the enduring potential to declare a state of exception within the current legal provisions. It was not necessary to pass any new legislation in order to treat this as an exceptional legal situation, only for the government to issue guidance that the law should be interpreted onerously. The simulacra of menacing criminal hoards was sufficient to invoke draconian powers. Existing police powers and criminal law contain within themselves the potential to arrest, charge, convict, and incarcerate swathes of the racialised working class during periods of resistance. As outlined in Chapter 2 and developed further in Chapter 4, under neoliberalism the third order simulacrum of hypercriminality absorbs the second order simulacra of race and the undeserving poor and reworks them in the context of meritocracy, such that poor communities are deemed responsible for their own disadvantage. While previously, colonial subjects were deemed as savage and requiring civilisation, under neoliberalism those discourses are reframed and used against domestic racialised communities. Therefore, Britain's colonial history is fundamental to contemporary processes of simulation and the construction of hypercriminals.

As discussed in Chapter 2 in relation to the work of Stuart Hall, in the 1970s the state and media created folk devils of Black 'muggers' and union activists. In the 1980s, Government and mainstream media discourses constructed Black 'rioters' and striking coal miners as folk devils. Arthur Scargill, the then president of the National Union of Mineworkers commented, 'police tactics in this dispute have revealed clearly to us what black and Asian communities throughout Britain mean by "police harassment"'.[90]

89 Owen Bowcott and Stephen Bates, 'Riots: Magistrates Advised to "Disregard Normal Sentencing"' *The Guardian* (15 August 2011) <www.theguardian.com/uk/2011/aug/15/riots-magistrates-sentencing> accessed 19 December 2024; Sarah Lamble, 'The Quiet Dangers of Civilized Rage: Surveying the Punitive Aftermath of England's 2011 Riots' (2013) 112(3) *Atlantic Quarterly* 577.

90 Chris Cunneen, *Defund the Police* (Polity Press 2023), 73.

In the twenty-first century, the s.60 powers used against Black 'knife carriers' are mirrored by the Public Order Act 2023 provisions aimed at environmental activists, as discussed at the end of this chapter. Under neoliberalism, racialised communities are constructed as ontologically suspect and are therefore prone to being abstracted as third order simulacra: hypercriminals. Generally, White people become simulacra of criminality only when they take action against the interests of neoliberalism or when they are considered proximate to Blackness, as will be discussed in Chapter 4.

State discourses relating to exceptional powers invoke arguments around the civilising mission and collective self-defence in an attempt to close the contradiction between the rhetoric of freedom, equality, and legality in neoliberal Western democracies, and the reality of the use of extra-legal powers. The use of exceptional powers against particular groups, or hyperreal suspect communities, is premised as necessary to safeguard democracy and the rule of law itself. By framing a group as terrorists or rioters who would deny rights to others, and have therefore placed themselves outside the law, the state is able to name them as non-citizens and use extraordinary powers against them, while still maintaining the illusion of the legitimacy of a fair justice system. As ungrievable populations are deemed unworthy of collective self-defence, uprisings are considered to be riots and are intelligible only as criminal actions. Legal sanctions are constituted as a civilising mission in relation to the ungrievable, and as collective self-defence for the grievable. Through these processes, the law constructs marginalised racialised communities as sources of danger. This latter point around racialisation and dangerousness will be developed further in Chapter 5.

The rest of this chapter will discuss s.60, a provision that could be considered as an exceptional power that has been normalised. However, as will be argued, rather than being exceptional and distinct from other stop and search powers, s.60 orders should be seen as a continuation of these racialised processes. The making and enforcement of a s.60 order is a performative practice that reproduces and intensifies racialised criminalisation. This operates as a process of simulation that frames those living in a particular area as hypercriminals, while using civilising mission discourses as a rationale. Whether deployed to justify imperialism overseas or exceptional powers against racialised communities in the metropole, civilising mission discourses serves as an accomplice to neoliberal hyperreality.

Hyperreal Section 60 and the Civilising Mission

Section 60 has been described as an exceptional provision, as it allows the police to stop and search individuals not suspected of any criminal offence.[91]

91 Shiner and Delsol, 37.

Under s.60 (as amended), a police officer of the rank of inspector or above can give authorisation that for up to 24 hours in a particular area[92] the police may stop and search any person or vehicle for weapons.[93] The conditions are that this officer believes that incidents involving serious violence may take place in the area and it is expedient to make an order to prevent their occurrence, that an incident involving serious violence has taken place and the weapon used is being carried in the area and it is expedient to make the order, or that persons are carrying weapons in the area without good reason.[94] A s.60 order can be extended by a further 24 hours by an officer of the rank of superintendent or above.[95] It will be argued below that s.60 orders construct poor racialised communities as pathologically violent, threatening, criminal, and ungrievable.

The s.60 powers were initially introduced in response to predicted violence at football matches.[96] Mark James and Geoff Pearson argue that s.60 was 'developed for the folk devils of the last Conservative government (striking miners, travellers and ravers) and in response to Labour concerns about binge drinkers' but later used 'as a means of regulating carnivalesque behaviour associated with football matches'.[97] While it is correct that the CJPOA signalled a general move towards criminalising certain lifestyles and communities, particularly travellers,[98] squatters,[99] and hunt saboteurs,[100] it appears that s.60 was initially premised in relation to football violence rather than this being a later use of the provision, as parliamentary discussions specifically referenced football-related disorder.[101] It is also notable that concerns about the potential for the provision to be used in racially discriminatory ways were voiced during its passage through the House of Lords.[102] During discussions in the House of Commons, similar concerns were raised, but

92 Criminal Justice and Public Order Act, s.60(1) as amended.
93 Ibid., s.60(4).
94 Ibid., s.60(1) as amended.
95 Ibid., s.60(3) as amended.
96 Equality and Human Rights Commission, 'Race Disproportionality in Stops and Searches under section 60 of the Criminal Justice and Public Order Act 1994' (Briefing Paper 5, 2012) <https://www.equalityhumanrights.com/sites/default/files/briefing-paper-5-race-disproportionality-in-stops-and-searches-under-s60-of-criminal-justice-and-public-order-act-1994.pdf> accessed 19 December 2024.
97 Mark James and Geoff Pearson, 'Regulating Anti-Social Behaviour and Disorder among Football Spectators' in Sarah Pickard (ed), *Anti-social Behaviour in Britain* (Palgrave Macmillan 2014), 303.
98 Criminal Justice and Public Order Act 1994, ss.77–78.
99 Ibid., s.73.
100 Ibid., s.68.
101 HL Deb 24 May 1994, vol 55, col 609–85, Lord Harmar-Nicholls, col 617.
102 HL Deb 24 May 1994, vol 55, col 609–85, Lord McIntosh of Haringey, col 609.

Michael Shersby MP suggested that the legislation could protect Black people from racially motivated attacks outside pubs, as well as football-related violence.[103] However, as will be discussed below, s.60 did not safeguard racialised people and instead, resulted in Black people being further targeted and criminalised. As will be argued in Chapter 4 in relation to hate crime, within a legal system rooted in colonialism and racial framing, criminal laws premised on the protection of racialised people result in the disproportionate criminalisation of those same communities. Under racial capitalism, the state cannot be relied upon to protect ungrievable populations.

While it may have been envisaged that s.60 would be used only in circumstances of serious violence, its use has been significantly extended by subsequent legislation, including the Knives Act 1997 and the Serious Crime Act 2007. As Peter Keeling writes, 'originally intended as a response to football hooliganism, s.60 became synonymous with crackdowns on knife crime and anti-gang operations'.[104] The implementation of amendments to the conditions required for s.60 orders, which made it easier to establish the grounds for an order and extended the length of orders, was part of the Conservative government's 'Beating Crime Plan' in 2021.[105]

Discourses around knife-related crime have reabsorbed and reformulated previous simulations around street crime, particularly the moral panic over muggings discussed in Chapter 2, and produced a moral panic around knife crime.[106] As Elaine Williams and Peter Squires argue, knife crime is a constructed category which, as with mugging, conflates various different offences and serves a symbolic function to reproduce Blackness as criminality.[107] Both of these moral panics can be seen as responses to crises in capitalism, and as attempts to divert public attention from the social consequences of increased poverty and inequality, and towards a law and order agenda.[108] This helped to reinvigorate and fortify the faltering legitimacy of the police through selective and misleading use of data.[109] The simulation of a knife crime epidemic requiring exceptional powers to safeguard the public enabled concerns about police racism, particularly racially disproportionate stop and search, to be pushed aside in the name of the 'war on knife crime'.[110] The apparent threat of serious violence by young Black

103 Criminal Justice and Public Order Bill Deb 12 April 1994, cols 76–77.

104 Peter Keeling, 'No Respect: Young BAME Men, the Police and Stop and Search' (Criminal Justice Alliance Briefing 2017), 4 <http://criminaljusticealliance.org/wp-content/uploads/2017/06/No-Respect-290617-1.pdf> accessed 19 December 2024.

105 UK Government, *Beating Crime Plan* (July 2021) <https://www.gov.uk/government/publications/beating-crime-plan> accessed 19 December 2024.

106 Stuart Hall and others, *Policing the Crisis: Mugging, the State, and Law and Order* (Macmillan 1978).

107 Elaine Williams and Peter Squires, *Rethinking Knife Crime* (Palgrave Macmillan 2021), 18.

108 Ibid., 236.

109 Ibid., 161.

110 Ibid., 115, 135, 171 and 209.

men gave the police a seemingly objective reason to stop and search racialised people in urban areas,[111] which increased the use of s.60 powers.[112]

Although reasonable suspicion is not required for a s.60 search, the Metropolitan Police Standard Operating Procedures made it clear that, 'the powers should not be used to stop and search persons and vehicles for reasons unconnected with the purpose of the authorisation'.[113] This reveals a tension within the provision itself – if it is to be used in situations relating to possession of weapons but it can be used without grounds for reasonable suspicion of such possession, then on what grounds are the police to select the people to stop and search for weapons? The government's own statistics show a correlation between being Black and being searched. In relation to searches under s.1, PACE, and s.60 combined during the year ending March 2024, Black people were 5 times more likely than White people to be stopped and searched.[114] However, when s.60 is considered in isolation, the figures are significantly starker, with a Black person 9.2 times more likely to be stopped and searched than a White person.[115] While statistics relating to stop and search may encounter methodological issues such as repeat stops on the same people, which may distort the figures in relation to the proportion of people stopped,[116] nonetheless these disparities are significant and demonstrate the racialised way that s.60 powers are enforced. Furthermore, it is little comfort that the numbers are distorted by repeated searches of the same people, as for those people it is a significant intrusion on their ability to go about their lives and exist in public spaces without state interference.

Searches under s.60 have a notably low success rate with only 4.1% resulting in arrest in the year ending March 2024, compared to 14.3% of searches under s.1, PACE during the same period,[117] and therefore arguments that s.60 searches are justified and more likely to yield results through temporal and spatial targeting are not borne out by the statistics. Searches requiring reasonable suspicion show less of a racial disparity and are more likely

111 Ibid., 10.

112 Ibid., 208.

113 Andy Walker, 'Section 60 Criminal Justice and Public Order Act 1994: Standard Operating Procedures' (Metropolitan Police 2012), 17 <www.met.police.uk/SysSiteAssets/foi-media/metropolitan-police/policies/search-powers-under-section-60-criminal-justice--public-order-act-1994-standard-operating-procedures-sop> accessed 19 December 2024.

114 Home Office, *Police Powers and Procedures: Stop and Search and Arrests, England and Wales, Year Ending March 2024* (26 September 2024) <https://www.gov.uk/government/statistics/stop-and-search-arrests-and-mental-health-detentions-march-2024/police-powers-and-procedures-stop-and-search-arrests-and-mental-health-detentions-england-and-wales-year-ending-31-march-2024> accessed 22 May 2025.

115 Ibid.

116 Equality and Human Rights Commission, 31–32.

117 Home Office, *Police Powers and Procedures*.

to result in arrest than searches under s.60. Research by Tony Jefferson on police practices concluded 'that where the legal structure was strong (clear/definite) it was able, effectively, to determine outcomes; where it was weak (unclear/discretionary), cop culture tended to take command'.[118] Put simply, the greater the discretion afforded to the police, the greater the racial disproportionality. Where the law is unclear and more reliant on interpretation by the police, racial framing is more pronounced, such that the sign of the hyperreal Black criminal prevails.

The lockdown rules during the Covid-19 pandemic are a further example of this. Many of the provisions were vague, such that police officers were afforded a high degree of discretion.[119] Returning to Patricia Williams' example of letting a flat in Chapter 1, it follows that within a racist legal system, tightly defined legal provisions can provide more of a safeguard to racialised people than those that are less specific. Where discretion exists, abstracted constructions of criminality have greater force and the simulacrum of the racialised hypercriminal dominates the interpretation of the provisions. During lockdown, the simulation of Black criminality was able to 'morph from the spectre of drug dealer to the virus spreader'.[120] Furthermore, not only were racialised people disproportionately impacted by Covid-specific Fixed Penalty Notices, but they were also subjected to high levels of disproportionality in relation to general policing techniques during the pandemic, particularly stop and search.[121] In other words, greater power to stop and search in relation to a specific purpose is likely to intensify street policing practices more generally, so that the increase in racially disproportionate policing is not limited to that specific purpose. Stop and search under s.60 can be seen as a further example of this, as illustrated by the case of *Roberts*.[122]

Ann Roberts was a 37-year-old Black female teaching assistant with no convictions or cautions. Following an allegation that she had not paid her bus fare and after she denied having identification, she was subjected to a bag search under s.60. After saying that she would prefer to be searched in a police station and keeping a tight hold of her bag, Ms Roberts was restrained and handcuffed. The s.60 order had been made on the grounds of gang-related activity in parts of the London Borough of Haringey. Ms Roberts argued that s.60 was incompatible with the right to respect for private life protected by Article 8 of the European Convention of Human Rights and

118 Tony Jefferson, 'Policing the Crisis Revisited: The State, Masculinity, Fear of Crime and Racism' (2008) 4(1) *Crime Media Culture* 113, 117.

119 Fatsis and Lamb, 42.

120 Scarlet Harris and others, *A Threat to Public Safety: Policing, Racism and the Covid-19 Pandemic* (Institute of Race Relations 2011), 15.

121 Ibid., 30.

122 *R (on the application of Roberts) v Commissioner of Police of the Metropolis and another* [2015] UKSC 79.

sought a declaration of incompatibility under s.4, Human Rights Act 1998 on the ground that the power was 'not in accordance with the law' as it was used in a discriminatory manner. The Supreme Court unanimously dismissed her appeal. They held that it was possible to decide whether the powers had been exercised lawfully, as the provisions required reasons to be given for the s.60 authorisation and for individual searches that took place, and that both the s.60 order and the search of Ms Roberts had been carried out legally. In essence, they decided that there were sufficient checks and balances to justify the restriction on liberty and that the provisions were 'in accordance with the law'.

Although it appears that the actual purpose of the search was to ascertain Ms Roberts' identity in relation to alleged non-payment of her bus fare, the court held that as the police officer thought that Ms Roberts was holding her bag tightly in what was considered to be a suspicious manner, she might have been carrying a weapon. The police officer stated that women of Ms Roberts' age would carry weapons for others. Yet, the reason for the involvement of the police was merely an alleged unpaid bus fare, and completely unrelated to knives. Notwithstanding police racism more generally, the existence of a s.60 order was the factor that prompted the police to view her actions as related to gangs and weapons. Racially disproportionate policing is officially sanctioned by a s.60 order covering areas where racialised communities live. The imposition of a s.60 order intensifies these racialising practices, such that not only young Black males but a middle-aged woman with no previous convictions is constructed as a criminal concealing a weapon.

A s.60 order serves a performative function as it racially frames those living in an entire geographical area as suspects for weapon-related offences. The police officer's contention that middle-aged women in the Tottenham area regularly carry weapons for others draws on narratives of sly, irresponsible single mothers from dysfunctional families colluding in the criminality of their gangster sons. It would seem inconceivable that a White, middle-aged, middle class woman would have been searched under the provisions. Ms Roberts was viewed as a simulacrum of Black criminality, such that she was abstracted rather than individualised. Her Blackness was the defining signifier, outweighing all other aspects of her identity. However, this intersected with her gender, such that the police viewed her as a Black matriarch and facilitator of male knife crime. This portrayal of Black women harks back to Lord Scarman's report following the unrest in Brixton, South London, in 1981. Scarman characterised Black families as matriarchies, where absent fathers and lack of discipline resulted in criminal children.[123] This discourse essentialised Black families as the undeserving poor, marked by a failure to comply with patriarchal, heteronormative expectations, with the insinuation

123 Gilroy, 133.

that women were using motherhood as an excuse to claim welfare benefits and avoid work, while their unruly sons were engaged in criminal activities.

In the *Roberts* case, the s.60 authorisation applied to the predominantly Black, working class areas of the London Borough of Haringey, including Tottenham, while excluding the more affluent areas of that borough. Research by Megan McElhone used geographical information system software to map every s.60 order imposed in London between 1 August 2019 and 31 July 2020, with preliminary results showing a correlation with areas where Black communities live, including Tottenham.[124] This reflects the binary distinctions in the colonial project that designates White spaces as respectable and civilised, and Black spaces as savage and uncivilised.[125] In a process of simulation that belies its colonial roots, areas inhabited by racialised communities become simulacra for criminality, such that they are subjected to spatial containment.

Although the Supreme Court was keen to point out that the UK does not have a system of identification cards allowing the police to arbitrarily stop people and ask them to account for themselves,[126] they argued that there are some instances where stopping people is 'necessary for the protection of the public from terrorism or serious crime'.[127] Yet, the targeting of Black communities by s.60 orders, such that a woman suspected only of non-payment of a bus fare could be subjected to demands to be searched in public, constitutes a significant restriction of the ability of racialised communities to exist and travel in public areas. As Rinaldo Walcott argues, street checks can be seen as 'part of the long history of travel passes, which date directly back to plantations and urban slavery'.[128] Laws premised around safety that target racialised communities such that they are denied control over their own possessions and bodies in public spaces are a continuation of colonial practices of surveillance and exclusion.[129]

The Supreme Court decision demonstrates the limits of human rights laws for Black people. The judgment stressed how the police are prohibited from using their powers in a racially discriminatory manner.[130] Yet the very use of s.60 frames Black people as criminals, and the statistics cited earlier in

124 Megan McElhone, 'In Conversation with Dr Megan McElhone' (Birkbeck Students' Union, 25 May 2022) <www.youtube.com/watch?v=dcSIPJvVSw4> accessed 19 December 2024.

125 Carol Azumah Dennis, 'Decolonising Education: A Pedagogic Intervention' in Gurminder K. Bhambra, Dalia Gebrial and Kerem Nişancıoğlu (eds), *Decolonising the University* (Pluto Press 2018), 192.

126 *Roberts*, para 1.

127 Ibid., para 2.

128 Rinaldo Walcott, *On Property: Policing, Prisons, and the Call for Abolition* (Biblioasis 2021), 32.

129 Ibid., 34.

130 *Roberts*, para 42.

this section illustrate that searches under s.60 are racially disproportionate. The preceding paragraph of the judgment exposes how the Supreme Court Justices racialised knife crime, stating that 'many of these gangs are largely composed of young people from black and minority ethnic groups' and then argues that it is in the interests of Black people to have such searches as they are the main victims of inner city gang violence.[131] The Supreme Court's argument is that disproportionate searches are in the interests of the communities targeted, despite the extremely low arrest rates in relation to s.60 searches. This civilising mission discourse positions racialised communities as backward, detached from rationality or reason, and prone to violence and self-destruction if not monitored, contained, and disciplined. In this way, increased surveillance and interference with the normal life of racialised communities is deemed to be for their own good. This attitude by the judiciary and law enforcement agencies conjures up imagery of colonialism and White superiority, within which savage populations require the force of White rule to keep them in order. Similarly, the mainstream media justify racially disproportionate stop and search as the preferable option for Black people, on the basis that the alternative is falling victim to knife crime committed by other Black people.[132] The civilising mission is a fundamental element of the simulacrum that positions Whiteness as progressive and protective. Expressed in terms of human rights discourses, 'the right not to be stopped and searched for no reason' becomes 'the right to have your community protected from itself by the police stopping and searching you for no reason' – the right for the racialised poor to be protected from themselves by White saviours.

Earlier in this book, it was argued that under neoliberalism, human rights discourses constitute third order simulacra. Human rights circulate as signs that communicate the message that Western societies have transcended discrimination. Courts bestow legitimacy on provisions such as s.60 by naming them as compliant with human rights. These discourses are self-referential and performative – by appearing to give rights to individuals from marginalised groups, they name those individuals as having rights. Then, the apparent rights granted to individuals from historically oppressed groups allow the simulacrum of meritocracy to appear as real. As Baudrillard argued, 'it is always the same with rights: the right to water, the right to air, the right to existence, etc. It is when all these fine things have disappeared that the law appears to grant their disappearance official recognition'.[133] Human rights discourses proliferate, yet inequalities persist, wealth differentials between rich and poor become more pronounced, and the incarceration of racialised

131 Ibid., para 41.
132 Williams and Squires, 181.
133 Jean Baudrillard, *The Illusion of the End* (Chris Turner tr, Polity Press 1994), 80.

poor populations increases. Relying on human rights laws to bring about equality mistakenly sees them as real rather than as hyperreal.

An analysis of s.60 must consider the state's need to create scapegoats in times of political and economic crisis, but also how this is grounded in colonial discourses. This not only applies to the use of stop and search powers but also to the decisions by senior police officers to make a s.60 authorisation in a particular location at a particular time. Neoliberal managerialism uses discourses around risk management to justify focusing police resources in particular areas, yet, as argued below, conceptions of risk are constructed through the racial frame. Operating within this framing, s.60 can be understood as a process of simulation that intensifies processes of racialised criminalisation. Returning to the case of *Roberts*, the pre-existing racial framing was intensified by the hyperreal s.60 authorisation, which meant that the entire Black community were seen as knife crime suspects. Ms Roberts became a hypercriminal – within the simulated conditions of s.60, the truth of whether or not she actually had a knife was superseded by the simulation of a community of knife carriers.

Earlier in this chapter, it was argued that exceptional techniques of control used against colonial subjects 'boomerang' back to the originating nation to be used against domestic racialised communities. In this way, as Alpana Roy writes, 'the ideological effects of colonial laws continue to have contemporary relevance as they *continue* to be used as an instrument of control in this postcolonial world'.[134] John Moore argues that:

> the exclusionary exceptions of liberalism have consequently been relocated to the metropole where in the guise of the 'New Punitiveness', they are used disproportionally against the direct descendants of the subjugated populations of the colonized periphery where they were tested.[135]

Racialised communities, whose ancestors were subjected to the violence of slavery and colonialism, are living with the continuation of these processes and reproduced as ungrievable populations, where the ability to simply exist in public spaces is curtailed.

Carceral provisions premised on the threat of terrorism, such as those used at Guantanamo Bay, deploy the civilising mission to render invisible the violence of Western imperialism. In relation to domestic racialised communities, the civilising mission is linked to another project of capitalist expropriation

134 Alpana Roy, 'Postcolonial Theory and Law: A Critical Introduction' (2008) 29 *Adelaide Law Review* 315, 319 (original italics).

135 John Moore, 'Is the Empire Coming Home?' (2014) 14 *Papers from the British Criminology Conference* 31, 40 <http://britsoccrim.org/new/volume14/pbcc_2014_moore.pdf> accessed 19 December 2024.

– the gentrification of urban areas. Under neoliberalism, housing is increasingly seen as a capital asset rather than as a home, with private 'buy to let' landlords amassing property portfolios, and the continuing decline of social housing which increasingly serves as a signifier for the undeserving poor.[136] Squatting in residential buildings was criminalised from September 2012, during a period when the value of residential property rose significantly.[137] Landlords were deemed worthy of state protection to defend their assets, while discourses around housing needs were silenced. Research by Brett Christophers found that between 1979 and 2018 the equivalent of about 10% of Britain's entire land was sold into private hands by the state,[138] which he compares to enclosure.[139] Just as discourses around enclosure defined common land as inefficient and backward, so neoliberal discourses do the same with public land and social housing, with enclosure and privatisation considered as useful, efficient, and profitable.[140] These processes have led to 'Britain's growing transformation into a "rentier" type economy – one increasingly dominated by rents paid by the many to the affluent, landowning few; and widespread social dislocation'.[141]

As discussed in Chapter 2, discourses around the perceived inefficiency of the public sector are racialised and linked to conceptions of the undeserving poor. The ownership of land gives the power to exclude and denote usage, such that it is a means of containing and disciplining particular communities. Justin Hansford likens gentrification to 'eighteenth-century colonialism, with inner cities our current "unclaimed" frontiers of the past – holding the promise of great wealth as long as the hordes of uncivilized natives are first tamed'.[142] The 'colonial mentality' of racial neoliberalism designates areas where poor racialised people live as places of squalor that require White elites to bring regeneration.[143] Both Conservative and Labour governments have presided over periods of rising house prices and sharp decreases in the availability of social housing.[144] As Ida Danewid argues, gentrification does not simply reflect colonial processes but can be seen 'as the continuation of

136 Ida Danewid, 'The Fire This Time: Grenfell, Racial Capitalism and the Urbanisation of Empire' (2020) 26(1) *European Journal of International Relations* 289, 295.
137 Legal Aid, Sentencing and Punishment of Offenders Act 2012, s.144.
138 Brett Christophers, *The New Enclosure: The Appropriation of Public Land in Neoliberal Britain* (Verso Books 2018), 2.
139 Ibid., 11–14.
140 Ibid., 11–12.
141 Ibid., 4.
142 Justin Hansford, 'Community Policing Reconsidered: From Ferguson to Baltimore' in Jordan T. Camp and Christina Heatherton (eds), *Policing the Planet* (Verso Books 2016), 223.
143 Danewid, 298.
144 Williams and Squires, 174.

distinctively colonial techniques for organising urban space'.[145] The racialised poor have persistently been confined to particular areas and to displacement, but under neoliberalism these processes of spatial exclusion are linked to urban policing techniques that seek to 'clean up' an area such that it is ripe for redevelopment.[146] Provisions such as s.60 serve a performative function by deeming racialised communities as backward, undeserving, ungrievable, and surplus; an obstacle to rationality, market forces, and neoliberal progress. Gentrification and the use of intensified police powers against the racialised poor may be seen as a necropolitical process whereby the expulsion of those communities, and expropriation of those areas, is deemed to be for the greater good of neoliberal capital accumulation.[147] The second order simulacrum of the undeserving poor under early capitalism has mutated into a third order simulacrum under neoliberalism, as discussed further in the next chapter.

The ways that s.60 denotes a community as criminal can be compared with the CTA and HCA considered in Chapter 2. However, s.60 occurs in a more abstracted form. Rather than specifically name Black people as criminal, which would be contrary to the purported colour-blind meritocracy of neoliberalism, s.60 appears to be based on risk management factors. As will be argued in Chapter 5, apparently neutral risk factors are racialised. The decision to impose a s.60 order is grounded in colonial discourses that equate Black communities with criminality and violence. The imposition of a s.60 order creates a situation where there are more arrests in those areas due to increased stop and search, then this is wrongly equated with increased criminality in those areas, which leads to the imposition of further s.60 orders, thus creating the impression that racially disproportionate criminality is real. As Patricia Ugwudike points out, studies in the United States have shown that where the disproportionate policing of Black communities led to exaggerated crime figures in those areas, 'it triggered an algorithmic self-reinforcing feedback loop whereby the algorithm repeatedly targeted those locations for high crime-risk prediction (overprediction), encouraging even more policing in those areas'.[148] This served to legitimate the simulation that the inhabitants of those areas were disproportionately criminal. Similar discourses and narratives of risk prediction are used to justify the imposition of s.60 orders. This constructs the appearance that poor racialised urban communities are disproportionately criminal while rendering invisible the colonial discourses that lead to their disproportionate policing. Therefore, the narratives that

145 Danewid, 302.

146 Ibid., 299.

147 Elijah Adiv Edelman, 'Walking While Transgender' in Jin Haritaworn, Adi Kuntsman and Silvia Posocco (eds), *Queer Necropolitics* (Routledge 2014), 76–77.

148 Patricia Ugwudike, 'Algorithms, Policing, and Race' in Chris Cunneen and others (eds), *The Routledge International Handbook on Decolonizing Justice* (Routledge 2023), 150–151.

lead to s.60 orders being imposed are themselves based on processes of simulation. In this way, s.60 can be viewed as hyperreal – a simulacrum based on a previous simulacrum. It is a self-referential provision that constructs its own apparent reality by creating the appearance of racialised criminality.

From Section 60 to the Public Order Act 2023

Section 60 was originally considered to be an exceptional provision, but it has become increasingly commonplace and normalised, such that particular poor racialised communities are dehumanised by the increased surveillance powers and interference with their ability to exist in public spaces. In this way, s.60 can be viewed as part of the permanent state of exception in neoliberal criminal law. Those areas subjected to s.60 orders have been appropriated from the communities that live there, such that they are dispossessed of public spaces during the operation of the order. The use of s.60 powers can be seen as contradiction-closing – by framing racialised poor communities as inherently criminal and ungrievable, it provides a rationale for the intense policing of the areas where they live and appears to account for racially disproportionate outcomes in an ostensibly colour-blind criminal legal system.

To understand s.60, one needs to consider the continuance and perpetuation of the colonial discourses that frame racialised communities as violent, and in need of control and management. It is worth returning to the quote from Achille Mbembe cited earlier in relation to terror suspects: 'the suspension of the rights and lifting of the guarantees that protect individuals are presented as the condition of the survival of those same rights'.[149] The judgment in the *Roberts* case relied upon the narrative of the need to suspend the right to enjoy a public space free from police violence so that the community could be protected against its own knife-related violence. These civilising mission discourses reproduce domestic racialised communities as colonial subjects, whose areas need to be occupied by those representing sovereign powers, and as criminal suspects rather than full citizens. Through the use of hyperreal provisions, which are simultaneously both legal and extra-legal, racialised communities are dehumanised. In this way, s.60, along with other stop and search powers, should be seen as a process of continued colonisation by the state of the areas where racialised communities live. Those areas can be seen as spaces where racialised people are subjected to occupation by the police.

As Dylan Rodríguez contends, it is a categorical error to frame the most extreme examples of police practices as 'police brutality', as this feeds into reformist agendas that the problems with policing can be solved within the

149 Mbembe, 33.

neoliberal carceral state.[150] He writes, 'it's not police brutality if the state sanctions the violence. At that point, you move from calling it "police brutality" to calling it "policing"'.[151] For the same reason, narratives that racialised communities are 'over policed and ...under protected'[152] are problematic as they frame neoliberal law enforcement as having the potential to protect poor racialised communities. Such discourses fail to understand how policing is embedded in colonialism, and serve to legitimate 'normal' police practices by attempting to distinguish between legal and illegal police powers without recognising that most harmful police behaviour is permitted by the law.[153] Similarly, as Arun Kundnani points out, many of the torture techniques used at Guantanamo Bay, such as lengthy solitary confinement and sensory deprivation, were previously used at US supermax prisons.[154] There is no clear division between regular and apparently exceptional forms of incarceration. The carceral state, in all its forms, is a source of violent harm against marginalised people.

In the same way, when describing s.60 as an exceptional power, one must be wary of feeding into reformist discourses that frame other stop and search powers as neutral and justified. Rather than being distinct from other stop and search laws, s.60 needs to be viewed as part of a continuum. Other stop and search laws may officially require reasonable suspicion, but the concept of reasonable grounds is viewed through the racial frame, and therefore these laws are also processes of simulation that reproduce racialised criminalisation. Where s.60 differs is that it makes this lack of reasonable grounds official, and in this sense it is exceptional. Against a backdrop of neoliberal punitivity and the gentrification of inner city areas, s.60 intensifies the creation of hypercriminals by not even requiring a pretence of reasonable grounds, such that the simulacra of racialised knife carriers take precedence. As argued below, rather than being an outlier, s.60 shares similarities with subsequent criminal provisions.

The Public Order Act 2023 (POA 2023) strengthened police powers to curtail the right to protest and introduced new offences such as locking-on (attaching oneself to buildings, objects, or other people).[155] It extended stop

150 Dylan Rodríguez, 'Abolition as Praxis of Human Being: A Foreword' (2019) 132 *Harvard Law Review* 1575, 1602.

151 Dylan Rodríquez, 'It's Not Police Brutality' (Critical Resistance 2017) <www.youtube.com/watch?v=ylEUT2BvvtM> accessed 19 December 2024.

152 Home Office, *Report of the Stephen Lawrence Inquiry*, Cm 4262 (1999) para 45.7.

153 Dylan Rodríquez, 'The Obsolescence of "Police Brutality"' in Chris Cunneen and others (eds), *The Routledge International Handbook on Decolonizing Justice* (Routledge 2023), 124–125.

154 Arun Kundnani, *What Is Anti-racism? And Why It Means Anti-capitalist* (Verso Books 2023), 18.

155 Public Order Act 2023, s.1.

and search powers, with wording derived from s.60, enabling an officer of the rank of inspector or above to give authorisation for an order allowing stop and search without reasonable suspicion in a specified locality for a specified period.[156] The links between s.60 and the POA 2023 can be analysed in similar terms to Stuart Hall's theorisation of moral panics in the 1970s, as discussed in Chapter 2 and referred to earlier in this chapter.[157] The policing of racialised communities is linked with the policing of political activists, particularly in times of economic crisis where government legitimacy is wavering, such that both groups are framed as enemies of the state by the government and the mainstream media. In order to shore up support for the government and for neoliberal policies, criminal law is deployed as a tool to name the racialised poor, and those resisting the harm caused by the profit motive of racial capitalism, as being against the interests of society. In this way, the use of criminal law and the expansion of the carceral state are presented as tools of collective self-defence.

Both s.60 and the POA 2023 trade on images of hypercriminality and serve to obscure the causes and perpetrators of significant material social harm. In the latter case, environmental activists are constructed as more of a threat than climate change and the destruction of the environment. Having normalised the use of suspicion-less stop and search powers against racialised poor communities, the state had the confidence to deploy them against another group constructed as enemies of civilised White society. In this way, the exceptionality of not even premising stop and search on grounds of reasonable suspicion becomes increasingly routine. While the POA 2023 provisions have been used against protestors, notably at the coronation in May 2023 when they were deployed against anti-monarchy demonstrators, given the racialised use of s.60, it seems inevitable that the POA 2023 will be used against poor racialised communities. Of course, protestors and racialised communities are not mutually exclusive groups, and increased police powers may lead to the targeting of Black activists.

Although the repeal of s.60 would be welcome, the problem is far deeper than one piece of legislation. The racial framing and hypercriminalisation of Black communities through s.60 need to be considered alongside discourses around gangs, dangerousness, and character, which are discussed in Chapters 5 and 6. Prior to that, Chapter 4 will consider several other provisions that operate in a comparable way to s.60. The hate crime provisions are a further example of how criminal legislation premised at protecting racialised individuals and communities has the effect of disproportionately criminalising them. Criminal Behaviour Orders, gang injunctions, and Knife Crime Prevention Orders (KCPOs) enable the state to impose restrictions on the

156 Ibid., s.11.
157 Hall and others.

lives of racialised people on the premise that it is in their own interests and those of their communities. Additionally, KCPOs are hyperreal, self-referential provisions that frame racialised communities as knife carriers, even when they have never possessed a knife, and therefore this provision creates knife-related hypercriminals. In this way, the narratives underpinning s.60 can be seen as permeating other neoliberal criminal laws. All of these provisions are situated within colonial discourses around race and the undeserving poor, including the civilising mission, and all of them operate to construct hypercriminals. As will be argued in Chapter 7, these processes of simulation can be interrupted by a refusal to see hypercriminality as reality, as part of a strategy of working towards social justice solutions to social problems rather than relying upon the purported solutions of the carceral state.

Chapter 4

Neoliberal Social Control

This chapter will consider a number of criminal legal constructions that not only rely upon previous discourses around the undeserving poor but rework these discourses in the context of neoliberal narratives around meritocracy and operate as means of social control. This includes hate crimes, Anti-social Behaviour Orders (ASBOs), Criminal Behaviour Orders (CBOs), gang injunctions, and Knife Crime Prevention Orders (KCPOs). These provisions are processes of simulation that advocate carceral solutions to social problems. Such narratives reinforce the simulation of neoliberal society as equal and colour-blind, and render invisible the anti-social actions of the neoliberal state. The portrayal of marginalised communities as backward and intolerant obscures underlying material inequalities, disappears the racism of the state, and individualises social issues. As with the s.60 orders considered in the previous chapter, these processes are intrinsically linked with civilising mission discourses. Furthermore, these legal constructions are hyperreal: they are self-referential processes of simulation that create their own apparent reality by naming legal subjects as ontologically anti-social or criminal. Such constructions are third order simulacra that build upon the second order simulacra of race and the undeserving poor discussed in Chapter 2.

Although much of the legislation discussed in this chapter was introduced some years ago, these discourses continue. At the time of writing, the Starmer government is proposing the imposition of measures similar to ASBOs. Additionally, knife crime continues to be a dominant racialised folk devil discourse, and the hate crime provisions are ongoing. Therefore, the issues discussed in this chapter continue to be pertinent in relation to narratives around criminal law and processes of racialised criminalisation.

The Undeserving Poor Revisited: The Chav Discourse

The distinction between the deserving and undeserving poor is a racialised concept rooted in colonialism and imperialism, as discussed in Chapter 2. In Robbie Shilliam's words, 'elite actors have racialized and re-racialized the historical distinction between the deserving and the undeserving poor

DOI: 10.4324/9781003602873-5

through ever more expansive terms that have incorporated working classes, colonial "natives" and nationalities'.[1] Slaves in the colonies were framed as the undeserving poor: lazy, working only because they were forced to do so, and prone to rebellion.[2] The slave analogy was then used to 'blacken' the English rural poor, who had lost access to communal land through the enclosure system and became the urban poor.[3] The distinction between the deserving and undeserving poor is subject to constant redefinition and renegotiation depending on the interests of racial capitalism. The second order simulacrum of the undeserving poor has morphed into the third order simulacra of the White chav and the Black hypercriminal under neoliberalism.

Categories of racialisation are unstable, and when it is useful to White elites, they will shift discourses such that particular sections of the working class are given access, albeit limited, to the psychological benefits and some of the economic benefits of White privilege so that their loyalty is assured. The concessions to voting rights by the Reform Act 1867 can be seen in this context: 'as the deserving English workingman became enfranchised they also became racialized as Anglo-Saxon'.[4] The ways that poor populations are racialised depend on the interests of White elites and whether their own interests are best served by attempting to co-opt sections of the poor or by demonising them.[5]

During debates around the UK's withdrawal from the European Union (Brexit), the 'White working class' were constructed as a category of deserving people whose interests had been neglected, and this discourse was used to shore up nationalism and anti-immigration policies.[6] As Reni Eddo-Lodge argues, 'affixing the word "white" to the phrase "working class" suggests that these people face structural disadvantage because they are white, rather than because they are working class'.[7] Following the Brexit vote in the UK and the first election of Trump in the United States, discourses focused on the perceived neglect of the White working class by the Left in favour of so-called identity politics. Such discourses misapprehended not only the socio-economic composition of those who voted for Brexit and Trump but also created a false dichotomy between class on the one hand and race and gender on the other, rather than recognising that the working class is racialised and

1 Robbie Shilliam, *Race and the Undeserving Poor* (Agenda Publishing 2018), 6.
2 Ibid., 24.
3 Ibid., 31.
4 Ibid., 46.
5 Ibid., 133–134.
6 Ibid., 162.
7 Reni Eddo-Lodge, *Why I'm No Longer Talking to White People About Race* (Bloomsbury Publishing 2017), 202.

gendered.[8] Since then, politicians have continued to refer to White working class males being disadvantaged, intimating that this is due to the advancement of Black people and of women, again implying that racial and gender equality are in opposition to class equality.[9] These discourses fail to understand, or seek to obscure, that racial capitalism structures class relations through processes of racial differentiation and patriarchal practices.

Discourses around the deserving and undeserving poor were central to immigration, welfare, and criminal law policies under the Blair government, which introduced the anti-social behaviour provisions. This administration was characterised by the acceptance of neoliberalism, and some commitment to human rights, such as the Human Rights Act 1998, combined with a strong paternalistic and moralistic message that rights had to be balanced by responsibilities. As discussed in previous chapters, rather than demonstrating that neoliberal societies remain unequal, human rights discourses name such societies as having transcended inequality. In this way, human rights discourses are consistent with, and serve to justify, the simulacrum of meritocracy, such that it appears as real.

New Labour premised itself on following a 'Third Way' distinct from both previous Labour governments and the Conservative party.[10] Clause IV of the Labour Party constitution, adopted by the party in 1918, had set out stated aims of securing for the workers the 'full fruits of their labour' and 'common ownership of the means of production, distribution and exchange', which was seen as a commitment to nationalisation, redistribution of wealth and income, and socialist principles in general. In 1995, this was replaced by a new version of Clause IV, which removed the above words, and included reference to enabling all 'to realise our true potential' such that 'power, wealth and opportunity are in the hands of the many, not the few' and 'where the rights we enjoy reflect the duties we owe'.[11] This was a shift from a commitment to 'equality of outcome' to the meritocratic 'equality of opportunity'.[12] While there were similarities between Blair's discourse and the explicitly right-wing, racist 'underclass' theory that was developed in the United States

8 Sarah Keenan, '"Identity Politics" and Property in the Trump/Brexit Era' (2018) 7(2) *feminists@law* <http://journals.kent.ac.uk/index.php/feministsatlaw/article/view/457/1170> accessed 20 December 2024.

9 Raquel Jesse, 'The UK Race Class Narrative Report' (Centre for Labour and Social Studies 2022), 40–41 <https://guerrillafoundation.org/wp-content/uploads/2022/07/Narratives-4_Race_Class_Narrative_Report-CLASS-v27.pdf> accessed 31 December 2024.

10 Anthony Giddens, *The Third Way: The Renewal of Social Democracy* (Polity Press 1998).

11 Tudor Jones, 'Labour's Constitution and Public Ownership: From "Old" Clause Four to "New" Clause Four' in Brian Brivati and Richard Heffernan (eds), *The Labour Party: A Centenary History* (Palgrave Macmillan 2000), 292–321.

12 Shilliam, 121.

during the 1990s,[13] New Labour repackaged it as the more palatable theory of social exclusion.[14] This paved the way for blaming economic problems on those elements of the working class perceived to be feckless, criminal, irresponsible, and workshy, with a shift from using welfare to rectify inequalities to using social policy as an instrument of the legal system and a means of social control.[15]

As David Downes and Rod Morgan argue, there was a '"law and order" arms race' between the two main political parties in the 1990s, with New Labour designating itself as the party of 'zero tolerance' of criminal behaviour, and criticising the Conservatives for being overly lenient rather than unduly punitive.[16] The Crime and Disorder Act 1998 (CDA) was introduced during a period when Left Realist concepts of crime were informing government discourses.[17] This theoretical approach, associated with Jock Young and John Lea, argued that social and environmental conditions, including relative as well as absolute poverty, were a significant cause of crime.[18] The CDA was a key element of Blair's promise to be 'tough on crime, tough on the causes of crime'.[19] New Labour criminal law policies were premised on ensuring that 'problem families' got their just desserts so that respectable families were able to live in peace, thus drawing a clear distinction between working class perpetrators and working class victims of crime. However, as will be argued later in this chapter, rather than being 'tough on the causes of crime', ASBOs did little to address the problems experienced by marginalised communities and instead shifted the blame onto individuals within those communities through a meritocratic framing that reproduced classed and racialised constructions of criminality while justifying this through the hyperreal figure of the chav.

The chav discourse was fundamental to the construction of legal subjects under the anti-social behaviour legislation. The chav became a new folk devil, presented in the media and popular culture as White, working class, living on

13 Richard J. Hernstein and Charles Murray, *The Bell Curve* (Basic Books 1994).

14 John J. Rodger, *Criminalising Social Policy: Anti-social Behaviour and Welfare in a De-civilised Society* (Routledge 2008), 3.

15 Ibid., 3.

16 David Downes and Rod Morgan, 'Waiting for Ingleby: The Minimum Age of Criminal Responsibility – A Red Line Issue?' in Tony Newburn and Jill Peay (eds), *Policing: Politics, Culture and Control* (Hart Publishing 2012), 247.

17 Ian Brownlee, 'New Labour – New Penology? Punitive Rhetoric and the Limits of Managerialism in Criminal Justice Policy' (1998) 25(3) *Journal of Law and Society* 313, 318–321.

18 John Lea and Jock Young, *What Is to Be Done About Law and Order?* (Penguin Books 1984).

19 Tony Blair, Speech to the Labour Party Conference (Brighton, 1995) <www.britishpoliticalspeech.org/speech-archive.htm?speech=201> accessed 20 December 2024.

welfare, and lacking social graces.[20] Poor marginalised communities, including many suffering from the effects of deindustrialisation, were stigmatised as chavs by these performative discourses that provided justification for neoliberal policies of increasingly punitive criminal laws combined with welfare cuts.[21] Discourses around female chavs centred around sexuality, with working class females portrayed as immoral, and single mothers presented as both a product and a cause of degeneracy.[22] These gendered discourses around working class lifestyles were epitomised by media headlines around women relentlessly having children by different fathers in order to claim benefits and avoid work.[23] Such discourses attempted to distinguish the authentic working class, characterised as hard-working, White and male, from the chav.[24]

While initially the chav discourse may have been premised on separating the undeserving poor from the 'authentic' deserving working class, it became an avenue for middle and upper class Whites to express their contempt and disgust towards the poor more generally as a means of defending their own privilege.[25] Through constant repetition in the media and on the internet, these discourses operated performatively to portray chavs as 'disgusting'.[26] This updated version of class snobbery intersected with racism and sexism to name poor communities as animalistic and immoral. The 1990s characters of Wayne and Waynetta Slob from BBC television comedy series, *Harry Enfield and Chums*, chain smoked, claimed benefits, lived on a council estate, rarely washed and displayed behaviour designed to be read as vulgar.[27] Some years later, the character of Vicky Pollard, played by a privately educated man in another BBC television show, *Little Britain*, which aired from 2003 to 2006, was seen to epitomise the female chav: aggressive, overweight, work-shy, poorly dressed, over made-up, and inarticulate.[28] The neoliberal middle class ideal of women as White, educated, upwardly mobile, feminine, and respectable was juxtaposed with the Vicky Pollard character.[29]

20 David Gillborn, 'The White Working Class, Racism and Respectability: Victims, Degenerates and Interest-Convergence' (2010) 58(1) *British Journal of Educational Studies* 3, 15–20; Owen Jones, *Chavs: The Demonization of the Working Class* (London 2011), 102.
21 Imogen Tyler, *Revolting Subjects* (Zed Books 2013), 165.
22 Rhian E. Jones, *Clampdown: Pop-Cultural Wars on Class and Gender* (Zero Books 2013), 17–27.
23 Gillborn, 'The White Working Class', 17.
24 Jones, *Clampdown*, 26.
25 Imogen Tyler, 'Chav Mum, Chav Scum' (2018) 8(1) *Feminist Media Studies* 17, 22–24.
26 Ibid., 24–25.
27 Tracy Fisher, 'Sex in the Nation: White Women, Brown Babies, and the Politics of Belonging' in Kia Lilly Caldwell and others (eds), *Gendered Citizenships: Transnational Perspectives on Knowledge Production, Political Activism and Culture* (Palgrave Macmillan 2010), 174.
28 Tyler, *Revolting Subjects*, 164.
29 Tyler, 'Chav Mum, Chav Scum', 30.

As discussed in Chapter 1, White privilege varies across time and space and cannot be reduced solely to skin colour.[30] The gaze upon chavs constituted them as a lesser form of Whiteness – 'White but not quite'.[31] They were seen as inhabiting a 'contaminated whiteness', with their music, clothes, and dialect influenced by Black popular culture.[32] The framing of female chavs as sexually indiscriminate was also linked to race, particularly in relation to giving birth to mixed-race children.[33] One particular episode about the Slob family featured a storyline where Waynetta told Wayne that she would have to leave him because she wanted a 'brown baby' like all the other mothers on the estate.[34] The transmission of this as a comedy sketch on primetime television was possible due to a White gaze that dehumanised and abstracted mixed-race children as a signifier of irresponsible parents. This narrative silenced discussions around 'the ways in which white mothers of mixed race children demonstrate a keen awareness of how their children are racialized, create a community for their children, and, in the process, negotiate and contest racial hierarchies'.[35] The implication was that the baby would be the product of a short-lived liaison between a promiscuous White mother and a soon-to-be absent Black father, thus reinforcing racist conceptions of irresponsible Black men reduced to their physical attributes, and dysfunctional matriarchal racialised families. The mixed-race baby was reduced to a signifier of a chav mother, with the unspoken insinuation that sexual activity with Black men was for lower status White women.

This illustrates how chavs were deemed to be situated within 'a whiteness polluted by poverty and contaminated by territorial proximity to poor black and migrant populations'.[36] Such narratives aroused anxieties over poor people producing many children[37] and echoed the rhetoric around immigrants having large families.[38] Margaret Thatcher's discourse of respectable White communities being 'swamped' by those of a different culture raised spectres of reproduction as well as immigration.[39] This played upon 'the fear that the wrong kinds of population will be reproduced', with excessive sexual activity

30 Noel Ignatiev, *How the Irish Became White* (Routledge 1995), 2–3.
31 Ricky Lee Allen, 'What About Poor White People?' in Williams Ayers, Therese M. Quinn and David Stovall (eds), *Handbook of Social Justice in Education* (Routledge 2009), 214 (as cited in Gillborn, 'The White Working Class', 22).
32 Tyler, 'Chav Mum, Chav Scum', 25–26.
33 Ibid., 26.
34 Fisher, 173.
35 Ibid., 174.
36 Tyler, *Revolting Subjects*, 188.
37 Matt Wray and Annalee Newitz, *White Trash: Race and Class in America* (Routledge 1997), 2.
38 Tyler, 'Chav Mum, Chav Scum', 26.
39 Margaret Thatcher, *Granada, World in Action* (27 January 1978) <www.margaretthatcher.org/document/103485> accessed 20 December 2024.

linked with the 'racially lesser'.[40] Such narratives can be understood as the continuation of colonial discourses that frame racialised people as animalistic and corporal rather than cerebral. This is discussed further in Chapter 5 in relation to sexual danger.

The reaction of right-wing historian David Starkey to the 2011 uprising illustrates how White elites viewed Blackness as a contaminant:

> What's happened is that a substantial section of the chavs ... have become black. The whites have become black. A particular sort of violent, destructive, nihilistic, gangster culture has become the fashion ... It is about black culture, that is the enormously important thing, it is not skin colour, it is culture.[41]

In this way, poor Whites were differentiated from respectable Whites, while Black communities were located within a culture of criminality, thus bolstering the privilege of White elites on both fronts. As David Gillborn argues, 'the existence of poor Whites is not only consistent with White supremacy, it is actually an essential part of the processes that sustain it'.[42] Through the chav discourse, White elites were able to render invisible the classist, racist, and patriarchal narratives underpinning their disgust towards working class communities by refashioning the narrative as legitimate criticism of those too lazy, dishonest, or disreputable to embrace the opportunities for social mobility.[43] The argument that such opportunities were unavailable to poor communities, who experienced an increase in economic inequality during this period, was absent from this discourse.[44] The economic basis of class was denied and replaced by signifiers around morality and respectability.[45]

These discourses operated to abstract poor individuals and communities as signs of failure. Therefore, rather than being contradictory to the New Labour project of meritocracy, the chav discourse entrenched the view that poor communities had only themselves to blame for their situation due to their own poor choices.[46] This enabled the concept of meritocracy to circulate as a sign indicating that class had been overcome and social mobility was available to those who chose to avail themselves of it. Such discourses were hyperreal – they were an implosion where class was denied yet class division

40 Gargi Bhattacharyya, *Rethinking Racial Capitalism* (Rowman and Littlefield International 2018), 39.
41 David Starkey, *BBC Newsnight* (13 August 2011) (as cited in Tyler, *Revolting Subjects*, 188).
42 Gillborn, 'The White Working Class', 6.
43 Tyler, 'Chav Mum, Chav Scum', 32.
44 Ibid., 31–32.
45 Jones, *Clampdown*, 12.
46 Tyler, *Revolting Subjects*, 161.

was intensified and White privilege was bolstered. In this way, the boundaries of truth and falsity were collapsed.

The concept of the undeserving poor around the period of industrialisation can be viewed as a second order simulacrum based on discourses around economic utility and worthiness. While sharing these discourses around morality and the lack of work ethic, the neoliberal reworking of the undeserving poor has become a third order simulacrum. As Imogen Tyler argues, 'the mediating agencies of popular culture, newspaper journalism, television and the Internet ...transformed New Labour's symbolic abjection of class into the figure of the chav'.[47] Characters such as Vicky Pollard and the Slob family constructed the sign of the chav, such that young, working class females were derided as 'real life' Vicky Pollards.[48] One young woman shamed by the media as a 'real life Vicky Pollard' was a 19-year-old from Tyneside, an area of high unemployment and deprivation, who was excluded from her own home by an ASBO.[49] Such narratives were hyperreal: they 'dissolve[d] the difference between fiction and reality'.[50] There was no 'real' Vicky Pollard, so these discourses referenced a copy without an original: a third order simulacrum that served to create its own apparent reality. Tyler notes that working class women were acutely conscious of the signs constructing the chav simulacrum, and keen to differentiate themselves from that image by, for example, stressing that they were keen to engage in paid employment or that they were not the birth mother of the children they were looking after.[51]

In Chapter 1, it was argued that police 'reality' television shows mediate not only the behaviour of the parties involved in the incidents filmed but also the behaviour of other people towards the police based on the belief that the images are a true version of policing. The belief that the simulacrum of the chav was real led to a circular, self-referential, and self-perpetuating process of simulation whereby the response of the media and government to working class communities was mediated by this simulated image. The characters of Wayne and Waynetta Slob pre-dated the CDA and although the Vicky Pollard character came after the imposition of the CDA, it nevertheless impacted on the discourses that fed into the implementation of these policies, such that there was a symbiotic effect between these provisions and the simulacra of chavs. For poor young people wearing items of clothing deemed as chav signifiers, the material consequences of the chav discourse included exclusion from particular shopping centres

47 Ibid., 163.
48 Ibid., 164–165.
49 *The Guardian*, 'No But Yeah But No' (12 May 2005) <https://www.theguardian.com/media/2005/may/12/pressandpublishing.penal> accessed 27 February 2025.
50 Ibid.
51 Tyler, *Revolting Subjects*, 169.

and bars through the imposition of dress codes.[52] Thus, the simulacrum of the chav caused people to act on the basis that anti-social behaviour and chavs were inseparable and served to create its own reality. This process of simulation allowed those deemed to be chavs, as well as racialised young people wearing similar clothes, to be discriminated against and their movements restricted.

Imogen Tyler argues that, 'in the context of shifting class definitions, the vilification of the chav can be interpreted as a symptom of a middle class desire to re-demarcate class boundaries within the context of contemporary consumer culture'.[53] Therefore, as Keith Hayward and Majid Yar write, middle class condemnation of chavs 'focuses not on the inability to consume, but on the *excessive* participation in forms of market-orientated consumption which are deemed *aesthetically* impoverished'.[54] The poor are simultaneously told that they should aspire to consume, and ridiculed for doing so. As Baudrillard explains, 'this pursuit of status and social standing, are all based on signs ... they are based not on objects or goods as such, but on *differences*'.[55] For the wealthy, their rejection of particular types of consumption works to differentiate them from the lower classes.[56] Chavs are positioned as making poor choices in all aspects of their lives. Of course, for many working class people, their 'choice' of clothing is constrained by their limited means.

More fundamentally, these signifiers, such as dysfunctional single parent households headed by irresponsible matriarchs, laziness, reliance on welfare, living in social housing, wearing conspicuous jewellery and branded items, and drug consumption, are not solely related to class but are formed at the intersection between the traits associated with the undeserving poor and those embedded in the racial frame. As argued in Chapter 2, constructions of race and the undeserving poor have been linked throughout their genealogy. Such characteristics serve as a code for criminality and deviance and are a continuation of colonial constructions of Blackness. Naming Black people as chavs is superfluous, as the above signifiers are already used to deride racialised poor communities. The chav discourse seeks to 'blacken' poor White people in order to differentiate them from the privilege afforded to those who perform the hegemonic norms of the idealised White neoliberal subject.

52 Keith Hayward and Majid Yar, 'The "Chav" Phenomenon: Consumption, Media and the Construction of a New Underclass' (2006) 2(1) *Crime Media Culture* 9, 22–23.

53 Tyler, 'Chav Mum, Chav Scum', 22.

54 Hayward and Yar, 14 (original italics).

55 Jean Baudrillard, *The Consumer Society: Myths and Structures* (SAGE Publications 1998), 90 (original italics).

56 Ibid., 90–91.

It is useful to repeat the quote from Michelle Alexander cited in Chapter 2: 'What it means to be criminal in our collective consciousness has become conflated with what it means to be black, so the term *white criminal* is confounding, while the term *black criminal* is nearly redundant'.[57] It is unnecessary to name Black people as anti-social or chavs in order to criminalise them – they have already been subjected to this. Similarly, in relation to the phrase 'white trash', which is perhaps the nearest US equivalent to chav, the inclusion of the word 'white' indicates that 'trash' is conflated with Blackness.[58] Thus, as Philip Howard writes, rather than being a form of racism against White people, 'the term "white trash" actually serves to police the existing discursive boundaries between whiteness and degeneracy, and to entrench, quite effectively (and paradoxically), the white supremacist project'.[59] To argue that anti-white racism exists is to misunderstand the historical and material underpinnings of racism and to erroneously frame society as colourblind,[60] as will be argued below in relation to the hate crime legislation.

As outlined in Chapter 2, the language used to describe domestic poor urban communities in the nineteenth century drew on discourses relating to colonial subjects such that the former 'became known as the savages of the metropolis'[61] and as 'heathen races'.[62] Thus, the 'blackening' of working class communities has occurred throughout racial capitalism. While the concepts of race and the undeserving poor were both second order simulacra, as discussed above, under neoliberalism they have become simulations of simulations – third order simulacra.

When considering the chav as a simulacrum, it is useful to refer back to the work of Stuart Hall and Paul Gilroy considered in Chapter 2 in relation to the ways that Black young men were framed as 'muggers' in the 1970s at a time when the economy and state were in crisis. Similarly, the 2011 uprising occurred during a period of austerity, and was blamed upon bad behaviour by the folk devils of chavs and racialised gangs dressed in hoodies and sportswear, rather than on racist policing and the immiseration of working class communities. This narrative was used to justify militaristic policing and exceptional sentencing, as described in Chapter 3. The comments of David Starkey quoted above demonstrate that this was grounded in discourses of a degenerated White working class that had been led astray by

57 Michelle Alexander, *The New Jim Crow: Mass Incarceration in the Age of Colorblindness* (The New Press 2010), 385 (original italics).

58 Philip S.S. Howard, 'White Privilege: For or Against? A Discussion of Ostensibly Antiracist Discourses in Critical White Studies' (2004) 11(4) *Race, Gender and Class* 63, 69.

59 Ibid., 69.

60 Alana Lentin, 'Race' in William Outhwaite and Stephen Turner (eds), *The SAGE Handbook of Political Sociology* (SAGE Publications 2018), 872.

61 Preeti Nijhar, *Law and Imperialism* (Routledge 2009), 43.

62 Ibid., 42.

Black influences, thus foregrounding Black people as the main instigators.[63] The racialisation of so-called riots is discussed further in Chapters 5 and 6. As Robbie Shilliam suggests, Black disorder was essentialised whereas White disorder was seen as the result of this negative influence and therefore not immutable.[64] Similarly, Preeti Nijhar argues that the key difference in relation to race and the undeserving poor is that 'a distinction was made between the minority ethnic groups judged irredeemable and an indigenous criminal class which could be reformed – made modern'.[65] Thus, poor White communities had the potential to be rehabilitated, whereas Blackness and criminality were viewed as synonymous, such that poor White people were abstracted as chavs and poor Black people became hypercriminals.

Colour-Blind Hate Crimes

In addition to viewing the poor as workshy, promiscuous, and vulgar, discourses invoking perceptions of White middle class moral superiority position poor communities as containing the residue of hatred and prejudice that respectable society has surpassed. This positions White chavs and Black hypercriminals as holding insular attitudes and regressive views. It is argued below that hate crime laws are a third order simulacrum based on a denial of historically embedded racism, and are situated within narratives of neoliberal colour-blindness, and the attendant discourses of identity and difference. Such provisions individualise racism, position the state as protective, and seek to legitimate carceral responses to social problems.

The initial hate crime legislation under the CDA was premised on the need to protect Black people from racist attacks. One impetus for these new provisions was the aftermath of the racist murder of Stephen Lawrence, discussed in the next section. The Macpherson Inquiry into the case was ongoing as Parliament passed the hate crime legislation. However, the introduction of hate crime provisions was a wider international trend and therefore cannot be viewed solely as a reaction to the Stephen Lawrence case. Nevertheless, the narrative of working class White racists, of which the murderers of Stephen Lawrence were presented as the epitome, was crucial to the rhetoric behind the legislation, as the government attempted to disassociate itself from the racism stirred up by its own discourses around immigration, particularly in relation to asylum seekers.[66]

63 Shilliam, 132–133.
64 Ibid., 133.
65 Nijhar, 60.
66 Bill Dixon and David Gadd, 'Getting the Message? "New" Labour and the Criminalization of "Hate"' (2006) 6(3) *Criminology and Criminal Justice* 309, 324–325.

Anthony Giddens, a prominent sociologist and advocate of the Blairist 'Third Way' agenda, argued that the government should respond to right-wing populism around immigration by implementing policies that were 'tough on immigration, but tough on the causes of hostility to immigrants'.[67] However, rather than confront racism, such policies only strengthened the narrative that immigration was problematic. The links between discourses around restricting immigration and the consequent hostility to racialised communities were made invisible, as racism was blamed on the deficiencies of the working class. The media equated 'racism with a group of young, uneducated, foul-mouthed men who, despite almost never having worked, wear "smart clothes" and drive "smart cars"'.[68] In this way, the chav discourse was deployed to individualise racism.

Media and government discourses around chavs were contradictory. The chav was simultaneously viewed as being too close to Blackness and as the perpetrator of intolerance, including racism. This seeming contradiction was made possible by a post-racial narrative that viewed racism as a form of intolerance rather than as the outcome of colonial processes. The simulation of the racialised poor as the source of racist harm operated to disappear the state's historic and continued racist discourses. This demonstrated the state's ability to use poor White people 'as a kind of buffer, or safety zone, that secures the interests of elite Whites, especially when challenged by high profile race equality / civil rights campaigns'.[69] Rather than focusing on social justice, carceral solutions were presented as the remedy for hate. As Clara Lewis argues, 'within a society that actively seeks to define itself as both post-difference and perfectly tolerant, the intersecting processes of intra-white stereotyping and neoliberal constructions of crime are both essential'.[70] The underlying message was that racism was the preserve of badly brought up, ignorant poor people, and that the expansion of criminal sanctions was the solution.

Discourses around hate crimes cannot be reduced to a left-wing or right-wing position as there is academic debate for and against on both sides of the political spectrum, and perspectives from both sides were instrumental in establishing the legislation.[71] Those on the Right justify legislation with

67 Anthony Giddens, 'The Third Way Can Beat the Far Right' *The Guardian* (3 May 2002) <www.theguardian.com/politics/2002/may/03/eu.thefarright> accessed 20 December 2024.

68 Eugene McLaughlin and Karim Murji, 'After the Stephen Lawrence Report' (1999) 19(3) *Critical Social Policy* 371, 377.

69 Gillborn, 'The White Working Class', 7.

70 Clara S. Lewis, 'Tough-on-Crime Tolerance: The Cultural Criminalization of Bigotry in the Post-Civil Rights Era' (2012) 20(3) *Critical Criminology* 275, 288.

71 Valerie Jenness, 'The Hate Crime Canon and Beyond: A Critical Assessment' (2001) 12 *Law and Critique* 279, 283–285.

appeals to victims' rights and demands for increased sentencing powers,[72] while those on the Left point to the need to protect historically oppressed groups and to the particular harm caused by abuse based on discrimination.[73] For those against hate crime legislation, in broad terms those on the Right argue in favour of free speech.[74] Those on the Left argue that the individualisation of hate speech acts detracts attention from the racism, homophobia, and transphobia of the state, point to the practical effect on marginalised communities through increased criminalisation and division, and express doubt that the state can protect the same groups that it oppresses.[75] That latter position is adopted in this chapter. In Sarah Lamble's words:

> pro-criminalization policies can only be sustained on the myth that the criminal justice system punishes those who deserve it, and that imprisonment is about safety, justice and protection for all, and not about warehousing, caging and punishing particular targeted populations.[76]

As discussed below, where hate crime legislation is framed as a form of rights for marginalised groups, the CRT critique of rights can be used to analyse these provisions.

The hate crime provisions under the CDA introduced racially aggravated versions of a number of pre-existing offences. These aggravated versions carried higher maximum sentences than the standard versions of each offence. The offences were common assault, assault occasioning actual bodily harm, grievous bodily harm under s.20 Offences Against the Person Act 1861, criminal damage, harassment, and the least serious public order offences (ss.4,

72 Ibid., 284.

73 See for example, Mari J. Matsuda, 'Public Response to Racist Speech: Considering the Victim's Story' in Mari J. Matsuda and others (eds), *Words that Wound: Critical Race Theory, Assaultive Speech, and the First Amendment* (Westview Press 1993); Richard Delgado, 'Words That Wound: A Tort Action' in Mari J. Matsuda and others (eds), *Words that Wound: Critical Race Theory, Assaultive Speech, and the First Amendment* (Westview Press 1993); Mohamad Al-Hakim, 'Making Room for Hate Crime Legislation in Liberal Societies' (2010) 4 *Criminal Law and Philosophy* 356.

74 See for example, Melanie Phillips, 'Hate Crime: The Orwellian Response to Prejudice' in Paul Iganski (ed), *The Hate Debate* (Profile Books 2002), 130.

75 See, for example, Dean Spade and Craig Willse, 'Confronting the Limits of Gay Hate Crimes Activism: A Radical Critique' (2000) 21 *Chicano-Latino Law Review* 38; Leslie J. Moran, 'The Emotional Dimensions of Lesbian and Gay Demands for Hate Crime Reform' (2004) 49(4) *McGill Law Journal* 925; Sarah Lamble, 'Retelling Racialized Violence, Remaking White Innocence: The Politics of Interlocking Oppressions in Transgender Day of Remembrance' (2008) 5(1) *Sexuality Research and Social Policy* 24; Doug Meyer, 'Resisting Hate Crime Discourse: Queer and Intersectional Challenges to Neoliberal Hate Crime Laws' (2014) 22 *Critical Criminology* 113.

76 Sarah Lamble, 'Queer Investments in Punitiveness' in Jin Haritaworn, Adi Kuntsman and Silvia Posocco (eds), *Queer Necropolitics* (Routledge 2014), 155.

4A and 5, Public Order Act 1986 (POA 1986)).[77] Although initially only racially aggravated offences were introduced, these provisions were subsequently expanded to cover religious aggravation.[78] The hate crime legislation was expanded by the CJA, as amended, such that racial or religious hostility became an aggravating feature when determining sentence for all offences where there was not a specific racially aggravated version.[79] Additionally, hostility in relation to sexual orientation,[80] disability,[81] or transgender identity[82] became an aggravating feature when sentencing any offence, although unlike the specific aggravated offences, it did not increase the maximum sentence for the offence.[83]

Rather than reflecting the structural inequalities that were ostensibly the motivation behind the legislation, the law was framed in a neutral manner. Instead of referring to the victim's membership of a historically oppressed category, the legislation referred to 'the victim's membership (or presumed membership) of a racial or religious group'.[84] A 'racial group' was defined as 'a group of persons defined by reference to race, colour, nationality (including citizenship) or ethnic or national origins'.[85] The victim could be White, or from the same group as the perpetrator. Therein lay an apparent contradiction within the hate crime provisions. The laws were premised on the need to protect people from violence situated within historical inequalities, yet they were framed on the basis of the assumption of a post-racial society, where hate crimes were an aberration rather than a reflection of that society. This allowed for so-called anti-White racism, which defined racism as intolerance based on difference rather than ongoing material oppression rooted in colonialism.

In Chapter 3, it was argued that provisions that are framed as being neutral, or even as protecting racialised people from violence, lend themselves to being interpreted through the racial frame and result in racially disproportionate criminalisation. As Mark Tushnet argues, a critical legal theorist should ask: 'Are minorities more likely to be prosecuted under hate speech

77 Crime and Disorder Act 1998, ss.29–32.
78 Anti-terrorism, Crime and Security Act 2001, s.39.
79 Criminal Justice Act 2003, s.145.
80 Ibid., s.146(2)(a)(i).
81 Ibid., s.146(2)(a)(ii).
82 Ibid., s.146(2)(a)(iii) as amended by the Legal Aid, Sentencing and Punishment of Offenders Act 2012, s.65.
83 CJA, s.146 was repealed by the Sentencing Act 2020, and these provisions in relation to increased sentences for racial or religious aggravation and for hostility in relation to sexual orientation, disability, or transgender identity are now covered by the Sentencing Act 2020, s.66.
84 Crime and Disorder Act 1998, s.28(1)(a).
85 Ibid., s.28(4).

regulations than those who abuse minorities?'.[86] Some of the first prosecutions for incitement to racial hatred in the late 1960s were against Black defendants, particularly those involved in Black political movements at that time, yet Enoch Powell was not prosecuted for his 'rivers of blood' speech.[87] Hate crime laws in the UK are used to prosecute Black people for racially aggravated offences, both against White people and against other Black people.[88] When legislation is neutrally framed, it is likely to be used in ways that reflect existing practices of disproportionate criminalisation.

One response to the colour-blind framing of hate crimes has been to argue in favour of a definition that links hate to historical oppression. Mari Matsuda argues that speech should be defined as racist hate speech if the message is 'of racial inferiority', 'directed against a historically oppressed group' and 'persecutory, hateful, and degrading'.[89] She identifies how a neutral framing of rights can protect the freedom of speech of racist organisations such as the Ku Klux Klan, and argues for an outsider jurisprudence, such that hate crime legislation is 'founded not on an ideal of neutrality, but on the reality of oppression', which recognises structures of domination.[90] Critical race theorists who support hate crime legislation position their work as 'a pragmatic response' to protect 'victims of hate speech who are daily silenced, intimidated and subjected to severe psychological and physical trauma by racist assailants'.[91] They write that, 'as critical race theorists, we do not separate cross burning from police brutality nor epithets from infant mortality rates'.[92] Matsuda argues that racial hate speech requires legal intervention as it is situated within a historically racist society and causes particular harm through its ability to fortify White supremacy and communicate messages of Black subordination, resulting in psychic injury and material consequences.[93]

86 Mark V. Tushnet, 'The Critique of Rights' (1994) 47(1) *SMU Law Review* 23, 33.
87 See, for example, *R v Malik* [1968] 1 WLR 353 and *R v Sawh* (*The Times*, 29 November 1967).
88 Elizabeth Burney and Gerry Rose, *Racist Offences: How Is the Law Working? The Implementation of the Legislation on Racially Aggravated Offences in the Crime and Disorder Act 1998* (Home Office Research Study 244 2002), 30; Bill Dixon and David Gadd, 'Look Before You Leap: Hate Crime Legislation Reconsidered' (2012) 40 *South African Crime Quarterly* 25, 28.
89 Matsuda, 'Public Response to Racist Speech', 36.
90 Mari J. Matsuda, 'When the First Quail Calls: Multiple Consciousness as Jurisprudential Method' (1992) 14 *Women's Rights Law Reporter* 213, 216.
91 Charles R. Lawrence III and others, 'Introduction' in Mari J. Matsuda and others (eds), *Words that Wound: Critical Race Theory, Assaultive Speech, and the First Amendment* (Westview Press 1993), 7.
92 Mari J. Matsuda and Charles R. Lawrence III, 'Epilogue: Burning Crosses and the R.A.V. Case' in Mari J. Matsuda and others (eds), *Words that Wound: Critical Race Theory, Assaultive Speech, and the First Amendment* (Westview Press 1993), 136.
93 Matsuda, 'Public Response to Racist Speech', 20–26.

While acknowledging the limits of the law, she argues that it can be a weapon against hate speech and hate acts by using a definition that recognises historical and continuing oppression.

However, a reliance on the neoliberal state to protect racialised communities is problematic. As Judith Butler argues, hate speech legislation may result in the prosecution of the individual uttering the words but cannot prosecute the racist history that lies behind it.[94] The words are dislocated and abstracted from the colonial histories and ongoing racist discourses that produce them. This gives the appearance that the state and judiciary are dealing with hate speech by citizens, rather than being the producers and perpetrators of such discourses.[95] In other words, the terms of the debate are shifted so that the state is presented as the solution to racism rather than being implicated in its origins and perpetuation, such that 'the state then re-emerges as a neutral instrument to which we seek recourse to protect us from other citizens'.[96] The actions of the court are performative – they decide what constitutes hate speech[97] and define the boundaries.[98] This allows the state to discursively divorce legal definitions of hate crime from state racism, including colonialism, imperialism, nationalism, immigration laws, border controls, police violence, and the War on Terror, which are then disappeared. Charlotte Chadderton notes that in the context of citizenship education, non-racism and tolerance are presented as White British values.[99] Such discourses allow nationalism to be viewed as separate from racism rather than as intrinsically linked to it.[100]

The argument that hate crime legislation can be a tool to protect marginalised groups implicitly equates these provisions with human rights laws. As discussed previously, neoliberal human rights cannot be relied upon as a means of securing equality. Costas Douzinas writes that such a strategy 'transforms a political claim into a demand for admission to the law'.[101] As outlined in Chapter 1, the CRT critique of rights articulated by Derrick Bell warned of the dangers of a reliance on ostensible legal equality and explained how such laws can perform a contradiction-closing function. Hate crime legislation fails to resolve the socio-economic injustices or ongoing colonial processes behind racism. Equating rights claims with increased criminalisation legitimises criminal law and reframes it as progressive. Such narratives name the state as protective with any residual discrimination attributed to errant

94 Judith Butler, *Excitable Speech: A Politics of the Performative* (Routledge 1997), 50.
95 Ibid., 48.
96 Ibid., 82.
97 Ibid., 96.
98 Ibid., 101.
99 Charlotte Chadderton, *Judith Butler, Race and Education* (Palgrave Macmillan 2018), 15.
100 Paul Gilroy, *There Ain't No Black in the Union Jack* (Routledge 1987), 17–18 and 44.
101 Costas Douzinas, *The Radical Philosophy of Rights* (Routledge 2019), 102.

individuals. This positions carceral responses as the solution to hate crimes. As discussed in previous chapters, human rights discourses under neoliberalism can be seen as third order simulacra that operate to communicate the message that Western societies are post-racial and meritocratic. Hate crime legislation can be viewed as part of this process of simulation that serves to empty liberation movements of their transformatory potential.

In relation to homophobic hate crimes, Sarah Lamble writes that there has been an emergence of 'queer penality' whereby LGBTQ groups have argued for harsher sentences, particularly imprisonment, which has had a particular impact on marginalised young Muslim men.[102] Given the racial disproportionalities in a criminal legal system embedded in colonialism, 'queer investments in punishment are … investments in state racism and violence'.[103] Similarly, Dean Spade points out that the communities subjected to hate crimes 'are those targeted for cyclical abandonment and imprisonment in neoliberalism' and therefore hate crime legislation will impact hardest on those same marginalised communities.[104] Hate crime legislation frames the carceral state as providing safety for vulnerable groups, rather than as a source of significant violence towards them.[105] A demand for carceral solutions to homophobia and transphobia constitutes a demand for access to the full benefits of White privilege, including 'the spoils of colonialism'.[106] Homonormative narratives of hard-working, upwardly mobile, patriotic White gay families position them 'on the "right" side of the white innocence / black criminality divide'[107] and erase the existence and experiences of Black LGBTQ people.[108]

Hate crime legislation produces two types of simulated legal subjects. The constructed White working class are portrayed as backward, anti-social, racist chavs who lack the social graces of respectable British society. Racialised defendants are portrayed as uncivilised, lacking British values of tolerance, and culpable in the perpetuation of racism. Racism is framed as intolerance of difference, denying both its colonial roots and the continuing material inequalities under racial neoliberalism. Hate crime provisions are situated within hyperreal discourses of diversity where inequality and harm are dislocated from history. Within this simulation, 'identity and difference' have replaced 'otherness'.[109] Debates around whether hate crime legislation should

102 Lamble, 'Queer Investments in Punitiveness', 157 and 163.
103 Ibid., 161.
104 Dean Spade, 'Laws as Tactics' (2011) 21(2) *Columbia Journal of Gender and Law* 40, 64.
105 Dean Spade, *Normal Life* (Duke University Press 2015), 47.
106 Morgan Bassichis and Dean Spade, 'Queer Politics and Anti-Blackness' in Jin Haritaworn, Adi Kuntsman and Silvia Posocco (eds), *Queer Necropolitics* (Routledge 2014), 199.
107 Ibid., 199.
108 Ibid., 197.
109 Jean Baudrillard, *The Perfect Crime* (Chris Turner tr, Verso Books 2008), 109.

be extended to cover subcultures such as goths[110] are illustrative of this focus on difference.[111] The underlying post-racial neoliberal logic of hate crime provisions consolidates White supremacy. These laws are third order simulacra that are located within, and performatively reproduce, the equal right of everyone to be a victim due to their difference.[112] If everyone is a potential victim, then racism is disappeared and privilege appears to be a meaningless concept.

Hate crime provisions perform a contradiction-closing function, as they appear to explain away the continuance of racist speech and actions in a post-racial society by externalising racism through naming marginalised communities as uncivilised and positioning the carceral state as the solution to racism. In order to maintain the illusion of post-racial, colour-blind criminal laws, the state needs to have a 'hater' who is positioned as being outside respectable society.[113] The legislation allows 'the right amount of racism'[114] to continue such that the post-racial myth can persist and White privilege is not only unchallenged but is consolidated. Racial hatred under neoliberalism is individualised and privatised. Thus, hate crime legislation can be seen as a form of interest convergence – it appears to protect Black people but functions to make state racism seem unintelligible, while using discourses that reproduce the construction of a backward White working class, as well as separatist Black communities. Chavs and racialised poor people serve as signifiers of ignorance and intolerance. These performative processes of simulation associate racism with the uneducated poor, such that 'the White middle class is assumed to represent the normal, moral core of society providing economic and social leadership despite the burden of lesser groups'.[115] Although the hate crime provisions are premised on making racialised people grievable, they perpetuate conceptions of the ungrievable racialised undeserving poor requiring punitive interventions. Hate crime prosecutions are part of the civilising mission discourse, whereby the British state is presented as progressive and morally superior and, as with

110 See, for example, Jon Garland, '"It's a Mosher Just Been Banged for No Reason": Assessing Targeted Violence Against Goths and the Parameters of Hate Crime' (2010) 17 *International Review of Victimology* 159; Jon Garland and Paul Hodkinson, '"F**king Freak! What The Hell Do You Think You Look Like?"' (2014) 54 *British Journal of Criminology* 613; Jon Garland, Neil Chakraborti and Stevie-Jade Hardy, '"It Felt Like a Little War": Reflections on Violence Against Alternative Subcultures' (2015) 49(6) *Sociology* 1065.

111 Neil Chakraborti and Jon Garland, 'Reconceptualizing Hate Crime Victimization Through the Lens of Vulnerability and "Difference"' (2012) 16(4) *Theoretical Criminology* 510.

112 Baudrillard, *The Perfect Crime*, 138.

113 Lewis, 276.

114 Richard Delgado, 'Review Essay: Derrick Bell and the Ideology of Racial Reform: Will We Ever Be Saved?' (1988) 97 *The Yale Law Journal* 923, 923.

115 Gillborn, 'The White Working Class', 21.

s.60, the legislation is deemed necessary to protect the undeserving poor from each other.

Hate crime laws are simulacra that make the simulation of colour-blind neoliberal societies appear as real. In this way, hate crime provisions perform a hyperreal function. Just as the portrayal of Watergate as a scandal was deployed to sustain the simulation that the rest of capitalist political activity was moral,[116] so convictions for hate crimes serve a symbolic purpose to maintain the simulacrum that neoliberal society has transcended racism. In order for this process of simulation to succeed, people of all races need to be convicted of hate crimes. Therefore, the conviction of Black people for hate crimes is not merely the outcome of a racially disproportionate system of law enforcement but is necessary to maintain the legitimacy of colour-blindness in criminal law, and to make the hyperreal post-racial society appear real.

In this process of simulation, Black people can be perpetrators of racism in the same way as their White neighbours. The simulation that racial equality has been achieved and White supremacy no longer exists is seemingly proved by the conviction of Black people for hate crimes. In this way, hate crimes serve a performative function by asserting that race is just a matter of cultural and ethnic difference rather than a fundamental inequality. Those convicted of hate crimes are those deemed too backward to embrace the wonderful world of neoliberal colour-blind diversity. The hate crime legislation is a process of simulation that appears to challenge racism, makes the post-racial state appear real, and in so doing reproduces and consolidates White supremacy, and disappears White privilege. Racial hatred cannot be overcome by the very relations of power that reproduce and sustain it; it can only be dismantled by a coalition of progressive abolitionist politics working towards carceral abolition and transformative socio-economic justice.

The Stephen Lawrence Case

The Stephen Lawrence case illustrates the ability of the state to use hate crimes to perform a contradiction-closing function. Stephen Lawrence, a Black student from London, was murdered on 22nd April 1993 in an unprovoked racist attack by five White youths.[117] He had been waiting at a bus stop with his friend, Duwayne Brooks. The police viewed both young men through a racial frame that marked them as criminals rather than victims, which had repercussions for the way that the investigation was carried out, with the police later admitting that they had assumed that the incident was

116 Jean Baudrillard, *Simulacra and Simulation* (Sheila Faria Glaser tr, University of Michigan Press 1994), 14–15.

117 Home Office, *Report of the Stephen Lawrence Inquiry*, Cm 4262 (1999), paras 1.2–1.9 and 2.5.

an inner-city gang fight rather than a racist attack.[118] The botched police investigation into the brutal, racist murder of a Black teenager became such an embarrassment to the government that they were forced to take action to bolster the simulation of a post-racial society. The exhausting campaign fought by Stephen's family and their supporters shone a spotlight on police racism, secured an official inquiry, and led to the Metropolitan police force being labelled as 'institutionally racist' by the Macpherson Report.[119]

As discussed above, the individualisation of racism by the colonial state operates to render invisible the ways that racism pervades life under racial neoliberalism. In the context of the education system, David Gillborn has argued that the Stephen Lawrence case is 'the supreme example of a contradiction-closing case in the UK' – although it achieved some change, ultimately it was used to support government and media discourses that racism had been diagnosed, treated, and overcome.[120] The Macpherson report included consideration of racism in the education system and made a number of recommendations.[121] However, this led to little substantive change in practices or in educational outcomes for racialised students, while giving the impression that racism in education had been dealt with.[122]

In relation to criminal law, the case also performed a contradiction-closing function. The contradiction between a colour-blind justice system and ongoing police racism was seemingly resolved by securing two convictions for murder and by the Macpherson Report making recommendations for surface changes to the police force, such as diversity training[123] and recruitment of more Black officers.[124] The Macpherson Report recommended no reduction in the use of existing stop and search powers, stating that these were 'required for the prevention and detection of crime and should remain unchanged',[125] and limited its comments on the matter to suggesting that stop and searches should be recorded accurately.[126] As discussed in Chapter 3, stop and search provisions are situated within colonial discourses, particularly the civilising mission, and enable the police to occupy the areas where racialised communities live.

118 Biko Agozino, *Counter-Colonial Criminology: A Critique of Imperialist Reason* (Pluto Press 2003), 195–196.
119 David Gillborn, *Racism and Education: Coincidence or Conspiracy?* (Routledge 2008), 134.
120 Ibid., 120.
121 Ibid., 122.
122 Ibid., 120–145.
123 Home Office, *Report of the Stephen Lawrence Inquiry*, recommendations 48–54.
124 Ibid., recommendations 64–66.
125 Ibid., recommendation 60.
126 Ibid., recommendations 61–63.

Not only did the state use the Stephen Lawrence case to apparently close contradictions in the criminal legal system, but it was used as a justification for an increase in processes of criminalisation more widely. One of the recommendations of the Macpherson Report was consideration of a relaxation of the double jeopardy rule, which had prevented individuals being retried for the same offence following an acquittal.[127] Subsequently, the CJA 2003 modified the double jeopardy rule in certain circumstances.[128] In relation to a number of serious offences, the prosecution may apply to the Court of Appeal for an order that the original acquittal is quashed[129] and that a retrial for the original offence takes place.[130] The Court of Appeal must make the order[131] if there is 'new and compelling evidence'[132] and it is in the interests of justice to make the order.[133] Following new forensic evidence, two of the original suspects in the Stephen Lawrence case, Gary Dobson and David Norris, were charged with murder. As Dobson had been acquitted of this offence previously, it was necessary to invoke the new double jeopardy law so that he could be tried again, and he was subsequently convicted.[134] The Court of Appeal held that the double jeopardy interests of justice test were met despite the substantial time lapse, then 18 years from the murder and 15 years from the first trial,[135] and the significant adverse publicity during that period.[136] While one may have little sympathy for Dobson, the judgment in that case suggests that the provisions may be used many years after the original trial and where substantial prejudicial media coverage has occurred, notwithstanding the consequent impact on the reliability of the evidence. This gives the state considerable power to pursue individuals.

The use of bad character evidence against David Norris during the trial was significant, as it involved an incident that post-dated Stephen Lawrence's murder. Although this was not the first case where character evidence post-dating the offence was ruled admissible,[137] the bad character evidence was particularly prejudicial due to the adverse publicity against the defendants.[138] The evidence consisted of a DVD recording of Norris and his friends showing that he 'held racist views which extended to the approval of racially moti-

127 Ibid., recommendation 38.
128 Criminal Justice Act 2003, s.76.
129 Ibid., s.76(1)(a).
130 Ibid., s.76(1)(b).
131 Ibid., s.77(1).
132 Ibid., s.78(1).
133 Ibid., s.79(1).
134 *R v Dobson* [2011] EWCA Crim 1255.
135 Ibid., para 91.
136 Ibid., para 92.
137 See *R v Adenusi* [2006] EWCA Crim 1059.
138 *R v Norris* [2013] EWCA Crim 712, para 31.

vated serious violence, including the use of knives against black people' and that he associated with people who held similar views.[139] Again, Norris may not elicit much sympathy but then, for many people, neither do racialised defendants who are presented by the prosecution as gang members. The use of gang membership and of rap and drill music as bad character evidence are discussed in Chapter 6. Given that, as argued in that chapter, bragging, references to violence, and fictionalised accounts are all tropes of that genre of music, the use of comments that post-date the offence as bad character evidence is likely to disproportionately impact racialised defendants.

In the Stephen Lawrence case, the state needed convictions to advance the simulation that the legal system and law enforcement were post-racial and colour-blind. Therefore, the eventual successful prosecution of two White racists appeared to close the contradiction between discourses of post-rights equality and continued racism in the criminal legal system. The police had initially tried to discredit and smear the Lawrence family,[140] but once it became clear that this would not work, government and mainstream media discourses presented Stephen Lawrence's parents as deserving immigrants, to be differentiated from asylum seekers and drug dealers. This allowed racist state discourses around immigration, gangs, and racialised criminality to continue unabated.

Ultimately the state used the case to individualise racism, and to position the carceral state and criminal law as the solution to racism. Extending the power of the neoliberal carceral state not only fails to keep racialised communities safe but amplifies practices of racialised criminalisation. Racism cannot be prosecuted away. Accountability and safety require carceral abolition and practices of collective, transformative justice, which are incompatible with neoliberalism.

From Anti-Social to Criminal

Situated within discourses around chavs and the undeserving poor, the CDA introduced ASBOs. Anti-social behaviour was seen as a cause of wider problems, such as the decline of particular areas, rather than as symptomatic of the economic issues experienced by deprived communities, particularly in post-industrial towns.[141] While the anti-social behaviour provisions described below may have been premised on protecting 'authentic' working class

139 Ibid., para 23.

140 Adam Elliott-Cooper, *Black Resistance to British Policing* (Manchester University Press 2021), 55–56.

141 Jessica Jacobson, Andrew Millie and Mike Hough, 'Tackling Anti-social Behaviour: A Critical Review' (Institute for Criminal Policy Research, King's College London 2005) <https://research.edgehill.ac.uk/en/publications/tackling-anti-social-behaviour-a-critical-review-2> accessed 20 December 2024.

communities, they served the interests of capital. Narratives around 'cleaning up' communities were linked with gentrification of urban areas, as with the s.60 provisions. Anti-social behaviour legislation borrowed from the US 'broken windows' policing deployed by Mayor Rudy Giuliani in New York from the early 1990s, that focused police attention on minor infractions and 'converted areas of concentrated poverty into quasi-correctional spaces'.[142] In the UK context, the simulacrum of the chav was pivotal to constructions of anti-social behaviour.

An ASBO could be imposed on a person aged ten years or over who had acted 'in a manner that caused or was likely to cause harassment, alarm or distress to one or more persons' where an order was 'necessary to protect persons ... from further anti-social acts by him'.[143] It prohibited the recipient from carrying out certain activities[144] and lasted for at least two years,[145] although it could be discharged earlier if both parties agreed.[146] Breaching an ASBO condition could result in a sentence of up to five years' imprisonment. This maximum sentence applied even if the condition was not in itself a criminal offence, or if it was a criminal offence but with a lower maximum sentence. The Police Reform Act 2002, s.64 amended the CDA by inserting s.1C, which enabled courts to impose an ASBO on an individual convicted of a criminal offence, whether or not an ASBO was applied for, if the test was met.[147] ASBOs were a blurring of the lines between civil and criminal law, as they were civil orders but with criminal sanctions for breaching them. The civil rules on admission of hearsay evidence applied, such that hearsay was admissible. Although the court could decide what, if any, weight to give to the hearsay evidence, nonetheless this enabled evidence to be adduced that may have been inadmissible in criminal proceedings.

ASBOs were disproportionately imposed on marginalised individuals, including young people with learning disabilities,[148] homeless people,[149] and

142 Alex S. Vitale and Brian Jordan Jefferson, 'The Emergence of Command and Control Policing in Neoliberal New York' in Jordan T. Camp and Christina Heatherton (eds), *Policing the Planet* (Verso Books 2016), 164.

143 Crime and Disorder Act 1998, s.1.

144 Ibid., s.1(4).

145 Ibid., s.1(7).

146 Ibid., s.1(9).

147 The test for this was the same as for the standalone ASBOs save for it was to protect anyone in England and Wales from further anti-social acts by the person, rather than being confined to acts within a local authority area.

148 Rachel Fyson and Joe Yates, 'Anti-social Behaviour Orders and Young People with Learning Disabilities' (2001) 31(1) *Critical Social Policy* 102; Kate Varnfield, 'Vulnerable Young People and the Misuse of Anti-social Behaviour Orders' (2005) 4(1) *Safer Communities* 33.

149 Will McMahon, 'Concern Over ASBOs' (2005) 59 *Criminal Justice Matters* 43 <https://www.crimeandjustice.org.uk/sites/crimeandjustice.org.uk/files/09627250508553047.pdf> accessed 20 December 2024.

those experiencing mental illness.[150] Homeless people arrested for begging under the Vagrancy Act 1824 could be given anti-social behaviour sanctions.[151] The alcohol-dependent homeless person, the mentally ill individual exhibiting behaviour deemed unusual or erratic, and the teenager with learning disabilities creating noise were all categorised as anti-social. These concepts of anti-social behaviour were constructed through an ableist lens, where vulnerable people requiring support were judged to be ungrievable: not only surplus to the requirements of racial capitalism but disruptive to the neoliberal order and an obstacle to gentrification.

Recipients of ASBOs were punished for what they were perceived to be, rather than for what they had done. In this way, ASBOs were a move towards character-based liability, particularly propensity. The criteria set out in the CDA referred to both past and anticipated future conduct, thus inviting the court to infer that such future conduct was likely. The relatively lengthy period of orders, particularly significant in the context of the life of a young person, implied that such character traits were enduring. Furthermore, some of the conditions imposed under ASBOs, such as restricting association with particular individuals, fed into discourses around gang membership, something that later became admissible as evidence of propensity towards criminal conduct under the hyperreal bad character provisions considered in Chapter 6. ASBOs acted performatively to create abstracted legal subjects based on neoliberal constructions of anti-social behaviour.

Research by Sarah Isal for the Runnymede Trust found a lack of data on race in relation to ASBOs, and therefore she was unable to assess whether ASBOs were disproportionately imposed on Black people.[152] Given that Black people are more likely to be convicted of criminal offences in general, she suggested that ASBOs on conviction may have impacted most on Black people.[153] However, during interviews with practitioners, she found that they perceived that ASBOs were imposed predominantly on White individuals but was unable to say whether this was empirically true.[154] The signs of the chav were enmeshed with conceptions of behaviour deemed to be anti-social, such that the two were inseparable in those discourses. However, research by

150 Judy Nixon and others, 'Anti-social Behaviour and Disability in the UK' (2007) 2(1) *People, Place and Policy Online* 37 <https://ppp-online.org/wp-content/uploads/2013/06/anti_social_behaviour_disability_uk.pdf> accessed 20 December 2024.

151 Chloe Hadjimatheou, 'Beg, Get Arrested, Go to Court, Repeat…' *BBC News* (28 August 2018) <https://www.bbc.co.uk/news/stories-45301449> accessed 20 December 2024.

152 Sarah Isal, 'Equal Respect – ASBOs and Race Equality' (The Runnymede Trust 2006), 19 <https://cdn.prod.website-files.com/61488f992b58e687f1108c7c/617bfdf0ddbc2b83ff9ea3ba_Final%20Report%20Equal%20Respect.pdf> accessed 20 December 2024.

153 Ibid., 19.

154 Ibid., 20.

the Youth Justice Board sampled 137 young people who received an ASBO between January 2004 and January 2005 and found that 22% were from racialised backgrounds.[155] The study makes clear that the data was a sample obtained from Youth Offending Teams in particular areas and therefore cannot be seen as representative of the national picture.[156] Nonetheless, this suggests that although the majority of ASBO recipients were White, a disproportionate percentage were Black.

ASBOs were abolished by the Anti-social Behaviour, Crime and Policing Act 2014 and replaced with three new provisions – injunctions, which were broadly similar to ASBOs,[157] Community Protection Notices,[158] and Criminal Behaviour Orders (CBOs).[159] The latter are similar to ASBOs but can only be imposed on conviction for a criminal offence.[160] The 2014 Act also included dispersal powers whereby a police officer of the rank of inspector or above may issue an order allowing the police to ask members of the public to leave the area and not to return for a specified period.[161] The grounds for imposing such a draconian condition are fairly loose – that 'it may be necessary for the purposes of removing or reducing the likelihood of' harassment, alarm, distress, crime, or disorder.[162] Thus, the risk of a fairly low level of public disorder will suffice, and this can be seen as restricting access to public spaces, with clear similarities to the ways that s.60 produces racialised legal subjects, as considered in Chapter 3. The same Act also included the power to impose Public Spaces Protection Orders (PSPOs), which shared similarities with ASBOs as they enabled local authorities to prohibit or impose limits on specified activities in public places if they were satisfied that those activities 'have had a detrimental effect on the quality of life of those in the locality' or if it was likely that such activities would take place.[163]

The definition of anti-social behaviour (for both ASBOs and CBOs) as causing harassment, alarm, or distress appears to be taken directly from s.5, POA 1986, which is a non-imprisonable offence punishable by a fine or discharge. Thus, ASBOs and CBOs were unnecessary in order to criminalise such behaviour, as there was an existing offence designed to cover exactly that. The key difference is that breach of an ASBO or CBO could carry

155 Aikta-Reena Solanki and others, *Antisocial Behaviour Orders* (Youth Justice Board 2006) <http://news.bbc.co.uk/1/shared/bsp/hi/pdfs/02_11_06_asbo_summary.pdf> accessed 31 December 2024.
156 Ibid.
157 Anti-social Behaviour, Crime and Policing Act 2014, s.1.
158 Ibid., s.43.
159 Ibid., s.22. This has been repealed and replaced by Sentencing Act 2020, s.330.
160 Sentencing Act 2020, s.331(1).
161 Anti-social Behaviour, Crime and Policing Act 2014, ss.34–35.
162 Ibid., s.34(2).
163 Ibid., s.59.

custody and therefore these provisions allowed the courts to circumvent the prohibition on custody for this conduct, and send individuals to prison for non-imprisonable offences. Indeed, CBOs are used in onerous ways, including banning young Black males from making drill music, which will be discussed below. It is less the *conduct* that is being censured, as that could have been dealt with by s.5 POA 1986; it is the *individual* who is deemed to need a strong deterrent to keep out of trouble.

The imposition of an ASBO or CBO acted performatively to name a person as 'anti-social' or 'criminal', which then subsumed their identity. ASBOs were hyperreal, as they produced a simulated construction of anti-social behaviour. In other words, discourses around definitions of anti-social behaviour were formed on the basis of the conduct censored by these orders, such that this simulation was self-referential but appeared as real. Those labelled in this way were dehumanised and abstracted, such that they became hypercriminals. Their identity as an ASBO or CBO recipient determined their treatment by the criminal legal system and differentiated them from those not so named. Minor public order acts became imprisonable for those named as anti-social or criminal, but remained non-imprisonable for everyone else. While a person's criminal record is a factor relevant to sentencing more generally, these provisions changed the maximum sentence for a particular act depending on whether it was prosecuted as a normal crime or as an act of anti-social or criminal behaviour. Thus, the framing of the individual legal subject defined the available penalties – being constructed as an ASBO or CBO hypercriminal could result in imprisonment. The implementation of the sentence then served to reproduce them as anti-social or criminal, in a self-perpetuating and circular process of simulation.

Once these definitions of anti-social behaviour and criminality are interrogated, it is clear that they could be used against the government, corporations, and the police. As Emma Bell argues, the kettling of protesters on demonstrations could be described as causing 'harassment, alarm or distress'.[164] Yet due to the way that these constructions of crime and legal subjects are produced and reproduced within neoliberalism, it is unintelligible to the criminal law that the provisions could be used in such a way. Similarly, one could argue that repeated racialised stop and searches by police officers have a 'detrimental effect on the quality of life of those in the locality', with those in the locality being the young Black males who are frequently stopped, yet PSPOs are not imposed on the police officers carrying out those practices.

These performative discourses, through their repeated naming of particular classed and racialised subjects as anti-social or criminal, ensure that this neoliberal framing not only persists but becomes increasingly insidious, thus

164 Emma Bell, 'The Anti-sociality of Anti-social Behaviour Policy' in Sarah Pickard (ed), *Anti-social Behaviour in Britain* (Palgrave Macmillan 2014), 234.

appearing neutral and becoming normalised. These provisions are simulacra – they name the poor and vulnerable as anti-social and criminal while ignoring the material damage to those communities caused by the global reorganisation of capitalism and the corresponding material inequalities of neoliberalism. In this way, they fulfil a smoke and mirrors effect. Anti-social behaviour is a simulacrum framed as actions by the poor rather than as destruction of the environment, lack of affordable homes or cuts to healthcare. The discursive links between concepts of anti-social behaviour and poor communities mean that society's values are deemed to accord with those of White elites, and the devastating harm caused by the redistribution of wealth upwards is made invisible. The legislation both relies upon and reproduces these processes of simulation, and therefore can be viewed as hyperreal.

It may appear that CBOs are less objectionable than civil orders as they have to be preceded by a criminal conviction rather than standing alone. However, there is no requirement for there to be any nexus between the facts of the offence and the conditions imposed by the CBO. This allows CBOs with onerous conditions curtailing the recipient's freedom, such as exclusion from particular areas and restrictions on associating with named people, to be imposed for minor breaches of the law, such as possession of cannabis or low value criminal damage. CBOs enable courts to impose conditions that go beyond the sentencing powers for the conviction, and can be seen as a means of spatial containment and social control of racialised young people. All that is required is that the defendant has, to the criminal standard of proof, engaged in behaviour that caused or was likely to cause harassment, alarm, or distress[165] and that the court 'considers that making the order will help in preventing the offender from engaging in such behaviour'.[166] The requirement is not that such an order is necessary but only that it will 'help', which allows significant discretion in relation to the imposition of an order that, if breached, can result in lengthy incarceration. Further, to posit that a CBO will help someone to desist from particular behaviour relies upon a framing that considers restrictions on their liberty and the deterrent of custody as a positive influence on them. Such a narrative is intelligible only when marginalised communities are presented as lacking responsibility, and requiring onerous consequences to make them regulate their behaviour. They are deemed to be unworthy of being trusted with the freedoms associated with responsible adult society.[167] As with the s.60 provisions considered in Chapter 3, this echoes colonial civilising mission discourses of deficient populations requiring firm governance by White elites.

165 Sentencing Act 2020, s.331(2)(a).

166 Ibid., s.331 (2)(b).

167 It should be noted, as mentioned earlier, that of some of the recipients of these Orders are actually children.

This contradictory link between welfare and punishment can be seen as going to the heart of the neoliberal project. Sentencing provisions under New Labour included Drug Treatment and Testing Orders (DTTOs) that were a combination of rehabilitation and coercion, such that the continuation of a drug habit could be punished more onerously than an offence of drug possession.[168] Such measures led to the 'social exclusion of offenders who fail[ed] to take responsibility for their reformation'.[169] The hyperreal undeserving poor were deemed to have made bad choices, such that the state needed to intervene and compel them to make good choices. These discourses portrayed the state as benevolent rather than punitive, assisting the anti-social to reform while protecting the rest of society from their actions. This forced rehabilitation is an example of how 'penal violence finds its most subtle equivalent in re-socialisation and re-education'.[170] The continuing drug user was defined as ontologically criminal, such that their very existence became illegal and they were abstracted as a hypercriminal. The simulacrum of the irresponsible drug addict overrode the poverty, mental illness and lack of social care facing poor communities. Within this meritocratic hyperreality, the state appeared to recognise deprived individuals as grievable by offering assistance, but these punitive provisions further entrenched their ungrievability and exclusion.

Another form of social control introduced during this period were the gang injunction provisions introduced by the Policing and Crime Act 2009. Gang injunctions for adults came into force in January 2011 and were extended to cover 14–17 years old from January 2012. These are civil orders whereby the police or a local authority can apply for an injunction against someone who is deemed, on the balance of probabilities rather than the higher criminal standard of proof, to be involved in 'gang-related violence, or gang-related drug-dealing activity'.[171] For these purposes, 'violence' includes threats of violence.[172] The imposition of a gang injunction allows courts to impose both requirements and restrictions on the activities of an individual[173] in order to prevent them from engaging, encouraging, or assisting gang-related violence or drug-dealing, or to protect them from gang-related violence or drug-dealing.[174] As with the provisions considered above, such a framing is premised on marginalised communities requiring the colonial state to protect them from themselves. The Serious Crime Act 2015 amended the legislation to make the definition 'gang-related' looser

168 Emma Bell, *Criminal Justice and Neoliberalism* (Palgrave Macmillan 2011), 83.
169 Ibid., 92.
170 Jean Baudrillard, *Symbolic Exchange and Death* (Iain Hamilton Grant tr, SAGE Publications 2017), 190.
171 Policing and Crime Act 2009, s.34(2) as amended by Serious Crime Act 2015, s.51.
172 Ibid., s.34(6).
173 Ibid., s.34(4).
174 Ibid., s.34(3).

and easier to establish. Gang-related activities are defined as those pertaining to a group that consists of three or more people, and has 'one or more characteristics that enables its members to be identified by others as a group'.[175] It seems almost trite to point out that this is sufficiently wide to include many friendship groups, bands, pop groups, clubs, societies, campaign groups, and professional associations. As discussed below, this has enabled it to be used against drill musicians.

While chavs may have been racialised in the popular media as White, crimes involving knives, guns, and drugs have been racialised as Black, and these are increasingly the focus of the orders that followed ASBOs. Both CBOs and gang injunctions have been used in relation to drill music, and to attack basic freedoms, such as being able to make and perform music without state censorship or surveillance. This has included bans on recording or performing drill music without police permission, requirements to allow police officers to attend any such performances, and prohibitions on writing lyrics referencing gangs or deemed by the police to incite, encourage, threaten, or claim to commit violence.[176] In January 2019, two drill musicians, Skengdo and AM, were given nine-month prison sentences suspended for two years for breaching a gang injunction by performing one of their songs at a large, mainstream concert venue in Camden, London.[177]

Forms of music, theatre, writing, and art associated with White artists and audiences, from classical literature and Shakespeare plays to the present day, have always included references to weapons and violence, with opera being a pertinent example.[178] To label these forms of art, which have already been named as the highest forms of White culture, as criminal would be unintelligible in the context of White privilege. The legal regulation of drill music is possible only because of the existing racial framing and processes of simulation that link young Black working class culture with violence, gangs, guns, drugs and knife crime, and in turn these legal provisions create hyperreal legal subjects through criminalisation of culture. Rap and drill are genres that rely upon 'storytelling, symbolism, metaphors and boasting'.[179]

175 Ibid., s.34(5).

176 Ian Cobain, 'London Drill Rap Group Banned from Making Music Due to Threat of Violence' *The Guardian* (15 June 2018) <www.theguardian.com/uk-news/2018/jun/15/london-drill-rap-gang-banned-from-making-music-due-to-threat-of-violence> accessed 20 December 2024.

177 Dan Hancox, 'Skengdo and AM: The Drill Rappers Sentenced for Playing Their Song' *The Guardian* (31 January 2019) <www.theguardian.com/music/2019/jan/31/skengdo-and-am-the-drill-rappers-sentenced-for-playing-their-song> accessed 20 December 2024.

178 Nicholas Stoia, Kyle Adams and Kevin Drakulich, 'Rap Lyrics as Evidence: What Can Music Theory Tell Us?' (2017) 8 *Race and Justice* 1, 2.

179 Abenaa Owusu-Bempah, 'Part of Art or Part of Life? Rap Lyrics in Criminal Trials' (London School of Economics 2000) <https://blogs.lse.ac.uk/politicsandpolicy/rap-lyrics-in-criminal-trials/> accessed 20 December 2024.

As outlined above, a gang injunction can be imposed where it is shown to the civil standard of proof that there are threats of violence. This allows fictional lyrical content involving bragging and bravado to be presented as factual in order to fulfil this test. Additionally, drill music, along with many other art forms, tends to be a collective rather than individual enterprise, which has been deployed by the state to argue that drill musicians fit the gang injunction definition of three or more people who can be identified as a group.[180] The treatment of rap and drill music ignores the distinctions between criminal confessions and artistic expression. In this way, these provisions can be seen as collapsing the boundaries of truth and falsity through a reliance on signs of perceived racialised criminality, such that Black musicians are named as criminals regardless of whether or not they have committed any crimes. In this way, they are hypercriminals.

As will be discussed in Chapter 6, the gang discourse, which frames groups of young Black people as gangs rather than friends, plays a key role in the way that cases are prosecuted and presented at trial. The rules of evidence confine the ways that these discourses can be challenged at trial such that the only way left to challenge them may be outside the trial process, using art forms as a counternarrative. However, CBOs and gang injunctions enable the law to determine not only the scope of the racialised narratives that take place within court hearings but also the scope of culture more widely, refusing to recognise particular styles of music as having cultural legitimacy, thus silencing the voices of racialised legal subjects both in and out of the courtroom. Culture is an integral part of what it means to be human, so this silencing of counternarratives is a process of dehumanisation that reproduces racialised young people as ungrievable subaltern: those spoken about rather than those allowed to speak. Again, this is grounded in a genealogy of colonialism and the civilising mission discourse, which interprets Black self-expression as aggressive, subversive, and criminal. The simulacrum of the Black gangster appears more real than the teenager writing lyrics about their lived experiences of disproportionate stop and search. The criminalisation of rap and drill music is considered further in Chapter 6 in relation to bad character evidence.

While initial discourses around anti-social behaviour focused on the constructed White working class, the effect of these provisions was felt across the racialised working class. As the provisions have shifted from anti-social (ASBOs) to criminal (CBOs), both in terms of their titles and their framing, it is noteworthy that the focus has moved from poor White to Black people. While poor White people have been characterised as feckless and irresponsible, poor Black communities have been demonised as dangerous

180 Adèle Oliver, *Deeping It: Colonialism, Culture and Criminalisation of UK Drill* (404 Ink Limited 2023), 63.

gang members armed with deadly weapons. In this way, the behaviour of White legal subjects is portrayed as merely anti-social, albeit often subject to criminal sanctions, whereas similar activity by Black subjects is named as fully criminal. Furthermore, these legal provisions rely upon racialised and classed concepts of risk, which are rooted in colonial discourses around suspect populations. These performative processes of simulation name racialised communities as ontologically criminal, regardless of whether or not they have actually committed a crime, and therefore can be seen as producing simulated legal subjects, or hypercriminals, whereby the effect of racial framing overrides their actions or non-actions. These processes have intensified through a racialised moral panic over knife crime, as discussed below.

Hyperreal Knife Carriers

In Chapter 3, knife crime was discussed as a socially constructed and racialised simulacrum that has been, and continues to be, the subject of a moral panic. In addition to the stop and search practices described in that chapter, Knife Crime Prevention Orders (KCPOs), introduced by the Offensive Weapons Act 2019, are a further provision aimed at young racialised people and premised on the simulacrum of a knife crime emergency. Echoing the discourses linking welfare and punishment discussed above, the Home Office guidance describes these as a diversionary tool to be used by the police to prevent young people being involved in knife crime.[181] KCPOs can be made on an individual as young as 12.[182]

There are two different types of KCPOs – those made on conviction and freestanding orders. They can be made on conviction where the substantive offence involved violence or the threat of violence, or where the defendant or a co-defendant used or was in possession of a bladed article during commission of the offence.[183] Therefore, a defendant may receive an order even if they were not themselves in possession of a knife or where a knife was not used. For a non-conviction order, the test is that the person had a bladed article without lawful authority in a public place, school, or college within the past two years on at least two separate occasions[184] and the standard of proof is the civil standard of the balance of probabilities rather than the criminal standard.[185] The conditions imposed can include exclusion from

181 Home Office, *Knife Crime Prevention Orders: Practitioners' Guidance* (5 January 2022) <www.gov.uk/government/publications/knife-crime-prevention-orders-kcpos/practitioners-guidance-accessible-version> accessed 20 December 2024.

182 Offensive Weapons Act 2019, ss.14(1) and 19(1).

183 Ibid., s.19(10)-(11).

184 Ibid., s.14(3)-(4).

185 Ibid., s.14(3).

particular areas, curfews, not to participate in particular activities, not to associate with particular individuals, not to use the internet to facilitate or encourage knife crime, or to participate in particular activities.[186] The activity requirements are similar to those imposed under community order sentences, yet one can receive a KCPO without meeting the criminal standard of any offence. Breaching the requirements of a KCPO can result in a criminal conviction with a maximum sentence of two years' imprisonment.[187]

In respect of both types of order, there is also the condition that a KCPO is necessary to protect the public or protect particular persons, including the defendant, from the risk of harm from a knife or to prevent the defendant from committing a knife-related offence.[188] The framing that a KCPO may be for the protection of the recipient again reproduces civilising mission narratives that racialised communities are incapable of looking after themselves. Colonial discourses name racialised populations as pathologically inferior, and in need of control, re-education, and civilisation from the White ruling elite, while neoliberal discourses that link welfare and punishment allow a framing that constraints on racialised communities and individuals are in their own interests, and are to reform and protect them from each other, as with s.60 and the CBOs and DTTOs discussed above. As was outlined in Chapter 3, such civilising mission provisions need to be seen in the context of the gentrification of urban areas, and the need to present them as sanitised and safe, where safety is equated with middle class Whiteness, and Blackness signifies danger.

KCPOs constitute a symbiotic process whereby one must be viewed as a criminal or future criminal in order to receive a non-conviction KCPO, and in turn, the imposition of the KCPO names that individual as a criminal. This is only possible due to previous performative processes of simulation that have already named those racialised young people as criminals. In this way, the imposition of a KCPO is hyperreal – a simulation without an original. It names individuals as knife criminals even where they have never possessed a knife. It constructs these third order simulacra through racially framed discourses around knife crime that categorise the racialised poor as violent, dangerous, and a threat to the wellbeing of society, such that action must be seen to be taken against them. This is based on earlier processes of simulation rooted in colonialism that equate Blackness with savagery. The symbolic image of the knife-wielding young Black male appears more real than what they have, or have not, done – they are a hypercriminal.

186 Ibid., s.21(2)-(4).
187 Ibid., s.25(2). Note that the standard of proof required for a conviction for breaching a KCPO is the criminal standard of beyond reasonable doubt.
188 Ibid., ss.19(4) and 14(6).

Non-conviction KCPOs have been viewed as 'pre-criminal' and compared to counter-terror policing and immigration policy, as they rely upon racialisation, guilt by association, and character-based liability.[189] The phrase 'pre-crime' comes from science fiction: the police force in *Minority Report* whose mission is to catch those who are going to commit crime before it happens.[190] The state imposes restrictions on someone who may have done nothing wrong because they are deemed at risk of harming others, such that 'the possibility of forestalling risks competes with and even takes precedence over responding to wrongs done'.[191] Gabe Mythen and Sandra Walklate link pre-crime to s.44, Terrorism Act 2002, which led to young Muslim men being disproportionately stopped on the basis of anticipatory risk.[192] They argue that 'in a climate of "hyper-riskality" it is cultural representations and political narratives of risk that mould material decisions about crime and security regulation'.[193] These provisions are used against those that the state considers to be 'risky populations': poor racialised communities.[194] Such constructions of risk mean that pre-crime interventions are conspicuous by their absence in relation to environmental and financial crime, despite the harm caused by these practices.[195]

Jude McCulloch and Dean Wilson also link 'pre-crime' with counter-terror policies, citing the War on Terror as a pre-emptive intervention that shifted the discourse around criminal law provisions.[196] They argue that:

> The organizational allocation of police resources to particular geographic locations where marginalised people live and congregate ... along with the exercise of individual police discretion in ways that equate non-white identities in particular with offending, are instrumental in producing criminal identities that conform to, reproduce and reinforce widely held views about who and what constitute criminal groups and criminal activities.[197]

189 Gargi Bhattacharyya and others, *Empire's Endgame: Racism and the British State* (Pluto Press 2021), 37.
190 Gabe Mythen and Sandra Walklate, 'Pre-crime, Regulation, and Counter-terrorism: Interrogating Anticipatory Risk' (2010) 81(1) *Criminal Justice Matters* 34, 34; Philip K. Dick, *Minority Report* (Gollancz 2002). This was made into a Steven Spielberg film starring Tom Cruise.
191 Lucia Zedner, 'Pre-crime and Post-criminology?' (2007) 99(2) *Theoretical Criminology* 261, 262.
192 Mythen and Walklate, 35.
193 Ibid., 35.
194 Ibid., 35–36.
195 Ibid., 35.
196 Jude McCulloch and Dean Wilson, *Pre-crime: Pre-emption, Precaution and the Future* (Routledge 2015), 2, 18–19 and 56–73.
197 Ibid., 25.

These acts of arresting, charging, and convicting racialised individuals serve to confirm the prediction that they were criminal all along, and thus these are self-serving and confirmatory processes that reproduce colonial power relations against racialised domestic populations.[198] These practices create their own reality of racially disproportionate criminality – they are hyperreal. Additionally, there is evidence to show that the moral panic over knife crime has resulted in some young people becoming scared and carrying knives for their own protection, such that the simulation mediates their behaviour.[199]

KCPOs have been described as not only 'pre-criminal' but also 'post-criminal'.[200] They are an implosion, whereby the past, present, and future co-exist in the construction of the hypercriminal. The criminal legal system identifies them as a knife carrier in need of intervention prior to the order, performatively confirms them as a knife carrier through the making of the KCPO, and declares them a future knife carrier by imposing conditions on them. A KCPO recipient becomes subject to criminal sanctions, including potential incarceration, by breaching the requirements of the order that they received for suspected rather than actual commission of a crime. Therefore, a person who has never carried a knife may not only receive a KCPO but also be liable for breaching a KCPO. Their initial simulation as a knife carrier by the KCPO is made to appear real by the breach. In this way, KCPOs are self-referential orders that construct their own hyperreality and destroy the boundaries between truth and falsity.

In the year April 2023 to March 2024, a person of Afro-Caribbean descent was 8.3 times more likely than a White person to be searched under PACE for offensive weapons in England and Wales.[201] As outlined in Chapter 3, knife crime has been the subject of a moral panic and framed by the media, the government, and law enforcement agencies as a young Black male inner city issue. Therefore, KCPOs are imposed in the context of the racial framing that reproduces this performative discourse and simulated legal subject, every time such an order is imposed. Whether or not the individual had actually carried a knife or been violent is deemed irrelevant compared to the risk that they are deemed to pose by being a member of a hyperreal suspect population; in other words, by being young, poor, and Black. As with counter-terrorism provisions such as Prevent, guilt is calculated through risk

198 Ibid., 25–27.

199 Elaine Williams and Peter Squires, *Rethinking Knife Crime* (Palgrave Macmillan 2021), 21.

200 Bhattacharyya and others, *Empire's Endgame*, 37.

201 Home Office, *Police Powers and Procedures: Stop and Search and Arrests, England and Wales, Year Ending March 2024* (26 September 2024), para 2.7 <https://www.gov.uk/government/statistics/stop-and-search-arrests-and-mental-health-detentions-march-2024/police-powers-and-procedures-stop-and-search-arrests-and-mental-health-detentions-england-and-wales-year-ending-31-march-2024> accessed 22 May 2025 .

assessments that present as colour-blind, rational, and value-neutral.[202] These practices of creating guilt are simulations constructed through the racial frame while vanishing their colonial roots.

The negative consequences of naming young, racialised people as 'pre-criminal' are evident from similar US policies. Under the Juvenile Delinquency Prevention and Control Act 1968, young people who were deemed 'potentially delinquent' were put into programmes run by police officers whereas they had previously been eligible for similar provisions from welfare services.[203] Elizabeth Hinton points out that these schemes focused on poor, Black areas, where 'the label of "predelinquent" was a prerequisite to benefit from fundamental social services that ought to have been universal', and this initiated contact between many racialised people and law enforcement agencies.[204] This expanded the reach of the carceral state, with a corresponding disinvestment in public services.[205] It created a self-fulfilling prophecy where Black young people had more contact with the police, which made them seem disproportionately criminal and appeared to justify the initial 'predelinquent' label.[206] Crime statistics included arrests, rather than only convictions, such that racist policing created the appearance of racially disproportionate criminality.[207] A hyperreal Black crime problem appeared more real than the racist provisions that constructed this simulation. This in turn led to increased policing of Black areas.[208] Thus, the simulation of Black criminality was a self-referential, intensifying process, as with UK provisions such as s.60.

The Juvenile Justice and Delinquency Prevention Act 1974 fed this hyperreality by increasing punitive measures for those deemed to be youth criminals, which impacted most on Black young people, and redefined many White offenders as 'troublesome' rather than criminal, such that they received non-custodial rehabilitative programmes.[209] This Act also linked signs of poverty, such as living in a family in receipt of benefits, with being 'potentially delinquent', and law enforcement agencies were given powers to monitor young people in poor communities, such that poverty and criminality were seen as synonymous.[210] Again, the simulacra of the undeserving poor was bound up with hypercriminality. This was a driver of increased racial disproportionality

202 James Trafford, *The Empire at Home* (Pluto Press 2021), 100.
203 Elizabeth Hinton, *From the War on Poverty to the War on Crime* (Harvard University Press 2016), 119.
204 Ibid., 122.
205 Ibid., 223.
206 Ibid., 123.
207 Ibid., 224.
208 Ibid., 219–220.
209 Ibid., 221–222.
210 Ibid., 222.

in imprisonment.[211] Thus, the belief that Black hypercriminality was real had material consequences for poor, racialised communities.

In Chapter 2, it was argued that the War on Drugs operated 'to *produce* race itself, giving material form to old ideas about humanity and sub-humanity in this supposedly post-racial era'.[212] Similarly, the simulated 'war on knife crime' is a hyperreal and self-legitimising construction, whereby the racialisation of knife-related violence appears to justify racially disproportionate stop and search in a post-Macpherson, apparently colour-blind criminal legal system. In doing so, it deems working class racialised communities as an unwelcome, threatening presence who are unworthy of inclusion in increasingly gentrified, privatised urban spaces, such that it reproduces colonial discourses around the undeserving poor. In the UK, while funding of youth services has fallen dramatically since 2010, grants to knife crime prevention organisations and campaign groups have risen sharply, such that it is now a multi-million pound industry attracting entrepreneurs.[213] Given that this 'knife crime industry' is dependent upon the continuation of a moral panic around knife crime to legitimise its own existence,[214] it is itself part of the process of simulation, and therefore such organisations have a vested interest in maintaining, and even amplifying, the belief that an epidemic of Black youth knife crime is real.

Knife crime is either portrayed as Black-on-Black violence whereby racialised communities require protection from themselves or as involving White victims and Black perpetrators such that increasingly gentrified White communities require protection from residual uncivilised presences. Discourses around White perpetrators are conspicuous by their absence despite evidence that White young men constitute the majority of those carrying knives.[215] The knife crime discourse and the legal practices that it serves to legitimate can be seen as reproducing race and colonial relations in apparently post-racial times. In this way, the knife crime simulacra perform a contradiction-closing function by giving an apparently rational reason for continuing to stop and search young Black people at a disproportionate rate.

While the knife crime epidemic is a simulacrum, of course knives do cause serious physical harm and death. However, a moral panic bears little or no relation to levels or types of interpersonal violence, and it frames surveillance, harassment, and incarceration of poor racialised communities as the solution to harm. Youth clubs, housing, community services, and education

211 Ibid., 240.
212 Kojo Koram (ed), *The War on Drugs and the Global Colour Line* (Pluto Press 2019), 17 (original italics).
213 Williams and Squires, 253.
214 Ibid., 281.
215 Ibid., 181.

are defunded, while resources are diverted to anti-knife crime organisations that further the framing of hyperreality as reality. As will be argued in the final chapter of this book, the belief in the neoliberal carceral state as the solution to harm is instrinsically linked to the hyperreality of racialised criminalisation, and to overcome this process of simulation we need to respond with community solidarity, socio-economic justice, and mutual aid.

Class, Racism and Hypercriminality

Hyperreal constructions of inherent criminality enable discourses of meritocracy to continue to circulate during periods of working class immiseration. Conceptions of criminality that are centred on ontology not only compound racial disproportionality in the criminal legal system but rely upon and reproduce simulations of criminality whereby the racialised legal subject is abstracted to the point of simulacra. The provisions considered in this chapter intensified these processes of simulation and can be seen as means of social control of poor racialised communities suffering deprivation. The hyperreal simulacra reproduced by these provisions were, and continue to be, deployed by White elites to justify the expansion of the carceral state in a circular and self-referential process.

The term 'chav' was ubiquitous in the early twenty-first century but has fallen out of popular usage in recent years. However, while the chav discourse may seem to have disappeared, this simulacrum has been absorbed into ongoing narratives around class and anti-social behaviour. Therefore, the concept of chavs continues to inform criminal legal processes and practices, while appearing to have been erased from criminal narratives, enabling the media and politicians to continue to use increasingly abstracted undeserving poor discourses without incurring allegations of snobbery. The construction of anti-social behaviour has remained and is used to refer, almost exclusively, to actions by people from poor communities, with increased policing, surveillance, arrests, and evictions framed as solutions. At the time of writing, the forthcoming Crime and Policing Bill proposes the introduction of Respect Orders, which could include mandatory requirements to attend various programmes, with breaches punishable by imprisonment. The title of these orders suggests that the problem is lack of respect for society, again feeding into narratives that poor communities require instruction, control, and civilisation rather than social justice and material equality. The Bill also includes provisions relating to knife crime and public protest.

As described in this chapter, the chav discourse, with its framing of the constructed White working class as anti-social, has obscured processes of racialisation. In David Gillborn's words, 'Although the "degenerate" discourse trades on images of the *White* working class ... the policy impacts will likely hit minoritised groups the hardest'.[216] In a similar way to s.60, the legal provisions discussed above may have been premised as targeting the constructed White working class, but they impact most upon Black communities. As discussed above, when discourses shift from anti-social to criminal, legal subjects are increasingly racialised as Black. In other words, poor White people are viewed as anti-social, racist chavs; poor Black people are framed as criminals and knife carriers. While White criminality is seen as degenerate yet rectifiable, Black criminality is viewed as essential and irredeemable. These discourses around Black criminality are located within colonial narratives around Black lawlessness and savagery that find their contemporary expression in legislation around gangs, violence, weapons, and drill music, as discussed further in the following two chapters. The rise of these simulacra of criminality has occurred during a period when both relative and absolute poverty have increased. The defunding of public services, previously framed as a temporary austerity measure to get the country through a hyperreal economic crash, has become normalised. Wealth continues to be redistributed upwards while millions of children go to sleep cold and hungry every night.

The next two chapters will consider two significant changes to the law made by the CJA that amplified racialised hypercriminalisation – dangerousness and bad character.

216 Gillborn, 'The White Working Class', 22 (original italics).

Chapter 5

Dangerousness

The concept of dangerousness is a process of simulation used to justify the neoliberal carceral state. Discourses around danger and self-defence are key to the operation of the criminal legal system, particularly in relation to surveillance, stop and search, arrests, incarceration, and police violence against racialised people. Constructions of dangerousness take different forms depending on the needs of particular stages of racial capitalism. However, one recurring theme is racialisation. The words and phrases used to describe those considered dangerous have their roots in racial discourses – 'thug' from thugees in colonial India, 'hooligan' from an Irish surname.[1] Such forms of naming 'came to represent actions categorized as "un-English" or "un-British"'.[2]

Dangerousness can be understood as a biopolitical or necropolitical discourse that categorises racialised people as ungrievable. As outlined in Chapter 1, Michel Foucault argued that populations deemed as a threat to the state were vulnerable to being killed or expelled in order to defend the social body.[3] Naming someone as dangerous, and as a threat to society, justifies the use of force against them or their exclusion from society. Individual self-defence by grievable individuals, and collective self-defence on behalf of elite groups or the state, is considered legitimate force against dangerous, ungrievable individuals and populations. Grievability and the right to use self-defence are constructed within colonial discourses, including the civilising mission, such that self-defence of grievable populations can be considered as defence of Whiteness.

The CJA 2003 introduced the concept of dangerousness as a specific category in relation to sentencing, as well as the sentence of indefinite Imprisonment for Public Protection (IPP). This chapter will analyse the two

1 Mike Brogden and Graham Ellison, *Policing in an Age of Austerity: A Postcolonial Perspective* (Routledge 2013), 134.
2 Ibid., 134.
3 Michel Foucault, *Society Must be Defended* (David Macey tr, Penguin Books 1997), 255–258.

DOI: 10.4324/9781003602873-6

main types of dangerousness that this sentence purported to address – violent danger and sexual danger. These categories are constructed through the racial frame and create hyperreal legal subjects. In order to understand these processes, it is necessary to consider first the genealogy of the concept of dangerousness in criminal law.

A Short History of Dangerousness

Discourses around dangerousness have moved from concepts of dangerous populations to dangerous individuals, and back to populations. During all these periods, notions of dangerousness remain situated within processes of simulation and racialisation. Dangerousness has moved from a second order simulacrum in previous periods of racial capitalism to a third order simulacrum under neoliberalism.

Colonial subjects and slaves were named as feral and wild, such that dangerousness was part of the process of racialised simulation that justified their control and enslavement. Laws premised on conceptions of dangerousness have their origins in the nineteenth century in relation to those seen to be a danger to the community due to their habitual offending.[4] Discourses around dangerousness and criminality developed during the Victorian period, as illustrated by the CTA in colonial India and the HCA in Britain discussed in Chapter 2. In India, those determined to be members of 'criminal castes' were viewed as inherently barbaric, such that 'the colonial subject was first and foremost a body, to be known and controlled'.[5] Biopolitical discourses determined that the health of the social body required the exclusion or containment of those groups considered a threat.[6] As Foucault argued, 'once the mechanism of biocriminal was called upon to make it possible to execute or banish criminals, criminality was conceptualised in racist terms'.[7] The criminal was 'not an erring individual but a specimen of a dangerous biological milieu, a separate race'.[8] Those deemed to be criminally insane were likened to 'savage tribes'.[9] Preeti Nijhar writes that 'by attributing racial characteristics to biological differences, criminological science turned

4 John Pratt, *Governing the Dangerous: Dangerousness, Law, and Social Change* (The Federation Press 1997), 9.

5 Nicholas B. Dirks, *Castes of Mind: Colonialism and the Marking of Modern India* (Princeton University Press 2001), 193.

6 Foucault, *Society Must be Defended*, 61–62.

7 Ibid., 258.

8 Colin Gordon, 'Governmental Rationality: An Introduction' in Graham Burchell, Colin Gordon and Peter Miller (eds), *The Foucault Effect* (The University of Chicago Press 1991), 39.

9 Martin J. Wiener, *Reconstructing the Criminal: Culture, Law, and Policy in England, 1830–1914* (Cambridge University Press 1990), 26.

savagery and civilisation into fixed and permanent conditions'[10] such that, 'scientific racism legitimized the notion of dangerousness'.[11] Not only was biological racism a process of simulation, but the very concept of using biology and medicine to categorise individuals was itself a simulation based on Enlightenment discourses that created and imposed ordering and classification, which normalised the concept of different types of human beings with distinct characteristics.

The 'pathologification' of crime that occurred in the nineteenth century[12] used psychiatry to 'seek out pathological stigmata which may mark dangerous individuals: moral insanity, instinctive insanity, and degeneration'.[13] During this period, the focus shifted from punishing the seriousness of the crime to considering the culpability of the individual, with the increased use at trial of medical and psychiatric experts to determine a person's dangerousness,[14] and attention given to future risk.[15] Discourses around protection from risk were intrinsic to modernist views that events could be defined, managed, and controlled scientifically, rather than being acts of God or luck.[16] There was a move from narratives around 'the supposed threat to social order posed by the dangerous classes' during the first part of the nineteenth century to a focus on individual dangerous recidivists by the end of that century.[17] The criminal legal system shifted from punishing defendants solely for the act that they had committed to punishing them for their innate criminality, with the crime being 'no more than the event which signals the existence of a dangerous element ... in the social body'.[18] Biography became central to the notion of the dangerous individual, as 'it establishe[d] the "criminal" as existing before the crime and even outside it'.[19] Such discourses constructed second order simulacra and can be seen as the precursors of the third order simulacra that defined racialised individuals as simultaneously 'pre-criminal', 'criminal', and 'post-criminal', such as the KCPOs considered in the previous chapter. Although conceptions of dangerousness during the nineteenth century were individualised, they remained situated within the categorisation of populations. As discussed in Chapter 2, the HCA focused on individuals

10 Preeti Nijhar, *Law and Imperialism* (Routledge 2009), 74.
11 Ibid., 71.
12 Michel Foucault, 'About the Concept of the "Dangerous Individual" in 19th-Century Legal Psychiatry' (1978) 1 *International Journal of Law and Psychiatry* 1, 6.
13 Ibid., 10.
14 Ibid., 13–14.
15 Ibid., 16.
16 Pratt, *Governing the Dangerous: Dangerousness, Law, and Social Change*, 1.
17 John Pratt, 'Dangerousness and Modern Society' in Mark Brown and John Pratt (eds), *Dangerous Offenders: Punishment and Social Order* (Routledge 2000), 36.
18 Foucault, 'About the Concept of the "Dangerous Individual"', 2.
19 Michel Foucault, *Discipline and Punish – The Birth of the Prison* (Penguin Books 1977), 252.

but was embedded within discourses around the undeserving urban poor. These processes served a performative function to name vulnerable individuals from marginalised communities as inherently inferior and dangerous, and thus ungrievable.

The ways that concepts of dangerousness continued to be constructed within racist discourses are illustrated by twentieth-century risk prediction methods. As Bernard Harcourt explains, 'throughout most of the twentieth century, race was used *explicitly* and *directly* as a predictor of dangerousness'.[20] The Burgess method of prediction, developed in the United States in the late 1920s, used the nationality or race of one's father as a predictor of parole breaches.[21] This was used in decision making by Parole Boards in Illinois from 1933.[22] The use of race as a predictor of parole violation continued until the late 1960s, with California introducing a similar actuarial prediction method in the 1970s.[23]

Neoliberal formations of dangerousness have seen a return to racialised communities being viewed as a threat to civilised society, as discussed in Chapter 3 in relation to s.60. Colonial discourses have been absorbed into neoliberal constructions of danger. These simulated processes have become more abstracted, with conceptions of dangerousness premised on risk management and apparently colour-blind statistical factors, thus rendering invisible their colonial origins. Concepts of risk appear to be neutral but constitute a code based on earlier simulations of race. As such, dangerousness has become a simulation of a simulation and has therefore moved from a second order to a third order simulacrum – dangerousness is hyperreal.

Statistics and algorithms may present as objective, but many of the factors used to assess risk are synonymous with measures of socio-economic disadvantage, such as education, accommodation, employment, and financial status.[24] The effects of racism, such as deprivation, mental health issues, and contact with law enforcement, are used to denote dangerousness. While quantitative research may present as colour-blind, some quantitative research in the field of education has been shown to 'normalize racial inequality' and give 'supposedly "objective" support to Eurocentric and White Supremacist

20 Bernard E. Harcourt, 'Risk as a Proxy for Race' (2015) 27(4) *Federal Sentencing Reporter* 237, 238 (original italics).

21 Ibid., 238.

22 Ibid., 238.

23 Ibid., 239.

24 Jamie Bennett, 'The Social Costs of Dangerousness: Prison and the Dangerous Classes' (Centre for Crime and Justice Studies 2018) 10 <https://www.crimeandjustice.org.uk/publications/social-costs-dangerousness> accessed 21 December 2024; Lisa M. Saccomano, 'Defining the Proper Role of "Offender Characteristics" in Sentencing Decisions: A Critical Race Theory Perspective' (2019) 56(4) *American Criminal Law Review* 1693, 1728–1729.

ideas'.[25] Similarly, in the criminal justice system, statistical methods of prediction can naturalise and perpetuate racial inequalities. This 'data colonialism' operates to 'reconstitute human experiences and attributes as data points and uncritically posit them as objective reflections of reality'.[26] In this way, statistical prediction techniques can be seen as hyperreal: racialised inputs are laundered and reproduced as impartial knowledge such that hypercriminality appears real.

An example of this is the use of previous convictions to denote criminality and dangerousness.[27] The use of antecedents to indicate guilt is discussed in detail in Chapter 6. Algorithms used to inform pre-trial bail decisions in the United States are premised as colour-blind but perpetuate the simulacra of Black criminality by using factors that are themselves grounded in racial disproportionality in the legal system, such as past arrests and pending charges, that 'are more reflections of historic, racial inequalities rather than predictions of a defendant's propensity for future crime'.[28] Predictions of future criminality are constructed within a legal system where racial bias occurs at every stage of the process, from stop and search onwards.[29] This is a self-referential hyperreal process whereby the consequences of living in a racist society are deemed risk factors. In Texas, Duane Buck was initially sentenced to death[30] after a psychologist agreed with counsel when asked in cross-examination: 'The race factor, black, increased the future dangerousness for various complicated reasons, is that correct?'[31] An assessment of future dangerousness was shown to be a consideration in death penalty decisions in both Texas and South Carolina.[32]

25 David Gillborn, Paul Warmington and Sean Demack, 'QuantCrit: Education, Policy, "Big Data" and Principles for a Critical Race Theory of Statistics' (2018) 21(2) *Race Ethnicity and Education* 158, 170.

26 Patricia Ugwudike, 'Algorithms, Policing, and Race' in Chris Cunneen and others (eds), *The Routledge International Handbook on Decolonizing Justice* (Routledge 2023), 152.

27 Harcourt, 239–240.

28 Ngozi Okidegbe, 'The Democratizing Potential of Algorithms?' Cardozo Legal Studies Research Paper No. 655 (2020), 1, 20 <https://papers.ssrn.com/sol3/papers.cfm?abstract_id=3835370> accessed 21 December 2024.

29 Nicole Gonzalez Van Cleve and Lauren Mayes, 'Criminal Justice Through "Colorblind" Lenses: A Call to Examine the Mutual Constitution of Race and Criminal Justice' (2015) 40(2) *Law and Social Inquiry* 406, 410 and 422.

30 The US Supreme Court ruled that the case should be retried following which Duane Buck reached a plea deal with the prosecution and was sentenced to life imprisonment – see Alex Arriaga, 'Texas Death Row Inmate Duane Busk has Sentence Reduced to Life After Supreme Court Orders Retrial' *Texas Tribune* (3 October 2017) <https://www.texastribune.org/2017/10/03/high-profile-death-row-case-comes-end-guilty-plea/> accessed 5 January 2025.

31 Michael R. Cavanaugh, Marilyn McShane and Frank P. Williams III, 'Confronting the Demons of Future Dangerousness' 2014 2(2) *Journal of Law and Criminal Justice* 47, 51.

32 Ibid., 48–50.

Legal practices that name racialised defendants as dangerous are performative, as each one 'reinforces the cultural stereotype of black as dangerous and legitimizes the use of the criminal justice system as a mechanism of racial control on an institutional level'.[33] Conceptions of danger and risk are reproduced within the racial frame while giving the appearance of colour-blindness and neutrality. These simulations simultaneously rely upon and perpetuate previous simulations of threat, criminality, and danger in ever more abstracted forms, such that their colonial origins are absorbed and no longer visible. The second order simulacra of dangerousness in the nineteenth century laid the foundation for the third order simulacra of dangerousness under neoliberalism. Poor, racialised communities are constructed as sites of danger, as illustrated by the s.60 provisions considered in Chapter 3. Danger is defined as hyperreal racialised defendants who need to be disposed of by execution or contained by indefinite state incarceration, rather than as the violence of the carceral state and the precarity of life under racial neoliberalism.

Neoliberal Dangerousness and Indefinite Imprisonment

As Judith Butler argues in the context of the War on Terror and determinations of dangerousness by military tribunals, 'what counts as "dangerous" is what is deemed dangerous by the state, so that, once again, the state posits what is dangerous, and in so positing it, establishes the conditions for its own pre-emption and usurpation of the law'.[34] Naming someone as dangerous frames them as a security risk.[35] This is then used to justify the use of force against them as a means of collective self-defence. As discussed in Chapter 3, such discourses seek to legitimise the use of extraordinary legal provisions. Those deemed dangerous are reduced to beasts who are 'out of control, in need of total restraint'.[36] Being dangerousness means being ungrievable and not entitled to use self-defence, as discussed below in relation to Rodney King.

While dangerousness in general terms has long been relevant to conviction and incarceration,[37] the concept of dangerousness as a specific category in sentencing in the UK was brought to the fore by the CJA. A dangerous offender could be sentenced to a new type of indefinite custodial sentence: Imprisonment for Public Protection (IPP), or be made subject to an extended

33 Van Cleve and Mayes, 422.

34 Judith Butler, *Precarious Life: The Powers of Mourning and Violence* (Verso Books 2004), 76.

35 Ibid., 76–77.

36 Ibid., 78.

37 Estella Baker, 'Dangerousness, Rights and Criminal Justice' (1993) 56(4) *The Modern Law Review* 528, 543.

sentence where the licence period after release was extended. Under the IPP provisions, those who would previously have been sentenced to determinate sentences with a fixed release date were instead imprisoned until the Parole Board deemed them suitable for release, and then released on life licence. As with life sentences, they could apply to the Parole Board for release only after the expiration of their tariff, which was the minimum term that they could serve. The imposition of an IPP sentence acted performatively to draw a binary distinction between the dangerous, ungrievable defendant subjected to indefinite incarceration for 'public protection' and the public who required this protection.

The IPP provisions were so widely used that by December 2006, there were fewer prisoners serving sentences of under a year than there were prisoners serving indeterminate sentences (including both IPP and life sentences).[38] This extensive use differentiated them from previous preventative detention measures, such as those under the Prevention of Crime Act 1908, which were used infrequently.[39] The Legal Aid, Sentencing and Punishment of Offenders Act 2012 abolished the IPP sentence but was not retrospective.[40] As of 31 March 2024, there were 2,796 IPP prisoners – 1,180 who had never been released and 1,616 who had been recalled.[41] Of those who had never been released, 98% had served more than two years over their tariff, 91% had served more than four years above their tariff, and 80% had served more than twice their tariff.[42] One hundred and ninety prisoners with comparatively short tariffs of under two years had been in prison for over 10 years more than their tariff.[43]

Delays in the parole process,[44] as well as the lack of availability of courses that IPP prisoners are required to complete in order to satisfy the Parole Board, have led to many being in limbo and unable to apply for parole for years past their tariff.[45] The British Psychological Society have highlighted that IPP sentences have a particularly detrimental effect on prisoners' mental health due to their indefinite duration, such that 'IPP sentences are in

38 Joe Sim, *Punishment and Prisons: Power and the Carceral State* (SAGE Publications 2009), 113.
39 Arie Freiberg, 'Guerillas in Our Midst?' in in Mark Brown and John Pratt (eds), *Dangerous Offenders: Punishment and Social Order* (Routledge 2000), 56.
40 Legal Aid, Sentencing and Punishment of Offenders Act 2012, s.123.
41 Jacqueline Beard, 'Sentences of Imprisonment for Public Protection' (Briefing Paper No. 6086, House of Commons Library 22 October 2024), 6 <https://researchbriefings.files.parliament.uk/documents/SN06086/SN06086.pdf> accessed 21 December 2024.
42 Ibid., 17.
43 Ibid., 17.
44 House of Commons Justice Committee, *IPP Sentences, Third Report of Session 2022–23* (22 September 2022), 31, para 84. <https://publications.parliament.uk/pa/cm5803/cmselect/cmjust/266/report.html> accessed 16 February 2025.
45 Ibid., 24–26, paras 66–71.

themselves psychologically harmful'.[46] IPP prisoners have a higher rate of self-harm and suicide than those serving other types of custodial sentence.[47] This is particularly pronounced in relation to female IPP prisoners, whose self-harm rate is more than double that of other female prisoners.[48]

The level of prisoners recalled may suggest that those prisoners were in fact dangerous. However, between 2010 and 2021 the reasons for recall were due to the commission of a further offence in only 24% of recalls, with other reasons including non-compliance with licence conditions (39%), failure to reside at the specified address (14%), drugs and alcohol use (9%), and failure to keep in touch (6%).[49] The precarity of life following release is likely to have been a factor in many recalls. Many of those recalled felt that their licence conditions were unduly onerous and that they were given insufficient support,[50] with one prisoner commenting that, 'More effort goes into catching you than helping you out'.[51] Additionally, if those prisoners had received a definite term rather than an IPP sentence, their licence period would have been shorter so far fewer of them would have been recalled to prison.

Chapter 2 included a discussion of how neoliberal discourses of risk management reproduce hypercriminality for the racialised poor through post-release supervision and surveillance. The life licence requirements of IPP sentences ensured that even those released could not escape the threat of further incarceration. Their punishment for being an IPP recipient was enduring. As with the provisions considered in Chapter 4, their status as a hyperreal legal subject defined their treatment in the criminal legal system. The sign of the dangerous hypercriminal prevailed. Although an IPP recipient could apply to the Parole Board to have the life licence revoked ten years after their first release, there was no guarantee that the Parole Board would decide to do this. However, this was amended by the Victims and Prisoners Act 2024, s.66. From 1st November 2024, termination of the licence became automatic if the applicant had been released over five years ago and had not been recalled in the previous two years. Additionally, from 1st February 2025, the period to make an application for termination of the licence was reduced from ten years to three years after release. Rather than revoking all IPP licences, this provision assisted the 'reformed' IPP recipient while failing

46 The British Psychological Society, *BPS Briefing: Imprisonment for Public Protection (IPP) Sentences* (2024) <https://cms.bps.org.uk/sites/default/files/2024-11/BPS%20Briefing%20-%20Imprisonment%20for%20Public%20Protection%20Sentences.pdf> accessed 16 February 2025.

47 House of Commons Justice Committee, *IPP Sentences*, 17–19, paras 40–48.

48 Ibid., 18, para 44.

49 Ibid., 38, para 106.

50 Ibid., 35–36, paras 95–97.

51 Ibid., 36, para 97.

to help many vulnerable individuals who remained subject to the revolving door of custody recall and insecure release.

The Sentencing Act 2020 replaced the dangerous provisions in the CJA with comparable provisions in relation to extended sentences, so the concept of dangerousness persists in criminal legislation.[52] In assessing dangerousness, the sentencing judge can take into account not only information about the offence itself[53] but also previous convictions,[54] any pattern of behaviour in relation to the previous convictions,[55] and any other information about the defendant.[56] This may include previous conduct that has not been proved at a criminal trial, such as alleged acts that previously led to an ASBO being imposed, as in the case of *Hillman* where the Court of Appeal described such incidents as 'hard information'.[57] This indicated a move away from tested evidence, giving judges substantial discretion in determining dangerousness. As discussed in Chapter 3, provisions that allow greater discretion increase the impact of processes of racialised simulation. Where the rules of evidence are vague or undefined, simulacra of criminality predominate.

In a similar way to the ASBOs, CBOs, and KCPOs considered in the previous chapter, the dangerousness provisions required the court to take a view relating to both past and future behaviour, such that the legal subject was being punished for what they *might* do. The concept of dangerousness discounted the situational aspect of offending, decontextualised the background, and conceptualised the perceived character traits behind particular actions as pathological and immutable. Abstractions of criminality took precedence and the individual was disappeared. In this way, once named as dangerous, the defendant became a hypercriminal, where what they had done was less relevant than what they were seen to signify.

Dangerousness provisions were passed in other jurisdictions, including the United States, Australia, New Zealand, and Canada, mainly in the early 1990s and sharing the criteria that those deemed dangerous had committed crimes defined as violent or sexual, and were likely to commit similar offences in the future.[58] These provisions were premised on discourses around focusing limited public spending on incarcerating those considered statistically most likely to reoffend, and therefore intrinsically linked with neoliberalism's increased managerialism and cost saving through risk management and

52 Sentencing Act 2020, ss.306–308.
53 Ibid., s.308(2)(a).
54 Ibid., s.308(2)(b).
55 Ibid., s.308(2)(c).
56 Ibid., s.308(2)(d).
57 [2006] EWCA Crim 690. Note that this case pre-dates the Sentencing Act 2020 and therefore relates to the equivalent provisions in the CJA.
58 John Pratt, 'Governing the Dangerous: An Historical Overview of Dangerous Offender Legislation' (1996) 5(1) *Social and Legal Studies* 21, 21.

rationalisation of resources.[59] However, they may be seen more accurately as what David Garland describes as 'value rational' which, rather than being cost effective, may incur increased public expenditure in order to convey a message, even where that does not reduce crime effectively and therefore does not fit with the economic rationalist project.[60] As discussed in Chapter 2, although the neoliberal project is premised on the basis of economic rationality, the increase in punitivity, even where this incurs cost to the state, should be seen as an intrinsic part of neoliberalism, rather than a deviation from it.

The concept of dangerousness serves to maintain the simulation that it is the racialised poor and not the state that constitutes the threat to the wider population. In order to dispose of surplus populations and advance the neoliberal project, constructions of danger operate to uphold the belief that racially disproportionate criminality is a reality. Not only do conceptions of risk name the racialised poor as a risk to (White) society, but they obliterate recognition that poor communities experience ungrievable lives subsumed in risk. As Nils Christie argues, the real issue is not one of dangerous citizens but of 'dangerous states ... where mass incarceration is based on triviality, seven bottles of milk, two grams of some sort of drugs'.[61] In 1996, more Californian defendants were given 'three strikes' imprisonment for possession of cannabis than for murder, rape, and kidnapping combined.[62] Risk management constitutes a hyperreal code that absorbs previous Enlightenment and colonial constructions while appearing neutral and post-racial. Ungrievable populations are 'erased from view' in indefinite detention or subjected to such insecurity that they lack access to the basic requirements of life.[63] In this way, they are subjected to necropolitical discipline. The harm and preventable deaths caused by the state, corporations, and material inequalities are not considered as danger.[64]

I will now discuss two specific forms of dangerousness – violent danger and sexual danger. As the main categories in the original dangerousness provisions in the CJA, they are worthy of particular analysis. Situated within racial framing and civilising mission discourses, these two categories of dangerousness construct hyperreal racialised legal subjects.

59 Ibid., 32–33.

60 David Garland, *The Culture of Control* (Oxford University Press 2001), 191.

61 Nils Christie, 'Dangerous States' in Mark Brown and John Pratt (eds), *Dangerous Offenders: Punishment and Social Order* (Routledge 2000), 190.

62 Paul Butler, '(Color)Blind Faith: The Tragedy of "Race, Crime, and The Law"' (1998) 111 *Harvard Law Review* 1270, 1275.

63 Judith Butler, *The Force of Non-Violence* (Verso Books 2020), 24.

64 Victoria Canning and Steve Tombs, *From Social Harm to Zemiology: A Critical Introduction* (Routledge 2021), 27, 39–40 and 68–71.

Violent Danger

Judith Butler cites Frantz Fanon's description of how a White girl pointed and exclaimed, 'I'm frightened!' upon seeing him, a Black man.[65] This pointing of the observer can be seen as 'the schematic foreshadowing of an accusation, one which carries the performative force to constitute the danger which it fears and defends against'.[66] Although this act names Fanon as dangerous, 'the black body is circumscribed as dangerous, prior to any gesture'.[67] Those deemed dangerous are vulnerable to being subjected to force in order to contain this perceived threat. Thus, the naming of racialised subjects as 'a risk' not only reproduces their criminalisation but simultaneously makes them 'at risk' from potentially lethal violence by the state.[68] Such narratives have absorbed colonial discourses that equate Blackness with violent danger.[69]

This framing of Black bodies as dangerous allowed the defence lawyers for the police officers on trial for assaulting Rodney King to state that he was 'endangering' the police.[70] Yet these words were not just oral submissions made to the jury in a case where the only available evidence was the testimony of the parties. This was commentary to the playing of a video that showed an unarmed man lying on the ground being beaten with batons by police officers.[71] Butler argues that the acquittal of these officers was 'not the consequence of ignoring the video, but, rather, of reproducing the video within a racially saturated field of visibility'.[72] The effect of this racial framing was so strong that the jury 'saw' a dangerous Black man; a threat who justified the use of self-defence by the officers rather than a citizen being brutally assaulted by the police.[73] This 'seeing' or 'reading' of the video could only take place against a background where Whiteness was equated with vulnerability and the need to be kept safe, whereas the Black male was 'the site and source of danger, a threat'.[74] This precluded the police officers' violence from being seen as violence – it was read as defence of Whiteness.[75]

65 Judith Butler, 'Endangered/Endangering: Schematic Racism and White Paranoia' in Robert Gooding-Williams (ed), *Reading Rodney King / Reading Urban Uprising* (Routledge 1993), 18.
66 Ibid., 18.
67 Ibid., 18.
68 Mary Beth Oliver, 'African American Men as "Criminal and Dangerous": Implications of Media Portrayals of Crime on the "Criminalization" of African American Men' (2003) 7(2) *Journal of African American Studies* 3, 3.
69 Van Cleve and Mayes, 419–420.
70 Butler, 'Endangered/Endangering', 15.
71 Ibid., 15.
72 Ibid., 15.
73 Ibid., 16.
74 Ibid., 18.
75 Ibid., 18.

The evidence was constructed through a process of simulation that relied upon and reproduced previous simulacra of racialised danger.

In this way, violence by the state against Black people is considered self-defence: 'They are in a war against black people in which they constantly imagine that those upon whom they inflict violence are the true source of violence'.[76] Butler refers to this phenomenon as 'racial phantasmagoria', whereby Black bodies are 'cast phantasmagorically, as states of imminent danger: as if those bodies are about to spring to kill, to inflict mortal danger on the police who are, in fact, inflicting mortal danger'.[77] This narrative is reproduced every time a court acquits a White police officer of assaulting a Black person on the basis of self-defence.[78] Each such acquittal is performative – it reinforces the notion that White people need to be protected from Black violence and amplifies fear of the hyperreal aggressive Black person.

In the UK, racialised people are disproportionately likely to die in police custody, particularly where restraint is used.[79] An independent review into deaths and serious incidents in police custody commissioned by the government commented that Black men were frequently stereotyped as 'dangerous, violent and volatile'[80] and Black men with mental health issues were 'effectively dehumanised' with symptoms of mental illness and vulnerability interpreted as violence and aggression.[81] Overall, there was evidence that restraint and excessive force were more likely to be used on Black people.[82] Through racialised conceptions of danger, 'some lives are figured as pure violence or as an imminent threat of violence, whereas others are regarded as entitled to self-defence and to the preservation of their lives'.[83] The third order simulacrum of the dangerous Black male requiring restraint can be viewed as an abstracted form of the colonial discourses that equated Black slaves with animalistic physicality rather than intellect, and with savagery rather than rationality. Under neoliberalism, these discourses are reworked as risk management, as discussed above, and operate to racially differentiate populations into those who are at risk and those who constitute the risk. Butler argues that:

76 Judith Butler and Brandon M. Terry, 'The Radical Equality of Lives' *Boston Review* (7 January 2020) <http://bostonreview.net/philosophy-religion/brandon-m-terry-judith-butler-radical-equality-lives> accessed 21 December 2024.

77 Ibid.

78 Ibid.

79 Nadine El-Enany, 'From Love to Justice: Families' Interrogation of Racial State Violence' (2022) 32 *Social and Legal Studies* 1, 5; INQUEST, 'BAME Deaths in Police Custody' (2023) <www.inquest.org.uk/bame-deaths-in-police-custody> accessed 21 December 2024.

80 Elish Angiolini, *Report of the Independent Review of Deaths and Serious Incidents in Police Custody* (HM Government 2017), 87.

81 Ibid., 88.

82 Ibid., 33.

83 Butler, *The Force of Non-Violence*, 143.

> those whose lives are not considered to matter, whose lives are perceived as a threat to the life that embodies white privilege can be destroyed in the name of that life. That can only happen when a recurrent and institutionalized form of racism has become a way of seeing, entering into the presentation of visual evidence to justify hateful and unjustified and heartbreaking murder.[84]

As argued in Chapters 1 and 3, being entitled to use self-defence means being deemed grievable rather than disposable. The denial of the right to self-defence for Black people has its genealogy in slavery, with the Virginia Slave Codes 1705 prescribing whipping as a punishment for any Black person using physical force against a White person.[85] The notion of entitlement to self-defence is both individual and collective. It is present in wider issues of racist policy, such that war rhetoric is used not only to justify killing in wars but also used against refugees, who are perceived as a danger to national security.[86] When viewed through the lens of biopolitics, 'the self' is defined not only as the individual but also as the nationality, race, or class under threat from those categorised as outsiders.[87] This racial framing of collective self-defence impacts on issues of individual self-defence in court, such that those with lives deemed to be worth defending, those who have the privilege of entitlement to self-defence against a perceived threat, are more likely to be believed when they claim to be acting in self-defence.[88]

While the simulacrum of the dangerous Black body is frequently associated with males, this hyperreality also results in police violence against Black women who are 'often figured as aggressive, dangerous, out of control or drugs mules'.[89] This can be illustrated by the *Roberts* case discussed in Chapter 3, where such a framing was intensified by the s.60 order. In 1985, during police searches of their respective homes in London in connection with male relatives, Cynthia Jarrett died, and Cherry Groce was shot causing permanent paralysis from the waist down.[90] Neither woman was a suspect but that did not stop them from being subjected to police violence.[91] Joy Gardner was killed in 1993 when an immigration officer and five male Metropolitan

84 George Yancy and Judith Butler, 'What's Wrong With "All Lives Matter"?' *The New York Times* (12 January 2015) <https://opinionator.blogs.nytimes.com/2015/01/12/whats-wrong-with-all-lives-matter/> accessed 21 December 2024.

85 Theodore W. Allen, *The Invention of the White Race* (Verso Books 2021), Volume 2, 250.

86 Butler, *The Force of Non-Violence*, 62.

87 Ibid., 12 and 62–63.

88 Ibid., 12.

89 Ibid., 120.

90 Adam Elliott-Cooper, *Black Resistance to British Policing* (Manchester University Press 2021), 44–45.

91 Ibid., 44–45.

Police officers attended her address to deport her.[92] She was restrained with a leather body belt and attached handcuffs, and gagged with 13 feet of adhesive tape around her head, such that she was unable to breathe and later died of brain damage.[93] The police narratives around her death described her as 'mentally deranged' and 'very, very strong',[94] as well as using her immigration status to attempt to discredit her and deem her ungrievable.[95] As Simon Pemberton argues, these claims were 'likely to be accepted as "truths" because they [were] interpreted through the popular and official discourses of race, which associate "blackness" with violence, disorder and criminality'.[96] Again, the abstraction of racialised dangerous criminality appeared real, such that distinctions between truth and falsity were collapsed.

As in the Rodney King case, even a viewpoint that appears to be neutral, such as CCTV or police body-worn cameras, occurs through the racial frame where the racialised person appears as a simulacrum of danger. Such footage cannot capture the totality of encounters between the police and racialised communities. It lacks the historical context of such encounters and constructs racialised bodies not in terms of what they do but as abstracted signs. As Amanda Glasbeek, Mariful Alam, and Katrin Roots argue, while the recordings may show 'an *absence* of racism, whether through the non-utterance of offensive language or through the privileging of temporally limited encounters over longer histories of state violence against racialized communities' they cannot show 'the historical and deeply racialized nature of the relationship between the surveillance state and its subject populations'.[97] The seemingly objective footage is decontextualised. It cannot show the colonial origins of policing, nor can it show the number of prior occasions the person has been stopped and searched. The actions of the parties are viewed through a process of simulation, with the police constituted as post-racial, and the racialised subject constructed as the threat. In this way, the suspect appears not as a person but as a third order simulacrum of criminality – a violent Black body reduced to an abstraction of danger.

Additionally, body-worn cameras can be seen as a form of 'point of view' imagery (POV) – a device used in gaming, films, and television that allows the

92 Simon Pemberton, 'Demystifying Deaths in Police Custody' (2008) 17(2) *Social and Legal Studies* 237, 249.
93 Ibid., 249.
94 Ibid., 249.
95 Ibid., 251.
96 Ibid., 256.
97 Amanda Glasbeek, Mariful Alam and Katrin Roots, 'Seeing and Not-Seeing: Race and Body-Worn Cameras in Canada' (2020) 18(3) *Surveillance and Society* 328, 339 (original italics) <https://ojs.library.queensu.ca/index.php/surveillance-and-society/article/view/13259> accessed 21 December 2024.

viewer to identify with that character and see the world through their eyes.[98] As Carolyn McKay and Murray Lee argue, in body-worn footage:

> it is a police officer's singular perspective, evidenced by the camera's POV, that is captured; the officer is rendered absent, bar perhaps moving limbs. This absence is filled by the viewer of the footage – and like in any modern video game, the viewer becomes the officer avatar or character.[99]

In this way, the medium of POV technology enters into the content through the way that it frames 'reality', and it is viewed through the subjective perspective of the police officer. To quote Marshall McLuhan's well-known phrase, 'the medium is the message'.[100]

Baudrillard argued that McLuhan's theory 'pushed to its limit' resulted in the conclusion that:

> there is not only an implosion of the message in the medium, there is, in the same movement, the implosion of the medium itself in the real, the implosion *of the medium and of the real* in a sort of hyperreal nebula, in which even the definition and distinct action of the medium can no longer be determined.[101]

McLuhan's view of technology as 'extensions of man' had become 'expulsions of man'.[102] With POV technology, the medium goes further than merely privileging the experiences of the police officers – the technology 'becomes an art of disappearance',[103] such that the police officer disappears, and their view no longer seems to be their view. It appears as neutral and objective. For the police officer, the eyes of the camera 'relieve him of his

98 Carolyn McKay and Murray Lee 'Body-worn Images: Point-of-view and the New Aesthetics of Policing' (2020) 16(3) *Crime, Media, Culture* 431, 437–440.
99 Ibid., 440.
100 Marshall McLuhan, *Understanding Media: The Extensions of Man* (McGraw Hill 1964). Baudrillard was influenced by this concept – see Jean Baudrillard, *Simulacra and Simulation* (Sheila Faria Glaser tr, University of Michigan Press 1994), 30, 81; Jean Baudrillard, *Symbolic Exchange and Death* (Iain Hamilton Grant tr, SAGE Publications 2017), 85; Jean Baudrillard, *Screened Out* (Chris Turner tr, Verso Books 2014), 205. However, he criticised McLuhan's formulation as overly optimistic regarding the role of technology – see Jean Baudrillard, *The Transparency of Evil: Essays on Extreme Phenomena* (James Benedict tr, Verso Books 1993), 33; Jean Baudrillard, 'Review of Marshall McLuhan's "Understanding Media"' in Gary Genosko (ed), *The Uncollected Baudrillard* (Mike Gane tr, SAGE Publications 2001), 39–44.
101 Baudrillard, *Simulacra and Simulation*, 82 (original italics).
102 Jean Baudrillard, *The Perfect Crime* (Chris Turner tr, Verso Books 2008), 37.
103 Ibid., 41.

own production'.[104] POV technology appears independent and author-less but rather than viewing it subjectively with their own interpretation, the jury are looking through the police officer's eyes, yet it appears to be an independent viewpoint. This simulacrum of what happened through the now invisible eyes of the officer means that 'the medium itself is no longer identifiable as such ... there is no longer a medium .... It is now intangible, diffused, and diffracted in the real'.[105] The image is hyperreal such that the footage and the officer's viewpoint cannot be separated but are fused into one simulation, thus collapsing the distinction between the objective and the subjective. What Baudrillard described as the 'perfect crime', the obliteration of subjectivity, has been achieved through the vanishing of the officer.[106] This mutation of human and technology can be described as 'no more fiction or reality, it is hyperreality that abolishes both'.[107] The viewpoint of the police officer and the history of colonial policing are rendered invisible yet amplified, such that the recording appears objective while being seen through the White supremacist gaze of the carceral state. Such technologies serve to give legitimacy to the simulation of a post-racial, colour-blind criminal legal system.

These hyperreal processes silence the voice of the racialised suspect in epistemic terms. The officer's perspective is deemed neutral through the disappearance of its subjectivity. The suspect is constructed as the subaltern and positioned as the third party; the one spoken about rather than the one speaking. The experiences of both the racialised individual and their community vis-à-vis law enforcement are absent from the footage. Michelle Brown writes that in such cases:

> the murderous carceral state is grounded in spectral qualities of white, antiblack visuality. The ghost, then, is not the oft-cited specter of Black criminality but the ghosts and phantoms produced by white optics and a visuality rooted in colonialism and conquest.[108]

The hyperreal image of the racialised criminal is constructed as reality. It is dislocated from contemporary police racism, and from the colonial imprints that underpin this, through a process of hyperreal abstraction. It is not a matter of simulated criminality overcoming the evidence in a case but of the evidence being constructed through processes of simulation embedded in colonial White supremacist discourses.

104 Ibid., 43.
105 Baudrillard, *Simulacra and Simulation*, 30.
106 Baudrillard, *The Perfect Crime*, 101.
107 Baudrillard, *Simulacra and Simulation*, 111.
108 Michelle Brown, 'The Specter of White Supremacy' in Michael Fidler, Theo Kindynis and Travis Linnemann (eds), *Ghost Criminology* (New York University Press 2022), 97.

This construction of hypercriminality can be seen in the jury's decision that the police officers were not guilty of assaulting Rodney King. The simulacrum of him as a dangerous Black man rather than as a victim was constructed as reality, such that factual accuracy becomes irrelevant through the hyperreal corporal threat of the Black man. The King case is sometimes compared with the O.J. Simpson trial, with arguments that the 'juries ignored visual and "scientific" evidence to acquit the accused, and in both cases the juries operated along racial lines'.[109] However, as Douglas Kellner points out, the verdict in the Rodney King case was 'a validation of the existing form of hegemonic power, while the O.J. Simpson verdict represented a challenge to it'.[110] Furthermore, while there were issues regarding police contamination of evidence in the Simpson case that could justify a not guilty verdict on the basis of reasonable doubt,[111] the footage in the King case showed him being beaten by the police, and therefore they were not directly comparable.[112]

The framing of the Simpson acquittal as an example of jury nullification[113] demonstrates the way that White supremacist discourses negate the concept of Black innocence and make the verdict intelligible only as an act of bias and irrationality, such that 'false claims were used to perpetuate racial stereotypes about a largely African-American jury'.[114] The view that the acquittal of a Black man by a predominantly Black jury must be illegitimate is a reflection of two intersecting processes of simulation operating within the racial frame. Firstly, the implication that the jury made the wrong decision is located within the colonial gaze of those who argue that counternarratives are emotional responses that lack the rigour of objective knowledge, as discussed in Chapter 1. Such a position frames White supremacist viewpoints and outcomes as logical and neutral, and therefore as legitimate knowledge, and silences the counternarratives of racialised communities by naming them as lacking credibility. Such counternarratives could include knowledge about police behaviour that challenges the view that evidence is always collected accurately or that the police never put pressure on a suspect, for example. The lived experiences of racialised jurors may give them this knowledge about police practices and the effect of these practices on the reliability of evidence.

Secondly, media narratives around jury nullification are rooted in the belief that 'normal' (racially disproportionate) jury verdicts of guilt are

109 Douglas Kellner, *Media Spectacle* (Routledge 2003), 107.

110 Ibid., 108.

111 Nancy S. Marder, 'The Interplay of Race and False Claims of Jury Nullification' (1999) 32 *University of Michigan Journal of Law Reform* 285, 290–293.

112 Kellner, 124.

113 Jury nullification can be defined as when a jury chooses to acquit a defendant even though they are legally guilty.

114 Marder, 286.

accurate and that acquittals of racialised defendants are abnormal and suspicious. Contemporary media reinforces the stereotype of Black men as dangerous and violent through the way that crime is reported, both in relation to the overrepresentation of Black people as perpetrators and White people as victims, and the construction of the narrative about the incident.[115] For dehumanised racialised defendants, rather than benefitting from the statutory presumption of innocence, 'a presumption of dangerousness looms large in judgments about Black defendants, and especially those with darker skin tones and greater Afrocentric features'.[116] Trial verdicts cannot be separated from racialised narratives around what it means to be a criminal. This results in hypercriminals being convicted due to signifiers of criminality rather than as a result of their actions. The abstraction of racialised dangerous criminality appears real, such that distinctions between truth and falsity are no longer meaningful.

As described in Chapter 2, violent crime has been racialised to the extent that discourses can appear to be colour-blind while invoking images that serve as a code for race.[117] In the UK, public unrest in 1981[118] and 1985[119] was characterised as being predominantly perpetrated by Black people despite the involvement of significant numbers of White youths. The simulacra of the inner cities as locations of violence, as illustrated by the use of s.60 orders discussed in Chapter 3, were the dominant narrative. This cannot be divorced from the simulacra of Black muggers discussed in Chapter 2 or the gangs discourse considered in Chapter 6. In all of these cases, areas of deprivation are deemed to be sites of violence perpetrated by racialised populations. Paul Gilroy notes the change in the term 'race riots' over time – initially it was used to describe riots by racists against racialised groups, but the discourse shifted, and it became used to denote public disorder perceived to be carried out by Black people.[120] Despite Home Office statistics showing that over two thirds of those arrested in connection with the 1981 unrest were White, the incidents were racialised as Black.[121]

In relation to the 2011 uprising, Sarah Lamble describes how a media photograph of a male in a hoodie and a scarf with 'the aura of stigmatised blackness' was used to symbolise rioters, and was juxtaposed with images

115 Mark W. Bennett and Victoria C. Plaut, 'Looking Criminal and the Presumption of Dangerousness: Afrocentric Facial Features, Skin Tone and Criminal Justice' (2018) 51(3) *UC Davis Law Review* 745, 768–769; Oliver 5–11 and 15–16.

116 Bennett and Plaut, 803.

117 Michael Rowe, *The Racialisation of Disorder in Twentieth Century Britain* (Ashgate Publishing Limited 1998), 157.

118 Paul Gordon, *White Law* (Pluto Press 1983), 105.

119 Rowe, 135–159.

120 Paul Gilroy, *There Ain't No Black in the Union Jack* (Routledge 1987), 26 and 122.

121 Ibid., 178.

of a White woman clearing up after the unrest.[122] Government and media discourses acted as performative simulations to reproduce the image of a rioter as a young Black male. Ingrid Hoofd argues that media narratives of the 2011 uprising constructed '"unruly" phantom collectives', such that 'the destruction endemic to capitalism' was 'projected onto "risky" populations in need of further technologically enhanced containment'.[123] As demonstrated by the discourses around public disorder, the concept of dangerousness operates performatively to name whole racialised communities, rather than just individuals, as violent and out of control.

Whereas the events described above were portrayed as mindless savagery and associated with the hyperreal construction of rioters of Afro-Caribbean descent, disorder blamed on Asian males relied upon a distinct narrative that focused specifically on young Muslim men.[124] The unrest in Bradford in 1995 was presented as 'youth alienation and a racialized cultural incompatibility ... made more overtly threatening with the overarching spectre of religious fundamentalism'.[125] Similarly, the media narrative around the 2001 disorder in deindustrialised Northern English towns presented a picture of Muslim separatism and a failure to assimilate into the 'British' way of life.[126] Claire Alexander explains how discourses around racism were silenced, both in relation to material inequalities and the activities of the far-right in the area.[127] The hyperreality of the violent Muslim extremist rendered invisible the policy shift from 'multiculturalism to a home-grown cultural re-colonization'.[128] These simulations framed Muslim communities as uncivilised and hostile to Britain, such that they constituted a violent threat necessitating the use of state force as collective self-defence. As argued in Chapter 3, Muslims in Britain have been constructed as a 'suspect community'.[129] These narratives later fed into the moral panic over 'grooming gangs' described in the next section of this chapter.

In a 1983 interview, Foucault argued that whereas the dangerous criminal had previously been seen as an individual psychopath who committed unusually brutal forms of homicide, there had been a move to considering

122 Sarah Lamble, 'The Quiet Dangers of Civilized Rage: Surveying the Punitive Aftermath of England's 2011 Riots' (2013) 112(3) *Atlantic Quarterly* 577, 577.
123 Ingrid M. Hoofd, 'The London Riots and the Simulation of Sociality in Social Media Data Research' (2014) 7 *Journal of Critical Globalisation Studies* 122, 126.
124 Claire Alexander, *The Asian Gang* (Berg 2000), 4.
125 Ibid., 10.
126 Charlotte Chadderton, *Judith Butler, Race and Education* (Palgrave Macmillan 2018), 169.
127 Claire Alexander, 'Imagining the Asian Gang: Ethnicity, Masculinity and Youth After "The Riots"' (2004) 24(4) *Critical Social Policy* 526, 543.
128 Ibid., 544.
129 Christina Pantazis and Simon Pemberton, 'Restating the Case for the "Suspect Community"' (2011) 51 *British Journal of Criminology* 1054.

whole racialised communities as dangerous and as breeding grounds for criminality.[130] Under neoliberalism, the focus has shifted from the dangerous individual to the individual from a dangerous population; the criminal from a racialised community whose interests are not those of (White) society. Entire racialised communities are essentialised and framed as dangerous such that the area in which they live is sufficient to deem them as criminal, as illustrated by the s.60 provisions analysed in Chapter 3, the children and young people deemed 'at risk' of becoming involved in knife crime discussed in Chapter 4, the discourses about public disorder considered above, and the Gangs Matrix covered in Chapter 6. This happens in increasingly abstracted ways, such that racialised communities become third order simulacra – violent, ungrievable hypercriminals. This relies upon and reproduces the racial frame constructed through historical colonial discourses and repackaged as risk management under neoliberalism, where risk and danger are viewed as being located within the bodies of racialised populations. The differentially racialised discourses that portray men of African descent as pathologically violent, and Muslim men as sources of violent danger due to cultural factors, are mirrored in the racialisation of sexual danger, as discussed below.

Sexual Danger

In this section, it will be argued that conceptions of sexual danger are historically specific and differentially racialised, such that Black men of African descent are viewed differently to Muslim men.[131] However, both are linked to concerns about White purity, and both position the racialised male as corporal, oversexualised, and uncivilised. The simulacra of the Black rapist and the Muslim paedophile not only disappear the colonial and imperial discourses that underpin these processes of simulation, but they revitalise civilising mission narratives. Moreover, they render invisible the sexual violence of the carceral state.

Sexual danger has been conceptualised as existing within the bodies of historically contingent folk devils. In the mid-twentieth century, gay men were viewed as dangerous and a threat to family life, with homosexuality categorised as a form of deviance.[132] Recently, the religious Right and trans-exclusionary radical feminists have promoted a transphobic narrative that trans women pose a danger to cis women, and called for trans women to be excluded from women-only spaces, such as toilets, shelters, and prisons, a

130 Michel Foucault, Jonathan Simon and Stuart Elden, 'Danger, Crime and Rights: A Conversation Between Michel Foucault and Jonathan Simon' (2017) 34(1) *Theory, Culture and Society* 3, 17.

131 Gargi Bhattacharyya, *Dangerous Brown Men* (Zed Books 2008), 98 and 104.

132 Pratt, 'Governing the Dangerous: An Historical Overview of Dangerous Offender Legislation', 26.

view ratified by the Supreme Court in 2025. Yet, trans women are far more likely to be victims than perpetrators of sexual violence in prison.[133] Those who do not conform to patriarchal heteronormative conventions are portrayed as sources of sexual danger rather than vulnerable to danger.

The family continues to be seen as the haven against predators, despite much sexual abuse taking place within the domestic setting and only a small percentage being committed by complete strangers.[134] Loïc Wacquant argues that in the context of neoliberalism, this discourse of the family as a safe haven against the sexually deviant stranger is a means of bolstering the hegemonic role of the family when it is undermined materially through job insecurity and the pressure of increased working hours.[135] In this way, the construction of the paedophile as a stranger outside the home 'serves to symbolically purify the family and reassert its established role as a haven against insecurity even as accelerated neoliberal trends in the culture and the economy undermine it'.[136] The simulacrum of the dangerous predator or pervert operates to erase the location of most sexual danger.

Further, as David Garland writes, the obsession with child sexual abuse in media and political discourses frames this as the primary social harm to children, and thus acts as a distraction from the immense harm caused by child poverty.[137] The trauma suffered by children through family separation resulting from border controls and parental incarceration is also absent from these debates. Risk and danger are constructed as immediate bodily harm rather than wider societal harm, thus silencing discourses around the impact that socio-economic disadvantage, environmental harm, racist practices, and the defunding of healthcare, education, and social services have on children. Neoliberal constructions of sexual danger individualise harm, and, it will be argued below, this operates to legitimise and strengthen carceral solutions as a means of racialised, patriarchal social control.

Not only is sexual danger positioned as outside the family, but it is also constructed as being outside civilised Whiteness. Images of Black people, and young Black males in particular, as savage and dangerous have their roots in slavery and colonialism.[138] Enlightenment civilisation discourses named the European White as rational and the Black Other as an uncivilised

133 Vic Parsons, 'Ministry of Justice Dispels Bigoted Myths Around Trans Prisoners and Sexual Assault with Cold, Hard and Indisputable Facts' *Pink News* (21 May 2020) <https://www.thepinknews.com/2020/05/21/trans-prisoners-victims-sexual-assault-more-than-perpetrators-ministry-of-justice-liz-truss/> accessed 29 December 2024.

134 Loïc Wacquant, *Punishing the Poor* (Duke University Press 2009), 235.

135 Ibid., 235.

136 Ibid., 235.

137 Garland, 136.

138 Bennett and Plaut, 760.

'hyperphysicalised black body'.[139] Anthropologists from that period described colonised people as having excessively large sexual organs.[140] Frantz Fanon describes how White Europeans reduced Black men to 'a beast' with 'sexual potency'.[141] White slaveowners and colonialists were able to justify their use of violence, including sexual violence, by presenting slaves and native populations as oversexed and in need of control.[142] Such a narrative was perpetuated in early twentieth-century literature, which portrayed Black males as sexually aggressive and animalistic, and a threat to the chastity and purity of White women.[143] The 1915 film, *The Birth of a Nation*, described as the United States' first 'blockbuster',[144] was 'the first film to dwell (not once but twice) on the theme of the rape of white women by black men' and 'presented the Ku Klux Klan as the "heroic" rescuers of whites threatened by "black terror"'.[145] As argued below, these second order simulacra that reduced Black people to sexual aggression were used to justify both the lynching of Black men and the rape of Black women in order to maintain White supremacy.[146]

While deploying discourses around protecting White women, lynching was a means of protecting White privilege in the postbellum era, by preventing Black people from collectively resisting their continued oppression and from achieving material equality.[147] The simulacrum of the 'Black rapist' attacking White women was constructed to legitimise lynching.[148] White men could claim to be acting to safeguard 'their' women, even though only a minority of lynch victims were accused of sexual offences.[149] C.L.R. James argued that lynching was 'rooted in the economic system' and 'conditioned by the specific class relations of the two races'.[150] He differentiated between lynchings carried out in Black Belt areas and those in more rural areas.[151] In the former, which were areas dependent on Black labour, lynchings were carried out by wealthy Whites or their agents to preserve White landlord and Black tenant

139 Bhattacharyya, *Dangerous Brown Men*, 98.
140 Gargi Bhattacharyya and others, *Empire's Endgame: Racism and the British State* (Pluto Press 2021), 104.
141 Frantz Fanon, *Black Skin, White Masks* (Pluto Press 2008), 130–131.
142 Joshua M. Price, *Prison and Social Death* (Rutgers University Press 2015), 79; Elliott-Cooper, *Black Resistance to British Policing*, 185.
143 Bennett and Plaut, 763.
144 Melvyn Stokes, *D.W. Griffith's The Birth of a Nation* (Oxford University Press 2007), 3.
145 Ibid., 255.
146 Angela Y. Davis, *Women, Race and Class* (Penguin Random House 1981), 166–168.
147 Ibid., 166–167.
148 Ibid., 166.
149 Ibid., 168–171.
150 Ibid., 35.
151 C.L.R. James, 'The Economics of Lynching' in Scott McLemee (ed), *CLR James On the 'Negro Question'* (University Press of Mississippi 1996), 34–35.

relations.[152] In the latter, they were carried out by poor Whites who saw Black labourers as competition.[153] Lynching increased during periods when poor White communities experienced economic hardship,[154] and there was a correlation between falling cotton prices and higher incidences of lynching.[155] Stewart Tolnay and E.M. Beck argue that lynching performed three functions – to impose terror over Black communities as a means of social control, to limit competition for economic resources and status, and to preserve White socio-economic structures and the privileges of White elites.[156] It maintained racial boundaries, which prevented poor White people from combining with Black people to collectively resist class inequality.[157] Thus, both race and class structures were maintained and consolidated, benefitting White elites. Lynching was effectively sanctioned by the state through the lack of action against perpetrators.[158] In the early twentieth century, lynchings or 'lynch law' sometimes took place in front of courthouses with police complicity.[159]

Patrick Wolfe argues that factors such as competition over jobs cannot account for the horrific brutality of lynchings, often including sadistic mutilation and 'an open trade in commemorative postcards and souvenir body parts'.[160] Black people who did not 'know their place' in the Southern states became targets.[161] As described in Chapter 2, hangings of working class individuals in the early capitalist period served to communicate to the whole London working class: 'Respect Private Property'.[162] Similarly, lynchings in the postbellum United States transmitted the message: 'Respect White Supremacy' to Black communities. Therefore, while premised as defence of women, this can be seen as collective self-defence of Whiteness,[163] such that 'by defending the honor of their women, men were able to naturalize a racially exclusive social group'.[164] In this way, 'racism would be the glue that bound white society together, and lynching was the public affirmation of

152 Ibid., 34.
153 Ibid., 35.
154 Stewart Tolnay and E.M. Beck, *A Festival of Violence: An Analysis of Southern Lynchings, 1882–1930* (University of Illinois Press 1995), 24–25 and 213.
155 Daniel Kato, *Liberalizing Lynching: Building a New Racialized State* (Oxford University Press 2016), 5–6.
156 Tolnay and Beck, 18–19.
157 Ibid., 26–27.
158 Kato, 6.
159 Chris Cunneen, *Defund the Police* (Polity Press 2023), 33.
160 Patrick Wolfe, *Traces of History: Elementary Structures of Race* (Verso Books 2016), 13.
161 Ibid., 16.
162 Peter Linebaugh, *The London Hanged* (2nd edn, Verso Books 2006), xxii.
163 Elsa Dorlin, *Self Defense: A Philosophy of Violence* (Kieran Aarons tr, Verso Books 2022), 99.
164 Ibid., 106.

that fraternal bond'.[165] For Black people, to view these murders of members of one's community was 'to carry the unwelcome image around as a constant reminder of the precariousness of life'.[166] This sustained the racialised division between grievable and ungrievable populations.

As Angela Davis argues, it is crucial that anti-rape activists 'develop an understanding of the degree to which rape and the racist use of the fraudulent rape claim are historically inseparable'.[167] Ida B. Wells-Barnett, who led anti-rape and anti-lynching campaigns in the 1890s, recognised the link between 'the myths that Black men were rapists and Black women could not be raped'.[168] Both the lynching of Black men and the rape of Black women were intrinsically linked to White patriarchal capitalist property relations while relying upon the simulacrum of Black oversexualisation. Therefore, 'the struggle to defend Black men from fraudulent rape charges was directly linked to the defence of Black women who were targets of rape ... rape and the racist manipulation of the rape charge were fundamentally connected'.[169] The simulacrum of the Black rapist was deployed to erase the rape of Black women by White men, thus consolidating the White male patriarchy, such that White men retained their sense of sexual entitlement over both White and racialised women. From Roman law onwards, conceptions of rape have been 'framed wholly within a context of male ownership of female sexuality'.[170] Under slavery, 'the right claimed by slaveowners and their agents over the bodies of female slaves was a direct expression of their presumed rights over Black people as a whole'.[171] Male ownership of women's bodies and White ownership of Black people's bodies intersected in the violent sexual abuse of Black female slaves by White male slaveowners.

During the postbellum period in the Southern states, being a 'real' woman worthy of male protection was defined as being ladylike, fragile, vulnerable, and White.[172] Thus, the construction of gender was fundamentally racialised and, as described above, served to consolidate racial privilege.[173] To be ungrievable is to be unrapable – the dehumanisation of Black women meant that consent to sex was assumed due to essentialised promiscuity, or was unrequired as 'only those considered "human" can be raped ...as consent

165 Tolnay and Beck, 27.
166 Bhattacharyya, *Dangerous Brown Men*, 114.
167 Angela Y. Davis, *Women, Culture and Politics* (The Women's Press 1990), 43–44.
168 Mariame Kaba, *We Do This 'Til We Free Us* (Haymarket Books 2021), 50.
169 Angela Y. Davis and others, *Abolition. Feminism. Now.* (Penguin Books 2022), 98.
170 Yvette Russell, 'Thinking Sexual Difference Through the Lens of Rape' (2013) 24(3) *Law and Critique* 255, 263.
171 Davis, *Women, Race and Class*, 158.
172 Dorlin, 105–106.
173 Ibid., 106.

requires the participation of subjects in possession of full personhood'.[174] The continued rape of Black women operated in tandem with the lynching of Black men as a 'strategy of racist terror' to ensure the maintenance of White supremacist economic relations.[175] Violence against Black women, from that perpetrated by slave owners and the Ku Klux Klan to that by police officers and prison guards, was and continues to be used to remind Black women of their place in a patriarchal White supremacist society.[176]

In the UK, racist discourses around post-Second World War Windrush migration from the Commonwealth were permeated with anxieties about the effect of Black sexuality, particularly in relation to poor White women, with reports expressing fears that Liverpool could become 'a "new Harlem" ...characterised by black pimps and white prostitutes, and high crime rates'.[177] These narratives around Black male pimps meant that 'race was fixed in a matrix between the imagery of squalor and that of sordid sexuality'.[178] Such discourses reproduced colonial notions of White femininity as innocence that needed to be protected by White men against violent Black males. However, where White females were themselves cast as 'fallen' rather than 'innocent', they were produced as doubly tainted – both sexually promiscuous and racially impure through their association with Black males who sullied their Whiteness. This framed Blackness as a contaminant that diminished White racial purity, as discussed in Chapter 4.

These narratives around racialised sexual predatory behaviour and the corruption of tainted poor White females continue in recent discourses around grooming, with the new folk devils of 'Muslim grooming gangs'[179] preying on White young women and girls.[180] The moral panic over 'muggings' discussed in Chapter 2 was used in a similar way in the 1970s to associate Blackness with deviance, criminality, and danger.[181] While the simulacrum of the Black mugger relied upon images of Black assailants and White victims, the moral

174 Jackie Wang, *Carceral Capitalism* (Semiotext(e) 2018), 115.
175 Ibid., 166.
176 Davis, *Women, Race and Class*, 158–159; Angela Y. Davis, *Are Prisons Obsolete?* (Seven Stories Press 2003), 68.
177 Ali Rattansi, 'On Being and Not Being Brown/Black-British: Racism, Class, Sexuality and Ethnicity in Post-Imperial Britain' in Jo-Anne Lee and John Lutz (eds), *Situating Race and Racisms in Space, Time, and Theory: Critical Essays for Activists and Scholars* (McGill-Queen's University Press 2005), 50.
178 Gilroy, 97.
179 Ella Cockbain and Waqas Tufail, 'Failing Victims, Fuelling Hate: Challenging the Harms of the "Muslim Grooming Gangs" Narrative' (2020) 61(3) *Race and Class* 3, 4.
180 Aisha K. Gill and Aviah Sarah Day, 'Moral Panic in the Media: Scapegoating South Asian Men in Cases of Sexual Exploitation and Grooming' in Shulamit Ramon, Michele Lloyd and Bridget Penhale (eds), *Gendered Domestic Violence and Abuse in Popular Culture* (Emerald Publishing Limited 2020), 188.
181 Cockbain and Tufail, 5.

panic around sexual exploitation followed a narrative of immigrant Muslim male predators and White female victims.[182] In both cases, White society was deemed to be under physical threat from racialised men.

Media discourses have suggested, and continue to suggest, that Pakistani Muslim grooming gangs are the main source of sexual danger to children in the UK, yet this is not supported by data. In 2023, 3.7% of child sexual abuse reported to police was group-based abuse.[183] Of this type of abuse, 17% (so less than 1% of reported child sexual abuse overall) involved grooming gangs and 26% took place in family settings.[184] For all group-based sexual abuse, of those suspects who had a self-defined ethnicity, 83% were White.[185] A 2020 Home Office report found that the available data on the ethnicity of perpetrators was of poor quality and often subject to generalisation and bias, such that it was not possible to reliably conclude that Asian people were overrepresented, and that 'it seems most likely that the ethnicity of group based CSE (child sexual exploitation) offenders is in line with CSA (child sexual abuse) more generally and with the general population, with the majority of offenders being White'.[186]

Despite this, in April 2023, the then Home Secretary Suella Braverman asserted that 'overwhelmingly white girls' were being sexually abused by 'grooming gangs' consisting of 'groups of men, almost all British-Pakistani, who hold cultural attitudes completely incompatible with British values'.[187] Just a few days later, it was reported that twenty-one people had been convicted of multiple child sexual abuse following the largest such investigation ever conducted by West Midlands police.[188] All of those convicted were White, yet this barely impacted on discourses around grooming gangs. As discussed in Chapter 1, one aspect of White privilege is the individualisa-

182 Gill and Day, 181–183.

183 Hydrant Programme and Child Sexual Exploitation Taskforce, Group-Based Offending Publication (November 2024) <https://www.hydrantprogramme.co.uk/assets/Documents/CSE-Taskforce-Group-Based-Offending-Publication-November-2024.pdf> accessed 4 January 2024.

184 Ibid.

185 Ibid.

186 Home Office, *Group-based Child Sexual Exploitation* (December 2020), para 81 <https://assets.publishing.service.gov.uk/government/uploads/system/uploads/attachment_data/file/944206/Group-based_CSE_Paper.pdf> accessed 21 December 2024.

187 Suella Braverman, 'My Mission to Ensure There Really is No Hiding Place for the Evil Gangs Grooming our Vulnerable Young Girls' *The Daily Mail Online* (1 April 2023) <https://www.dailymail.co.uk/debate/article-11928629/SUELLA-BRAVERMAN-mission-ensure-really-no-hiding-place-gangs-grooming-young-girls.html> accessed 21 December 2024.

188 Jessica Murray, 'Twenty-one Convicted in West Midlands Child Sexual Abuse Inquiry' *The Guardian* (5 April 2023) <www.theguardian.com/uk-news/2023/apr/05/twenty-one-convicted-in-west-midlands-child-sexual-abuse-inquiry> accessed 21 December 2024.

tion of harm caused by White people. In contrast to the narratives around 'Muslim grooming gangs', discourses around systematic child sexual abuse by wealthy White male celebrities, including Jimmy Savile, completely disregarded race and culture as factors.[189]

As with the discourses around the unrest in Northern towns discussed in the previous section, child sexual abuse is presented as a cultural problem related to the failure of Muslim men to assimilate. The framing of the debate around sexual exploitation cannot be disassociated from narratives around the War Against Terror, with Muslims portrayed as culturally distinct from the White majority and from Western values.[190] Muslims are presented as bound to their culture, religion, and community.[191] In relation to domestic violence, where a White man claims to have killed his wife on account of her infidelity, it is seen as the act of an individual, but where a Muslim man does the same, it is viewed as an 'honour crime' linked to his 'pre-modern' cultural background.[192] Research by Caroline Braunmühl found that references to 'culture' in law reports almost always referred to racialised defendants, but were largely absent when the defendant was White.[193] Such discourses enable gender oppression to be 'subtly explained as symptomatic of an essentialist, non-Western barbarism',[194] with Islam presented as an outdated ideology from bygone eras that needs to 'catch up' with Western democracy, and has 'not yet ... arrived at the idea of the rational human'.[195] In contrast to these portrayals of Islam, the extensive sexual abuse perpetuated by Christian clergy, both Catholic and Protestant, has not led to discourses that generalise Christian beliefs, values, or communities as backward, barbaric, or deviant.

Narratives around sexual abuse and Islam can be understood as part of the civilising mission discourse linking the War on Terror with liberating Muslim women and safeguarding Western women, and by implication protecting Western values around perceived individual freedom from dangerous 'barbarian hordes'.[196] By deploying imperialist discourses, used to justify military invasions of predominantly Muslim countries in order to

189 Shamim Miah, 'The Groomers and the Question of Race' (2015) 1 *Identity Papers: A Journal of British and Irish Studies* 54, 55; Bhattacharyya and others, *Empire's Endgame*, 119.

190 Bhattacharyya and others, *Empire's Endgame*, 120.

191 Sherene H. Razack, 'Imperilled Muslim Women, Dangerous Muslim Men and Civilised Europeans: Legal and Social Responses to Forced Marriages' (2004) 12(2) *Feminist Legal Studies* 129, 148.

192 Ibid., 152.

193 Caroline Braunmühl, *Colonial Discourse and Gender in U.S. Criminal Courts* (Routledge 2012), 25.

194 Judith Butler, *Gender Trouble: Feminism and the Subversion of Identity* (2nd edn, Routledge 1990), 5.

195 Judith Butler, *Frames of War: When Is Life Grievable?* (Verso Books 2016), 125.

196 Bhattacharyya, *Dangerous Brown Men*, 49.

'rescue' women, patriarchy was framed as a backward way of living, in contrast to Western society, which was framed as post-patriarchal.[197] Gargi Bhattacharyya argues that there was a shift from 'the demonised figure of the "dangerous black man"' to 'the brown man from a backward and misogynistic culture, anti-feminist, sexually frustrated by traditional culture, addicted to honour killing and viewing women as tradable objects'.[198] This reinforced images of White superiority through combining discourses around backward cultures and dangerous terrorists with those around racialised sexualisation.[199]

While the colonial second order simulacrum of the Black rapist of African descent persists, under neoliberalism the racialisation of sexual danger has mutated into the third order simulacrum of the Muslim predator. This is a repurposing of the use of racialised discourses around danger.[200] In the US postbellum era, the crude biological simulated image of the Black rapist served the interests of White supremacy by constraining Black advancement through the maintenance and consolidation of White racial interests over class interests. Under neoliberalism, the ostensibly colour-blind and post-patriarchal cultural narratives used to justify Western invasions of the Middle East simultaneously name Muslim men as a danger to women in the UK.[201] The colonial trope of 'White men saving brown women from brown men'[202] has expanded to encompass 'White men saving White women from Muslim men'.

Many of the abused girls and women were initially viewed by the police as deviant, beyond control, and engaging in sexual relations voluntarily,[203] with many labelled as prostitutes.[204] Misogyny shaped the responses to them. Some of the girls had been in social services care, with the state failing to exercise its duty of care for their welfare.[205] Although abandoned by the neoliberal state when they were in need, they were subsequently portrayed as being rescued by civilised society and were reclaimed as the property of White men. In this way, 'the interaction between patriarchal violence and state neglect, which led to so many young people being harmed, was minimised and obscured'.[206]

197 Braunmühl, 41.
198 Bhattacharyya, *Dangerous Brown Men*, 96–97.
199 Ibid., 104.
200 Ibid., 97.
201 Ibid., 104.
202 Gayatri Chakravorty Spivak, 'Can the Subaltern Speak?' in Patrick Williams and Laura Chrisman (eds), *Colonial Discourse and Post-Colonial Theory: A Reader* (Routledge 1994), 93.
203 Bhattacharyya and others, *Empire's Endgame*, 116.
204 Ibid., 179–180; Becka Hudson, 'Statues and Gangs' in Koshka Duff (ed), *Abolishing the Police* (Dog Section Press 2021), 103.
205 Gill and Day, 181.
206 Bhattacharyya and others, *Empire's Endgame*, 118.

Their systematic abuse was deemed less a crime against them personally but was reframed as a crime against White society. Meanwhile, a further consequence of the racialisation of sexual abuse was that non-White victims were virtually absent from government and media discourses.[207] As Shamim Miah argues, the imagery of vulnerable White girls and Muslim predators diverted attention from institutional failures and public services cuts that affected abuse victims from all communities.[208] The simulacra of Muslim grooming gangs deflected attention from the impact of neoliberal austerity on social services.[209]

These discourses around grooming gangs present themselves as post-patriarchal, but are inherently patriarchal. They share the racist narrative of the White male saviour of White femininity used to justify lynching in the United States. White female bodies are deemed to be a form of White space that White men are entitled to access, but racialised men are not. Not only do such discourses objectify White women, but Asian men are framed as marauding forces, linked to images of immigration and Islamic fundamentalism. In January 2025, the Shadow Justice Secretary, Robert Jenrick explicitly linked grooming gangs with immigration, stating that: 'The scandal started with the onset of mass migration. Importing hundreds of thousands of people from alien cultures, who possess medieval attitudes towards women, brought us here'.[210] As Yvette Russell has argued in relation to the criminalisation of street harassment, 'women's bodies are often at the vanguard of the symbolic fight in which nostalgia for empire becomes the ideological outlet for a new proto-nationalism'.[211] By assuming the role of protector of White females and the family, the state is able to reassert patriarchal and racial relations of power.[212]

A narrative that child sexual abuse stems from 'affording *too much* respect to "inferior" migrant cultures' continues to be exploited by right-wing politicians and media outlets, and by the far-right.[213] The disorder in many UK towns in summer 2024 was fuelled by inaccurate reports that the man who had murdered three young girls and stabbed several other people was a Muslim refugee who had recently come to the UK. This anti-immigrant violence was premised on intersecting narratives that Muslim men were raping

207 Gill and Day, 171; Bhattacharyya and others, *Empire's Endgame*, 117.

208 Miah, 59 and 62.

209 Cockbain and Tufail, 22.

210 Robert Jenrick, X (4 January 2025) <https://x.com/RobertJenrick/status/1875549435926581584> accessed 11 January 2025.

211 Yvette Russell, 'Criminal Law to the Rescue? "Wolf-Whistling" as Hate Crime' *Critical Legal Thinking* (20 July 2016) <https://criticallegalthinking.com/2016/07/20/wolf-whistling-as-hate-crime/> accessed 21 December 2024.

212 Bhattacharyya and others, *Empire's Endgame*, 123.

213 Gill and Day, 191 (original italics).

or murdering 'our' White girls and that immigration was the cause of poverty and cuts to public services. Some of the perpetrators acted almost as lynch mobs, checking cars to see if the occupants were White and setting fire to hostels housing refugees and mosques. As with the simulated moral panic over Muslim grooming gangs, much of these events happened in poor, post-industrial towns in the North and the Midlands where communities had suffered the effects of decades of neoliberal austerity. Deploying a similar narrative as the hate crime provisions discussed in Chapter 4, the state individualised the violence as being perpetrated by racist thugs, who were hastily locked up despite prison overcrowding, and continued to advance the discourse that immigration was problematic, while doing little to address material inequality. The violence tailed off when larger counter-protests by anti-racists took back the streets.

In contrast to grooming gangs discourses, rape and sexual abuse by White police officers have been minimised and individualised. In the same week that police officer Wayne Couzens was sentenced for the kidnap, rape, and murder of Sarah Everard,[214] environmental activist Kate Wilson won a tribunal claim against the Metropolitan Police.[215] Wilson had a two-year relationship with someone she believed to be a fellow activist, who was a married police officer spying on environmental groups. This was not an isolated case, with a number of undercover police officers having deceptive intimate relationships with female political activists from the 1970s onwards, including fathering children in at least three cases.[216] This systemic sexual abuse of women in environmental, animals rights, socialist, anarchist, trade union, and anti-racist organisations existed within a framing by the police that such women were enemies of the state and unworthy, and thus ungrievable and unrapable. While criticised by the media, these relationships based upon fundamental deceit were not framed as rape, either legally or discursively. The undercover police officers involved were not charged with rape, nor were they described as a grooming gang or as dangerous predators.

Since the murder of Sarah Everard, further incidents of police sexual violence against women have been exposed with David Carrick sentenced

214 BBC News, 'Sarah Everard Murder: Wayne Couzens Given Whole-Life Sentence' *BBC News* (30 September 2021) <https://www.bbc.co.uk/news/uk-england-london-58747614> accessed 21 December 2024.

215 BBC News, 'Deceived Activist Kate Wilson Wins Tribunal Against Met Police' *BBC News* (30 September 2021) <https://www.bbc.co.uk/news/uk-england-nottinghamshire-58749590> accessed 30 December 2024.

216 Rob Evans, 'Spy Cops Joked About Sexual Relationships with Women, Inquiry Told' *The Guardian* (7 May 2021) <www.theguardian.com/uk-news/2021/may/07/spy-cops-joked-about-sexual-relationships-with-women-inquiry-told> accessed 21 December 2024.

in February 2023 for 85 offences, including 48 rapes.[217] Baroness Casey's March 2023 report found that the Metropolitan Police were 'institutionally sexist', with 'prejudiced assumptions, stereotypes and rape myths, often unchallenged, expressed openly by officers'.[218] Even on its own terms, the legal system fails to deal with sexual violence. In the UK, only around 16% of rapes, attempted rapes, and sexual penetrations are reported to the police,[219] and conviction rates for rape are so low that Dame Vera Baird KC commented that the offence had effectively been decriminalised.[220]

As Françoise Vergès argues, violence against women cannot be solved where 'the role of protector is entrusted to the male, rapist state'.[221] As was discussed in Chapter 3, police practices are embedded in colonialism. More specifically, 'policing in its various forms was gendered and imposed the patriarchal relations of the colonising society'.[222] In this way, 'policing reflects a pervasive colonial norm that reproduces cultures of both racism and patriarchy'.[223] Police violence, including sexual violence, against women under neoliberalism finds its origins in the treatment of female slaves and colonial subjects.[224] This is absorbed into contemporary policing practices. As argued below, neoliberal carceral practices fail to provide safety from physical and sexual violence, as well as being a source of harm.

Dangerousness, the Carceral State, and Gender

The belief that some people are dangerous is key to the belief in carceral solutions to social problems.[225] The simulacra of dangerous racialised men

217 Vikram Dodd and Emine Sinmaz, 'David Carrick Jailed for Life Over a Series of Rapes While Met Police Officer' *The Guardian* (7 February 2023) <www.theguardian.com/society/2023/feb/07/david-carrick-jailed-life-rapes-met-police-officer> accessed 21 December 2024.

218 Baroness Casey, 'An Independent Review into the Standards of Behaviour and Internal Culture of the Metropolitan Police Service' (March 2023) 164 <https://www.met.police.uk/SysSiteAssets/media/downloads/met/about-us/baroness-casey-review/update-march-2023/baroness-casey-review-march-2023a.pdf> accessed 21 December 2024.

219 Office for National Statistics, *Crime Survey for England and Wales* (2021) <www.ons.gov.uk/peoplepopulationandcommunity/crimeandjustice/articles/natureofsexualassaultbyrapeorpenetrationenglandandwales/yearendingmarch2020> accessed 21 December 2024.

220 Haroon Siddique, 'We are Facing the "Decriminalisation of Rape", Warns Victims' Commissioner' *The Guardian* (14 July 2020) <www.theguardian.com/society/2020/jul/14/we-are-facing-the-decriminalisation-of-warns-victims-commissioner> accessed 21 December 2024.

221 Françoise Vergès, *A Feminist Theory of Violence* (Melissa Thackway tr, Pluto Press 2022), 25.

222 Cunneen, *Defund the Police*, 39.

223 Adam Elliott-Cooper, '"Our Life is a Struggle": Respectable Gender Norms and Black Resistance to Policing' (2012) 51(2) *Antipode* 539, 542.

224 Cunneen, *Defund the Police*, 39.

225 Kaba, 24.

render invisible the violence of criminal law and the dangers inherent in racial capitalism. The name of the original dangerousness sentence under the CJA, 'imprisonment for public protection' is illustrative of the narrative behind these severe powers. Indeterminate incarceration was presented as necessary to safeguard the public against the violent or sexually dangerous hypercriminal. Such practices obscured the material dangers caused by neoliberalism, such as poverty, lack of healthcare, and housing insecurity, through processes of simulation that located risk and danger within the bodies of racialised hypercriminal populations. In relation to violence against women, the simulacra of the dangerous male looms large. As outlined below, many prominent mainstream women's organisations have advocated for a carceral feminist approach, calling for increased police powers, more convictions, and higher sentences in response to sexual violence.[226] Yet, such an approach not only fails to address gendered violence but leads to further significant harm.[227]

Carceral feminism has been described as 'a drift from the welfare state to the carceral state as the enforcement apparatus for feminist goals'.[228] It can be seen as 'the depoliticization of a social movement with politically radical roots'.[229] Violence against women is reconceptualised through the lenses of neoliberal discourses of individualism and criminal law solutions, rather than as a wider social issue.[230] As Aya Gruber argues in the US context, 'carceral feminism is colonial', as it aligns itself with the interests of the inherently colonial criminal legal system, and it silences the voices of racialised and indigenous women in relation to alternative ways of dealing with harm and criticisms of pro-criminalisation policies.[231]

Although aspects of carceral feminism have existed throughout the history of White Western strands of feminism, neoliberal trends have exacerbated this and, in some cases, diluted previously progressive feminist practices.[232] In both the UK and the United States, neoliberal austerity, particularly the defunding of support services, has driven some anti-violence

226 Leah Cowan, *Why Would Feminists Trust the Police?* (Verso Books 2024), 9.

227 Ibid., 8–10; Aviah Sarah Day and Shanice Octavia McBean, *Abolition Revolution* (Pluto Press 2022), 82–83.

228 Elizabeth Bernstein, 'The Sexual Politics of the "New Abolitionism"' (2007) 18(3) *Differences: A Journal of Feminist Cultural Studies* 128, 143.

229 Mimi E. Kim, 'From Carceral Feminism to Transformative Justice: Women-of-color Feminism and Alternatives to Incarceration' (2018) 27(3) *Journal of Ethnic and Cultural Diversity in Social Work* 219, 221.

230 Ibid., 221–222.

231 Aya Gruber, 'Colonial Carceral Feminism' in Chris Cunneen and others (eds), *The Routledge International Handbook on Decolonizing Justice* (Routledge 2023), 240–241.

232 Ibid., 240.

organisations to accede to the state's crime and punishment agenda as a funding strategy.[233] In Chapter 4, the links between youth organisations securing funding and co-option to the government's knife crime agenda were discussed. Similarly, many UK women's organisations have adhered to government policies, such as Prevent, as a means of gaining funds.[234] Situating services within such a framing reproduces discourses that link terrorism and misogyny and reinforces the simulacrum of racialised men as the main source of sexual harm.

In the United States, the simulacrum of the Black rapist from the post-bellum period has been reabsorbed into neoliberal narratives around sexual harm. As Kristin Bumiller writes:

> This marking of the rapist was inextricably tied to the history of lynching black men. What had begun as a new feminist sensibility that 'any man could be a rapist' was transformed primarily into a campaign driven by fear of dangerous strangers, who were implicitly or explicitly marked as dark-skinned men.[235]

Processes of simulation locate sexual danger within racialised bodies. The simulacra of the Black rapist and culturally backward Muslim predator are embedded in colonial and imperialist civilising mission discourses, which are reworked into a narrative that neoliberal White feminism, in collusion with the carceral state, is the saviour of women.

Where support services are defunded and unavailable, calling the police may seem to be the only option available to those experiencing domestic violence or sexual abuse. However, the criminal legal system can further disempower and even criminalise women who report abuse. This has a disproportionate impact on racialised working class women.[236] For women who are undocumented migrants, reporting violence against them may result in their arrest, detention, and deportation.[237] In relation to domestic assaults, mandatory arrest policies mean that women who call the police risk being the arrested party if they have acted in self-defence in the UK[238] and the United

233 Kristin Bumiller, *In an Abusive State: How Neoliberalism Appropriated the Feminist Movement Against Sexual Violence* (Duke University Press 2009), 4; Cowan, 126 and 129–136.

234 Cowan, 143.

235 Bumiller, 10.

236 Davis and others, *Abolition. Feminism. Now.*, 109.

237 Aviah Sarah Day and Aisha K. Gill 'Applying Intersectionality to Partnerships Between Women's Organisations and the Criminal Justice System in Relation to Domestic Violence' (2020) 60 *British Journal of Criminology* 830, 838–841.

238 Ibid., 841–842.

States.[239] When an abusive partner is charged, the prosecution is brought by the state so if the survivor of violence decides that they no longer want to proceed with the court case, it may continue anyway. In the UK, if a survivor refuses to attend the trial, they may be witnessed summonsed to attend court, and if they continue to refuse, the court has the power to issue a warrant for their arrest, allowing the police to bring them to court. Refusal to answer questions when testifying can result in a conviction for contempt of court, an imprisonable offence. While it is rare for women reporting sexual violence to be imprisoned for refusing to testify, it has happened.

Carceral responses individualise gendered violence and capitulate to the patriarchal, racist state, which cannot provide safety and security for women and girls. The concept of the protective state is a neoliberal simulacrum manifesting itself as post-racial and post-patriarchal, but embedded in colonial simulacra of White purity and White male superiority. The focus on increased criminalisation as a policy goal diverts resources away from addressing the practical and emotional needs of those who have experienced abuse, such as secure housing, financial assistance, counselling, childcare, and healthcare. Ultimately, the criminal legal process can be traumatising for all parties, and the adversarial system works against perpetrators accepting accountability for their actions. A carceral approach is inconsistent with promoting rehabilitation, healing and transformation, and cannot be a solution to gendered sexual violence.

Dangerousness as a Continuation of Colonialism

Although concepts of dangerousness have persisted in earlier incarnations of criminal law, both in the UK and other jurisdictions, these provisions take a particular form under neoliberalism. By linking violent and sexual offences, which are viewed through the racial frame, with concepts of dangerous criminality, a seeming rationale is provided for the incarceration of those from racialised communities. Statistical predictions and risk management policies are framed as neutral, logical, and efficient, thus leading to the inference that racial disparities in relation to legal outcomes must be the result of racially disproportionate criminality.[240] However, these measures of risk are themselves based on simulations of racialised criminality, such that they are a simulation of a simulation. These neoliberal codes construct third order simulacra of dangerous hypercriminals. Rather than racially disproportionate outcomes being a threat to the simulacrum of neoliberal colour-blind neutrality, they bolster White supremacy by reinforcing colonial and imperialist

239 Bumiller, 11–12.
240 Van Cleve and Mayes, 412–413 and 420–421.

discourses around the undeserving poor and the dangerous subject who falls outside civilised society and needs to be contained, controlled, or excluded.

The second order simulacra that were deployed by colonial discourses to justify slavery and conquest are subsumed into contemporary criminal laws and practices. As Frantz Fanon described the colonial position, 'confronted with a world ruled by the settler, the native is always presumed guilty'.[241] Just as colonial subjects under the rule of the British Empire were seen through the racial frame as corporal rather than cerebral, so racialised people under neoliberalism are dehumanised, and are viewed as ungrievable, dangerous bodies. However, this racial framing is made invisible as racialised criminality is constructed in ever more abstracted ways. Neoliberal risk management purports to be neutral and colour-blind but is embedded in this genealogy. The third order simulacrum of the dangerous racialised criminal builds upon previous orders of simulacra while denying those processes. Concepts of dangerousness can be seen as absorbing and rendering invisible their colonial roots, while serving a contradiction-closing function within neoliberalism and acting performatively to reproduce this imagery and so consolidate White supremacy. In this way, narratives of dangerousness appear to close the contradiction between discourses of colour-blind legal equality and racially disproportionate criminal outcomes, such that racially disproportionate criminality appears real.

Each stop and search of a young Black man on an inner city street in London finds its genealogy steeped in the history of colonialism, yet this is disappeared through processes of simulation. In the United States, each restraint by the police is located within the history of slavery, segregation, and lynching, which are absorbed into contemporary police practices. Each unjustified stop and search or unnecessary use of force is performative as it re-inscribes these racial distinctions, which are continually reabsorbed into contemporary criminal practices, becoming ever more insidious, and constructing racialised people as dangerous hypercriminals.

Nothing in this chapter should be taken as denying or underplaying the harm caused by violence and sexual abuse in all forms. The aim of this chapter has been to illuminate how neoliberal discourses around danger fail to contextualise harm, ignore the significant harm caused by neoliberalism and its institutions, and create racialised folk devils as a means of distraction, such that concepts of danger are constructed by colonial discourses – they are simulacra. This simulation serves to erase from discourses the ways that the colonial state, the Church, the police, and prisons are all sources of violent and sexual danger rather than the remedy to this danger. Ultimately, the institutions that cause harm cannot be the solution to harm. Neoliberal discourses embedded in colonialism produce constructions of dangerousness

241 Frantz Fanon, *The Wretched of the Earth* (Penguin Books 1961), 41.

that simultaneously bolster the carceral state and disappear the danger and harm caused by law enforcement, the military, poverty, and inequality.[242] Carceral solutions 'are offered as antidotes to the precarities and insecurities of the contemporary neoliberal political order, by protecting against the dangerous others'.[243] As Dean Spade argues, social movements can promote change by politicising concepts such as 'violence' and 'danger' and redefining them as the harm caused by racial capitalism.[244] While it is not possible to remove danger and risk from our lives, the abolition of the carceral state and the dismantling of racial neoliberalism, and their replacement by practices of social justice and mutual aid, can significantly reduce the danger of harm.

The next chapter will consider another provision that punishes defendants for what they are perceived to be, rather than what they have done, and again finds its genealogy in colonial discourses – bad character evidence.

242 Reina Gossett and Dean Spade, 'No One is Disposable (Part 4): Gun Control and Producing Dangerousness' (Barnard Center for Research on Women 2014) <https://bcrw.barnard.edu/videos/reina-gossett-dean-spade-part-4-gun-control-producing-dangerousness/> accessed 4 January 2025.

243 Sarah Lamble, 'Queer Investments in Punitiveness' in Jin Haritaworn, Adi Kuntsman and Silvia Posocco (eds), *Queer Necropolitics* (Routledge 2014), 152.

244 Reina Gossett and Dean Spade, 'No One is Disposable (Part 3): What About the Dangerous People?' (Barnard Center for Research on Women 2014) <https://bcrw.barnard.edu/no-one-is-disposable/> accessed 4 January 2025.

Chapter 6

Bad Character Evidence

In this chapter, it will be argued that bad character evidence under the Criminal Justice Act 2003 (CJA) is another racialised provision situated within neoliberal discourses of colour-blindness and meritocracy. There are a number of similarities with the dangerousness provisions. As with dangerousness, bad character evidence serves a performative function, as it names racialised individuals as threatening and criminal. Such legal categories frame those criminalised in an essentialised and pathological manner that excludes the possibility of change. Character is deemed permanent and irredeemable rather than situational, such that discourses around bad character silence the material, social, and practical context in which acts take place. Although these discourses may take distinct forms in different contexts, they retain the imprint of colonialism and act performatively to reinterpret and perpetuate racism within neoliberal criminal law and evidence. Concepts of bad character are viewed through the racial frame, most pertinently in relation to gangs and to rap and drill music. Again, these provisions can be analysed as contradiction-closing devices that are deployed to explain away racial disparities in convictions, and as processes of simulation that construct hypercriminals.

The CJA defines 'bad character' as 'evidence of, or of a disposition towards, misconduct',[1] which is described as 'the commission of an offence or other reprehensible behaviour',[2] such that bad character evidence is not restricted to previous convictions, nor to criminal offences. The CJA significantly extended the admissibility of bad character evidence, leading Scott Baker LJ to comment that it was clear that Parliament's intention was to increase the use of bad character evidence at trial.[3] The wide definition of character under the CJA has enabled prosecutors to use these provisions to adduce the associations and culture of racialised defendants as evidence of

1 Criminal Justice Act 2003, s.98.
2 Ibid., s.112(1).
3 *R v Edwards* [2005] EWCA Crim 3244 [1] (Scott Baker LJ).

DOI: 10.4324/9781003602873-7

bad character. This reproduces the colonial discourses that view Black collective expression as violent and uncivilised.

Prior to the CJA, bad character evidence was admissible at trial where a charge, for example, driving whilst disqualified, required a previous conviction; where a defendant raised their own good character; where the defence attacked the character of a prosecution witness; and in relation to 'similar fact' evidence, as discussed below.[4] Under the CJA, a defendant's bad character is admissible in the following circumstances: all parties agree;[5] it is adduced by the defendant;[6] it is important explanatory evidence;[7] it is relevant to an important matter in issue between the defendant and the prosecution;[8] it has substantial probative value in relation to an important matter in issue between the defendant and a co-defendant;[9] it is evidence to correct a false impression given by the defendant;[10] or the defendant has attacked another person's character.[11] These are known by lawyers as the gateways for admission.

Of these provisions, the most significant extension to the admissibility of bad character evidence is s.101(1)(d) CJA, which makes evidence of the defendant's bad character admissible if 'it is relevant to an important matter in issue between the defendant and the prosecution'. A matter in issue is a point on which the prosecution and defence disagree. Under the CJA, important matters in issue include propensity to commit offences of the kind with which the defendant is charged[12] and propensity to be untruthful.[13] The general rule in relation to the admissibility of any evidence in criminal trials is that firstly, the evidence is not deemed inadmissible for any reason and secondly, that it is relevant to a matter in issue between the prosecution and the defence. Therefore, the only difference in relation to the admissibility of bad character evidence is that it must be relevant to an 'important' matter in issue rather than merely a matter in issue. Arguably, most points in contention at a trial are important in relation to the direction that the trial takes, such that s.101(1)(d) makes bad character potentially admissible in relation to all but the most peripheral matters.

4 Mike Redmayne, 'The Relevance of Bad Character' (2002) 61(3) *Cambridge Law Journal* 684, 684.
5 Criminal Justice Act 2003, s.101(1)(a).
6 Ibid., s.101(1)(b).
7 Ibid., s.101(1)(c).
8 Ibid., s.101(1)(d).
9 Ibid., s.101(1)(e).
10 Ibid., s.101(1)(f).
11 Ibid., s.101(1)(g).
12 Ibid., s.103(1)(a).
13 Ibid., s.103(1)(b).

Further, s.98 CJA states that any evidence that 'has to do with the alleged facts of the offence with which the defendant is charged'[14] or 'is evidence of misconduct in connection with the investigation or prosecution of that offence'[15] is not deemed to be bad character evidence. Thus, if the prosecution can convince the judge or magistrates that the alleged 'misconduct' is related to the facts of the allegation itself, the evidence will be admissible subject to the usual conditions of relevance and admissibility. In other words, if evidence is admissible under s.98, it does not need to meet the conditions of one of the bad character gateways listed above. It is no exaggeration to say that evidence that presents the defendant's character in a negative way, whether under the bad character gateways or under s.98, is now widely admissible.

Distinctions between good and bad character are located within colonial narratives of racial hierarchy that categorise racialised populations as barbaric and savage, and equate good character with Whiteness. As with dangerousness, the second order simulacra of these colonial discourses have morphed into third order simulacra under neoliberalism. Bad character evidence appears to be based on objective factors but operates through the circulation of racialised signifiers. The seeming permanence of such categories names racialised subjects as irredeemably bad and operates as a process of dehumanisation that seeks to justify mass incarceration. The gang discourse absorbs colonial discourses around dangerous hordes and reworks them into a contemporary signifier for criminality. These processes have been intensified by the Gangs Matrix, and by the use of social media and YouTube footage as character evidence. Factors such as living in proximity to gangs, fashion styles, or involvement in rap or drill music function as codes for racialised criminality. This allows the police, prosecution lawyers, and judges to appear to be racially neutral when presenting cases or reaching decisions while relying upon abstracted colonial tropes. It will be argued that these practices construct simulacra, such that not only gang membership but signifiers of what is considered to constitute gang membership are used to frame racialised subjects as criminals, such that this form of evidence is hyperreal.

From Striking Similarity to Simulation

The shift to hyperreality can be analysed by considering the genealogy of bad character evidence, and how it has become increasingly abstracted. In the 1915 case of *Smith*, the defendant was charged with murder by drowning his wife in the bath after she had left him a substantial sum in her will, and evidence that two of his previous wives had also drowned in the bath in

14 Ibid., s.98(a).
15 Ibid., s.98(b).

similar circumstances was ruled admissible.[16] This relied upon 'the improbability that each of his "wives" was by chance accident-prone and, moreover, accident-prone in a "strikingly similar" way and in strikingly similar circumstances'.[17] In the later cases of *Sims*[18] and *Boardman*,[19] it was ruled that it was necessary for there to be 'striking similarity' between the previous and current allegations in order for the previous allegations to be admissible as evidence.[20] Therefore, there was a requirement for a clear factual nexus between the alleged conduct in the current case and previous alleged conduct. However, the requirement for the previous allegations to be 'strikingly similar' was removed in the 1991 judgment of Lord Mackay in *DPP v P*, where a father had abused two daughters in similar but not strikingly similar circumstances, and the evidence was ruled cross-admissible.[21]

Under the CJA, although similarity is more likely to make the evidence admissible, there is no requirement for the conduct to be similar, only for it to be relevant to an important matter on which the prosecution and defence disagree. As outlined above, this can include propensity to commit offences of the kind with which the defendant is charged[22] and the propensity to be untruthful.[23] However, s.101(1)(d) is not limited to evidence relating to propensity. Bad character evidence can be considered 'relevant to an important matter in issue' if it concerns the defendant's state of mind, such as motive or intention, or if it could be used to rebut the defendant's account.

Bad character evidence has changed from striking similarity to similarity under the pre-CJA case law, and then to relevance under the CJA. In this way, the factual basis of the previous allegations adduced as character evidence can be seen as moving further away from the offence charged, such that bad character law has become increasingly abstracted. The striking similarity rule required that the previous conduct reflected the offence charged. In this way, it can be seen as a first order simulacrum: a 'good appearance' of the conduct alleged, such that it was 'the reflection of a profound reality'.[24] As the requirement shifted to similar conduct, the previous actions had to represent the appearance of, rather than match the alleged offence. In this way, bad

16 *R v Smith* (1915) 11 Cr App R 229.

17 P.B. Carter, 'Forbidden Reasoning Permissible: Similar Fact Evidence a Decade After Boardman' (1985) 40 *Modern Law Review* 29, 32.

18 *R v Sims* (1946) 31 Cr App R 158.

19 *DPP v Boardman* (1975) AC 457.

20 Richard Webster, 'Trawling and Similar Fact Evidence' (Select Committee on Home Affairs Memorandum 2002), 71 (CA 104) <https://publications.parliament.uk/pa/cm200102/cmselect/cmhaff/836/836m72.htm> accessed 21 December 2024.

21 [1991] 2 AC 447.

22 Criminal Justice Act 2003, s.103(1)(a).

23 Ibid., s.103(1)(b).

24 Jean Baudrillard, *Simulacra and Simulation* (Sheila Faria Glaser tr, University of Michigan Press 1994), 6.

character evidence became a second order simulacrum that 'mask[ed] and denature[d] a profound reality', as it was no longer a requirement to replicate the facts of the allegation.[25]

Under post-CJA case law, bad character evidence can constitute signs of wider character traits deemed relevant to an important matter in issue. It 'plays at being an appearance', such that it is a third order simulacrum that 'masks the *absence* of a profound reality'.[26] Particular examples of this are the use of evidence relating to rap music and gang membership, as considered below. Bad character evidence under the CJA is founded on a simulacrum of what the legal subject committing such acts is deemed to be. It is a copy without an original, as there is no original misconduct matching the allegations. In this way, bad character evidence under the CJA can be considered a hyperreal evidential provision. Bad character evidence masks that the apparent link between Blackness and criminality is hyperreal rather than real, and makes this simulation of racialised criminality appear real through the use at trial of signifiers embedded in colonial discourses. As was argued at the end of Chapter 2, this process of masking hyperreality, so that it appears as reality, performs a contradiction-closing function in criminal cases and operates to naturalise racially disproportionate outcomes in the criminal legal system. The bad character provisions amplify the legal processes that appear to close the contradiction between those outcomes and the simulacrum of colour-blind criminal evidence.

The concept of relevance is particularly significant in relation to the hyperreality of character evidence. As outlined above, two of the main ways that evidence relating to 'misconduct' is admissible are that it is relevant to an important matter in issue (s.101(1)(d)) or that it is connected with the facts of the case and relevant to a matter in issue (s.98). Abenaa Owusu-Bempah points out that rap and drill music have been ruled relevant in relation to motive, intention, presence, and association (including that relating to gang membership), propensity for violence and propensity to use weapons.[27] In this way, the courts are replacing direct evidence with codes for criminality. This is discussed further in the section below on rap and drill music. As argued previously, as legal and evidential provisions become more abstracted, they impact most on dehumanised, ungrievable communities. Processes of racialised criminalisation are intensified as signifiers predominate and the individual person is disappeared. Moreover, these signifiers are themselves constructed through the colonial racial frame such that bad character law

25 Ibid., 6.
26 Ibid., 6 (original italics).
27 Abenaa Owusu Bempah, 'Prosecuting Rap: What Does the Case Law Tell Us?' (2022) 41(4) *Popular Music* 427, 436; Abenaa Owusu-Bempah, 'The Irrelevance of Rap' (2022) 2 *Criminal Law Review* 130, 130–151.

both relies upon and reproduces concepts of racialised criminality, and racialised defendants become hypercriminals.

Good Character and Whiteness

A critical approach to bad character law entails interrogating what we mean by 'character'. This requires consideration of why criminal law equates bad character with factors such as convictions, Black culture, or social connections with poor racialised people; and why good character is linked with factors bound up with heteronormative patriarchal White privilege, such as lack of convictions, the heterosexual two-parent family, secure employment, or social connections with those considered to be of high status. Character as a concept in criminal law followed a similar genealogy to the dangerousness provisions considered in Chapter 5. Nineteenth-century statutes such as the CTA, HCA, and Vagrancy Act constructed the racialised poor as having inferior character traits and inherent criminality.[28] People from such communities were criminalised due to their associations and perceived character.[29] As discussed in Chapter 2, this concept of 'habitual criminals' was central to Victorian domestic and colonial criminal law.[30] However, discourses linking race and character predate this period. As outlined in Chapter 1, Linnaeus's eighteenth-century classification of human beings changed from purely physical characteristics in earlier editions of his book to character traits in later versions.[31] Further, he ordered the four categories into a hierarchy, with Black Africans ranked last.[32] He described the Black African character as 'crafty, lazy, careless', in contrast to the White European character, which was 'governed by law'.[33] Thus, concepts of character are intrinsically linked to Enlightenment theories of race, with the rule of law seen as synonymous with Whiteness.

In the nineteenth century, theories drawing on Morton and Lombroso's phrenology and on Darwinian anthropology were used to argue that Black people were of inferior character and pathologically criminal.[34] Enlightenment classification and categorisation fused with colonial racism

28 Preeti Nijhar, *Law and Imperialism* (Routledge 2009), 54–56.

29 Ibid., 32.

30 Ibid., 54.

31 Nikki Sullivan, *A Critical Introduction to Queer Theory* (Edinburgh University Press 2003), 57.

32 Ibid., 57.

33 Kehinde Andrews, *The New Age of Empire* (Allen Lane 2021), 8.

34 Lisa M. Saccomano, 'Defining the Proper Role of "Offender Characteristics" in Sentencing Decisions: A Critical Race Theory Perspective' (2019) 56(4) *American Criminal Law Review* 1693, 1706–1710.

to create a pseudo-scientific biological racial hierarchy.[35] Although sentencing practices became more individualised over time, they remained situated within a racialised conception of criminality, focusing on perceived moral failings rather than on the effects of poverty and disadvantage.[36] Crime was viewed as 'the expression of a fundamental character defect' and convicts were punished for who they were deemed to be, rather than solely for their actions.[37] As Katy Sian argues, contemporary programmes such as Prevent treat propensity to terrorism as pathological, identifiable from non-criminal behaviours and therefore measurable and predictable, harking back to these racist Lombrosian criminology categorisations.[38] Such narratives are based on binary distinctions between 'good' and 'bad' populations, and are located within the racially differentiating practices deployed by racial capitalism to maintain White supremacy.

In the United States, during the late nineteenth and early twentieth century, the use of character evidence in sentencing coincided with anthropological discourses on 'racial character'.[39] At the National Congress on Penitentiary and Reformatory Discipline held in Ohio in 1870, Zebulon Reed Brockway presented a paper arguing that 'the true basis of classification for prisoners is *character*, not conduct'.[40] In this context, 'character' is related to inherited racial qualities, with good character equated to progress and civilisation.[41] Criminal law discourses in Britain, the colonies, and the United States shared the view that criminality was a manifestation of the lack of civilisation, rationality, and the capitalist work ethic.[42] In other words, good character was defined as reflecting the values and norms attributed to racial capitalism. Bad character was framed as backwardness and laziness – the values that the colonialists had attributed to those they enslaved and colonised, as discussed in Chapter 2. The law was viewed as a means of 'character building' and as a civilising influence on the racialised undeserving poor.[43] Therefore, references to character in criminal law are, from their inception, steeped in discourses of racial capitalism, colonialism, and the civilising mission.

To be considered of good character is synonymous with the benefits conferred by White privilege. Under neoliberalism, as with earlier stages of racial

35 Nijhar, 69.
36 Martin J. Wiener, *Reconstructing the Criminal: Culture, Law, and Policy in England, 1830–1914* (Cambridge University Press 1990), 46.
37 Ibid., 46.
38 Katy Pal Sian, 'Born Radicals? Prevent, Positivism, and "Race-Thinking"' (2017) 3(6) *Palgrave Communications* 1.
39 Saccomano, 1711.
40 Ibid., 1707 (original italics).
41 Ibid., 1709.
42 Wiener, 47.
43 Ibid., 52–91.

capitalism, the notion of character is saturated in discourses of what it means to be civilised, to be Western. A pertinent example of such a narrative was given in a television interview by Margaret Thatcher in 1978:

> People are really rather afraid that this country might be rather swamped by people with a different culture and, you know, the British character has done so much for democracy, for law and done so much throughout the world that if there is any fear that it might be swamped people are going to react and be rather hostile to those coming in.[44]

This quote about immigration juxtaposes British and non-British character. British colonialism is framed as a benign and civilising gift to the world, with Britishness equated to lawfulness. The suggestion that the 'different culture' of immigrants would swamp a 'character' that 'has done so much for democracy, for law' names non-British character as undemocratic, unlawful, uncivilised, and a threat to perceived British values.

There is a significant overlap between the use of concepts of character in immigration law and criminal law. Immigration status is a weapon that the state deploys against racialised people, and in doing so determines their presence in Britain as a privilege and a concession that is contingent on 'good character'.[45] Those with convictions may be stripped of their right to live in the UK and deported, even where they were born or brought up in the UK, if they do not possess British citizenship.[46] Deportation on the basis of criminality 'marks them as uncivilised, as unworthy of legal rights because they have not met the standards for inclusion set by the colonial state'.[47] Furthermore, the case of Shamima Begum demonstrates that even lifelong British citizenship and lack of convictions cannot be relied upon as a safeguard for racialised individuals wanting to reside in the UK.[48] Ms Begum was deprived of her British citizenship on national security grounds, having travelled to Syria when she was a 15-year-old child.[49] Such practices illustrate the historical and continuing links between concepts of character and processes of racialisation, with Whiteness, Britishness, and constructions of good character being intrinsically linked, both discursively and legally.

44 Margaret Thatcher, *Granada, World in Action* (27 January 1978) <www.margaretthatcher.org/document/103485> accessed 21 December 2024.

45 James Trafford, *The Empire at Home* (Pluto Press 2021), 92–93.

46 Dan Godshaw, 'Becoming an Immigrant? Border Harms and "British" Men with Previous Convictions in British Immigration Centres' (2020) 28 *Critical Criminology* 225.

47 Nadine El-Enany, *(B)ordering Britain: Law, Race and Empire* (Manchester University Press 2020), 93–94.

48 *R (on the application of Begum) v Secretary of State for the Home Department* [2021] UKSC 7.

49 Ibid.

Evaluation of character continues to be fundamental to sentencing practices. Lisa Saccomano explains that, 'judges tend to infer good character from facts related to socioeconomic disadvantage and dangerousness from facts related to socioeconomic disadvantage, which reflects a cultural belief in meritocracy'.[50] As she argues, this reflects White elite norms and values.[51] Contemporary legal discourses around character are embedded in neoliberal concepts of meritocracy and colour-blindness, where material success is reified and property ownership confers respectability.[52] Thus, signs of social disadvantage, such as unemployment and lack of secure housing, are deemed to indicate negative character traits.[53] These factors present as colour-blind under the managerial risk assessment of neoliberalism, yet they are the material effects of racism.[54] They serve as signifiers of bad character, reproducing the third order simulacra of the racialised undeserving poor under neoliberalism as hypercriminals.

It will be argued below that in criminal trials, evidential provisions relating to character are increasingly abstracted, such that they appear meritocratic and colour-blind; reabsorbing and rendering invisible their colonial genealogy. Character evidence can be seen as a third order simulacrum – a simulation with no original. The notion of character is intrinsically linked with the simulacra of race and the undeserving poor. There is no original or neutral concept of character in criminal law and evidence that is not tied to processes of racialisation. As outlined in Chapter 1, Cheryl Harris has described Whiteness as an asset, and therefore a form of property,[55] that obscures the operation of White privilege.[56] Similarly, good character can be viewed as an asset that is akin to property and is intrinsically linked with Whiteness, and therefore unavailable to racialised defendants. The concept of character in law is constructed within the realms of Whiteness and is a colonial simulacrum. It therefore follows that any extension to the use of character evidence at trial will impact disproportionately on Black defendants. This has been borne out by the ways that these provisions have been used, as discussed below.

Bad Character and Blackness

As with dangerousness, any provision wholly or partially reliant upon previous convictions will by definition impact disproportionately on those already

50 Saccomano, 1699.
51 Ibid., 1721 and 1733.
52 Ibid., 1702.
53 Ibid., 1720.
54 Ibid., 1732.
55 Cheryl I. Harris, 'Whiteness as Property' (1993) 106(8) *Harvard Law Review* 1707, 1709.
56 Ibid., 1715.

criminalised. Where Black people are more likely to be stopped, searched, arrested and prosecuted, their level of previous convictions will reflect this.[57] As Paul Butler argues, 'if the police concentrated their enforcement of the drug laws at Harvard Law School ... the percentage of Harvard law students under criminal justice supervision would rise appreciably'.[58] In the UK context, one might substitute 'Oxbridge' (or perhaps more specifically, 'the Bullingdon Club') for 'Harvard'. At the most basic level, any law that is dependent on prior treatment in a racially disproportionate legal system will not be racially neutral. Bernard Harcourt writes that, 'risk today has collapsed into prior criminal history, and prior criminal history has become a proxy for race'.[59] In this way, as with the dangerousness provisions, the concept of bad character is a self-referential process of simulation, where signs of race, criminality, future risk, and disadvantage are entangled with each other. The character provisions are embedded within a racially disproportionate legal system where racialised individuals are more likely to be stopped, searched, arrested, charged, and convicted, such that they are deemed 'of bad character'. Then, the admission of this bad character evidence in future cases makes them more likely to be convicted again, thereby compounding disadvantage and serving to entrench the belief that they are of bad character, such that the simulation creates its own hyperreality.

Additionally, as outlined above, bad character evidence under the CJA can include the propensity to be untruthful, in other words the credibility of the defendant. If a defendant has been untruthful in a previous case, the jury may take that into account when deciding whether or not they are telling the truth in the current case. In other words, if the defendant previously pleaded not guilty, gave evidence, and was disbelieved in a previous case, that can be held against them in future cases. It is not difficult to understand how this can reproduce and compound disproportionality within the trial process. By resisting criminalisation in a previous case and being disbelieved by a jury, judge, or magistrates located within a system of White privilege and discourses of Black criminality, the racialised defendant is named as a liar not only in that case but also in future cases.

However, the issue is not merely that previous racial disparities are disproportionately reproduced by the admissibility of bad character evidence but that the very issues of propensity and credibility are located within the racial frame and colonial discourses. It will be argued below that credibility in court proceedings is a White asset that Black people do not possess. By

57 Saccomano, 1722.

58 Paul Butler, '(Color)Blind Faith: The Tragedy of "Race, Crime, and The Law"' (1998) 111 *Harvard Law Review* 1270, 1287.

59 Bernard E. Harcourt, 'Risk as a Proxy for Race' (2015) 27(4) *Federal Sentencing Reporter* 237, 237.

designating credibility as a form of evidence, the law defines credibility as a rational, measurable quality that can be assessed at trial. This acts as a simulation to abstract and render invisible the colonial genealogy of concepts such as reliability and credibility.

The behaviour for which Black defendants are penalised includes discomfort or nervousness in the courtroom setting, despite this being a rational and reasonable response to a stressful, intimidating, and alien atmosphere.[60] Thus, the treatment of witnesses is presented as colour-blind but is situated within a system of White supremacy that normalises White privilege and criminalises or disbelieves the racialised defendant or witness who does not enjoy the privilege of feeling comfortable in White spaces. As Judith Butler writes in relation to the subject attempting to give an account of themselves: 'dispossession in language is intensified by the fact that I give an account of myself to someone, so that this narrative structure of my account is superseded by the *structure of address* in which it takes place'.[61] Amanda Carlin argues that the courtroom is a 'White space' that privileges the testimony of White witnesses, and 'others' and discredits Black witnesses, yet maintains a façade of colour-blindness.[62] She describes how certain types of demeanour are seen to signify credibility, such that Black witnesses are penalised for styles of speech or behaviour that differ from the 'White norm', and are perceived as evasiveness or untruthfulness.[63] By 'performing blackness on the stand' rather than providing 'the white legal narrative the courtroom has come to expect', a racialised witness is excluded from being seen as credible.[64] Discomfort in the courtroom environment is deemed to signify lack of credibility.

Any point that requires an explanation at trial, such as the reason for fleeing from the police or not answering questions in interview, puts a defendant in the position of having to testify if they want to counter it. Further, if evidence of previous convictions has been admitted at trial, the defendant will need to give evidence if they want to explain, contextualise, and mitigate this bad character evidence. For racialised defendants, this means exposing themselves to being cross-examined in the context of a courtroom which operates under White norms and where their unease in that setting or negative views of the police are likely to be used as evidence that they lack credibility, and as an indicator of criminality. Thus, defendants are placed in an impossible position – either remain silent, with that silence framed as having

60 Amanda Carlin, 'The Courtroom as White Space: Racial Performance as Noncredibility' (2016) 63 *UCLA Law Review* 450, 480.

61 Judith Butler, *Giving an Account of Oneself* (Fordham University Press 2005), 39 (original italics).

62 Carlin, 458–459 and 466.

63 Ibid., 468–469.

64 Ibid., 484.

no explanation to give to the prosecution allegations due to guilt; or give evidence and risk their prior negative experiences of the legal system being used, together with their performance of Blackness in court, to frame them as guilty. Due to these considerations, the potential admissibility of bad character evidence puts pressure on defendants to plead guilty. A defendant may decide not to risk contesting the case if bad character evidence is likely to be admitted, and effectively 'self-convict' in order to receive a lower sentence.

There are ways of mitigating the perception of Blackness as bad character. Defence expert witnesses may be a means of giving credibility to the defendant's evidence. Jasmine Gonzales Rose contends that the admission of defence expert evidence can be used to make the jury aware of the lived experiences of racialised communities.[65] She argues that this evidence should be admissible on the grounds that it is knowledge that falls outside the life experience of White jury members, such that it meets the criteria for expert evidence.[66] She considers how running away from the police is seen as evidence of guilt.[67] However, Black defendants may have legitimate reasons unconnected with the allegations for fleeing from the police, such as fear of police violence, disproportionate stop and search practices, or concerns regarding immigration status.[68] Thus, the decontextualisation of evidence disproportionately disadvantages Black defendants.[69] Failing to stop for the police can be seen as an admission of guilt when law enforcement practices are viewed through the lens of White privilege as neutral and fair, but may be a rational response for communities with negative experiences of being stopped by the police.[70] The challenge is to disrupt the White supremacist narrative in order that the lived experience of the racialised defendant may be heard rather than silenced. Defence expert evidence could be used to illustrate to juries why members of racialised groups might run away from the police for innocent reasons.[71] In this way, the defendant can be humanised and their account given credibility, thus tempering the prejudicial effect of the prosecution evidence.

Mikah Thompson discusses what she refers to as 'stereotypical Blackness' whereby the way that a case is presented in court plays to the bias of the jurors.[72] She argues that in order to counter this, evidence should be adduced

65 Jasmine B. Gonzales Rose, 'Toward a Critical Race Theory of Evidence' (2017) 101 *Minnesota Law Review* 2243, 2309 and 2311.
66 Ibid., 2309.
67 Ibid., 2253 and 2269.
68 Ibid., 2253, 2269–2270, and 2277.
69 Ibid., 2280.
70 Ibid., 2279.
71 Ibid., 2281.
72 Mikah K. Thompson, 'Blackness as Character Evidence' (2015) 20(2) *Michigan Journal of Race and Law* 321, 337.

in rebuttal to humanise the racialised person.[73] Positive character evidence can serve as a counternarrative to challenge racialised prosecution narratives such as the gang discourse. Assertions of good character could include such factors as being a good son, a partner, a parent, an employee, and so on. As argued above, many of the categories signifying good character at trial themselves play on patriarchal heteronormative White privilege and socio-economic advantages, such that 'good character' in law is intrinsically linked to Whiteness, White privilege, and the neoliberal simulacrum of meritocracy. Notwithstanding this, anything that contextualises the lives of racialised defendants may be useful in countering the racial framing deployed in prosecution case theories.

However, under s.101(1)(f) CJA and the earlier common law provisions, presenting good character evidence if one has previous convictions can be considered as giving a false impression of the defendant's character, which can lead to an application to adduce the defendant's bad character. As Mikah Thompson argues in the context of similar US provisions, this leaves a defendant with previous convictions in the difficult tactical position of being unable to adduce any positive evidence about their own character for fear of their bad character going before the jury.[74] This means that they are effectively silenced in relation to presenting evidence of their own good character, and this may be exploited by the prosecution in the way that they present their case at trial.[75] The defendant is denied a reply to this process of racialised simulation, such that they are prevented from naming their racialised criminalisation as hypercriminality.

Moreover, even where a defendant can adduce evidence of their own good character in law and even if expert evidence in rebuttal were admitted, this fails to overcome the fundamental problem of the courtroom as a White, colonial space. Viewing Blackness as bad character is part of the racial gaze of the law. In a legal system situated within discourses where Whiteness is seen as rationality, reliability, and credibility, measures such as evidence in rebuttal can only mitigate the effects of the racial framing that equates Blackness with a lack of those qualities.

Hyperreal Gang Discourses

One of the most striking examples of the racialised use of the bad character provisions is in relation to alleged gang membership. Bad character evidence under s.101(1)(d) (important matters in issue between the prosecution and the defence) can include evidence that a defendant is a gang member.

73 Ibid., 346.
74 Ibid., 322 and 324.
75 Ibid., 322 and 324.

Authority for this can be found in the case of *Smith*,[76] where it was held that evidence that the defendant was a member of a gang involved in drugs and firearms was admissible as bad character evidence to assist the jury in deciding whether he was in possession of a firearm used in a murder. Similarly, in the case of *Elliott*,[77] it was held that evidence of gang membership was admissible in relation to charges of possession of firearms and supply of cocaine. Both of these cases were relied upon in *Lewis*,[78] when the Court of Appeal commented that, 'it is now well established that evidence of membership of, or association with, a criminal gang may be admissible under gateway (d)'.[79]

The use of gang membership as evidence at trial is not exclusive to the bad character provisions. Research by Patrick Williams and Becky Clarke demonstrates how the criminal law doctrine of joint enterprise is linked to the 'gang discourse'.[80] The police are disproportionately likely to label Black individuals as gang members,[81] and this categorisation is more likely to be deployed in the way that the prosecution presents the case against them in court compared to White defendants, particularly in joint enterprise cases.[82] Whereas White people who socialise together are more likely to be seen as friends, Black people are more likely to be seen as gang members.[83] The research also found that most of the defendants who were presented by the prosecution at trial as gang members denied that they were in a gang.[84] The use of the gang discourse at trial has a disproportionate criminalising effect on Black people, particularly young men.[85] The non-criminal interactions and associations of young Black males are viewed through the racial frame as gang related. This naming of racialised people as gang members at trial then reproduces and embeds the narrative of Black males as gang members, and of gang members as criminals. This can be seen as a process of simulation – a self-referential practice that creates hypercriminals.

In the same way that young Black men were demonised as muggers in the 1970s, so the contemporary narrative of criminal gangs serves a similar

76 [2008] EWCA Crim 1342.
77 [2010] EWCA Crim 2378.
78 [2014] EWCA Crim 48.
79 Ibid., para 80.
80 Patrick Williams and Becky Clarke, 'Dangerous Associations: Joint Enterprise, Gangs and Racism' (Centre for Crime and Justice Studies 2016) <www.crimeandjustice.org.uk/publications/dangerous-associations-joint-enterprise-gangs-and-racism> accessed 21 December 2024.
81 Ibid., 19–20.
82 Ibid., 20.
83 Ibid., 18.
84 Ibid., 15 and 20.
85 Ibid., 20–21.

purpose.[86] In this way, 'the primary function of the gang industry in England and Wales is to secure the normative boundaries of the imagined (white) society against the incursion of black and brown bodies'.[87] Through deployment of the gang discourse, poor racialised communities are reproduced as inherently criminal, enabling the state to justify their disproportionate surveillance.[88] The definition of gang membership is itself a racialised concept that performatively reproduces racially disproportionate criminalisation. As Patrick Williams argues, there is a 'race-gang nexus' whereby the construction of the Black or Asian gang operates as 'a latent racialised signifier that subverts any acknowledgement of racism'.[89] This leads to inferences that Black communities have 'the "propensity" to crime', which performs a contradiction-closing function in relation to racially disproportionate rates of arrest, charge, and conviction, such that Black criminality appears as real.[90] In the New Zealand context, Simone Bull argues that a hyperreal 'Māori-crime nexus' has been constructed.[91] In particular, facial tattoos involving a contemporary reworking of traditional designs have become signifiers for gang-related criminality.[92] Again, this nexus is self-perpetuating, with the intense policing of Māori communities leading to more arrests, such that the hyperreality of disproportionate Māori criminality appears real.[93]

The gang discourse also contributes to the racialisation of public disorder. Media and government narratives following the 2011 uprising in England identified gangs as a 'driving force'.[94] Yet even the police's own statistics demonstrated that gangs did not play a significant role.[95] Despite this, in 2012 the Metropolitan Police and Boris Johnson introduced the Gangs Matrix, a database containing the personal details of over 3,800 people suspected by the police of being gang members, gang associates, or 'at risk' of being gang

86 Patrick Williams and Becky Clarke, 'The Black Criminal Other as an Object of Social Control' (2018) 7(11) *Social Sciences* 1, 5 <www.mdpi.com/2076-0760/7/11/234> accessed 21 December 2024.

87 Ibid., 2.

88 Ibid., 5.

89 Patrick Williams, 'Criminalising the Other: Challenging the Race-Gang Nexus' (2015) 56(3) *Race and Class* 18, 32.

90 Paul Gilroy, 'The Myth of Black Criminality' (1982) 19 *The Socialist Register* 52 <https://socialistregister.com/index.php/srv/article/view/5474> accessed 21 December 2024.

91 Simone Bull, 'Crime and Māori in the Media' in Antje Deckert and Rick Sarre (eds), *The Palgrave Handbook of Australian and New Zealand Criminology, Crime and Justice* (Springer 2017), 744.

92 Ibid., 743.

93 Ibid., 745.

94 Williams and Clarke, 'The Black Criminal Other', 7.

95 Alan Travis, 'UK Riots Analysis Reveals Gangs Did Not Play Pivotal Role' *The Guardian* (24 October 2011) <www.theguardian.com/uk/2011/oct/24/riots-analysis-gangs-no-pivotal-role> accessed 21 December 2024.

members, with the vast majority being Black males and the youngest aged 12 years.[96] The Matrix assessed 'propensity for violence' through traffic light scores, with red for individuals deemed the highest risk.[97] It therefore relied upon a prediction of future conduct, as with the bad character and dangerousness provisions.

The information behind the Gangs Matrix was compiled from various sources, including previous convictions, dress style, mobile phone data, algorithmic analysis of social media, and stop and search data.[98] Therefore, the Matrix relied on codes for criminality rather than commission of criminal offences, and constituted a further process of simulation. In this way, the Matrix constructed abstracted legal subjects. It was not just that gang membership served as a signifier for criminality, regardless of whether or not the gang member had committed any criminal offences. The abstraction was taken a step further such that signifiers of gangs were used as markers of criminality, regardless of whether or not the person was in a gang. Signs such as music, address, or social media presence were used to denote gang membership, which was then used as a code for criminality. Not only was the question of whether they had committed a criminal offence irrelevant, but whether or not they were a gang member became irrelevant, as the process of simulation relied upon signs of gang membership. In this way, the hyperreal Gangs Matrix constructed hypercriminals.

The Gangs Matrix and the stop and search provisions were symbiotic practices that interacted to reproduce racialisation and criminalisation. Data gathered from stop and search could be used as police intelligence to justify inclusion on the Matrix, and narrative accounts of family members suggested that they believed that young Black men were stopped and searched as a means of collecting such data.[99] Furthermore, presence on the Matrix could lead to being stopped and searched,[100] such that 'being matrixed emerged as a powerful process of criminalisation'.[101] Thus, it was a circular process and self-fulfilling prophecy whereby a simulation of criminality was created by practices of stop and search. This constructed 'criminality' was then used to justify further stop and searches on the basis that those young people were on the Matrix and therefore criminal. In this way, the Matrix was hyperreal, as

96 Patrick Williams, 'Being Matrixed: The (Over)Policing of Gang Suspects in London' (StopWatch 2018), 5 and 8 <www.stop-watch.org/what-we-do/research/being-matrixed-the-overpolicing-of-gang-suspects-in-london/> accessed 21 December 2024.

97 Amnesty International, 'Trapped in the Matrix' (2018) 2 <https://www.amnesty.org.uk/files/2018-05/Trapped%20in%20the%20Matrix%20Amnesty%20report.pdf?VersionId=lJSxllcKfkZgr4gHZsz0vW8JZ0W3V_PD> accessed 21 December 2024.

98 Williams, 'Being Matrixed', 8.

99 Ibid., 21.

100 Ibid., 26.

101 Ibid., 32.

it defined as criminal those people that it had constructed as criminal whether they had committed a crime or not, thus collapsing the boundaries between truth and falsity. This simulacrum of criminality appeared real and had material consequences for those on the Matrix.

The Gangs Matrix was deployed by state agencies to control, contain and restrict the lives of racialised communities, which could include restrictions on their opportunities in relation to education, employment and accommodation.[102] As well as being subjected to more frequent stop and search,[103] some of those on the Matrix were denied entry to schools and colleges,[104] placed in local authority care, and had their family moved out of their community.[105] The Matrix constructed a causal link between existing in a certain way in particular communities and gang membership, and then constructed a further link between gang membership and criminal activities. Over a third of those on the Matrix had never committed a serious offence.[106] In many cases, 'it was their non-criminal presence in police-defined risky areas which simplistically served to affirm to the police a gang suspect status'.[107] Living in a place that was deemed by the police to be a high crime area was sufficient to name someone as a gang member, and by implication a criminal. Repeated stop and search and other interactions between the police and racialised communities were performative – they made this hyperreality seem real.

Even within existing definitions of crime, those communities named as high crime areas by the police did not match the statistics, with racialised communities disproportionately viewed by the police as 'high crime'.[108] Being poor and Black was sufficient to be named as a gang member, a criminal and of bad character when using public spaces. This harked back to nineteenth century discourses around 'dangerous classes' and habitual criminal communities, who were 'defined and signified not in terms of their offences, but rather in terms of their propensity to commit crimes, by the nature of their characters, their appearance, their physical location and their associations'.[109] Under neoliberalism, racialised poor communities in urban areas are named as being of bad character due to those same factors. The people that they socialise with, the areas in which they live, and the music that they write, perform, and listen to is used as evidence of bad character.

102 Ibid., 26.
103 Ibid., 28–30.
104 Ibid., 42–45.
105 Ibid., 39–42.
106 Ibid., 26.
107 Ibid., 35.
108 Williams and Clarke, 'The Black Criminal Other', 8–9.
109 Nijhar, 10.

There are significant parallels between these practices and s.60 CJPOA, considered in Chapter 3, which relies on the same processes of racial framing and spatial containment. In Chapter 4, it was argued that KCPOs are hyperreal, as they construct racialised young people as knife carriers whether or not they have carried a knife. The 'pre-crime' simulation of the KCPO creates its own perceived reality by targeting those individuals, with their subsequent arrest appearing to confirm that they were a criminal all along. The gangs discourse operates in a similar way, such that 'gang members are imagined as criminal in being, as predisposed to criminality and as unreformable'.[110] Signifiers of gang membership are used to construct racialised legal subjects who are deemed to be ontologically criminal, and therefore of bad character.

In November 2022, after a legal challenge by Liberty, the Metropolitan Police agreed to overhaul the Gangs Matrix by removing large numbers of people and allowing those who asked to be told if they were on the database, unless certain limited exceptions applied.[111] The case was brought on behalf of Awate Suleiman, a musician and writer who experienced debilitating anxiety after being frequently arrested.[112] He had spent months trying to find out if he was on the Matrix.[113] He described the Matrix as 'a relic of colonialism, brought back to the home of Empire and used against people the Met Police thinks nobody cares about'.[114] Use of the Matrix was discontinued in February 2024.[115] However, much harm had already been done and the Matrix had entrenched perceived links between gangs, race, and crime, with the use of the gangs discourse continuing at criminal trials. Further, the police moved to other forms of surveillance and social control, including the Violence Harm Assessment.[116] Even before the Matrix had been discontinued, the Metropolitan Police had already started to profile young racialised

110 Lisa Marie Cacho, *Social Death* (New York University Press 2012), 66.

111 BBC News, 'Gang Violence Matrix: Met Police to Overhaul Controversial Database' *BBC News* (12 November 2022) <https://www.bbc.co.uk/news/uk-england-london-63568880> accessed 21 December 2024.

112 Liberty, 'Met to Overhaul "Racist" Gangs Matrix After Landmark Legal Challenge' *Liberty* (11 November 2022) <https://www.libertyhumanrights.org.uk/issue/met-to-overhaul-racist-gangs-matrix-after-landmark-legal-challenge/> accessed 21 December 2024.

113 Ibid.

114 Ibid.

115 Metropolitan Police, 'Gangs Violence Matrix' (2025) <https://www.met.police.uk/police-forces/metropolitan-police/areas/about-us/about-the-met/gangs-violence-matrix/> accessed 5 January 2025.

116 Metropolitan Police, 'Violence Harm Assessment' (2025) <https://www.met.police.uk/police-forces/metropolitan-police/areas/about-us/about-the-met/violence-harm-assessment/> accessed 5 January 2025.

people through Project Alpha, a unit set up in 2019 to monitor drill music, as discussed below.[117]

An example of how discourses around signifiers of gang membership play out in court is the case of *Elliott*, where the court stated that 'proof of (gang) membership will almost inevitably involve the prosecution putting forward evidence of a number of circumstances from which gang membership could be inferred'.[118] This means that evidence of gang membership is likely to be hearsay, circumstantial and uncertain, which heightens the difficulties involved in challenging it. The Court of Appeal justified this by arguing that 'violent gangs ... are unlikely to issue membership cards',[119] thus effectively allowing a lower standard of evidence in relation to establishing gang membership by stating that the surrounding circumstances are sufficient to demonstrate such membership. This means that signifiers, rather than evidence around conduct, are used to construct gang membership, and in turn construct bad character and criminality. In this way, the bad character provisions interact performatively with the gang discourse to intensify the ways that Black people are reproduced as criminals. Bad character evidence on the basis of gang membership is a simulation whereby concepts of truth and falsity are no longer meaningful as they are subsumed by codes for criminal gangs.

In the case of *Lewis*, which involved an incident during the 2011 uprising, evidence was adduced in relation to gang membership in order to support the prosecution case that the defendants were present at the scene, were acting with common purpose and had the propensity to commit offences of the kind charged. While there was other evidence against the defendants, such as cell site analysis, surveillance and CCTV, the bad character evidence around gang membership was central to the Crown's case theory, and the admission of this bad character evidence was the basis of the majority of the appeals against conviction. Previously, courts had stressed the undesirability of the central issue of guilt being overshadowed by satellite arguments over character at trial.[120] However, where trials include an assertion of gang membership, the appellate courts seem keen to categorise this as a central rather than secondary issue. Not only is gang membership deemed to constitute bad character, but it is considered as part of the main prosecution trial narrative, which is a significant and racialised reframing of the use of bad character evidence. At trial, the prosecution called police officers as expert witnesses to

117 Wil Crisp and Vikram Dodd, 'Met Police Profiling Children "On a Large Scale", Documents Show' *The Guardian* (3 June 2022) <https://www.theguardian.com/uk-news/2022/jun/03/met-police-project-alpha-profiling-children-documents-show> accessed 21 December 2024.

118 *Elliott*, para 31.

119 Ibid., para 31.

120 *R v Mitchell* [2016] UKSC 5, para 53.

give evidence around gang membership in Birmingham and used YouTube videos to support their contention that the defendants were gang members who were involved with firearms and had negative attitudes towards the police. The use of police officers as expert witnesses is analysed later in this chapter.

In *Lewis*, Sir Brian Leveson set out four questions to be considered in cases involving the admissibility of gang membership as bad character evidence to demonstrate propensity:

1. Is the evidence relevant to an important matter in issue between a defendant and the prosecution?
2. Is there proper evidence of the existence and the nature of the gang or gangs?
3. Does the evidence, if accepted, go to show the defendant was a member of or associated with a gang or gangs which exhibited violence or hostility to the police or with links with firearms?
4. If the evidence is admitted, will it have such an adverse effect on the fairness of the proceedings that it ought to be excluded?

Particularly troubling in the *Lewis* test was the phrase 'hostility to the police'. Aside from the ambiguities involved in defining what this constitutes, to show hostility to the police may be a logical response for someone stopped and searched on a regular basis. To define this as criminality is to interpret the everyday experiences of young Black men through the lens of White privilege rather than through their lived experiences. Hostility to those enforcing a racist legal system is deemed bad character, thus reinforcing the boundaries of White supremacy by equating resistance with criminality. As the 2011 uprising was a reaction to the police shooting dead a racialised man in North London, those involved were by definition hostile to police tactics and practices. Those resisting or protesting against the violence of the state are framed as feral gangs threatening civilised society. The imagery of the gang discourse cannot be divorced from colonial narratives of uncivilised, hostile, and ungovernable racialised populations. Such discourses reinforce the hegemony of White privilege by decontextualising public unrest and framing it in such a way that it is unintelligible as legitimate resistance, and intelligible only as gang-related violence, which is an ostensibly colour-blind code for Black criminality. Those resisting state violence are named as criminal in order to uphold the legitimacy of the state and its monopoly on lawful violence.

Rap and Drill Music: Simulations of Criminality

In Chapter 4, the use of CBOs and gang injunctions in relation to drill music was considered, particularly in relation to the way that this frames the music and culture of young Black males as violent criminality and silences their voices by criminalising their self-expression. Rap and drill music have also been used as bad character evidence against racialised subjects in criminal trials to demonstrate evidence of propensity to commit offences of the kind charged, to disprove a defence such as alibi, or to establish an element of the offence, such as intention. As Adèle Oliver argues, Patrick Williams' concept of the 'race-gang nexus' outlined above now finds its expression in a 'drill-gang nexus', where participation in drill music, or even a liking for the genre, is viewed as intrinsically related to gang activities.[121]

Historically, one way of oppressing racialised communities has been through the criminalisation of music and poetry. The Irish Penal Code described in Chapter 2 is an example. Contemporary forms of Black music such as rap, grime and drill are not the first to be targeted by the state. The music of previous generations of Black communities in the UK was subjected to heavy handed practices as a means of social control, including police raids on blues house parties and on venues playing reggae sound systems.[122] Adèle Oliver explains that, 'Black music has not been traditionally considered an expressive art form but a dangerous call to arms'.[123] The criminalisation of rap and drill relies upon a conception of valid forms of music that is embedded in a history of 'colonial epistemologies of European tonal superiority'[124] that draws a binary distinction between White music and Black noise.[125] White supremacist norms refuse to consider rap and drill as legitimate art forms but only as an adjunct to crime, and as the soundtrack to gang culture. This refusal stems from the colonial racial framing of Black communities as barbaric and feral, with danger located in their bodies, their culture, and their associations.

In the case of *O*,[126] the Court of Appeal upheld a conviction for possession of firearms with intent after the prosecution admitted evidence of YouTube videos where the defendant, along with others, was rapping lyrics including references to gangs and guns. However, in *Alimi*,[127] the Court of Appeal quashed the defendant's conviction and ordered a retrial on the basis that the defendant had been present in videos but had not rapped and was effectively an extra, such that the third question in *Lewis* set out above was answered in the negative. The prosecution offered no evidence against Mr Alimi prior to

121 Adèle Oliver, *Deeping It: Colonialism, Culture and Criminalisation of UK Drill* (404 Ink Limited 2023), 10.

122 Lambros Fatsis, 'Grime: Criminal Subculture or Public Counterculture? A Critical Investigation into the Criminalization of Black Musical Subcultures in the UK' (2019) 15(3) *Crime Media Culture* 447, 447–448.

123 Oliver, 45.

124 Ibid., 35.

125 Ibid., 47.

126 [2010] EWCA Crim 2985.

127 [2014] EWCA Crim 2412.

the retrial. However, the two co-defendants who had participated in the rapping had their convictions upheld on appeal. Again, signifiers of criminality were constructed as evidence of guilt.

In the case of *Awoyemi*,[128] YouTube videos including two of the defendants making gun symbols with their hands and using slang language for guns were admitted as evidence of gang membership and of their attitudes towards serious violence and firearms, on the basis that this was important explanatory evidence under s.101(1)(c) and evidence of propensity to commit offences of the kind charged under s.101(1)(d). Using two fingers to make a gun symbol can indicate positive endorsement of a music track and finds its origins in 1950s Jamaican music.[129] Yet, such nuances are lost on the criminal courts, where such a hand symbol is linked to the use of firearms or interpreted as gang affiliation.[130] Evidence was also admitted in relation to rap lyrics found in the bedroom of one of the defendants that referred to gangs, violence, firearms, and drugs. Rejecting the appeals against conviction, the Court of Appeal stated that the four-stage test in *Lewis* was particular to the facts in the *Lewis* case rather than having to be satisfied in every case involving allegations of gang membership.[131] Therefore, the admissibility of gang membership as bad character evidence became even less onerous to establish and rap lyrics were confirmed as admissible evidence at trial.

Research in the United States has found that rap music is viewed negatively compared to other music, which has implications for the ways that it is used at trial. In a study by Adam Dunbar, Charis Kubrin, and Nicholas Scurich, participants were shown identical lyrics referring to violence but one group was told that they were country music lyrics and the other group was told that they were rap lyrics.[132] The lyrics were actually taken from a 1960s folk song.[133] Those told that they were rap lyrics had a more negative reaction and considered the lyrics more in need of regulation than those who were told that they were country lyrics.[134] In a further study, there was no significant difference in results between a control group not told the genre of the music and those participants who were told that the lyrics were country music, which suggested that the differences in results between rap and country could not be explained by positive feelings towards country music, and were therefore indicative of a bias against rap music.[135]

128 [2016] EWCA Crim 668.
129 Oliver, 73.
130 Ibid., 72–74. See *R v Sode* [2017] EWCA Crim 705.
131 *Awoyemi*, para 35.
132 Adam Dunbar, Charis E. Kubrin and Nicholas Scurich, 'The Threatening Nature of "Rap" Music' (2016) 22(3) *Psychology, Public Policy, and Law* 280, 281.
133 Ibid., 284.
134 Ibid., 285.
135 Ibid., 286–287.

In a further experiment, Dunbar and Kubrin added heavy metal to country and rap to see whether metal might be a more effective comparator than country.[136] Again participants were shown the folk song lyrics and told it was a particular genre, and this time they were asked various questions, including whether the author of the lyrics was intelligent, threatening, intimidating, likeable, aggressive, honest, dangerous, violent, a gang member, involved in criminal activity, had a criminal record and owned a gun.[137] The answers were put together to create a composite 'bad character' score.[138] Those who were told that the genre was rap gave higher bad character scores than those who were told that the song was country or heavy metal, and this was particularly marked in relation to older participants.[139] This led the researchers to conclude that 'negative character assumptions, and particularly those related to criminal propensity, appear unique to rap'.[140] This indicates that the introduction of rap lyrics into a trial acts as a signifier for criminality and reprehensible behaviour.

Andrea Dennis considered training materials provided for US lawyers prosecuting 'gang' cases.[141] These materials noted that referring to gang signifiers, including lyrics, could shift the narrative of a trial and portray the defendant as of bad character, thus advantaging the prosecution.[142] In her words, 'when courts permit the prosecutor to admit rap music lyrics as criminal evidence, they allow the government to obtain a stranglehold on the case'.[143] Rap lyrics are used as evidence in ways that other genres of music are not,[144] and juries are invited to treat them literally and as confessions of guilt rather than as artistic expression.[145] Research found that such evidence was used to bolster weak cases to secure convictions and could lead to higher sentences, including nearly 30 death penalty cases in the United States.[146]

Similarly in the UK, the prejudicial use of rap and drill lyrics to establish gang membership, a propensity to be violent and a propensity to use

136 Adam Dunbar and Charis E. Kubrin, 'Imagining Violent Criminals: An Experimental Investigation of Music Stereotypes and Character Judgments' (2018) 14 *Journal of Experimental Criminology* 507, 515 <https://doi.org/10.1007/s11292-018-9342-6> accessed 21 December 2024.

137 Ibid., 525.

138 Ibid., 519.

139 Ibid., 519–520.

140 Ibid., 523.

141 Andrea L. Dennis, 'Poetic (In)justice? Rap Music Lyrics as Art, Life, and Criminal Evidence' (2007) 31(1) *Columbia Journal of Law and the Arts* 1, 1.

142 Ibid., 1.

143 Ibid., 2.

144 Ibid., 2–3.

145 Ibid., 3–8.

146 Erik Nielson and Andrea L. Dennis, *Rap on Trial: Race, Lyrics and Guilt in America* (The New Press 2019), 19 and 70.

weapons, constitutes a racialised, unreliable, and highly prejudicial form of evidence. Rap music acts as a signifier for Black criminality that allows prosecutors to deploy racist discourses around gang violence without appearing openly racist, and is used as a deliberate tactic to increase the prospect of conviction.[147] Abenaa Owusu-Bempah analysed 38 criminal appeal cases involving rap, grime, and drill music,[148] and found that the lyrics adduced often bore a tenuous relationship to the offence charged.[149] As she explains, 'the case law confirms that rap can operate as a "racialised signifier" to help build a gang narrative'.[150] In this way, the admission of rap music as bad character evidence constitutes the replacement of direct evidence by symbolic evidence at trial, such that involvement in, or a preference for rap music serves as a code for criminality.

Rap and drill music rely upon 'symbolism, figurative language, hyperbole, braggadocio and humour' as part of their art form.[151] Rather than inciting violence, aggressive lyrics may be used to deter threats from others or as a means of dealing with unresolved complex trauma.[152] References to violence and weapons are frequently used as metaphors and fictional tropes, and to gain commercial success.[153] Thus, prosecutors 'conflate art with character' by presenting lyrics as confessional.[154] While some tracks may have an autobiographical element whereby racialised young people narrate their lived experiences of poverty and police harassment, rap music trades upon fictionalised or exaggerated accounts of urban life where 'tales of criminality, violence, and misogyny are considered genre conventions, similar to action-packed Hollywood movies'.[155] As Robert Roks argues, rap creates its own hyperreality by 'blurring distinctions between the binary oppositions of "fiction or fact" and "real or fake"'.[156] Therefore, 'the importance of "keeping it real" in

147 Eithne Quinn, 'Lost in Translation? Rap Music and Racial Bias in the Courtroom' (The University of Manchester 2018) <http://blog.policy.manchester.ac.uk/posts/2018/10/lost-in-translation-rap-music-and-racial-bias-in-the-courtroom/> accessed 21 December 2024.

148 Owusu Bempah, 'Prosecuting Rap', 430.

149 Ibid., 437.

150 Ibid., 434.

151 Ibid., 430.

152 Beth Hall, Roxanne Khan and Mike Eslea, 'Criminalising Black Trauma: Grime and Drill Lyrics as a Form of Ethnographic Data to Understand "Gangs" and Serious Youth Violence' (2022) 7(2) *Genealogy* <https://doi.org/10.3390/genealogy7010002> accessed 21 December 2024.

153 Owusu-Bempah, 'Prosecuting Rap', 430–431.

154 Abenaa Owusu-Bempah, 'Part of Art or Part of Life? Rap Lyrics in Criminal Trials' (London School of Economics 2000) <https://blogs.lse.ac.uk/politicsandpolicy/rap-lyrics-in-criminal-trials/> accessed 21 December 2024.

155 Robert A. Roks, '"Keeping it (Hyper)Real": A Musical History of Rap's Quest Beyond Authenticity' in Dina Siegel and Frank Bovenkerk (eds), *Crime and Music* (Springer 2021), 282.

156 Ibid., 282.

rap culture has morphed into the act of "keeping it hyperreal," with a quest beyond authenticity in constructing street credibility'.[157] Rap and drill music can be seen as hyperreal forms of expression that are treated as expressions of reality by the state. Unlike other forms of art, the conventions of rap and drill music are deployed by the prosecution to signify criminality.

Because the form of address used by criminalised Black men as artistic expression has already been deemed by White norms as a confession of criminality, it is intelligible to the criminal law only in those terms. For the Black defendant to claim that their lyrics were a simulation of reality, not intended to be taken literally, is akin to Baudrillard's discussion of the simulated robbery that the police are unable to distinguish from reality, as described in Chapter 1 – 'the network of artificial signs will become inextricably linked with real elements'.[158] It is hyperreal, such that the boundaries between truth and fiction are collapsed. This inability to distinguish culture from criminal confessions is made possible through processes of dehumanisation and abstraction that deny Black self-expression as an art form, such that art is seen as the preserve of Whiteness.

Colonialism Gives Evidence: Police as Expert Witnesses

Patrick Williams writes that, 'the "gang industry" is … sustained through the perpetuation of mythologies parading as research truths, which facilitate the continuity and the (re)construction of the Black folk devil'.[159] Some academics, criminal practitioners, and community associations have been complicit in this process through uncritically accepting police narratives in relation to racialised gangs,[160] such that hyperreality is framed as reality. As outlined in Chapter 4, an example of this is the 'knife crime industry', whereby public and private organisations can apply for public funds for campaigns and interventions, such that adherence to socially constructed racialised narratives around knives and gangs is a means of securing funding.[161] As discussed in earlier chapters, knife crime is a racialised simulacrum, and therefore 'organising a response to violence through the language of "knife crime" will inherently reiterate racist understandings of criminality' and reproduce the simulation.[162] A further way that the hyperreal gang narrative is reproduced is through the use of police as expert witnesses on gangs and drill music.

157 Ibid., 282.
158 Baudrillard, *Simulacra and Simulation*, 20.
159 Williams, 'Criminalising the Other', 32.
160 Ibid., 31–32.
161 Elaine Williams and Peter Squires, *Rethinking Knife Crime* (Palgrave Macmillan 2021), 315.
162 Ibid., 281.

The general rule in criminal proceedings is that expert evidence is admissible only for matters outside the jury's knowledge, and unlike other witnesses, experts are permitted to express their opinion on the matters on which they give evidence rather than being restricted to factual points.[163] As mentioned above in relation to the *Lewis* case, police officers have been allowed to give evidence as expert witnesses at trial in relation to gangs. Similarly, in the case of *Rashid*,[164] the evidence of a police constable was deemed admissible in relation to gang association, with the Court of Appeal affirming that the point had been established in the cases of *Smith*, *Elliott* and *Lewis*. Defence counsel had argued that the police officer's evidence was based 'only on an interpretation of music videos, knowledge gained from social media and discussions with people who were not identified'.[165]

The prevalence of the practice of calling police officers as expert witnesses on gangs and music is illustrated by the resources that the Metropolitan Police have devoted to drill music with their own specialist unit, Project Alpha, which has over 30 staff.[166] The head of the project, PC Michael Railton, described their work as 'decod[ing] the hyper-local context of the lyrics, hand gestures and symbolism of the visual content used by aspiring rappers'.[167] In other words, the police attempt to interpret what they perceive to be codes for criminal behaviour in recordings and videos. They do this through the racial frame, such that their interpretation of these signifiers is through a lens that views drill music as an expression of criminality.

Framing police witnesses as experts is means of privileging and reproducing the discourses of those who enforce the law. It has been described as 'the prosecution calling itself to give evidence'.[168] Police narratives are presented as neutral expertise rather than as partial accounts located within racially disproportionate law enforcement practices embedded in colonialism. They are given superior epistemic status as their subjective opinions are produced as neutral, objective, and legitimate sources of knowledge, while the racialised defendant is presented as an object of study. The evidence given by those who police racialised communities is deemed colour-blind and accorded a similar status to forensic and medical evidence. This reinforces White privilege, reproduces racial framing, and silences the voices of

163 Criminal Procedure Rules 2020 Part 19.2.
164 [2019] EWCA Crim 2018.
165 Ibid., para 33.
166 Crisp and Dodd.
167 Ibid.
168 Sandra Paul and others, 'Tackling Racial Injustice: Children and the Youth Justice System' (Justice 2021) 41, para 2.51 <https://justice.org.uk/wp-content/uploads/flipbook/46/book.html> accessed 21 December 2024.

racialised communities, particularly in relation to the lived experiences of young Black males.

Although juries are not obliged to accept the evidence of expert witnesses, naming a witness as an expert seems likely to invite an interpretation that their evidence is superior to that of the lay witness. Such a positioning serves to remove the subjectivity of the police officer's account and reframe it as neutral expert evidence. As with the body-worn camera footage considered in Chapter 5, the police officer's subjectivity is disappeared, and the evidence appears objective. In the case of *Fender*, the Court of Appeal approved the use of a police report as expert evidence, on the basis that the officer had access to the Gangs Matrix and had worked at a gang unit.[169] As described above, the Gangs Matrix information was collected through police practices which already framed racialised communities as gang members and criminals, even where they had no previous convictions. Narratives around gangs are subsequently reproduced as 'truth' through the presentation of evidence in court. Such evidence can be seen as hyperreal and based on previous simulacra. In this way, 'information' created by the carceral state, such as the Gangs Matrix and Project Alpha, became evidence, such that it created its own reality and the simulacrum of the violent, Black gang member appeared real. Once the spectre of the gang discourse has been raised at trial, convincing the jury that this highly prejudicial evidence is hyperreal rather than real is a significant challenge. Defendants are faced with the prospect of opposing a narrative account constructed through the racial frame that presents itself as factual.

The use of police as experts on both gang membership and the culture of racialised communities bears the imprints of the colonial anthropologists who saw the subjects of the colonies as different, exotic, animalistic and part of nature. It silences racialised defendants as those who are misrepresented, and as those whose culture and associations are spoken about by others who profess to know more about it. Such evidence is constructed through the colonial gaze with police testimony presented as rational, objective, and quasi-scientific, and racialised defendants framed as savage, uneducated, and violent. In this way, racialised defendants are constituted as subaltern. If we view the concept of race as, in Patrick Wolfe's words, 'colonialism speaking',[170] then the third order simulacrum of bad character evidence given by agents of the neoliberal carceral state against the racialised poor can be seen not only as the prosecution giving evidence but as colonialism giving evidence.

169 [2018] EWCA Crim 2829.
170 Patrick Wolfe, *Traces of History: Elementary Structures of Race* (Verso Books 2016), 57.

Resisting Character Evidence: From Exclusion to Abolition

Because White norms view rap and drill music as intrinsically linked with inner city gang-related public disorder, drug dealing, and serious violent crime, these norms need to be disrupted in order for those lyrics to be intelligible in the same way as country lyrics or poetry. Andrea Dennis argues that defence expert evidence should be admissible to avoid the risk of juries seeing lyrics as confessions of guilt rather than as an art form, and therefore treating rap differently to other forms of music, poetry, and literature.[171] In the UK context, Eithne Quinn discusses the importance of calling defence experts to contextualise and explain rap and drill music as a counterbalance to the use of police expert witnesses.[172] As the norms of rap and drill music are beyond the knowledge of many jury members, this calls for specialist knowledge and meets the test for the admissibility of expert evidence.[173] Such testimony can enable juries to recognise and understand the conventions of the genre, such as the use of collective knowledge, boasting, metaphors, role playing, and fictional folk narratives.[174] In other words, this evidence can help the jury to see the defendants as hypercriminals rather than criminals.

Although this contextualisation by defence expert witnesses can be useful as a means of disrupting the racial frame, this only mitigates the effect of prejudicial evidence, and the better solution is to exclude this hyperreal form of evidence from trials altogether.[175] Defence expert witnesses can also be called to support a pre-trial legal application to exclude this evidence so that it does not go before the jury.[176] Various exclusionary provisions are available to the defence where admission is sought under s.101(1)(d). Under s.103(3), evidence can be excluded where it would be unjust to admit it and under s.101(3), evidence must be excluded where it appears to the court that admission of the evidence would have such an adverse effect on the fairness of the proceedings that the court ought not to admit it. Additionally, the general exclusionary provision under s.78, PACE is a potential means of excluding any prosecution evidence that would cause such unfairness that it should not be admitted at trial.

These provisions may give the appearance of fairness but have been shown to provide little respite to defendants in cases framed as gang related. For example, in the case of *O* outlined above, the court considered exclusion under s.101(3) but decided that slang references to the defendant's local area and to gangs were sufficient, notwithstanding that the defence argued that

171 Dennis, 14–16.
172 Quinn.
173 Dennis, 13 and 32.
174 Ibid., 20–23.
175 Nielson and Dennis, 155–157.
176 Quinn.

the video existed six months prior to arrest and involved no specific threat to anyone.[177] The Court of Appeal conceded that such evidence was necessarily prejudicial but nonetheless ruled that it was not unfair to admit it. This illustrates how, rather than making the law fairer, exclusionary provisions may operate as performative discourses to name the admission of the evidence as fair and just, and thus to silence debates around its unfairness. In this way, exclusionary provisions serve a comparable purpose to the human rights laws considered in the case of *Roberts* in Chapter 3 – they legitimise laws that are located within racialised processes of simulation.

Fundamentally, character law is rooted in colonial discourses and reproduces Blackness as criminality, whereas Whiteness is associated with the Enlightenment concepts of rationality and the rule of law. For this reason, as Adèle Oliver argues, 'the criminalisation of UK drill is not an exception to the rule of law; it is the rule'.[178] As bad character evidence has become increasingly dislocated from the factual basis of the allegation, and thus more abstracted, it has shifted from a first order to a second order simulacrum under pre-CJA case law, and then to a third order simulacrum under the CJA. Bad character laws are hyperreal; they rely upon codes for criminality, which they use to construct evidence of criminality at trial and so construct hypercriminals. Case law in respect of gang membership and music has demonstrated that bad character provisions have reproduced the racial frame of the Gangs Matrix, Project Alpha, and the gang discourse, as well as naming cultural expression by racialised communities as criminality rather than as art. The bad character provisions rely upon previous simulations of criminality, and reproduce and intensify these processes, such that teenagers singing along to music videos or making gestures become simulacra of violent criminality, and the boundaries between truth and falsity are destroyed.

As outlined earlier, the admission of bad character evidence can be seen as a contradiction-closing device. This is particularly true of cases that include discourses around gang associations and rap or drill music. The concept of a post-racial society can be seen 'as an ideological state ploy, which defines young Black Britons out of citizenship by delineating their activities as dangerous, threatening and criminal'.[179] The civil rights dream that people would be judged by their character rather than the colour of their skin has been appropriated by discourses of neoliberal post-rights colour-blindness.[180] This denial of racism leads to the conclusion that unequal outcomes must be due to the deficiencies or criminal character of racialised people. Character is a

177 O.
178 Oliver, 17.
179 Lambros Fatsis, 'Policing the Beats: The Criminalisation of UK Drill and Grime Music by the London Metropolitan Police' (2019) 67(6) *The Sociological Review* 1300, 1311.
180 Henry A. Giroux, *America on the Edge: Henry Giroux on Politics, Culture and Education* (Palgrave Macmillan 2006) 158; Andrews, xxvii–xxviii.

racialised concept that masquerades as being racially neutral to produce the simulation that the dream of overcoming racism has been achieved. Such narratives blame Black people for racial disparities in the criminal legal system. As Lambros Fatsis argues:

> instead of repairing the desolate environments that drill artists describe in their lyrics, the neoliberal state accuses residents for the deterioration in their surroundings; often attributing such decline to a lack of civility and a cultural propensity for gang violence.[181]

In the hyperreal neoliberal post-racial world, the simulacrum of meritocracy asserts that racially disproportionate outcomes cannot be due to the colour of a person's skin, so it must be due to their character. In this way, a seemingly objective reason is provided to justify and legitimise the disproportionate conviction and incarceration of the racialised poor.

The processes of simulation that view personal associations and musical taste as criminality also render invisible the most significant harm in society. Framing young racialised men as gangsters serves to 'rejuvenate the fiction of the real in the opposite camp';[182] to juxtapose them against White elite society, which is viewed as non-criminal and respectable. In this way, it acts as a simulation that equates Whiteness with lawfulness and conceals that the gangsters whose actions lead to the greatest social harm, those who carry out violent and premeditated attacks on those outside their circle for their own gain and that of their associates, are in the boardrooms of multinational corporations, in the police force, and in the government.

Bad character law, along with the other provisions discussed in this book, is both racialised and racialising. In other words, it is both a symptom and a cause of narratives around racialised criminality. Making bad character evidence inadmissible, particularly that relating to gangs and rap music, could reduce the criminalisation and incarceration of racialised young people. However, criminal law would find alternative means of adducing evidence that frames racialised people as being of bad character because the criminal legal system in a colonial state such as the UK is based on, and reproduces, the simulacra of Blackness as bad character and Whiteness as good character. These underlying processes of hypercriminalisation would continue in other guises. In the final chapter, I will argue that in order to challenge processes of hypercriminalisation, address social harm, and advance the project of social justice, it is necessary to confront racial neoliberalism and abolish the carceral state.

181 Fatsis, 'Policing the Beats', 1302.
182 Baudrillard, *Simulacra and Simulation*, 13.

Chapter 7

Hypercriminality and Carceral Abolition

The aim of this book has been to theorise how neoliberal criminal law and evidence create hyperreal racialised legal subjects through repeated performative discourses that collapse the boundaries between truth and falsity, and reproduce criminality in increasingly abstracted ways, so as to construct hypercriminals. From the slave patrols in the Southern US states to the operation of s.60 in North London, criminal law is a practice embedded in colonialism, racial capitalism, and the dehumanisation of racialised communities. Criminal law and evidence construct, reproduce, and naturalise simulations of racialised criminality. The problem is the belief that these simulacra are real. The question that needs to be posed is how to achieve a destabilisation and disruption of these ostensibly neutral symbols and categories, such that they are denaturalised. In other words, the task for critical legal scholarship is how to interrupt and challenge these processes of hyperreality.

As discussed in earlier chapters, concepts of harm are embedded in processes of simulation that identify the racialised poor as the source of harm and ignore the devastating social harm that is intrinsic to racial neoliberalism. To challenge mainstream definitions of harm and criminality, a zemiological approach focusing on social harm can assist in working towards social justice solutions and in breaking away from the purported sense of security of the carceral state.[1] Under hyperreality, the simulacra of racialised criminality appear as real. It is argued below that speaking back against this simulation can be a revolutionary act and a means of resisting the carceral state. Speaking back is not only a discursive practice but requires practical action that aims to build an alternative to racial capitalism through a different set of values that are not based on Whiteness or colonial norms but are founded in social justice and solidarity.

1 Paddy Hillyard and Steve Tombs, 'Beyond Criminology?' in Paddy Hillyard and others (eds), *Beyond Criminology: Taking Harm Seriously* (Pluto Press 2004), 10–29; Victoria Canning and Steve Tombs, *From Social Harm to Zemiology: A Critical Introduction* (Routledge 2021), 147–149.

DOI: 10.4324/9781003602873-8

Prior to considering those points in more detail, it is useful to summarise the main themes of previous chapters. Processes of simulation have taken place in relation to various legal provisions under neoliberalism, including s.60 orders, hate crimes, ASBOs, CBOs, gang injunctions, KCPOs, dangerousness provisions, and bad character evidence. Criminal law under racial capitalism is rooted in Enlightenment discourses of racial ordering that were deployed to justify slavery, colonialism, and imperialism. The law was a second order simulacrum, but neoliberal legal and evidential provisions, including those discussed in Chapters 3–6, are third order simulacra. Neoliberal processes of simulation include discourses of colour-blindness, meritocracy, and risk management. These discourses operate as codes that work to abstract, absorb, and disappear colonialism and racism, while erasing this act of disappearance. They rely upon racialised simulacra, such as the undeserving poor and the civilising mission, which are reworked into new forms under different periods of racial capitalism. Under neoliberalism, these simulations maintained and consolidated White supremacy and capital accumulation during the restructuring of global capitalism, and are a means of countering liberation movements and resisting progressive advances towards greater material equality and social justice. The norms and values of Whiteness are made to appear real and natural, thus making their partiality invisible.

A pervasive theme throughout this book is that populations have differential exposure to being constructed as hyperreal subjects. Processes of simulation are symbiotic with practices that deem particular communities as ungrievable. As argued in Chapter 2, being ungrievable is closely linked to discourses around the undeserving poor, and both are racialised. Being abstracted such that your history is disappeared, and you are considered to be a criminal rather than an individual, is not only a process of simulation but also a process of dehumanisation. To be abstracted, viewed through the racial frame, and named a criminal is to be deemed ungrievable. Performative discourses maintain this framing throughout the life of the ungrievable person. This includes subjection to heightened precariousness and denial of the use of lawful self-defence. These simulations operate through the performativity of legal and political discourses that are dislocated from their colonial genealogy and appear as neutral. The hyperreal realm extinguishes the boundaries between truth and falsity but appears real, and is believed to be real.

Even when criminal law is premised as protecting marginalised groups, it increases the criminalisation of those same groups, as illustrated by s.60 and the hate crime provisions. This cannot be attributed solely to racism by law enforcement agencies, although that is a factor, with police practices rooted in colonialism. Criminal law and evidence under neoliberalism construct hypercriminals through signs of criminality that appear as real. This construction of legal subjects is hyperreal as it relies upon previous colonial and racialised conceptions of criminality, which are abstracted and disappeared through neoliberal codes of colour-blindness and meritocracy. Processes of abstraction rewrite the effects of racism as evidence of inferiority and criminality. In this way, criminal law is both racialised and racialising. Locating criminality within poor racialised communities results in intense policing and surveillance of those areas as a technique of risk management, which then results in further criminalisation, which in turn appears to justify the disproportionate policing. This performs a contradication-closing function, as the perceived criminality of racialised poor communities appears to close the contradiction between apparently post-racial criminal laws and racially disproportionate outcomes in the legal system. Such laws are self-referential and hyperreal, as they construct their own perceived reality. Racialised poor people become third order simulacra of criminality – hypercriminals.

The Black Lives Matter movement has demonstrated the urgency and importance of speaking back against the discourses and practices that dehumanise racialised people.[2] Contending that racialised poor people are hypercriminals rather than criminals can be a means of disrupting processes of simulation. This assertion of hypercriminality speaks to the growing literature around zemiology, carceral abolition, and transformative justice. It can help to illuminate the ways that legal and criminological discourses equating harm with criminality are located within a history of racial capitalism and colonialism. In this way, the theory of hypercriminality can be seen as consistent with a zemiological approach that challenges dominant definitions of social harm. Furthermore, stating that racialised criminalisation is based on processes of simulation rather than reality calls into question the justification for the carceral state, and repositions it as a source of, rather than a cure for, social harm. The implication of this approach is that community-based initiatives around social justice are a more effective way of overcoming harm than the purported solutions offered by criminal law and punishment.

Criminalisation and the Carceral State

Slavoj Žižek's *Welcome to the Desert of the Real*[3] begins with an old joke about red ink.[4] Aware that his mail will be read by Soviet censors, a man tells his friends that the contents of his letters will be true if written in blue ink

2 David Theo Goldberg, 'Why "Black Lives Matter" Because All Lives Don't Matter in America' *Huffington Post* (25 September 2015) <https://www.huffpost.com/entry/why-black-lives-matter_b_8191424> accessed 20 December 2024.

3 The phrase 'the desert of the real' is taken from Jean Baudrillard, *Simulacra and Simulation* (Sheila Faria Glaser tr, University of Michigan Press 1994), 1. The phrase, 'Welcome to the desert of the real' is taken from *The Matrix* film (1999): Slavoj Žižek, *Welcome to the Desert of the Real* (Verso Books 2020), 17.

4 Žižek, 1.

but false if written in red ink. His first letter is written in blue ink and speaks of how great everything is but ends, 'the only thing you can't get is *red ink*'.[5] For Žižek, the point is that under Western neoliberalism, 'we lack the very language to articulate our unfreedom' as 'all the main terms we use ... "war on terrorism", "democracy and freedom", "human rights", and so on – are false terms, mystifying our perception of the situation instead of allowing us to think it'.[6] As Victoria Canning and Steve Tombs argue, the use of terms such as crime and criminality 'force thinking in a selective direction', which not only relies upon familiar images in relation to who constitutes a criminal and where harm lies in society but also constricts our response, such that we see conviction and punishment as the solution.[7] The language of criminal law and evidence refers to criminal behaviour, prevention, risk, anti-social behaviour, hate, danger, gangs, and bad character, all of which are constructed through discourses embedded in colonialism and racial capitalism, and serve to maintain inequality and exclude social justice solutions to harm. Hyperreality not only renders invisible the colonial genealogies of simulacra of racialised hypercriminality but hides the processes of simulation through which it achieves this disappearance of history.

The binary distinctions that label some as worthy and others as unworthy are a product of the Enlightenment logic of categorisation, which denies the humanity of racialised populations. Criminal law follows this logic by dividing legal subjects into innocent or guilty; victim or perpetrator; good character or bad character; vulnerable or dangerous; worthy of protection or anti-social; entitled to use self-defence or the threat requiring force. For the racialised poor, criminalisation and incarceration are made to appear 'natural' and pathological; for White elites, criminalisation appears 'unnatural'.[8] These simulacra conflate poverty with criminality and operate on the premise of protecting grievable populations from the dangerous, racialised undeserving poor. As Reina Gossett explains:

> The logic of the state, of the prison system, demands the idea that there are innocent people and guilty people, so that ... policing, prisons, imprisonment, deportation can be justified because some people are 'dangerous', or some people are 'guilty', or some people are the 'violent ones'.[9]

5 Ibid., 1 (original italics).
6 Ibid., 2.
7 Canning and Tombs, 118.
8 Dylan Rodríguez, 'Abolition as Praxis of Human Being: A Foreword' (2019) 132 *Harvard Law Review* 1575, 1586.
9 Reina Gossett and Dean Spade, 'No One is Disposable (Part 3): What About the Dangerous People?' (Barnard Center for Research on Women 2014) <https://bcrw.barnard.edu/no-one-is-disposable/> accessed 4 January 2025.

Not everyone is deemed culpable or held accountable for what they do, and this reflects how criminal law is rooted in colonial discourses and material inequalities.[10] These dichotomies between innocent and guilty people have their genealogy in processes of racialisation. Furthermore, this categorisation into criminal or victim, guilty or not guilty, is an attempt to make criminal law and criminalisation seem real rather than hyperreal. By employing discursive categories that divide individuals and communities into innocent or guilty, we are ourselves engaged in carceral strategies of imposing and maintaining boundaries, such that we are implicated in techniques of discipline. Moreover, we are enabling the hyperreality of criminal law to appear real – we are providing it with an alibi by accepting its premise that people can be divided into guilty and innocent.

As well as arguing that 'Disneyland is presented as imaginary in order to make us believe that the rest is real', Jean Baudrillard argued that 'prisons are there to hide that it is the social in its entirety, in its banal omnipresence, that is carceral'.[11] This carceral approach extends beyond the legal system, such that attributing blame and punishing others permeates our existence under neoliberalism, from school exclusions to shaming or blocking others on social media.[12] The carceral state includes biopolitical/necropolitical institutions and practices, from psychiatry to welfare benefit assessments, that seek to normalise and judge.[13] We have internalised the criminalisation processes that individualise harm, such that we effectively find others 'guilty', rather than seeing harm in its wider socio-economic context.[14] Thus, we apply carceral logic to everyday issues and social problems.[15] We consent to our own surveillance by the state and corporations, and allow CCTV and DNA collection to make us feel secure by protecting us from 'the bad guys'.[16] Relying upon criminal law as a solution to social problems is contradictory and doomed to failure, as the narrative that some people are criminals due to their 'personal moral failing' is part of the same neoliberal meritocratic logic as economic policies of privatisation and austerity, which increase inequality and perpetuate social problems.[17] Further, the apparition of hypercrime fuels the far-right through blaming harm, insecurity, and societal injustice

10 Ibid.
11 Baudrillard, *Simulacra and Simulation*, 12.
12 Sarah Lamble, 'Practising Everyday Abolition' in Koshka Duff (ed), *Abolishing the Police* (Dog Section Press 2021), 149–151.
13 Michel Foucault, *Discipline and Punish – The Birth of the Prison* (Penguin Books 1977), 298–308.
14 Lamble, 149.
15 Ibid., 149–150.
16 Victoria E. Collins and Dawn L. Rothe, *The Violence of Neoliberalism* (Routledge 2020), 90–95.
17 Alex Vitale, *The End of Policing* (Verso Books 2018), 227–228.

on racialised communities. White elites blame this increase in racism on poor Whites and deploy carceral responses against them while continuing to advance hyperreal constructions of racialised criminality.

As Yvette Russell argues, 'working towards abolition is an ongoing process of everyday practice, both personal and political, and one that decentres criminal justice'.[18] If we are to reject the racialised criminalisation that is fundamental to a system of criminal law and evidence that has absorbed the sign values of colonialism and the civilising mission, we need to move away from the constructed binary categories of criminal law to a more nuanced consideration of social harm. Mainstream constructions of crime ignore, for the most part, the immense harm caused by governments and corporations, as well as the harm caused by criminalisation and punishment, and in doing so maintain material inequalities in society.[19] This perpetuates the illusion that the inherent criminality of the racialised poor is real rather than hyperreal.

A zemiological approach, which considers harm rather than crime, can highlight ways that criminal law equates crime with harmful behaviour, even though many crimes are comparatively harmless.[20] Moving to a consideration of social harm can enable us to name racial capitalism, rather than criminalised marginalised individuals, as the problem. From the estimated nine million people a year who die due to hunger,[21] to the six million children a year who die due to lack of clean water,[22] to the 72 people who died in the Grenfell Tower fire due to inadequate health and safety,[23] much premature death is preventable and impacts upon those populations considered ungrievable, disposable, and surplus to the capital accumulation motive of racial neoliberalism. A zemiological analysis of the harm caused by capitalism needs to be situated within an understanding of capitalism as a colonial process.[24] For example, to gain an understanding of the Grenfell Tower fire, it is not sufficient to consider it only as a matter of class-based harm due to state-corporate capitalism.[25] Any analysis of harm needs to recognise that 'the arrangement of urban housing according to race is not merely one of the class, but one underpinned by a colonial logic of personhood'.[26] This

18 Yvette Russell, 'Criminal Injustice' in Illan rua Wall, Freya Middleton and Sahar Shah (eds), *The Critical Legal Pocketbook* (Counterpress 2021), 177.
19 Canning and Tombs, 25–30.
20 Ibid., 24–25.
21 Kehinde Andrews, *The New Age of Empire* (Allen Lane 2021), xi.
22 Canning and Tombs, 68.
23 Ibid., 4–5.
24 Edward J. Wright, 'Decolonizing Zemiology: Outlining and Remedying the Blindness to (Post)colonialism Within the Study of Social Harm' (2023) 31 *Critical Criminology* 127, 130.
25 Ibid., 133–135.
26 Ibid., 134.

cannot be separated from the gentrification of inner city areas, as discussed in Chapter 3, which can be seen as a continuation of the colonial processes that exclude the domestic racialised poor.[27]

Existing conceptions of criminality tend to focus on individual acts that are temporally and spatially proximate, such as shoplifting, while neglecting more fundamental harm, such as environmental damage caused by corporations seeking to increase their profits, and the subsequent impact on populations.[28] Although we all cause harm, degrees of harm vary, such that an act by an individual causing petty or minimal harm needs to be differentiated from the significant harm caused to marginalised populations who are denied the basics of life.[29] The discourses of the carceral state create the belief that the drug dealing criminal causing the most significant harm is the teenager selling cannabis on the street corner rather than the pharmaceutical company withholding medication from terminally ill patients; or that living standards are falling due to refugees and welfare claimants rather than due to corporations making millions of pounds in profit while paying wages so low that workers in the UK have to claim benefits or go to food banks and manufacturing workers in the Global South live in abject poverty. The simulacra reproduced by these narratives – dangerous, gang member, anti-social, violent, sexual predator, terrorist – disappear their colonial genealogy and obscure the origins and causes of social harm. A shift towards decarceration cannot be restricted to the decriminalisation of particular acts, such as drug use, but needs to encompass an understanding of criminalisation as a classed and racialised practice that targets particular populations.[30]

Any consideration of social harm must include the harm caused by criminalisation.[31] The stress of a court case and psychological effect of being branded a criminal can be significant. Furthermore, for those struggling financially, a fine or court costs are likely to lead to hardship for them and their dependants. As described in Chapter 2, the harm caused by a custodial sentence includes both imprisonment itself and the significant impact on life chances and experiences following imprisonment. The prison regime of surveillance,[32] violence or the threat of violence,[33] lack of dignity,[34] lack of

27 Ibid., 134; Ida Danewid, 'The Fire This Time: Grenfell, Racial Capitalism and the Urbanisation of Empire' (2020) 26(1) *European Journal of International Relations* 289, 302.
28 Canning and Tombs, 29 and 55–59.
29 Ibid., 25; Lamble, 157.
30 Angela Y. Davis, *Are Prisons Obsolete?* (Seven Stories Press 2003), 113.
31 Canning and Tombs, 28.
32 David Scott, *For Abolition: Essays on Prisons and Socialist Ethics* (Waterside Press 2020), 133–134.
33 Ibid., 75–98 and 127–129.
34 Ibid., 109.

security,[35] boredom and loss of hope[36] is a dehumanising process that denies meaningful human existence.[37] Prisoners are likely to have suffered trauma or significant disadvantage prior to their incarceration, such as time in the care system or childhood abuse, meaning that they are already vulnerable.[38] In other words, ungrievable people are prone to incarceration, where this lack of grievability is further accentuated.

Incarceration can be seen as 'social death', a term used by Joshua Price to describe the effect of prison, which builds upon Orlando Patterson's analysis of slavery as social death.[39] This comprises three main elements: 'generalized humiliation, institutional violence, and natal alienation', the latter referring to separation from families and communities.[40] As Zach Norris argues, from slavery and colonialism onwards, techniques of separation and isolation, such as boarding schools for indigenous populations, have been used as tools to weaken the bonds and cultures of racialised communities.[41] In the UK, the separation of racialised families persists through immigration law, deportation, and racially disproportionate care orders for children, in addition to imprisonment.[42] All of these can be seen as techniques of discipline and control that the neoliberal carceral state deploys against ungrievable populations.

For some of those incarcerated, their existence in prison is so unbearable that social death leads to physical death. During the period December 2023 to December 2024, 89 prisoners in England and Wales took their own lives, and there were 77,869 self-harming incidents involving 13,724 individuals between September 2023 and September 2024.[43] Neoliberal criminal law not only fails to provide the safety and security that it promises for all except the elite, but it also removes what little security exists for marginalised communities.

35 Ibid., 124.
36 Ibid., 141–153.
37 Ibid., 159.
38 Ibid., 125; Canning and Tombs, 18.
39 Joshua M. Price, *Prison and Social Death* (Rutgers University Press 2015), 5.
40 Ibid., 6.
41 Zach Norris, *Defund Fear: Safety Without Policing, Prisons, and Punishment* (Beacon Press 2020), 58–59.
42 Nadine El-Enany, 'From Love to Justice: Families' Interrogation of Racial State Violence' (2022) 32 *Social and Legal Studies* 1, 10.
43 Ministry of Justice, *Safety in Custody Statistics, England and Wales: Deaths in Prison Custody to December 2024, Assaults and Self-Harm to September 2024* (Ministry of Justice 30 January 2025) <https://www.gov.uk/government/statistics/safety-in-custody-quarterly-update-to-september-2024/safety-in-custody-statistics-england-and-wales-deaths-in-prison-custody-to-december-2024-assaults-and-self-harm-to-september-2024> accessed 23 May 2025.

The precarity of life under neoliberalism is such that the carceral state operates as a counterbalance to this, providing people with perceived security against dangerous hypercriminals. Discourses that link race, poverty, and criminality have led to a 'security state founded on fear, class privilege and updated notions of racial purity'.[44] The carceral state purports to keep individuals and communities safe from harm, thus enabling much of the harm caused by processes of criminalisation to be considered necessary in order to achieve its stated aims, or as a deviation from the norm that can be resolved by police and courts observing the correct procedures. Reformist approaches of merely replacing the death penalty with whole life imprisonment, or replacing imprisonment with supervision and surveillance, may provide some respite from the harshest aspects of the law, but are still significant causes of harm located within the carceral worldview and the perceived need to punish, contain, and monitor suspect communities.[45] This perpetuates the simulation that the racialised poor are the threat requiring monitoring and supervising.

The sense of security apparently provided by the carceral state is hyperreal. As outlined in Chapter 5, the existence of law enforcement agencies fails to prevent serious harm such as rape from occurring, with the Crime Survey showing around that around 1.6 million people in England and Wales had experienced a serious sexual assault since reaching the age of 16 years.[46] The neoliberal carceral state fails to keep communities safe from poverty, sickness, homelessness, harassment, sexual abuse, war, and environmental harm. Moreover, it creates many of these harms and maintains a system where harms are perpetuated. Rejecting the carceral state involves reconceptualising fear and safety and, as abolitionist scholars have argued, offering community-based social justice solutions to social problems, through building practices of mutual aid and assistance.[47] This goes beyond whether a particular defendant is innocent or guilty, but is about collective resistance against

44 Henry Giroux, 'The Biopolitics of Disposability' in Uli Linke and Danielle Taana Smith (eds), *Cultures of Fear: A Critical Reader* (Pluto Press 2009), 307.

45 Davis, 106–107.

46 According to data from the Crime Survey for England and Wales for the year ending March 2020, around 1.6 million people had been victims of rape or sexual penetration, or attempted rape or penetration, since reaching the age of 16 years: Office for National Statistics, *Crime Survey for England and Wales* (2021) <www.ons.gov.uk/peoplepopulationandcommunity/crimeandjustice/articles/natureofsexualassaultbyrapeorpenetrationenglandandwales/yearendingmarch2020> accessed 20 December 2024.

47 See, for example, Rodríguez, 1576; Norris, 93–96; Dean Spade, *Mutual Aid* (Verso Books 2020); Adam Elliott-Cooper, *Black Resistance to British Policing* (Manchester University Press 2021), 190; Mariame Kaba, *We Do This 'Til We Free Us* (Haymarket Books 2021), 97–101; Melanie Brazzell, 'Theorising Transformative Justice' in Koshka Duff (ed), *Abolishing the Police* (Dog Section Press 2021), 165–167; Aviah Sarah Day and Shanice Octavia McBean, *Abolition Revolution* (Pluto Press 2022).

the processes of simulation that differentiate, order, and demarcate populations. As Jackie Wang explains, 'when we rely on appeals to innocence, we foreclose a form of resistance that is outside the limits of law and instead ally ourselves with the state'.[48] Resistance to constructions of hypercriminality is about transcending binary distinctions of guilty and not guilty, and about working to dismantle carceral practices.

Hypercriminality as a Theory of Resistance

Neoliberal criminal law performs a hyperreal function: it maintains, abstracts, and amplifies the belief that racialised criminality is real. Racialised individuals are deemed 'guilty until proven innocent' at all stages of the legal process. Measures of culpability are constructed through codes of White norms and values, which appear neutral. Legal doctrines, such as bad character, appear neutral but serve as codes that disappear historical and continuing processes of racialised criminalisation. In conjunction with neoliberal simulations of colour-blind meritocracy, racialised people are deemed as criminals responsible for their own predicament. Therefore, the law cannot be used as a means of resisting oppression. It is not possible to decolonise criminal law as it is embedded in colonial processes of racialisation and situated within racial capitalism.[49] Rather than merely having a colonial history, neoliberal criminal law entails an implosion of the colonial past into the present, such that simulacra of criminality appear as 'real' criminality, while these processes of colonialism and racialisation are disappeared. Legal terms are situated within a simulacrum, such that it is impossible to peel away this simulation. There is no 'pure' law or 'truth' of law to uncover, but we can draw attention to the simulacrum and attempt to disrupt it by speaking back against it while recognising that we are ourselves situated within the simulation.

Under the neoliberal ideology of colour-blindness, racism becomes more insidious than under previous historical incarnations, such that its colonial roots are rendered invisible. In this way, the racism inherent in criminal law and evidence is abstracted to the point of disappearance. The simulacrum of racialised criminality with its genealogy of slavery, empire, colonialism, and imperialism allows neoliberalism to dislocate itself from its inherent social harm. Neoliberal criminal law constructs the premise that race is real, that racially disproportionate criminality is real, and that the carceral state is necessary to deal with this threat. It follows that a necessary condition for the abolition of the neoliberal carceral state is the negation of the belief that racialised criminality and indeed race and criminality themselves are real.

48 Jackie Wang, *Carceral Capitalism* (Semiotext(e) 2018), 116.

49 Aya Gruber, 'Colonial Carceral Feminism' in Chris Cunneen and others (eds), *The Routledge International Handbook on Decolonizing Justice* (Routledge 2023), 235.

Doing this entails accepting 'that whiteness is *nothing but* oppressive and false'.[50] The norms and values of Whiteness need to be exposed as a simulation used to justify a system of capital accumulation. Crime is situated within these constructions and has no ontological reality.[51] The concept of criminality is deployed as an alibi to advance White supremacy and justify the carceral state. Paul Gilroy's work articulated how 'Black criminality' is a myth.[52] The concept of hypercriminality enables us to name race and criminality as myths – they are simulacra.

Baudrillard's example of the simulated robbery, as discussed in Chapter 1, illustrates that using simulation as a technique to expose simulation itself is ineffective against the order of law.[53] This is not, however, due to law being 'real' as distinguished from the simulated robbery but due to the law itself constituting a simulacrum. According to Baudrillard, 'the worst error of all our revolutionary strategies is to believe that we will put an end to the system on the plane of the *real*'.[54] He goes on to argue:

> the only solution is to turn the principle of its power back against the system itself: the impossibility of responding or retorting. *To defy the system with a gift to which it cannot respond save by its own collapse and death.*[55]

Discourses of power are themselves simulacra.[56] Baudrillard argued that revolutionary aims were too often steeped in Enlightenment ideals of progress and rationality, and that they sought to resolve contradictions.[57] In this way, they were still wedded to the reality principle; accepting hyperreality as reality.[58] As has been argued throughout this book, contradiction-closing provisions are deployed by elites to make the inequalities inherent in racial capitalism appear natural and neutral, and to make the hyperreal appear real. Thus, a revolutionary movement should advance 'a principle anterior (or ulterior) to the reality principle' and 'take the form of interruption, rupture,

50 David Roediger, *Towards the Abolition of Whiteness* (Verso Books 1994), 13 (original italics).
51 Canning and Tombs, 21.
52 Paul Gilroy, 'The Myth of Black Criminality' (1982) 19 *The Socialist Register* 47 <https://socialistregister.com/index.php/srv/article/view/5474> accessed 20 December 2024.
53 Baudrillard, *Simulacra and Simulation*, 20–21.
54 Jean Baudrillard, *Symbolic Exchange and Death* (Iain Hamilton Grant tr, SAGE Publications 2017), 57 (original italics).
55 Ibid., 58 (original italics).
56 Jean Baudrillard, *Forget Foucault* (Nicole Dufresne tr, Semiotext(e) 2007), 50–51.
57 Jean Baudrillard, 'Police and Play' in Gary Genosko (ed), *The Uncollected Baudrillard* (Mike Gane tr, SAGE Publications 2001), 67.
58 Ibid., 67.

dysfunction and blockage'.[59] In this way, 'it aims not at the overcoming of its contradictions but at the abolition of separations'.[60] Baudrillard argued that:

> When a system manages to maintain its equilibrium by its own continual breakdown, when it manages to digest its own contradictions and profits from its own crises ... what remains but to interrupt it and raise the almost blind demand of the real pleasure principle, the radical demand of transgression, against the massive collusion under the sign of satisfaction?[61]

The destruction of the neoliberal carceral state cannot succeed on a material level if it cannot succeed on a symbolic level. The negation of the discourse that the police and prisons are necessary and that they are a source of security cannot be overcome within the confines of the law because such discourses are part of the construction of criminal law itself. Practices such as adducing defence expert evidence at trial may temper the worst excesses of criminal law and evidence, and may even shift the trial narrative and secure an acquittal in some cases, but cannot overcome the ways that neoliberal criminal law constructs hypercriminals. To resist the belief in the reality of race, the belief in the criminality of the racialised poor, and the belief in the need for the security of the carceral state, neoliberalism must be given a gift to which it lacks the language to respond. While the law deploys the device of contradiction-closing processes to maintain the simulation, revolutionary politics needs to be contradiction-opening.

The discourse of racial neoliberalism is that of division, private property, the profit motive, competition, meritocracy, risk management, managerialism, division, exclusion, control, and containment. Neoliberalism has no reply to those who are indifferent to the accumulation of wealth, those who eschew the toxicity of competitiveness for mutual co-operation, and those who reject the apparent protection of criminal law and perceived carceral solutions against those who have harmed them in favour of forgiveness and understanding. A code that operates on balance sheets and exclusion cannot respond to discourses around social justice and assistance. While one may argue that the neoliberal state has the ability to reply in both simulated and material terms, through deeming those who reject its code as backward and unintelligible and by criminalising them, it cannot speak back against discourses which refuse to accept this simulated criminalisation as real.

The assertion that the perceived criminality of racialised poor people is hypercriminality, not criminality, is an act of subversion that rejects the belief

59 Ibid., 67.
60 Ibid., 68.
61 Ibid., 67–68.

systems of racial capitalism, colonialism, and the rule of law. In this way, the theory of hypercriminality can contribute towards abolitionist goals. Speaking back against the violence of criminal law and the carceral state is a project of both discursive and material acts that rejects the values of Whiteness and racial capitalism and works to replace them with solidarity, community, mutual aid, and social justice.

Index

Kolibri 360 GmbH
Ferdinand-Jühlke-Straße 7
99095 Erfurt, Deutschland
produktsicherheit@kolibri360.de